About Island Press

Island Press is the only nonprofit organization in the United States whose principal purpose is the publication of books on environmental issues and natural resource management. We provide solutions-oriented information to professionals, public officials, business and community leaders, and concerned citizens who are shaping responses to environmental problems.

Since 1984, Island Press has been the leading provider of timely and practical books that take a multidisciplinary approach to critical environmental concerns. Our growing list of titles reflects our commitment to bringing the best of an expanding body of literature to the environmental community throughout North America and the world.

Support for Island Press is provided by the Agua Fund, The Geraldine R. Dodge Foundation, Doris Duke Charitable Foundation, The Ford Foundation, The William and Flora Hewlett Foundation, The Joyce Foundation, Kendeda Sustainability Fund of the Tides Foundation, The Forrest & Frances Lattner Foundation, The Henry Luce Foundation, The John D. and Catherine T. MacArthur Foundation, The Marisla Foundation, The Andrew W. Mellon Foundation, Gordon and Betty Moore Foundation, The Curtis and Edith Munson Foundation, Oak Foundation, The Overbrook Foundation, The David and Lucile Packard Foundation, Wallace Global Fund, The Winslow Foundation, and other generous donors.

The opinions expressed in this book are those of the author(s) and do not necessarily reflect the views of these foundations.

About the Growth Management Institute

The Growth Management Institute is a nonprofit organization established in 1992 by a group of distinguished practitioners and scholars recognized nationally as experts in the field of growth management. Under the guidance of Douglas R. Porter, the Institute encourages effective and equitable management of growth in human habitats and provides a forum for the constructive exchange of ideas and information about growth management. The Institute promotes strategies and practices to achieve sustainable urban development and redevelopment while preserving environmental quality. The Institute is based in Chevy Chase, Maryland.

Managing Growth in America's Communities

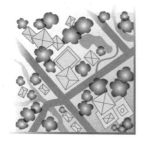

Managing
Growth in
America's Communities

Second Edition

Douglas R. Porter

ISLANDPRESS
WASHINGTON • COVELO • LONDON

Library of Congress Cataloging-in-Publication data.

Porter, Douglas R.
  Managing growth in America's communities / Douglas R. Porter. — 2nd ed.
    p. cm.
  Includes bibliographical references and index.
  ISBN-13: 978-1-59726-006-0 (hardcover : alk. paper)
  ISBN-13: 978-1-59726-007-7 (pbk. : alk. paper)
  1. Cities and towns—United States—Growth. 2. City planning—United States. 3.
Regional planning—United States. 4. Community development—United States. I.
Title.
  HT384.U5P67 2008
  307.1'2160973—dc22

                                        2007026189

British Cataloguing-in-Publication data available.

Printed on recycled, acid-free paper ✪

Design by Joan Wolbier

Manufactured in the United States of America

10 9 8 7 6 5 4 3 2 1

Contents

Preface   IX

CHAPTER 1
Introduction to Managing Community Development   1

CHAPTER 2
The Practice of Growth Management   37

CHAPTER 3
Managing Community Expansion: Where to Grow   65

CHAPTER 4
Protecting Environmental and Natural Resources: Where Not to Grow   113

CHAPTER 5
Supporting Growth by Managing Infrastructure Development   147

CHAPTER 6
Design to Preserve and Improve Community Character and Quality   179

CHAPTER 7
Managing Growth to Advance Social and Economic Equity   209

CHAPTER 8
Regional and State Growth Management   241

CHAPTER 9
Deciding How to Manage Growth   281

Notes   301

Index   313

Preface

When I began writing the first edition of this book ten years ago, growth management was on the increase in communities across America. As public officials sought to improve the quality of life in places where we live, work, and relax, jurisdictions of many shapes and sizes were adopting planning and regulatory techniques that had been invented and applied from the 1960s on. Growth boundaries, requirements for adequate public facilities, impact fees, conservation and farmland protection zoning, and other techniques increasingly found favor with public officials and the electorate. Professional and citizen planners were expanding their understanding of the vital linkages among development, the environment, and the social and economic conditions of everyday life.

The book's focus at that time was "to draw on community experiences to describe proven strategies, policies, programs, and techniques for managing growth in American communities," with the ultimate purpose of identifying and clarifying workable approaches to managing community development.

But new concepts were then gaining attention as well—concepts that championed goals both broader and more focused than growing communities had commonly pursued. Advocates of neo-traditional, new urbanist, and transit-oriented development renewed our interest in the significance of urbane designs for neighborhoods and town centers; supporters of sustainable development and smart growth reminded us about the critical principles of livable and sustainable communities; and conservationists touted the environmental and human benefits of green buildings and green infrastructure systems. Meanwhile, helping to transpose these concepts into reality, more Americans began to view urban centers as attractive living and working places. Innovations in the adaptive re-use of historic areas stimulated by the growing interest of empty nesters and young professionals in city rather than suburban lifestyles, the development of infill sites, and the redevelopment of disused properties added to the lexicon of public approaches to managing growth in many cities throughout the nation.

This edition is aimed particularly at demonstrating how these exciting concepts can be integrated within the framework of the policy and practice of managed community growth. More to the point, all of the concepts depend on communities establishing a supportive context of public policies and regulations that can enable the pursuit of innovative ideas—the essence of effective growth management.

My work over the past ten years has introduced me to many of these new concepts. I refer particularly to the research I pursued when writing my books *The Practice of Sustainable Development*, *Making Smart Growth Work*, and *The Power of Ideas*, all published by the Urban Land Institute. My published analyses of other pertinent subjects are noted throughout the book. In addition, I value the further education provided by the impressive volume of newsletters, books, and conferences issuing from a growing body of organizations dedicated to specific causes.

Finally, my heartfelt thanks to the contributors of the commentaries that add so much to the meaning of the text. All experts in the field, they include Christopher Duercksen, Robert Dunphy, Robert Lang, Lindell Marsh, Arthur (Chris) Nelson, Erik Meyers, Cara Snyder, Paul Tischler, and Richard Tustian. And of course, my appreciation for the patience of my wife, Cecelia, and our four offspring who put up with my travails in reworking this book about a changing universe of urban growth and change.

CHAPTER 1

Introduction to
Managing Community Development

Local governments endeavor to guide community growth and change through a host of plans, policies, programs, and regulations. Most are embodied in traditional planning documents, such as comprehensive or master plans, zoning ordinances, and subdivision regulations. However, beginning in the 1960s, public officials sought greater influence over the location, rate, and quality of development. They crafted and applied new types of planning and regulatory controls under the heading of "growth management." The techniques that evolved from these efforts, such as growth boundaries and adequate public facilities requirements, now offer public decision makers almost day-to-day opportunities to shape the direction and character of community expansion. What's more, such increasingly popular precepts as *sustainable development, smart growth, new urbanism,* and *green development* (terms defined and described later) are expanding the lexicon of growth management and increasingly influencing the form and function of community development.

The efforts of Fort Collins, Colorado, to manage community growth over a half century illustrate the roots and branches of public involvement in the development process. In the mid-1950s, the citizens of Fort Collins recognized that the city's growth was raising issues that needed attention. Founded in 1864 as a military outpost, Fort Collins developed into a small college town and a trade and shopping center for the surrounding area. Until the 1950s, the town boasted fewer than fifteen thousand residents, but then the college began expanding and new industries arrived; suddenly growth was everywhere. During the 1960s, the number of residents rose by 7 percent a year, and in the 1970s, by 5 percent.

As growth occurred, the town frantically annexed land to accommodate development, virtually doubling the incorporated area each decade.

Soon, growth brought traffic-clogged roads, overcrowded schools, the need for expanded sewer and water systems, and a scarcity of park spaces. The rudimentary zoning ordinance seemed inadequate to deal with these problems. Although a city-appointed task force recommended a program of short-term public investments, the larger issue of managing future growth remained unresolved. A "Plan for Progress" formulated in 1967 started the planning ball rolling, but to little effect on the ground. A follow-on planning effort produced a statement of goals and objectives but no consensus on where and what development should take place. Another task force, extensive public hearings, and a failed growth-limiting ballot initiative finally led to the city council's adoption in 1979 of a four-part comprehensive plan: a land use policies plan, an innovative land use guidance system that added flexible development standards to existing zoning, a city-county agreement defining an urban growth area, and a cost-of-development study.

Fort Collins's population growth continued to rise, from 43,000 in 1970 to 118,000 in 2000. The effects on spatial needs drove the city to adopt a new plan, called "City Plan," in 1997, shortly followed by a new zoning ordinance that wrapped many of the "flexible" development standards into zoning requirements. By 2002, however, when the plan was due for updating, significant opposition to rapid growth resulted in a plan that emphasized redevelopment and infill of the existing urbanized area instead of significantly expanding the established growth area. Subsequently, the city staff has proposed revisions to city codes and administrative policies to assist redevelopment and infill activities.

Fort Collins's experience over a half century of rapid growth mirrors the principal features of growth management programs in many communities:

- Sudden, unplanned development caused major problems in community livability, provoking citizens' concerns for improving public management of development.
- Agreement on measures for addressing growth problems evolved over many years as community leadership coalesced and various solutions were tested.
- City officials learned that a single solution—meeting infrastructure needs—fell short of satisfying wider community concerns.
- Continual involvement of many organizations, interests, and community leaders built strong support for public guidance of the development process.
- The city's program today represents an amalgam of conventional and

innovative planning and growth management components tailored to the city's particular character and needs.

In short, the citizens of Fort Collins discovered that managing growth is a time-consuming, politically messy, and constantly evolving process. At times exhilarating, the experience and guidance of urban growth also can be deeply frustrating. Easy solutions are elusive, and lingering opposition by property owners and the development industry to strengthening public guidance of growth can impede positive measures. In addition, the process usually requires multiple investments of time, energy, innovation, and follow-through actions. But citizens, public officials, and city planners in many communities are acquiring a long-term, comprehensive view of the challenges of community growth and change. They understand the need to anticipate problems before they overwhelm community resources; to recognize the interrelationships among urban design, environmental, transportation, social and economic, and other components of growth; and to incorporate a broad sense of shared values and concerns in public policies affecting community development.

These approaches all fall under the heading of *growth management*, an inclusive approach to defining community strategies for future development and acting on them.

Anticipating Community Growth and Change

America's population continues to grow. The U.S. Census Bureau counted 281 million residents in the United States in 2000 and estimates that that number increased to about 301 million by 2007. By 2020, the Census Bureau projects a U.S. population of 336 million, and by 2050, a population of 420 million—almost half again the 2000 population. Although fertility rates are not anticipated to rebound to earlier levels, the average life

BOX 1.1

Four Numbers Tell the Population Story

U.S. Census: 2007 Components of Population Growth

One birth every	eight seconds
One death every	thirteen seconds
One international migrant (net) every	twenty-seven seconds
Net gain of one person every	eleven seconds

Source: http://www.census.gov/population/www/popclockus.html

---

expectancy of residents probably will increase and the rate of immigration will continue to add substantially to the nation's population. The Census Bureau predicts that, by 2050, about half of all residents will represent what are now regarded as minority groups.

Almost 90 percent of new residents will remain in or move to metropolitan areas. About four out of five Americans live in metropolitan areas today, and the Census Bureau expects that the expansion of the urban and suburban population will continue well into the twenty-first century. And, since 1950, more than 90 percent of the growth in metropolitan areas has occurred in suburban places; many people are born, mature, work, and die all in the suburban environment. Indeed, Joel Kotkin claims that "most of the fastest growth 'cities' of the late twentieth century—Los Angeles, Atlanta, Orlando, Phoenix, Houston, Dallas and Charlotte—are primarily collections of suburbs."[1] Suburbs in many metropolitan areas are being transformed into major regional centers, the focus of metropolitan growth.

At the same time, some older central cities are attracting new residents drawn by appealing historic neighborhoods and access to entertainment and other center-city advantages. In fact, most large central cities have added population since 2000, although some, such as Boston and San Francisco, have been affected by regional economic shifts that have reduced center-city populations.[2] Even city downtowns, following twenty years of declining populations, have rebounded; a study of forty-four city downtowns showed that downtown populations grew by 10 percent during the 1990s and that the number of downtown households increased by 13 percent during that decade.[3]

Robert Lang and Arthur Nelson, of Virginia Tech's Metropolitan Institute, point out that the expansion of metropolitan areas is creating

BOX 1.2

Also Important: Shifts between Metropolitan Areas

Residents of metropolitan areas move about, not just to nearby suburbs but to other metropolitan areas as well, many apparently prompted by job opportunities and the availability of inexpensive housing. A 2005 analysis by Moody's Economy.com of net population movements into and out of the Washington area showed that during 2004, 8,900 more people from the metro areas of Boston, New York, Philadelphia, Chicago, and San Francisco moved into the Washington area than out of it. Meanwhile, a net movement of 15,892 people left the Washington metropolitan area for the Baltimore, Richmond, Tampa, Winchester, and Hagerstown metro areas—places where housing prices are considerably lower than Washington's.

Source: *Washington Post*, November 26, 2005, p. F1. n.a.

clusters of "megapolitan" regions that currently account for two-thirds of the U.S. population. They identify ten such regions—six east of the Mississippi River and four west of it—that are growing faster than the nation's population as a whole. The largest agglomeration is the Northeast Corridor, home to 50 million people, stretching from New England down the Atlantic coast to northern Virginia.[4]

Expanding suburbs and revitalized inner cities foster alterations in the built and social environment—some welcome, some not (for example, the displacement of existing residents in gentrifying city neighborhoods or the maturation of small-town centers into busy employment hubs). However, even metropolitan areas losing population experience change. As people move from inner-city areas and older suburbs to newly forming suburbs, they may better their quality of life while the continuing decline of their former neighborhoods creates other social and economic issues that need attention.

Many members of the baby boom generation are retiring to once-rural areas, many to find inexpensive housing; telecommuters, too, are moving farther away from cities. However, a substantial proportion of new homes in rural and remote areas constitute second homes of people otherwise still resident in urbanized areas.

Community growth and change challenge both citizens and governments to prepare for new circumstances. Fort Collins's history reveals a common process of urban formation, alteration, and adaptation to changing conditions. For close to a century, its small-town ways made few demands on public facilities. Its citizens saw no need to guide growth because, typically, small developments were easily assimilated into the social and economic fabric and the town's infrastructure systems. However, rapid growth generated disorienting alterations in the townscape: virtually overnight, it turned open farmland into subdivisions full of new houses and transformed rural crossroads into busy intersections lined with shopping centers.

In such circumstances, communities discover that highly visible new development is commonly accompanied by shifts in the social and economic aspects of daily life. New home owners arrive with expectations for services; some also have different ideas about lifestyles. Schools face new pressures on space and curricula. Often, growth also threatens the very environmental qualities that attract new residents. Low-density subdivisions and retail strips replace farms, meadows, and woodlands. Poorly designed development damages stream valleys and wetlands, disturbs wildlife habitats, and destroys historic and cultural features that link the community to its heritage.

Faced with new demands for public facilities and services, local public officials scramble to secure funding and establish administrations of ever-larger infrastructure systems. Often, they are overwhelmed and unprepared to envision new governmental responsibilities or take decisive steps to meet them. Slow to recognize emerging needs, they may neglect to insist on appropriate standards of development and instead resort to stopgap solutions and crisis-reactive actions. In so doing, local officials frequently miss opportunities for maintaining the special character of the community and for guaranteeing the long-term value of its ongoing development.

Community growth and change can be beneficial. New development can be a positive force for improving the lives of many residents. More and better employment opportunities may open up as new businesses and industries move to the area. Goods and services may become more conveniently available, and amenities in the form of special recreational sites, museums, and performance venues may increase. Residential development may provide wider choices of housing styles and prices to fit the preferences of a more varied population. New development may produce a sounder long-term fiscal base for the community.

But it takes foresight and incisive management of the resources at hand to answer the challenges of community expansion and change.

Public Guidance of Community Development

The United States traditionally has relied to an extraordinary extent on spontaneous economic forces (commonly termed the *free market system* or *free enterprise*) to build the places in which we live and work. The right of private individuals to own and determine how they will use real estate has been a cherished and constitutionally protected tradition. Unlike in ancient times when powerful governments founded cities and towns (especially in recently subjugated colonies), private developers and speculators have laid out and built the urban places where people lived. In Colonial America, great landowners such as William Penn and James Oglethorpe borrowed many of the ancient ideas of town building—a gridiron street pattern, systems of open spaces, highly visible civic buildings—in designing new towns. Since then, most communities in the United States have been developed as private ventures. The American Revolution helped the process by abolishing many of the feudal public claims on land ownership; soon after, the Ordinance of 1785 established the rectangular survey system that allowed speculators to identify and trade in land they never saw.[5]

But the public sector has always been a strong force in establishing the rules of the development game and participating in the development

BOX 1.3
Super Regions to Serve Super Growth

Robert E. Lang, Director and Arthur C. Nelson, Senior Fellow,
Virginia Tech Institute for Metropolitan Research

By 2040, the population of the United States is expected to add 100 million residents. We believe that most of these residents will live in twenty emerging
megapolitan areas, which include the fifteen largest metropolitan regions and thirty-six of the fifty most populous regions. These huge urban/suburban networks
were home to about 60 percent of the nation's population in 2005, yet they
account for only a tenth of the nation's land area. That computes to a density of
about half that of Japan and greater than that of the European Union. The notion
that Americans live in the wide-open spaces should fade fast. While metropolitan
areas have been decentralizing, the United States as a whole is undergoing a
concentration of its population.

By 2040, another 60 million residents could move into megapolitan areas. By
midcentury, it is likely that the twenty megapolitan areas will have merged into ten
megaregions, five east and five west of the 100th meridian line. Although suburban and fringe development will continue, overall the places where most people
live will see significant gains in density.

Remember that a little more than a century ago, the western settlement frontier closed. By the 1920s, more than half the nation's land was officially incorporated in metropolitan and micropolitan areas. The rise of the megapolitan areas,
and then the megaregions, continues this trend.

From an economic standpoint, megapolitan areas represent a concentration
of the nation's wealth. The ten most affluent metropolitan areas, the dominant
office markets and high-tech heartlands, and most of the nation's busiest airports
and seaports lie in megapolitan areas.

What will the nation look like with 400 million people? Our bet is that the metropolitan areas as we know them will expand but also grow denser. Most places
beyond them—such as the Great Plains and the northern Rocky Mountains—will
remain sparsely populated. The challenge is to enhance the increasingly urban
quality of life in growing megapolitan environments.

process. Governments provide the legal framework for land ownership and
contractual understandings. They support development by planning and
securing funding for necessary infrastructure and major capital facilities.
At times, governments participate in joint ventures to promote development that promises to meet economic and other public objectives.

Governments also prescribe standards for development and regulate the
character and location of development. The City Beautiful movement initiated by the Columbian Exposition of 1893 inspired cities to build imposing civic edifices and parks and to create wide boulevards—adding distinctive identities to urban places but also increasing the value of adjoining
private lands. The first two decades of the 1900s, however, saw the first stir-
rings of municipal interest and involvement in overseeing private develop-

ment activities. Stimulated by concepts of the City Beautiful movement and motivated by concerns over teeming slums in the major cities, civic reformers called for establishing housing and building standards and for devoting more attention to the quality of civic spaces such as roads and parks. Citizens began to understand the community-wide benefits of well-designed neighborhoods and cities. Committees of leading citizens commissioned well-known civic designers to provide plans for the future development of their up-and-coming cities. In 1916, New York City adopted the first comprehensive zoning law to regulate land use as well as building characteristics. Municipal zoning quickly spread across the nation, opening the door to increasing public regulation of development.

In recent decades, many local governments have increased their control over private development activities. Some, in response to voters' wishes to slow or even stop growth, have imposed limits on the amount or spread of development. Environmentalists and other interest groups have pressed for more rigorous standards to protect natural features and historic areas. Neighborhood residents have obtained special zoning protection against new developments in their vicinity. In addition, many local governments, constrained by limitations on powers of taxation and changing attitudes toward development, have shifted a significant proportion of the burden of financing development-related infrastructure to the private sector.

Today, local governments in the United States possess the most direct public powers to regulate development. Although some of the 19,000 municipalities and 3,100 counties throughout the nation are too small or lack the authority to enact development regulations, many local jurisdictions actively guide development through the adoption of official policies and regulations. Certainly, most cities with populations higher than twenty-five thousand persons as well as many suburban jurisdictions and towns with smaller populations are concerned with ensuring the quality of development. In addition, the townships in some states and some counties in other states also have power to regulate development, although some states deliberately limit county governmental powers to certain rurally oriented duties, such as highway maintenance and social services. Some states have also enabled combinations of cities and counties to jointly regulate development.

Thus thousands of local governments are engaged in governing the development process. In many metropolitan areas, dozens and even hundreds of municipalities and counties regulate development. In addition, regional agencies provide forums, and sometimes plans, to coordinate the development decisions of local governments, although few regional organizations have much influence on those decisions.

State and federal agencies also regulate development, although generally not in the same manner as local governments. State laws and regulations may require special permits for drilling wells or installing septic tanks in rural areas, for example, or for opening access from a property to a state highway or for developing certain types of facilities, such as airports and hazardous waste dumps. States commonly adopt building codes as guides for the codes of local jurisdictions. Both state and federal environmental laws require permits for development that affects wetlands, the habitats of endangered or threatened species, and water quality. Development that directly affects state or federal lands and facilities may require special evaluations or permits. Many states have also adopted state programs that require or encourage local governments to plan according to specified goals to improve the likelihood and quality of local planning. They may also offer financial carrots to local governments that work to achieve state goals.

The Emergence of Growth Management

The idea that public officials should employ hands-on techniques for managing community growth and change was hatched in the late 1960s, as the fast-paced development following World War II began to raise urgent concerns about the environmental, fiscal, and other effects of spreading, suburban-oriented development.

Pent-up demands for development, suppressed by the lean depression years of the 1930s and followed by restrictions imposed by the war, generated a burst of development unlike any that had gone before. The Federal Housing Administration and the Veterans Administration underwrote housing mortgages for the common citizen. Automobiles, which had just started to become popular prior to the war, poured onto the highways, taking their passengers to find homes in the countryside. Developers ushered in the era of big projects, including huge subdivisions of new houses on sites scraped clean of vegetation and the spread of innovative shopping centers and industrial parks. Development quickly reached beyond city boundaries into areas that were soon incorporated into separate suburbs.

During this period, every community considered growth a plus. Local progress was equated with the number of new houses built, the number of new jobs created, the increases in local spending, and the like. Growth expanded small communities into large ones that were a source of pride to the business community and most residents. Growth was expected to expand the local tax base, bring a broader range of goods and services, raise income levels and create job opportunities, provide a wider choice of housing, and lead to more and better community facilities to be enjoyed by all.

However, although developers were simply catering to the mass market (which became the baby boom generation), the picture generally was not a pretty one. The media—newspapers and magazines in those days—printed photo after photo of the new developments, usually using aerial angles guaranteed to highlight the immensity and bleakness of much suburban development. Standards of development were not high; the usual procedure was to bulldoze a site into building plots without worrying too much about stands of trees and stream valleys. Environmental sensibilities were virtually unknown. Many of the first postwar developments took place on small lots platted in the 1920s, planting houses a few feet apart with almost no attempt to retain landscape features. Then, as Randall Scott observes in his introduction to the book *Management and Control of Growth,* published by the Urban Land Institute in 1975, "the backlog of demand for more adequate and improved facilities could no longer be ignored: the 'catch-up' costs tended to be high, setting the stage for taxpayer reactions against increased costs, poor land use management, and further development."[6]

Adding strength to that reaction, Rachel Carson's work *Silent Spring,* published in 1962, opened many eyes to the degradation of the environment taking place on a national and global scale. The environmental movement thus set in motion led to the passage of the National Environmental Policy Act in January 1970. The environmental concerns that drove desires for managing development were reflected in the work of a national Task Force on Land Use and Urban Growth. The task force published *The Use of Land: A Citizen's Policy Guide to Urban Growth* in 1973—a highly influential publication for the next generation of environmental advocates. Wrote the task force: "There is a new mood in America that questions traditional assumptions about urban growth and has higher expectations of both government and new urban development. . . . It is time to change the view that land is little more than a commodity to be exploited and traded."[7]

Later in the report, the authors describe the consequences of six hundred thousand new residents settling in Nassau County on Long Island from 1950 to 1960, doubling its population, as "an unrelieved pattern of low-density single-family homes, shopping center sprawl, and haphazardly sited business, industry, and entertainment. Once-blue bays are polluted; once-common shellfish have disappeared, wetlands are bulkheaded and beaches are eroded; in many areas open space is virtually gone."[8]

These results of the postwar development boom, repeated in region after region across the nation, energized civic activists to demand better regulation of the development process. Even as the National Environmental Policy Act was being signed into law, local governments in widely scattered areas were formulating and adopting the first growth management acts.

Defining Growth Management

Managing the development process is one means our political institutions use to resolve issues associated with community development. Growth management programs help shape a strategy and policy framework to guide the many political decisions that otherwise would be made incrementally, without coordination. Public officials are practicing growth management, for example, when they seek community consensus on the composition, quality, and location of future urban development, including qualities advocated by supporters of sustainable development, smart growth, new urbanism, and green building. Public officials are managing growth when they determine specific policies, programs, and actions to implement that consensus.

Definitions of growth management have tended to describe an all-inclusive, concept. The swirl of publicity concerned with growth management innovations in the early 1970s gave the term a certain mystique in the land use and development field. Academics, researchers, and attorneys soon fashioned a theoretical construct that postulated growth management as a broadly comprehensive and meticulously detailed program enacted by public entities to control all aspects of development—the classic "management" scenario that rivaled corporate management styles.

However, the authors of *Constitutional Issues of Growth Management*, a 1977 publication that influenced an entire generation of planners and program administrators, preferred a more prosaic definition of growth management. For them, growth management is "a conscious government program intended to influence the rate, amount, type, location, and/or quality of future development within a local jurisdiction." The authors go on to note that practitioners intend growth management "to influence certain characteristics of growth and [to use] a variety of governmental policies, plans, regulations, and management techniques."[9]

The encyclopedic series of volumes called *Management and Control of Growth*, published by the Urban Land Institute from 1975 to 1980, stated that managed growth "means the utilization by government of a variety of traditional and evolving techniques, tools, plans, and activities to purpose-fully guide local patterns of land use, including the manner, location, rate, and nature of development."[10]

These broad definitions suggest that growth management programs can provide policy and implementation frameworks to influence a wide variety of development activities. In practice, most communities pick and choose among policies and actions to select those that most pertain to local conditions and needs.

In an influential article published in 1990, Benjamin Chinitz painted a more provocative picture of the functions of growth management: "Growth management is active and dynamic . . . ; it seeks to maintain an ongoing equilibrium between development and conservation, between various forms of development and concurrent provision of infrastructure, between the demands for public services generated by growth and the supply of revenues to finance those demands, and between progress and equity."[11] Condensing that statement provides a practical definition of growth management as "a dynamic process, incorporating a variety of plans, regulations, and programs, in which governments anticipate and seek to accommodate community development in ways that balance competing land use goals and coordinate local with regional interests."

This definition reflects the outlook and content of this publication. Several key aspects of the definition deserve further explanation.

- Growth management is a *public, governmental activity* designed to direct and guide public investments and the private development process. Growth management puts public officials in a proactive position regarding development and requires them to pay attention to development issues early and often. It also suggests that community development is too important to be left to developers alone.
- Growth management is a *dynamic process*, more than a onetime formulation of a plan and a follow-up action program. Growth management thrives on an evolving and ever-changing program of activities, a continual process of evaluating current trends and management results and updating both objectives and methods.
- Growth management intends to *anticipate and accommodate development needs*. Its principal purpose is to foresee and shape the scope and character of future development, to identify existing and emerging needs for public infrastructure, and to fashion governmental actions to ensure that those needs will be met.
- Growth management programs provide a forum and a process for

determining an *appropriate balance* among competing development goals. Public interests must be weighed against private property rights. Furthermore, individual public objectives are meaningless unless their value is weighed against the importance of other goals of growth management. Growth management programs must make the difficult choices of emphasis, priorities, and coordination that translate general intentions into workable plans for future action.

- Growth management is *more than a suburban concern*, although its genesis stemmed mainly from the issues raised by suburban development. Many rural towns, larger cities, urban counties, and even regional agencies are also affected by growth and change and can employ growth management approaches to guide development. The term *growth management* can be as inclusive as necessary to treat problems associated with development in every type of community.
- Local objectives in growth management must *relate to local and regional concerns*. Ideally, growth management encourages communities to reach beyond their individual interests in future development to also reflect regionwide needs and goals. Local governments' management of growth must recognize that communities function within a context of metropolitan economic and social activities, goals, and needs.

Thus growth management is both a political and a technical tool for guiding community development. It incorporates and builds on traditional planning approaches, embracing and extending the ideas of comprehensive planning, zoning, subdivision regulations, and capital improvement programs that are used quite commonly by local governments. For that reason, some urban planners think of growth management as a proactive form of conventional urban planning—an extension of legally sanctioned practices in regulating development. Other planners tend to view growth management as an integrated approach to implementing community strategies for future development. Both views have merit.

The business world well understands the benefits of managing future development. Corporate managers know that the success of private enterprises requires thoughtful strategies to guide future actions. In turn, strategies call for a rational sequence of actions: identifying conditions and trends, defining goals, determining workable approaches for achieving goals, and programming investments necessary to implement these approaches. Managers also understand that these strategies and related actions must be revisited time and again to keep their enterprises viable in a changing marketplace.

Management of community development follows a similar path, with two primary differences: (1) fashioning public strategies and actions to accommodate growth requires wide participation and consensus among the electorate, who act as "shareholders" or "stakeholders" in public decisions affecting community development; and (2) public management of the development process focuses greatly on guiding or influencing the activities of private developers, builders, and landowners who operate within changing economic markets.

Working through concerns about growth and development requires communities to acknowledge and reconcile conflicts and tensions existing among a wide universe of goals and needs—for successful economic development and environmental protection, for example. The process benefits from collaborative decision making among many community interests, including local elected officials, members of the development industry, residents of established neighborhoods, and property owners.

As in the business world, growth management involves technical processes that require specialized knowledge. Skilled professional staff must identify future development trends, define options for desirable forms of development, and draft policies, programs, incentives, and regulations to achieve the desired development. The tasks require an understanding of the complex relationships among geography, resources, social and economic institutions, the land development process, and other factors that contribute to a community's special character. Programmatic and regulatory approaches must also be understood. Growth management requires and benefits from technical competence and continual administrative coordination among the various agencies responsible for guiding development.

In summary, effective management of urban development fuses the interests of the public that makes up the community and of the industry that creates most of its physical form.

The Legal Foundation for Public Regulation of Development

The laws and ordinances enacted at federal, state, and local levels of government to regulate development have been tested in the courts, creating a large body of case law that continues to evolve. Regulation of land development by state and local governments is based on the police power—the right and obligation granted to states by the Tenth Amendment to the Constitution to protect the health, safety, and general welfare of citizens. Oddly, the police power is not a constitutional power of the federal government except in cases of interstate commerce, land in federal ownership, and private land subject to major federal public works, such as dams and irrigation systems. Rather, the police power is reserved for the states. Most states enacted legislation in the 1920s and 1930s that gave local governments the authority to regulate real estate development through use of the police power. Since then, local officials have become accustomed to thinking of these regulatory powers as rightfully theirs. Most firmly believe that regulations affecting the growth and character of their communities should be administered by local governments that are closest to the people and land most affected. Increasingly, however, states are moving to reassert a role in managing the development process through state growth management acts (as described in chapter 8).

Two early Supreme Court cases—*Welch v. Swasey* in 1909 and *Hadacheck v. Sebastian* in 1915—established the right of local governments to regulate development. (Complete citations for court cases referenced in this chapter can be found in box 1.4.) In 1926, a major judicial step supporting regulation of the police power occurred when the U.S. Supreme Court, in *Village of Euclid, Ohio v. Ambler Realty Co.*, upheld zoning as a valid form of regulation. Through countless decisions since, the courts have consistently upheld the right of local governments to regulate land use and development as long as they establish a legitimate public interest for the action and follow due process in adopting and administering it.

Traditionally, the courts have allowed local governments a wide latitude in adopting legislation under the police power. Under the doctrine of "legislative presumption of validity," the courts are inclined to back regulations that are properly enacted by local governments, generally holding them valid unless clearly proven otherwise. As a result, local governments' use of the police power to regulate development has grown considerably in scope and application.

Under the police power, governments may severely limit private property owners' rights to use of their property. In appropriate circumstances, governments legally may curtail or prohibit development to preserve such natural features as floodplains, wetlands, sand dunes, and habitats of endangered species, and they may restrict the amount or height of development to protect erodible hillsides, mountain views, access to beaches, solar access, and other public interests.

Courts, however, have established legal constraints on rights to use the police power. The courts' recognition of the right of local governments to exercise the police power is tempered by judicial concerns with safeguarding private property rights. The history of land use law in the United States demonstrates the working out of an uneasy—and continuously evolving—

BOX 1.4

Important Land Use Cases

Welch v. Swasey, 214 U.S. 91 (1909). The U.S. Supreme Court upheld Boston's height restrictions within districts.

Hadacheck v. Sebastian, 239 U.S. 394 (1915). The U.S. Supreme Court upheld a city ordinance prohibiting the continuance of brick manufacturing within designated areas as a nuisance to nearby residents as a proper exercise of the police power.

Village of Euclid, Ohio v. Ambler Realty Co., 272 U.S. 365 (1926). This was the first U.S. Supreme Court case to uphold zoning as a valid form of regulation of the police power.

Golden v. Planning Board of Town of Ramapo, 285 N.W.2d 291 (N.Y. 1972). This case is one of the first and most important cases upholding regulations of development timing, phasing, and quotas; in Ramapo, the court allowed the issuance of development permits to be contingent on the availability of adequate public facilities.

Southern Burlington County NAACP v. Mt. Laurel Township, 336 A.2d 713 (N.J. 1975) and 456 A.2d 390 (N.J. 1983). In these two cases, the state court ruled that Mt. Laurel Township and other New Jersey municipalities must provide for development of a fair share of lower-cost housing and imposed court oversight of the process.

Avco Community Builders, Inc. v. South Coastal Regional Commission, 132 Cal. Rptr. 386, 553 P.2d 546 (1976). The California Supreme Court held that Avco did not have vested rights to develop despite having secured local approvals and made expenditures of over $2 million. The decision led directly to the state development agreements act.

Penn Central Transportation Co. v. New York City, 438 U.S. 104 (1978). The U.S. Supreme Court upheld New York City's imposition of landmark status on Grand Central Station, which prevented construction of an office building over the station, as a justifiable regulation that required no compensation.

Kaiser Aetna v. United States, 444 U.S. 164 (1979). The U.S. Supreme Court upheld the owners of a private lagoon in their claim that a taking had occurred when they were forced to allow public use of the lagoon.

Agins v. City of Tiburon, 447 U.S. 255 (1980). This case was one of a series in which the U.S. Supreme Court held that the cases were not "ripe" for a decision, meaning that the plaintiffs had not exhausted the administrative procedures that might have resolved their complaint before going to court.

Nollan v. California Coastal Commission, 483 U.S. 825 (1987). The U.S. Supreme Court ruled that the California Coastal Commission had not established an appropriate connection between a requirement for an exaction and the cited public objective for the exaction.

First English Evangelical Lutheran Church of Glendale v. the County of Los Angeles, 482 U.S. 304 (1987). This decision was the first by the U.S. Supreme Court that a regulatory taking of property can require compensation to the owner even if the regulation has only a temporary effect.

Lucas v. South Carolina Coastal Council, 112 S.Ct. 2886 (1992). The U.S. Supreme Court ruled that damages are due in the relatively rare situations in which a governmental entity deprives a landowner of "all economically beneficial uses" of the land.

BOX 1.4

(Continued)

Dolan v. City of Tigard, 114 S. Ct. 2309 (1994). The U.S. Supreme Court ruled that the government has the burden of justifying permit conditions that require dedication of property without compensating the owner.

Tahoe-Sierra Preservation Council, Inc. et al. v. Tahoe Regional Planning Agency et al., 535 U.S. 302 (2002). The U.S. Supreme Court decided that moratoria (that prohibit or otherwise reduce issuance of development permits during some period of time) are well-established planning tools that do not automatically create a taking of property requiring compensation.

Kelo v. City of New London, 545 U.S. 469 (2005). The U.S. Supreme Court ruled that the use of eminent domain powers by the City of New London, Connecticut, to take private property to promote economic development satisfies the Fifth Amendment requirement that allows such a taking for a public purpose.

---

balance between the rights of local governments to protect the public's health, safety, and general welfare and the rights of individuals to enjoy unfettered use of private property. The balance has shifted as the courts have expanded their interpretations of "health, safety, and general welfare." Under certain conditions, private property rights now may be overridden by environmental, aesthetic qualities, and other concerns.

Nevertheless, the extent to which regulations can restrict the use of land remains an open and controversial legal question. Courts can view overly restrictive regulations as a "taking" of private property, which governments cannot do without compensating the property owners.

Four famous U.S. Supreme Court decisions in 1987, 1992, and 1994 sounded warning notes about overly expansive use of the police power. In *Nollan v. California Coastal Commission*, the Court ruled that the commission had not established an appropriate connection between a regulation and the public interest when it required property owner Patrick Nollan to allow public access along his beach frontage in order to provide public views of the ocean. The Court indicated that it would more closely scrutinize cases of this type to ensure that regulations were properly related to public purposes. Then, in *First English Evangelical Lutheran Church of Glendale v. the County of Los Angeles*, the Court ruled that if regulations are found to take property, the public authority may be required to compensate the owner. (In this case, however, a state court subsequently determined that the regulations, which prevented rebuilding of structures destroyed by a flood in a floodplain, did not constitute a taking.)

In 1992, in *Lucas v. South Carolina Coastal Council*, the U.S. Supreme Court held that a taking had occurred and that damages were due because the council's regulations against beachfront development deprived Lucas of all use of his two lots on the ocean. These decisions suggest that governments' regulation of development must follow strict rules, with due caution for the rights of private property owners. The Court's 1994 decision in *Dolan v. City of Tigard* determined that the government has the burden of justifying requirements for dedication of property for which the owner is not compensated.

Public opinion, as expressed through political processes, is the second important brake on governments' use of the police power. Many U.S. citizens own property and place great store in their rights to use it. Property owners in most areas are politically influential, including longtime residents, farmers on the outskirts of town, and developers who have purchased land in advance of development. Therefore, in writing and administering zoning regulations, city councils and public administrators typically take great care to allow property owners fair use of their property and to provide for special treatment of any hardships that regulations might impose on property owners.

Attitudes of public officials on this question, however, vary considerably from state to state and area to area. Regulatory restrictions that Californians might consider reasonable might be anathema for Virginians. Zoning actions in areas that have seen rapid growth over a long period of time are likely to be more restrictive than those in areas that have grown slowly or not at all, where growth is welcomed. Local attitudes are affected by such factors as past and present pressures for development, concerns about fiscal impacts, and implications for environmental conservation.

Elected officials and public administrators take these concerns very seriously, especially in making the most fundamental decision about managing growth in their communities: whether to plan for accommodating development or to limit growth. For some communities, accommodating projected growth generated by the local and regional economy presents a substantial challenge. Believers in controlling population increases dislike positive steps to accommodate growth. Longtime residents often complain about changes in the look and feel of their cities and towns. Public officials may worry about finding funds to expand infrastructure systems for growing areas. Fort Collins is not the only jurisdiction to decide that the continued geographic expansion of the city is not a worthwhile objective, although the city did propose actions to accommodate additional development within the existing growth boundary. Other communities, especially in growth-stressed California, have imposed limits on the amount of development they will permit, one effect of which is shifting growth to other jurisdictions.

Thus local governments have much latitude in determining how to regulate development. Enabling legislation passed by the state provides a starting point and court decisions form a legal framework, but final decisions often depend on the attitudes and political positions of local public officials and their constituents.

Managing Growth: An Expanding Universe

Local governments that at one time attempted to guide development with rather elemental planning and regulatory tools are now trying out more complex versions and grafting a variety of growth management techniques onto the regulatory structure. But over the past decade or two, urban designers and planners dissatisfied with the results of these efforts—especially the design character of spreading suburban growth—have proposed new ideas for guiding community development. Now, in the early years of the twenty-first century, sizeable constituencies have gathered around these fresh prescriptions for forms and functions of community development. They urge communities to embrace such principles and practices as sustainable development, smart growth, community visioning, new urbanism, neo-traditional development, conservation subdivisions, transit-oriented development, form-based zoning, green building, and green infrastructure.

Valuable as these concepts may be, the profusion of terms and their interrelationships can be confusing. And how do the concepts correspond to planning and growth management approaches that communities have employed for decades?

Untangling the Terminology

Box 1.6 distinguishes among emerging concepts that offer mostly general guidelines for developing desirable communities and those that propose specific forms and methods for achieving such goals. The sections below describe the concepts and their relationships.

Focusing on Long-term Principles: Sustainable Development and Smart Growth

The concepts of *sustainable development* and *smart growth* propose broad principles or policies intended to influence the form, character, and function of community development. Concerns about the sustainability of the global environment have stemmed from the explosive expansion of the world's population amid significant declines in biodiversity and air and water quality in recent decades. Recognizing that humanity's economic future and social fabric are linked to the integrity of natural systems, inter-

BOX 1.5

The Property Rights Issue

Erik Meyers, vice president for sustainable programs, The Conservation Fund

Few topics ignite such deeply held and poorly informed views as the conflict between property rights and regulation of development, especially restrictions for environmental objectives. Often a developer or landowner will claim that environmentally based land use regulation is an unwarranted, illegal, and even unconstitutional intrusion on his or her property rights. Some may seek compensation through the courts even for temporary restrictions. At the opposite end of the spectrum, public officials, environmental activists, and neighbors to a proposed project may claim that the community has a right to a clean environment and that the public's interest, which they naturally claim to represent, always trumps private interests in using or developing land. Legal reality floats between these two poles and is pushed back and forth by events in the courts, in the legislature, and across the landscape.

The pace of change in the United States has been dramatic in the past fifty years. Individual liberties and civil rights have experienced near-revolutionary change. Protection of the environment has moved from being a fringe, counter-cultural issue to becoming a core American value. Laws by the score have been enacted and billions of dollars expended to protect environmental features and qualities. At the same time, the consumption of the American landscape is at an all-time high. According to an authoritative 2006 report from the U.S. Forest Service, the United States is converting its landscape from field and forest to developed land at the rate of four thousand acres per day, or three acres per minute. The pace of land development accelerated during the 1990s despite considerable new local, state, and national environmental and land use regulation. The U.S. Census Bureau projects a U.S. population of 420 million by 2050, more than a third larger than the 300 million estimated in 2007. These immense changes point to continuing friction between those seeking to develop land with fewer restrictions and those concerned about such development's impact on the environment and general public welfare.

Often unacknowledged in this debate are the legal doctrines that determine the balance between private rights and public interests in land that have been evolving for centuries. Since the earliest days in the American colonies, the law has always recognized *shared* interests in land as between the individual owner and others. Private ownership of real property entails obligations to one's neighbors and society. One of the most enduring concepts in both American and English common law is the landowner's duty to use property in a manner that does not adversely affect his or her neighbor. While allowing the government to enact laws to protect public safety and health and to provide for the general welfare of the people, the U.S. Constitution also includes the Fifth Amendment (expressly extended to the states by the Fourteenth Amendment), which states in part: "nor shall private property be taken for public use, without just compensation." Known as the "Takings Clause," this phrase has been interpreted by American courts since the 1920s to apply even to validly enacted regulations and to require a governmental body to pay a landowner for a "taking" of private property if application to a particular parcel resulted in leaving the owner without a viable use of the property. This established doctrine, however, only starts the process of determining whether a particular law or regulation so severely restricts the use of a particular property that compensation is due its owner.

BOX 1.5

(Continued)

Law students encounter the concept of property as a "bundle of sticks" that includes the right to occupy and use property for an economically productive purpose, to exclude others, to convey title or ownership interests, and to convey by will the property to others. Each stick is limited by laws and limitation, and the loss of one stick does not automatically mean abrogation of one's property rights. The extent of a regulation's economic impact on property is generally the critical question. Regulations that protect water resources, hillside development, or scenic vistas, for example, can negatively affect the market value of a specific property. But, conversely, these and other land use regulations and environmental protection requirements often stabilize the value of other private property and protect public health and safety.

The Supreme Court's rulings in recent years have required governments to be specific on the public purposes for which regulations are enacted and has held that restrictions too attenuated from a legitimate public purpose could, in effect, "take" private property without just compensation. The Court's rulings make clear that an owner's expectations of value must be reasonable and backed by some investment. Through legislation and public initiatives, such as Oregon's Measure 37, some states have changed the point at which compensation is required for regulatory restrictions on private property. Further, although the sovereign may assert a public need and compel a private landowner to sell the government his or her property—a practice known as exercising *eminent domain*—legislatures and public initiatives have begun to place restrictions on the public purposes for which eminent domain powers can be used at the state and local level.

Despite these shifts in this legal landscape, the changes in rules and doctrines balancing between private property rights and society's interests to date have been evolutionary, not revolutionary. While valuing their property rights and constitutional freedoms, most Americans also place high value on environmental protection. More than ever, Americans are becoming willing to forgo some private prerogatives in the interests of the greater societal benefit, especially with their children in mind. Although the debate may continue, American law has shown a particular genius for adapting to society's evolving needs and expectations at a pace that both respects settled expectations and also accommodates change.

---

national efforts were initiated during the 1980s to promote economic development that respects the functions of natural systems while advancing social equity. The guiding spirit of sustainability was expressed by the 1987 report of the Brundtland Commission, sponsored by the United Nations: "Development that integrates environmental, economic, and social concerns can meet the needs of the present without compromising the ability of future generations to meet their own needs." This mission statement has launched many activities and interests focused on overcoming such issues as international trade barriers, widespread poverty, overpopulation, and global warming.

BOX 1.6
Untangling Terms: Emerging Concepts of Desirable Development

Goals and Directions of Development
 Sustainable development
 Smart growth principles
 Community visions

Desirable Products and Models of Development
 Traditional neighborhood design
 New urbanism
 Transit-oriented development
 Green building
 Green infrastructure

Processes and Tools for Implementation
 Form-based zoning
 Conservation subdivisions
 Greenways
 LEED for Neighborhood Development

Within the United States, sustainability concerns tend to arise from the undesirable effects of rapid growth in the nation's metropolitan areas. In these urban regions, development is intensifying pressures on vulnerable resources of land, water, air, wildlife, energy, and other components of the physical environment while escalating social and economic inequities between developed and newly developing areas. Advocates of sustainable practices push for more concentrated development that increases opportunities for access to jobs, affordable housing, and nonauto travel. They also promote building in ways that reduce dependence on nonrenewable resources, prevent pollution in all its forms, and expand the use of existing and renewable resources, such as solar energy.

Proponents of smart growth view urban development issues from a slightly different perspective. Smart growth principles chiefly focus on improving the physical qualities of development as supportive habitats for human activities. Smart growth calls for the following:

- compact, multiuse development that creates more livable neighborhoods, conserves natural lands and qualities, and expands choices of mobility and residence;
- adaptive reuse and infill of already built up areas, including historic buildings and areas, that restores existing neighborhoods and recycles

obsolete or poorly developed areas, thereby reducing the need to convert rural lands;

- improvement of existing infrastructure systems and efficient extensions to support development in areas adjoining urbanized areas;
- development of regions as interdependent collections of communities that contribute to social and economic equity throughout metropolitan areas;
- decision making about development through procedures that engage and respond to all community interests.

The value of smart growth principles lies in drawing attention to qualities of development in which many different interests—conservationists and home builders, public officials and business groups, and the general public—can find common ground.

The principles of smart growth and sustainable development clearly overlap, although sustainable development generally pertains to global, all-encompassing integration of environmental, developmental, and equity concerns whereas smart growth focuses mostly on community-scale forms of development. But definitions of smart growth appear to be evolving to incorporate many of the broader perspectives of sustainable development, such as greater recognition of the economic and social dimensions of development.

Translating Principles through Community Visions

The principles of sustainable development and smart growth suggest broad directions for future development that will be effective only when individual communities translate them into more specific descriptions of their long-term hopes for community growth and development. Traditionally, local comprehensive plans have stated long-range goals for community development. Together with associated policies, the plans designate areas for particular types of development and spell out the areas' desirable characteristics. As a foundation for these goals and policies, in recent years many communities have organized "visioning" processes to articulate residents' desires for the shape and quality of their future living environment. Broadly representative groups of citizens are brought together to define a brief description of the most desirable features of the future community.

The resulting "vision" is usually expressed in broad terms, generally touching on what residents value most about the community, such as neighborhood livability and appearance, convenient access to high-quality public and retail services, and a strong economic and job base. Some vision-

ing statements center on strengthening community relationships or economic advancement or conserving environmental and historic qualities. A
successful vision statement provides a constant reminder of citizens' desires
and expectations about the character of their future community.

Community visions and the stated objectives of countless local comprehensive plans and most state growth management programs address many
aims of sustainable development and smart growth. For example, most
local plans and state programs wish to cluster development to conserve
natural lands and allow public services and facilities to be managed more
efficiently. More and more vision statements and local plans are also
addressing the need for social and economic equity in development. But
the principles of sustainable development and smart growth act as a constant reminder of the larger, long-term concerns for guiding the development of individual communities.

Reviving Urban Design: Form and Function Matter

For much of the twentieth century, local governments commonly adopted
planning and regulatory devices that laid down restrictions for community and building development but provided little specific direction for the
forms, functions, and relationships of development. Public goals and policies expressed in comprehensive plans frequently promoted the benefits
of integrated designs for whole neighborhoods closely related to employment, shopping, and civic centers and interlaced with efficient transportation and other infrastructure systems. Zoning provisions established
rough guides as to the size of individual structures and their proximity
to adjoining development. But, in reality, the output of the development
process depended on the efforts of the individual developers and designers working to satisfy the shifting demands of the marketplace. Official
restrictions on their designs and desires typically allowed plenty of
options for where, how, and what to build.

Increasingly frustrated by the results of policy statements and regulatory
provisions—endless strip commercial centers, residential "neighborhoods"
made up of a hodgepodge of ill-related projects, job centers popping up
miles away from the homes of employees—public officials looked for ways
to improve the community-building process. Construction of large-scale
communities, such as the Irvine Ranch in California and Reston in
Virginia, has offered one means of promoting integrated development, but
relatively few market areas can support that scale of individual developments. To help knit together smaller developments that occur independently over time, planners have tried detailed neighborhood planning,

flexible zoning, design guidelines, and other variants of traditional plans and regulations to encourage the creation of multiuse neighborhoods interlinked with adjoining developments. Generally, the approaches have achieved only occasional successes.

Instead, widespread unhappiness with the clutter and aimlessness of much development since the mid-twentieth century has led architects and designers to champion new (or, rather, revived) forms of development—traditional neighborhood design (TND), new urbanism, and transit-oriented development—and to promote "green" building, which reduces impacts on land and water qualities and consumption of nonrenewable resources.

Urban design was once the essence of town planning. Such planners as Frederick Law Olmsted, Raymond Unwin, and John Nolan, working in the early decades of the twentieth century, designed cities and townscapes marked by grand civic spaces and handsomely formal neighborhoods. In later years, redevelopment projects in such places as downtown Philadelphia and Southwest Washington, D.C., were designed to re-create these landmark forms of urban development, although many project designs proved abject failures in this way and others.

City planners then became increasingly entranced with establishing broad policies to guide development, leaving urban form more or less to chance. Now, in the last decade or two, attention has turned again to urban design and, more particularly, to traditional neighborhood design as a model for development. The leading proponents of TND are the husband-wife team of Andrés Duany and Elizabeth Plater-Zyberk. The best example of this design approach is their 1981 plan for Seaside, Florida. During their years at Yale University, in New Haven, Connecticut, in the early 1970s, they delighted in the domestic architecture of the city: building fronts close to the street, front porches, gables and other decorative features, and garages on rear alleys—all the essence of many old city neighborhoods across the nation. At the time, they were students of renowned professor Vincent Scully, who observed that for Duany and Plater-Zyberk, the buildings came before the plan as a whole, as a means of shaping the New Haven grid street system into a three-dimensional space. Scully praised the revival of classical and vernacular traditions of architecture, "which have always dealt with questions of community and environment and their reintegration into the mainstream of modern architecture."[12] Elsewhere, he wrote: "It is not an architecture of individual buildings [but] an architecture of the community as a whole."[13]

Architect Peter Calthorpe became a proponent of traditional neighborhoods from a somewhat different direction—from a fascination for the devel-

opment opportunities presented by rail transit lines. Along with various associates, he proposed the concept of "pedestrian pockets" of dense, pedestrian-
friendly development clustered in rather formal designs around rail stations;
he then expanded that idea to a regional network of rail and bus corridors
with pods of development around a string of rail stations. His approval of the
TND concept was a short step from his notions of transit-oriented design.
Oddly, some of his well-known site designs, including the huge, ornate 1990
layout for Laguna West near Sacramento, lacked rail service.

Calthorpe's leadership, together with the Duany–Plater-Zyberk team
and a burgeoning number of eager advocates for design-oriented planning,
created a movement called new urbanism, committed to reinventing conventional styles of suburban development as well as promoting infill and
redevelopment in already urbanized areas. As the New Urbanism Web site
describes the concept: "New Urbanism is the revival of our lost art of place-
making, and is essentially a re-ordering of the built environment into the
form of complete cities, towns, villages, and neighborhoods—the way
communities have been built for centuries around the world."[14]

New urbanists hope to replace suburban sprawl with compact, pedestrian-
and transit-oriented neighborhoods, town centers, and communities with
well-defined public realms of streets, civic spaces, parks, and natural corridors (figure 1.1). New urbanist designs call for high densities in town centers; a range of uses within a ten-minute walk of the town centers;
increased use of transit, walking, and biking; and a high quality of architecture and urban design. Supporters of new urbanism formed the
Congress for the New Urbanism in 1993 as a nonprofit organization that
sponsors conferences and publishes information about the evolving concept.[15] Over the years, advocates have expanded the goals of new urbanism to incorporate principles of smart growth and sustainability.

TND and new urbanism also promote "smart codes"—also termed
"form-based zoning"—that prescribe specific standards for planning and
designing neighborhoods, development sites, and buildings. The standards,
which have been codified in several publications, typically require the small
lots, narrow streets, and civic spaces of TND plans but also establish relationships among types of buildings and prescribe certain architectural features, such as porches and roof styles. Form-based zoning (discussed further
in chapter 6) is intended to produce a specific form of development.[16]

Both new urbanism and smart growth emphasize *transit-oriented development* (TOD), a concept that has been promoted by transportation experts
and land use planners for decades, especially in metropolitan areas
involved in construction of new and expanding rail systems. TOD postu-

FIGURE 1.1

New urbanist designs typically plan moderate to high density development in a walkable environment—a gridiron pattern of pleasant streets with boulevards leading from major entrances to commercial and civic uses and spaces.

lates the clustering of a pedestrian-friendly density and mix of uses around stations and along transit corridors to encourage greater use of rail and bus travel and, not incidentally, to create bustling, attractive places as neighborhood and community centers. Long experience in older cities demonstrated that transit ridership benefited from locating residents and workers within walking distance of stations. It was also evident that the density, design, and mix of uses that best supported the use of transit could form interesting centers of activity in which to live and work. Successful examples of TOD (some of which will be featured in later chapters) have occurred in city and suburban areas in dozens of metropolitan areas. Their evolution and design attest to the value of this concept.

The Greening of Development

Careful attention to conserving natural qualities and resources as development occurs is a central theme of both sustainability and smart growth.

Environmental activists, architects, and planners are acutely aware of conservation needs (for sustainability) and benefits (for smart growth) and are becoming familiar with specific techniques for incorporating "green" attributes in development in the forms of green building, green infrastructure, and greenways.

The term *green building* generally refers to sustainable site and building designs that conserve rather than consume resources, support and restore rather than destroy natural systems, and mitigate rather than worsen development impacts on the environment. Green building looks beyond a building's physical shell of foundations, walls, and roofs to view building design as an integral part of the natural environment and of human, economic, and social institutions. Buildings can be designed for efficient use of floor space and materials, of energy-conserving windows and heating/ventilating equipment, and of reusable construction and recycled materials. For example, new types of high-performance window glass, passive and active solar heating, orientation of buildings to sun and shade, and greater use of natural light can significantly reduce energy requirements. These approaches can provide financial as well as ecological benefits.

Designers also can lay out developments to lighten environmental impacts and take advantage of the natural character of project sites. Not so many years ago, developers were not shy about disrupting the natural landscape and drainage system of new building sites, giving rise to the term *landscraper*. Topsoils, native vegetation, topographic features, stream valleys and wetlands, and wildlife habitats commonly were displaced or wiped out in the process of shaping street layouts and buildable lots. Now many site designers and developers are well aware of techniques for retaining natural systems and weaving them into the built environment—approaches that promote ecologically healthy natural settings for human settlements. Design concepts such as conservation subdivisions, which cluster buildings to retain and even enhance environmental features, offer nature-friendly alternatives to typical suburban subdivision layouts that pack as many lots as possible into development sites. The site selection criteria incorporated in the LEED for Neighborhood Development project evaluation process (described in chapter 6) awards points for clustering to conserve natural areas.

Sustainable designs also strive to maintain and improve the natural corridors that thread through development sites. Increasingly, such corridors are being recognized as *green infrastructure systems*, which incorporate many elements of ecological systems, such as a variety of park and recreation lands, conservation areas, and natural features. The use of the term *infrastructure* underscores the significance of natural landscapes and hydrological systems as an integral component of urban systems. It suggests that proactively conserving natural elements of communities is as important as constructing road networks and water and sewer systems as critical parts of community and regional growth plans. The concept of green infrastructure responds to the sustainable ideal of maintaining the environment as a fundamental contribution to human social and economic well-being.

Many public agencies and nonprofit groups are establishing green pathways—*greenways*—that play a central role in green infrastructure systems. Greenways connect stream valleys and wetlands, ridges and ravines, woodlands and meadowlands, and other elements of the natural landscape. Many are trails along unused railroad lines; others are put in place as pathways linking natural areas in development sites or as connections between developments. As trail systems, greenways offer opportunities for recreation, appreciation of natural features, protection of habitats and native vegetation, and even transportation by walking and biking.

Thus local governments' and regional agencies' purposes and practices for managing development are being enriched by the far-reaching goals and principles of sustainable development and smart growth, an increased emphasis on traditional design approaches for urban development, and a greater appreciation of the value of conserving the natural environment as an integral part of the urban development process. These increasingly recognized concepts challenge planners, designers, public officials, developers, and indeed the general public to adapt and incorporate them within public plans, programs, and regulations that guide the development process.

Folding New Concepts into the Growth Management Paradigm

Can the emerging principles and design ideas described in the previous section be factored into the mix of current planning and growth management techniques? Or do the new concepts stand outside, or even opposed to, the framework of planning and growth management programs that jurisdictions all across the nation have put in place?

The Go-it-alone Syndrome

Enthusiasts for new urbanism and other newly popular concepts tend to emphasize the benefits of the ideas while ignoring how they may relate to existing approaches to managing growth. Their slogan might be "down with the old, up with the new," possibly in the belief that they have created a new ball game with new rules for everyone. Peter Katz, for example, in an article in *Planning* magazine, approvingly cites Andrés Duany's advice that planners should "just throw your existing zoning in the garbage."[17] Apparently, both Katz and Duany assume that zoning is still stuck in its 1930s mode, although zoning ordinances these days are generally quite sensitive to the nuances of development forms and functions.

Similar thinking seems to affect advocates for smart growth, who hold up their principles as breakthrough thinking about community development, although city planners have routinely espoused many of the principles for decades. Advocates of transit-oriented development also overstate their case when they picture transit as the most effective answer to traffic congestion, downplaying the continuing ascendancy of the automobile as the primary means of travel for most Americans. Like advocates for many causes, intent on influencing existing attitudes, supporters of smart growth and TOD are prone to slip into "hard sell" language—and thinking—that undercuts the plausibility of their ideas.

In no small degree, timing has been crucial to the popularity of the new concepts. Real estate market trends in the mid-1990s began to bolster many principles of sustainability and smart growth. Recognition of the growing diversity of America's households, including empty nesters and young professionals, attracted attention to in-town living and provided a broader market segment for preserving historic buildings, undertaking brownfield redevelopments, and building denser, mixed-income housing. In cities and suburbs, developers found strong interest in mixed-use town centers, adaptive reuse of industrial buildings and old schools, and downtown residential developments. For an industry always alert to opportunities to increase density, the confluence of market tolerance for more intensive development and public support for smart growth has been fruitful. The time was ripe for persuasive packaging of the principles and the nationwide marketing campaigns that have won recent attention to the ideas.

An Uphill Endeavor

To be fair, advocates' emphatic sales pitches for emerging concepts arise in response to the uphill battles they face in overcoming business-as-usual attitudes about prevailing styles of development. For example, in jurisdictions across the nation, designers and developers of proposed TND projects confront zoning prohibitions against TND densities and mixes of uses, subdivision standards that dictate against narrow building setbacks and yards, and public works and fire departments that decry two-lane streets and reductions in off-street parking. (It is not uncommon that TND designers must arrange "show-and-tell" demonstrations for local fire officials and city engineers to prove the capabilities of their narrow, grid-system streets to handle traffic and fire trucks.) TND supporters invented smart or form-based zoning in part as a defense against these types of requirements ensconced in existing ordinances.

Developers of green or conservation subdivisions encounter similar problems in persuading local officials that clustered housing can be fiscally beneficial and that restored wetlands can be attractive as well as effective at controlling stormwater drainage, much less providing sewage treatment. One developer in a western state proposed to enhance a wetland to function both as a central design feature and a natural stormwater collector and filter but was ordered by the local public works director to fence it in—a "safety" measure that ruined the view.

Many developers and builders also view the compact forms of development propounded by supporters of TND, new urbanism, sustainable development, smart growth, and TOD as unresponsive to the desires of most consumers. They believe that demand for low-density suburban and rural subdivisions and highway-oriented retail centers is expanding rather than diminishing. Uninterested in changing their ways, they also perceive that the industry, the lenders, and the politicians have learned the ropes of local regulatory requirements and are reluctant to seek change.

In addition, developers of innovatively designed projects have learned to their regret that many neighbors of proposed projects object to them, because of either pocketbook worries (effects on property values) or social issues (introducing racial and class differences) or both. Fearing innovation, existing residents use the plans and zoning on the books to resist new forms of development.

A Niche in the Framework

It sometimes seems, however, that proponents of new concepts disregard the framework of established land use planning and regulation practiced by most communities. Although advocates touting the broad principles of smart growth and sustainable development, for example, can offer dozens of on-the-ground examples to illustrate their ideas, they seldom focus on how individual communities should translate the principles into forms of development that meet the communities' specific needs and goals. Inevitably, that requires further clarification to determine workable applications of the general principles.

Much of this process has to do with defining terms. For example, in community "X," what density of development is considered "compact" or "intensive"? After all, there is no universally accepted or "correct" density.

Appropriate density commonly is in the eye of the beholder: residents of subdivisions with quarter-acre lots may view eight townhouses per acre as high-density development, while owners of five-acre rural lots think of quarter-acre lots as practically urban. Smart growth calls for more intensive development than is generally provided in an area's conventional development. But density must be scaled to be compatible with the existing character of development in the vicinity. In most areas, densities can be increased by 20 to 30 percent without changing the general appearance of the area. High-quality design can achieve even greater density increases while maintaining desirable neighborhoods. The point is that communities must evaluate the acceptable scale and location of higher-density development, taking into account their individual character and projected development.[18]

Examples of other definitional issues are "conserving open space" and "mixing uses." What is "open space," anyway? Parks and farms? Woods and trails? Stream valleys and school playgrounds? Residential yards? How much open space should be conserved: a greenbelt around the town, a certain amount of acreage per person, or designated systems of parks and natural environments? Should uses be mixed in all areas or just within certain important places? What types and ranges of uses should be mixed, and within what scale of proximity? These are not easy questions to answer—although they are certainly more tractable than definitions of such principles as "reduced use of nonrenewable resources" and "social equity," which get short shrift in most community discussions about development.

Again, answers to these questions must be community specific, taking into account the current character of the community and its regional role, its prospects for growth and change, and its vision for the future. Not until a community has thoroughly deliberated on these matters should principles be transformed into adopted policies and actions.

Supporters of TND, new urbanism, TOD, and green development have their own answers to these questions. Indeed, many advocates appear to regard the generic form as the whole, rather than partial, solution to concerns for managing growth. Their proposals, in accord with the precepts of smart growth and sustainability, are intended to cluster people together, reduce dependence on automobiles, and conserve natural resources and environmental qualities. They design development at moderately high densities, grouped around centers shaped by civic place and uses mixed horizontally and vertically, all fronting along grids of walkable streets and bordered by swaths of open lands.

Advocates promote this model of urban development chiefly as an alternative to the conventional sprawling, automobile-dominated suburban development of the post–World War II era. According to the New Urbanist Charter, the new emphasis on design "is the attempt to apply the age-old principles of urbanism—diversity, street life, and human scale—to the suburb in the twenty-first century."[19] That focus on fashioning better suburban development has generated many designs for individual residential subdivisions, mixed-use town centers, and combinations of both, including plans for large-scale communities and neighborhoods. Many of the designs have been or are being developed, including such well-known projects as Seaside and Celebration in Florida, Kentlands in Maryland, Issaquah Highlands in Washington, Orenco Station in Oregon, and The Crossings in California. Others have been subject to significant design changes, reductions in size, or outright rejection by local officials. For example, the I'On development in Mount Pleasant, near Charleston, South Carolina, proposed a mixed-income residential community designed with an attractive new urbanist layout. Adamant opposition by Mount Pleasant residents to the proposed range of housing types and household incomes whittled the provision of affordable housing down to a few units on a side street. Today, I'On is a very successful, high-end residential enclave.

The TND–new urbanist model is also clearly evident in many designs for urban infill and redevelopment sites. Many of these proposals appropriately respect the established design themes and historic character of the area, such as the Holiday residential-commercial project in Boulder, Colorado; the small Grove Hall Mecca Mall in Boston's Roxbury District; and the Abercorn Common shopping center in Savannah, Georgia.

For the most part, the TND–new urbanist designs have been prepared for specific projects proposed by developers or public agencies. A few developments, such as the redevelopment of Stapleton on the site of Denver's old airport, are quite large, but most focus on a relatively limited range of urban uses and systems compared to the complexity of modern cities and metropolitan areas. For example, most such plans evince little interest in the major networks of transportation and utilities required to support them, and they shunt most industries and convention centers and other uses unsuited for neighborhood ambiance into districts of special uses. The designs offer little guidance about how their planned developments relate to existing city and regional systems and functions. Plus, like developers and designers everywhere, many proponents of new ideas are fixated on their latest project design and spend scant time and thought on how their designs might fit within a variety of project types coming on line over several years. Focused for the most part on reestablishing communal relationships within and among neighborhoods (certainly a worthy goal), they brush aside real planning for real growth in cities and regions. In essence, design practitioners tend to do what developers do, adding piece by piece to the urban constellation.

Second, the TND–new urbanist design palette is limited. It provides a particular physical solution to providing satisfying living and working environments but does not acknowledge the variety of built environments that Americans insist on having. Indeed, one important aim of smart growth and sustainable development is to widen access to people's choices for how they live and work as well as how they relate and travel. Widening choices suggest that some level of demand should be accommodated at city and metropolitan levels for single-family homes on quarter-acre or even larger lots, for industrial employment areas, for big-box and highway-oriented retailers, and for increased road capacity to serve them, all of which respond to the diversity of households, jobs, and personal desires of people across the nation. Even these divergent forms of development can be—and are being—improved and adapted to satisfy the growing appreciation for community-oriented design.

Advocates of innovative designs rightly believe that their proposals are well in the minority of development approaches. It is no secret that 80 to 90 percent of development continues to employ conventional designs dependent on the automobile. However, the challenge is to allow expressions of diversity while ensuring the avoidance or mitigation of their external effects. Doing so might well elevate the practices proposed by emerging concepts.

This is all the more reason to establish a niche for innovative approaches to development in a program of long-range, comprehensive growth management. Such a program can encompass the breadth of concerns and issues involved in the principles of sustainable development and smart growth and provide a supportive framework for promoting high-quality design and development. The descriptions of growth management techniques in chapter 2 suggest some ways in which evolving ideas for community development can be recognized and implemented through established growth management approaches.

Overall, the aspects of growth management discussed in this chapter describe evolving concepts and processes that are being continually transformed as conditions change and their implications for community development are better understood. Simultaneously, communities must tussle with ongoing issues about meeting goals and needs with the resources at hand and integrating new concepts and techniques with the existing approaches to managing growth. Growth management programs demand constant attention and adaptation, remaining open to tweaking and nudging current approaches and trying out new techniques that promise to be effective.

Nevertheless, for most people, managing growth beats the alternative: letting the marketplace dictate the future character of the community based on developers' senses of what form and quality of development will generate the greatest profits at any one point in time. The key, of course, is to apply effective techniques effectively, a management requirement in both public and private contexts.

In practical terms, growth management should be viewed as a community's collection of plans, programs, and regulations that will accomplish that community's development objectives. To the extent that community objectives are achievable through the use of such basic planning techniques as comprehensive plans and zoning, those techniques can constitute a satisfactory growth management program. However, if public officials desire a more "hands-on" approach for guiding the development process, or if innovative or experimental techniques are considered necessary, then the growth management program will extend standard planning and zoning to incorporate a larger package of techniques.

The hallmark of *effective* growth management is interlinking these individual techniques and their coordination synergistically, compared to the more commonly found incremental and independent approaches. Growth management programs also recognize that successful approaches to growth management depend as much on consensus-crafted leadership and skillful administration as on the adoption of specific policy or regulatory techniques and provisions. Effective management of urban development fuses the interests of the public, which makes up the community, and the industry, which creates most of a community's physical form.

In summary, growth management is a public response to the potential effects of growth and change on the physical, economic, and social qualities of communities. Communities of all kinds—large and small, urban and rural—use growth management approaches and techniques to resolve development problems before they become crises and to keep the public and private sides of the development process synchronized and in balance.

CHAPTER 2

The Practice
of Growth Management

The development of cities and suburbs takes place within a complex framework of public policies, regulations, restrictions, and incentives that collectively add up to programs for managing growth and change. This chapter identifies the most common techniques that communities currently employ and introduces the subsequent six chapters, which more fully describe practices to achieve the major goals of growth management.

Fundamental Components

The most popular devices used by most local governments to regulate development are zoning ordinances and subdivision regulations. These sets of legal requirements designate the appropriate locations and establish design standards for property development. They are often the first major regulations that cities, towns, and counties adopt to guide the character of growth and change in their communities. Many local governments also adopt comprehensive plans and capital improvement programs to guide long-term development.

These ordinances, plans, and programs may be said to constitute the four cornerstones of local governments' regulatory efforts to manage development. (Local jurisdictions also adopt building codes, of course, to ensure the quality of new construction.) Public officials are likely to be familiar with the general purposes and provisions of the ordinances and plans, if not the details. The salient characteristics of these cornerstones of growth management, briefly described below, can be further explored by referring to the noted publications.

Comprehensive Plans

Communities prepare and adopt comprehensive plans, sometimes known as general or master plans, to establish a vision and strategy to guide the amount, location, and character of future development. A comprehensive plan describes the desired ways a community should develop over a ten- to twenty-year time frame, including broad goals and specific policies for achieving the goals. Plan reports are supplemented with maps that delineate the proposed locational interrelationships of expected growth and change. The comprehensive plan is intended to guide local public officials' decision making about development issues and how to implement regulations and programs.

Comprehensive plans are distinctive for their long-range outlook and broad scope of development concerns. Plans may also incorporate or be accompanied by more detailed plans for specific elements of development, such as housing and infrastructure systems, or for particular areas of special significance, such as rapidly developing areas, redevelopment areas, and central business districts.

Local governments may or may not be required to adopt comprehensive plans, depending on specific state statutes and court decisions. Required subjects of plan policies may be specified. Plans may be merely advisory in nature or legally binding on public decisions. From state to state, and often from locality to locality, therefore, comprehensive plans differ greatly in content and significance. Public officials in many jurisdictions regularly consult their comprehensive plans as substantive policy documents and thus take pains to keep them up-to-date and focused on important issues. However, some local officials regard comprehensive plans as strictly advisory in nature. With little influence on development decisions, the plans may become obsolete and irrelevant to the development process.[1]

Zoning Ordinances

After zoning was invented in the early twentieth century, zoning regulations spread rapidly across the land. Public officials quickly recognized zoning as a powerful means of directing the location and characteristics of new development. Zoning is intended primarily to separate incompatible uses of land, including the activities and dimensions of the uses. In general, zoning ordinances separate housing from smoky or noisy industries and traffic-generating shopping centers; establish intensively developed areas apart from low-density areas; and prevent mixtures of tall buildings with low ones. Zoning also can protect new and old neighborhoods from unwanted uses. Today, most homeowners understand the importance of zoning in

BOX 2.1

Typical Elements of Comprehensive Plans

Requirements for Contents of Local Plans, State of Washington Growth Management Act

1. *Land use element*—including designations of areas for agriculture, timber production, housing, commerce, industry, recreation, open spaces, general aviation airports, public utilities, public facilities, and other land uses; plus population densities and projections, building intensities, and actions necessary to mitigate or cleanse drainage, flooding, and stormwater runoff
2. *Housing element*—including an inventory and analysis of existing and projected housing needs, a statement of goals, and identification of sufficient land for existing and project needs of all economic segments of the community
3. *Capital facilities plan element*—including an inventory of existing public facilities, a forecast of future needs, proposed locations and capacities of new and improved facilities, a six-year capital improvements plan, and a commitment to reassess the land use element if facility funding falls short of meeting existing needs
4. *Utilities element*—for the location and capacity of electrical, telecommunication, and natural gas lines
5. *Rural element*—required for counties, to permit rural development, forestry, and agriculture
6. *Transportation element*—including inventory of existing facilities, level of service standards, traffic forecasts and methodology, system needs to meet demands, and funding needs and capabilities
7. *Economic development element*—establishing local goals, policies, objectives, and provisions for economic growth and vitality
8. *Park and recreation element*—that implements needs for park and recreation facilities in the capital facilities element
9. *Optional elements*—such as conservation, solar energy, recreation, and sub-area plans.

Separately, the state Growth Management Act requires cities and counties to designate growth areas; agricultural, forest, and mineral resource lands; and critical areas, including wetlands, aquifer recharge areas, fish and wildlife habitats, floodprone areas, and geologically hazardous areas.

Source: Washington State Department of Community, Trade and Economic Development, *Growth Management Act and Related Laws—2002 Update*, April 2002, secs. RCW 36.70A.030, 060, 070, 080, 110, and 170.

defining the nature of their neighborhood, and most neighborhood associations routinely track rezoning proposals to fend off unwanted impacts of future development. Zoning is important enough that zoning issues occasionally dominate the outcome of local elections, and council members' positions on specific zoning cases can spell their defeat or victory at the polls.

Zoning ordinances include written requirements and standards that define the permitted uses for land and buildings, the height and size of buildings, the size of lots and yards around buildings, the supply of parking spaces, the size and type of signs and fences, and other characteristics of development. These provisions are spelled out for each of a number of individual zoning districts, which are delineated on maps. When a local

BOX 2.2

Selected Zoning Innovations

Conventional zoning, especially as practiced into the 1950s, has been supplemented by many special types of zoning to address needs for greater flexibility in regulating development. Some significant variations are summarized below. Usually such types of zoning are approved only after detailed reviews and special hearings.

Planned unit development (PUD). An optional procedure for project design that is usually applied to a fairly large site. It allows more flexible site design than ordinary zoning by providing optional standards or designs or by relaxing some requirements. A PUD commonly permits a variety of housing types and sometimes other uses. Usually, a PUD consists of an overall plan that is implemented in phases by specific subdivision plans.

Cluster zoning. Allows the reduction of minimum lot and yard sizes to promote grouping of dwellings in one part of a site to preserve open space or natural features on the remainder of the site.

Overlay zoning. A zoning district, mapped over one or more other districts, that contains additional provisions pertaining to special features or conditions in the district, such as historic buildings, wetlands, steep slopes, and downtown residential uses.

Floating zones. Zoning districts and provisions for which locations are not identified until enacted for a specific project. Such zones are used to anticipate the future development of certain uses, such as regional shopping centers, for which specific locations are uncertain until developers apply for zoning.

Incentive zoning. Zoning provisions that encourage but do not require developers to provide certain amenities or qualities in their projects in return for identified benefits, such as increased density or rapid processing of applications. For example, incentives are commonly used in downtown areas to gain open space, special building features, or public art in connection with approved developments.

Flexible zoning. Zoning regulations that establish performance standards and criteria for determining appropriate uses and site design requirements rather than prescribe specific uses and building standards. Rarely applied to all zoning districts, performance standards typically apply in selected locations or for specific types of uses, such as large-scale or planned-unit developments.

Form-based zoning. An emerging type of zoning aimed at creating a specific shape and structure of proposed development while allowing a fairly flexible mix of uses. Form-based zoning specifies building types, forms, and relationships to other buildings and streets and is typically applied to guide development of traditional neighborhood designs.

government adopts a zoning ordinance, every property within its jurisdiction is designated for a specific district and each property's use is regulated by the ordinance provisions for that district. The ordinances also establish procedures for changing zoning.

Through years of practical experience and litigation, single-family homes have emerged as the primary beneficiary of zoning. In most communities, zoning is largely a device for protecting residential neighborhoods from other uses viewed as incompatible. But zoning also can be employed to preserve areas suitable for economic development and to conserve natural areas from development. Because traditional zoning is rather inflexible, many alternative zoning approaches have been formulated (as summarized in box 2.2).

Professional city planners are taught that zoning should be based on a comprehensive plan. Zoning is viewed as the detailed application, in written and map form, of the general policies spelled out in a comprehensive plan. In states not requiring consistency between plans and zoning, however, zoning may vary from the plan, and often does, causing a great deal of unpredictability in the community development process. Some local governments also persist in treating both comprehensive plans and zoning regulations as transitory documents—essentially acting as baseline requirements from which to negotiate conditions on proposed developments. In such circumstances, plans and zoning are constantly amended and revised to meet short-term interests and pressures for development—again adding to the uncertainty about where and what development will occur.[2]

Subdivision Regulations

These regulations provide standards and procedures for divisions of land. The regulations require all subdivision developers to obtain approval of detailed plans before they can record and sell lots. For proposed developments, subdivision regulations state requirements governing the size and shape of lots; the design and construction of streets, water and sewer lines, and other public facilities; and such other concerns as parking requirements and design and protection of environmental features.

Subdivision regulations provide an important point in the development approval process for public officials to closely examine a proposed site design and its relationships to the surrounding planned or existing development. It is also quite common for subdivision approvals to be linked to annexation proposals, because many subdivisions located on sites outside municipal boundaries require or would benefit from municipal water and sewer systems, schools, and other public facilities. Revisions to zoning and comprehensive plans may also be required. In such circumstances, the subdivision review process offers opportunities for planning commissioners and elected officials to impose special conditions—for example, for construction of off-site road and utility improvements and other conditions related to expected impacts of the proposed development. In some jurisdictions, therefore, approvals of subdivision proposals may become quite complex and lengthy.[3]

Capital Improvement Programs

Local governments prepare programs of capital improvement needs to support future development indicated by comprehensive plan policies and zoning actions. Usually, local governments adopt annual six-year projected programs that identify and prioritize projected improvements for newly developing areas, needs for maintaining or upgrading existing systems, and proposed funding needs and sources. Effective programs provide financial accountability and predictability for implementing planned development.

Decisions about the location and nature of major public facilities can strongly stimulate types and locations of private development that are beneficial to community growth. Communities often fund construction and operation of convention centers, for example, to improve the local economic climate. To that end, they choose locations for convention centers that will stimulate interactions with existing and planned hotels, restaurants, and other convention-related private businesses. Similar approaches are applied to public participation in the construction of sports stadiums and arenas, colleges, performing arts centers, and other facilities that can boost community development.

However, establishing year-to-year timing and funding priorities for capital improvements can be subject to political wheeling and dealing by local officials interested in promoting improvements desired by their constituencies. In such circumstances, the programs are ineffective predictors of actual schedules of improvements and may interfere with achieving comprehensive planning goals. However, with the trend toward more private involvement in funding improvements, as well as with local governments' greater fiscal concerns, capital improvement programs may prove more significant in implementing long-range plans.

Public Participation in Development

The four basic regulatory tools described above constitute the principal framework used by many jurisdictions to manage growth. When skillfully structured and coordinated, they can function as an effective growth management program. But local governments may also choose to participate directly in the development process through involvement in public-private real estate ventures. Local governments partner with private developers to develop public-private projects of particular importance to the community

—a particularly proactive means of managing community development. This practice has proved valuable over and over, especially in promoting local economic and business opportunities, improving neighborhoods, and obtaining community amenities not otherwise attainable. For decades, federally assisted programs—such as urban renewal, new communities, housing subsidies, model cities, and urban development action grants— provided funds and processes for engaging in public-private development efforts. With cutbacks in federal aid, local governments have sponsored similar joint projects to develop or revitalize town centers, industrial areas, mixed-income residential areas, transit station areas, and even recreation areas. For example, the historic American Can Factory buildings in Baltimore, Maryland, were renovated by a development firm for use as a neighborhood retail and office center next to the Fell's Point neighborhood on the city's harbor front. The redevelopment, which opened in late 1998, was planned by the Southeast Community Development Corporation, working with community leaders, and the city cooperated by expanding the Baltimore Enterprise Zone to include the site. State grants and incentives assisted in leasing about one third of the office space to a technology business incubator and another third to the DAP Corporation.

Another example is the transit-oriented revitalization of downtown Plano, Texas, by city-sponsored redevelopment next to the planned Dallas Area Rapid Transit station. Based on a downtown revitalization strategy, the city assembled the 3.6-acre site and selected a developer, who completed the residential and retail project in 2002 in advance of the initiation of rail service to Plano. The city also sponsored other downtown private and public redevelopment to strengthen the role of downtown as well as to add riders to the transit system.

Local Regulatory Procedures

The regulations adopted by local governments establish procedures that require property owners and developers to obtain zoning, building, and occupancy permits. Depending on site conditions and circumstances, other permits for wells and septic tanks, the use of environmentally sensitive lands, and the provision of special uses may be required as well. Applications must be submitted for these permits, usually with supporting documentation. If the type of development is allowed "by right" according to zoning for the property, an administrative official can approve the proposal without further action. If the proposed development is allowed only under certain conditions or requires a change in zoning, special hearings and other procedures are necessary, which can be quite lengthy.

Development regulations have become more complicated and convoluted over the years, and applicants are faced with many decisions as they make their way through the permitting process. For a specific project, it may be necessary to request changes in adopted plans or zoning or to take advantage of special procedures that allow alternative uses or more flexible design treatment. A request for changes or special procedures usually exposes a project to closer scrutiny by public officials and the general public. It can also spur public officials to require additional amenities or private contributions to infrastructure.

The use of these special "discretionary" procedures has grown in recent years, in part because public officials have discovered that they can control the size and quality of development more directly through case-by-case reviews than through written regulations. Developers opt for discretionary procedures to avoid what they regard as overly restrictive regulations or to achieve greater flexibility in site design and development. But special interest groups and citizens' groups also have discovered that such procedures open opportunities for intervening in decisions. Thus negotiations over conditions of development approval can be quite lengthy, require additional special studies, and involve a number of interests in the process.

A time may come, however, when the local regulatory process clearly needs to be rethought and reorganized. Communities have frequently formed task groups, comprising both public and private interests, to review existing regulations and procedures and to recommend ways to streamline them. Complex or overlapping requirements and lengthy, bureaucratic procedures can be simplified to reduce wear and tear on both the public and private sectors in the permitting process. At the same time, design and construction standards can be brought in line with community objectives, particularly if reducing housing costs is a concern.

The public role in community development is ever changing, requiring local governments to revise plans and ordinances in response to emerging conditions and needs. To manage development effectively, however, most local governments have found it helpful to add other regulatory approaches—growth management techniques—to the four cornerstone regulatory mechanisms.

Pathbreakers for Emerging Growth Management

The idea that public officials should employ hands-on techniques for managing community growth and change was hatched in the late 1960s, as the fast-paced development following World War II began to raise urgent concerns about the environmental, fiscal, and other effects of spreading, suburban-oriented development. A growing awareness of the need to protect environmental quality was then sweeping the nation, and suburban development was increasingly viewed as a major threat to maintaining this quality. Such issues as finding funds and making plans for the infrastructure necessary to support new development, improving the design quality of development, and mitigating the exclusionary effects of suburban subdivisions added urgency to the concerns for managing growth more wisely.

Planners, land use attorneys, and public officials responded by eagerly inventing techniques—and variations on them—for influencing the amount, location, rate, and quality of development. Jurisdictions and consultants freely borrowed approaches and provisions from each other, tweaking them to satisfy local interests and legal constraints. An early study, published in 1975, identified fifty-seven such techniques, ranging, for example, from fee simple acquisition of parks to annexation, impact fees, and use of land use intensity rating systems.[4] Later lists of growth management techniques identified techniques within one or two dozen categories. Over time, some techniques have become well-known whereas others are employed by just a few communities. Yet invention continues, perhaps underlining the difficulties and shortcomings of applying established approaches.

Several early experiments with new forms of development regulations widely publicized some of the most restrictive approaches to growth management. In fact, these innovative approaches led to court decisions that established fundamental legal justifications for the techniques. The communities of Ramapo, New York; Petaluma, California; Boulder, Colorado; and Boca Raton, Florida, crafted approaches to growth management based on various ideas then circulating in the planning world. The innovations and early testing in the courts put them on the map as path breakers for the growth management movement.

Ramapo, New York

One of the best-known early growth management programs was adopted in 1969 by the town of Ramapo, New York, a semirural community within commuting distance of New York City. Following growth pressures created by the completion of two major highways in the vicinity, the town adopted a comprehensive plan that called for low- to moderate-density development. Then it amended the zoning ordinance to require that residential development take place only as public facilities were available to support it. Facility availability was programmed by an eighteen-year capital facilities budget that accompanied the amendment. Proposed development projects were rated according to a point system that awarded points based on availability of sewers, drainage, public parks, recreation facilities, major road facilities, and firehouses. Projects receiving fewer than fifteen points were to be postponed until facilities became available or the developer constructed them.

Ramapo's housing construction dropped by two thirds following adoption of the ordinance. Builders sued the town, but New York's highest court upheld the development control system in 1972, in *Golden v. The Planning Board of the Town of Ramapo*, 285 N.E. 2d 291 (1972). Although the system was criticized because the town itself controlled only provision of parks, sewage collection, drainage, and some roads, the ordinance's innovative requirements, positive judicial support, and widespread reporting of the case made the Ramapo approach a decisive influence in the spread of growth management. Ironically, some two decades later, the town decided to eliminate the system in order to stimulate economic growth.

Petaluma, California

The small community of Petaluma, California, with fifteen thousand residents in 1960, stood in the path of suburban growth pushing north from San Francisco. Between 1968 and 1972, two thousand new residents moved to the city each year. Although the town had planned for anticipated residential development and provided a full complement of urban services, by the early 1970s its sewer and water systems were operating at almost full capacity and elementary schools in newer parts of the city were on double sessions. In 1971, a moratorium was put in place to give the town council time to rethink the general plan. A year later, the town adopted a "residential development control system," applicable to any development of more than four units, that limited development to five hundred new housing units a year. (The ceiling was substantially lower than recent rates of development.) In addition, the system set quotas for various housing types and their distribution throughout the city and established an annual competitive evaluation of proposed projects according to such criteria as consistency with the plan, availability of services, urban design features, and provision of needed public facilities.

Home builders sued Petaluma in 1973 over the annual limit on new dwelling units. After lengthy court battles, including a decision by the federal district court against Petaluma's system, the U.S. Supreme Court settled the issue in 1976 by letting stand the residential development control system. Interestingly, Petaluma's pace of development after 1976 never again approached the five-hundred-unit limit. Although the system has been modified considerably over the years, especially focusing on design issues, the annual ceiling on growth has been maintained.

Boulder, Colorado

Boulder, Colorado, another city undergoing rapid growth during the 1960s and 1970s, adopted a growth limit in 1976. The move came in response to an initiative by the Boulder chapter of Zero Population Growth to halt development at the level of 40,000 housing units. The city's counter initiative, which won, called for the city to keep growth "substantially below" the 1960s growth rates. Following the work of a blue-ribbon commission, the city drafted an ordinance (patterned after Petaluma's) called the "Danish Plan" after its primary author and sponsor. It limited annual housing development to an increase of 1.5 percent, or an average of 450 units per year. Various exceptions to the limit allowed a rate of about 2 percent growth. As with Petaluma, subsequent growth rates generally fell below that limit, which remains in place. However, Boulder has continued to innovate many growth management techniques, some of which will be described in later chapters.

Boulder's success at controlling residential development was not paralleled by its regulation of nonresidential development. A lengthy boom in commercial and business growth prompted Boulder to adopt controversial limits on that type of development in 1995. The limits proved unsatisfactory, stopping expansion of desirable existing business, and were soon rescinded.

Boca Raton, Florida

Another example of early attempts to impose growth limits occurred in Boca Raton, Florida. Appalled at the rate of development in that resort community during the 1960s, citizens generated city action in 1972 to limit development to a maximum of forty thousand housing units, or a population of about 105,000 persons. The limit was implemented by adopting a moratorium on all but single-family and duplex residential development and by rezoning to reduce permitted densities. In 1979, a Florida court—in *City of Boca Raton v. Boca Villas Corporation* (371 So.2d 154 [Fla. App. 1979]) struck down the limit because it was not based on sound studies and deliberations (implying that better studies and improved procedures might have succeeded in winning approval). However, the court let the rezonings stand.

Outcome: Expanded Regulatory Powers

The court-blessed techniques applied by Ramapo, Petaluma, Boulder, and Boca Raton stretched to new heights the powers of local governments to control growth and development. All four cities won recognition of their right to significantly reduce the pace of development. Amid increasing dissatisfaction with conventional approaches for managing growth, this determination encouraged public officials and planners across the nation to establish more proactive public guidance of the community development process.

In particular, the courts' affirmation of local powers to regulate development, even to slow or stop growth under certain circumstances, became a rallying point for communities considering more restrictive requirements. Many local officials tended to view growth management primarily as a vehicle for limiting development. Based on the court decisions from the "pathbreaking" communities, and on many later cases, a range of techniques are now considered legally applicable for slowing or halting development, including temporary development moratoriums (also adopted under the rubric "interim development controls"), limits on building permit issuance (as in Boulder and Petaluma), downzoning to reduce the amount of permitted development (as in Ramapo), refusals to upzone or annex land to meet market demands, zoning or land acquisition to preserve open space (thus reducing the availability of developable land—as in Boulder), designation of restrictive growth boundaries or urban service limits (as in Boulder) and, more subtly, requirements for adequacy of public facilities coupled with a lack of scheduled funding and construction of such facilities (as in Ramapo).

All of these techniques remain in use today in various communities across the nation. All continue to be generally supported by court decisions, provided sufficient evidence has been assembled to demonstrate a legitimate purpose for the restrictions. Of course, the application of specific techniques depends on individual state legislative and judicial constraints on development regulation, as well as on local attitudes toward regulation of development.[5]

However, after considerable academic and practical exploration of the concept, growth management has come to be seen as a positive planning and administrative addition to traditional planning and zoning programs, with its primary goal being the accommodation and support of anticipated development. Indeed, in most places where growth management programs actually were adopted and functioned, growth management became a more mundane, practical concept. Selected techniques for more meticulous management of development were simply added to existing planning and zoning programs. Over time, they were tinkered with, revised, and extended to respond to specific community concerns. Today, growth management programs are considered helpful approaches to publicly guiding the development process—but a far cry from total public control over the development process. Property owners, developers, and others involved in private real estate market activities remain key players in that process. In addition, emerging principles and design approaches to development are adding to the techniques employed in the practice of managing growth.

Today: A Panoply of Practices

The following summary of today's most widely used techniques for managing growth introduces practices commonly employed to achieve six overall goals, which are the subjects of subsequent chapters. Each chapter further describes and details the techniques and cites examples of their applications in the practice of growth management. The terms used here are quite common across the nation but may vary from community to community. Also, techniques may be useful in more than one category— for example, "urban service districts" can be used to plan and schedule service extensions as well as to encourage growth in certain areas. The techniques build on the basic planning practices of comprehensive planning, zoning, subdivision regulations, and capital improvement programs.

Managing Community Expansion—Where to Grow

This category includes techniques that encourage development to occur in designated areas most suitable for community growth.

- *Urban growth boundaries,* which, through zoning and subdivision provisions, implement a policy to concentrate urban development within a specific area and discourage development in rural areas outside it;
- *Urban service limits*, which define areas where provision of urban services is planned for extension, including major highways and streets, sewer and water lines, schools, and other public facilities normally provided by local governments;
- *Designated growth areas* (a variation on urban growth boundaries), which delineate established urban neighborhoods and centers in which infill and redevelopment are encouraged as well as urbanizing areas intended for new development, and which may also indicate urban reserve areas expected to develop in the future;

- *Designated development centers,* which identify mixed-use town or regional centers, transit-oriented development, and such community centers as civic, arts, and convention activities for special planning and regulatory incentives and other support;
- *Infill and redevelopment programs,* which assemble properties and provide financial and other incentives to encourage development of vacant or underused sites in declining neighborhoods and in commercial and industrial areas, including so-called brownfields (polluted sites) and greyfields (obsolete developments);
- *Extra-jurisdictional controls,* which employ annexation policies, "extra-territorial" controls over development beyond municipal boundaries, or interjurisdictional agreements intended to influence the location and quality of development outside incorporated areas;
- *Limits on growth,* which establish temporary moratoriums on building or subdivision approvals or restrictions on the number of building permits issued each year in designated areas;
- *Threshold criteria,* which measure the extent to which proposed developments satisfy sustainability or smart growth principles as a condition for project approvals.

Techniques to Preserve Environmental Qualities and Natural Resources—Where Not to Grow

Techniques in this category are intended to encourage protection, conservation, and enhancement of environmentally sensitive lands, such as wetlands and wildlife habitat; natural resources, such as agricultural or forested lands; and significant natural features, such as ridgelines and dunes. (Urban growth boundaries, by limiting the spread of development, can accomplish this objective in addition to determining where growth should occur.)

- *Land acquisition* by governments, agencies, and land conservancies and other nonprofit organizations, either totally (in fee), by purchase of development rights or easements, or through donations;
- *Conservation planning and zoning* to identify conservation areas in which urban development will be discouraged by such measures as advance delineation of conservation areas, zoning for large lots, or subdivision requirements for developer set-asides of conservation areas;
- *Green infrastructure systems,* which thread through developed areas to connect and conserve open spaces and natural areas, such as greenways and other trail networks, community-related parks and recreation areas, stream valleys and floodplains, and environmentally sensitive areas;

- *Delineation of critical areas* having environmental qualities that could be degraded by development, such as wetlands, wooded areas, and wildlife habitats, which are designated for special protection measures as well as for detailed planning and management;
- *Mitigation of development impacts* by subdivision provisions that require clustered development, protection or enhancement of sensitive areas, or use of mitigation banks for off-site replacement of environmentally sensitive lands;
- *"Conservation" subdivisions*, which cluster development in part of a site to conserve environmentally sensitive or natural resource lands in the remaining area;
- *Agricultural land protection* using a variety of techniques to discourage conversion of farmland to urban uses, such as designation of agricultural districts, right-to-farm laws, large-lot zoning, and agricultural zoning that retains agriculture and associated uses as primary permitted uses;
- *Watershed planning and management* by public agencies charged with protecting water quality, reducing flood damage, and supporting water-related economic and recreational activities;
- *Environmental threshold standards*, which are established by some communities for air and water quality, energy consumption, preservation of important natural features, and other environmental qualities and are employed to evaluate potential impacts of proposed developments;
- *Transferable development rights programs*, which encourage the sale of development rights for properties in designated open space conservation areas and the transfer of such rights to designated urbanizing areas that allow increased densities;
- *Rural clustering provisions*, which allow some development in rural areas if it is grouped in hamlets or villages, perhaps using transferable development rights and similar programs.

Techniques for Efficient Provision of Infrastructure

These techniques encourage the construction of facilities and systems to serve new development in a timely and cost-effective manner.

- *Functional plans* for extending, improving, and maintaining the infrastructure systems that affect the location and timing of development, which are frequently prepared as supplements or elements of comprehensive plans and typically detail the current inventory and standards for schools, roads, parks, and other facilities, project future needs, and indicate priorities;

- *Adequate public facility requirements,* which specify that public facilities must have adequate capacity to support proposed development before building or before subdivision permits are issued to allow development;
- *Exactions and impact fees* imposed by local governments on developers to assist in funding infrastructure related to their developments, such as road improvements and parks;
- *Special taxing districts* established to fund basic development infrastructure by issuing bonds to be repaid by user charges from new residents and businesses in the affected developments (Tax increment financing, or TIF, districts, a popular method of funding improvements in infill and redevelopment areas, depend on revenues from increases in property values to repay bond issues.);
- *Roadway designs that enhance walkability and biking,* including attractive streetscapes, traffic calming devices, and sidewalk and pathway connections linking centers of activity;
- *Shared parking standards,* which allow joint use of parking spaces, thereby reducing needs for space;
- *Transportation demand management programs,* which provide incentives to reduce single-person automobile travel in favor of car pools; greater use of transit, walking, and biking; staggered work hours, and other techniques;
- *Use of natural systems to protect water quality,* such as measures that preserve and restore stream valleys and wetlands, require permeable pavements and wellhead protection, reduce or prohibit development on steep slopes, and so forth;
- *Location and design of schools and other community centers* to rely less on car and bus transportation by enhancing foot and bicycle access from surrounding neighborhoods.

Techniques to Create and Preserve Community Character and Quality

Intended to establish and maintain a desirable living and working environment, these techniques address the qualities of development.

- *Mixed-use zoning,* preferably by right rather than special review, that allows a mix of neighborhood-related residential, retail, civic, and selected employment uses in designated areas, possibly through the use of overlay districts;
- *Flexible planning and design options,* implemented through special procedures in zoning or subdivision regulations, to allow clustered or

small-lot development, variations in street standards, mixed uses, and other design aspects of development;

- *Form-based zoning* in designated areas to permit and guide TND–new urbanist forms of development by right;
- *Incentive or performance provisions* that encourage developers to meet public development objectives for mixing uses and high-quality design by offering density bonuses, fast-track permitting, and other incentives or by enabling the application of flexible or performance-based design standards;
- *Green building standards* to promote the location, design, and equipping of buildings to conserve energy, reuse materials, employ nontoxic materials, reduce water use, produce less solid waste, and reduce air pollution;
- *Project rating systems*, which evaluate the acceptability of projects according to such factors as neighborhood compatibility, design quality, provision of public facilities and amenities, and environmental conservation;
- *Design review procedures* that establish guidelines and procedures to enable the evaluation of proposed project designs, especially the specific qualities of design in such particularly desirable areas as historic districts, central business districts, and mixed-use developments;
- *Historic and architectural preservation standards*, to retain a community's unique character while offering opportunities for reuse and revitalization of older urban areas and reducing pressures for new development in fringe areas;
- *Neighborhood conservation and revitalization of declining areas* by adopting such devices as traffic calming, rehabilitation programs, targeted redevelopment, and infrastructure improvements to revitalize older neighborhoods, downtowns, arts districts, failing commercial centers, and other important areas;
- *Landscape design and preservation provisions* that establish standards for streetscapes and landscaped buffers and requirements for conserving trees and native vegetation in proposed developments.

Techniques to Improve Economic Opportunities and Social Equity

Governments at all levels as well as nonprofit organizations provide many social and economic development services to meet this objective. However, some growth management techniques that influence the location, quality, and timing of development can help expand local and regional economic opportunities and social equity in response to sustainability and smart growth principles.

- *Balancing of jobs and housing* in local jurisdictions and across regions by planning, zoning, and redevelopment programs, thereby increasing the likelihood of improving residents' access to a range of jobs and housing and reducing their travel costs;
- *Employment retention and expansion incentives* that provide zoning options and improve infrastructure systems to retain, expand, and improve existing businesses;
- *Brownfields remediation and reuse*, to eliminate neighborhood-blighting influences and helping improve the mix of jobs and housing;
- *Zoning to allow or require a mix of housing types and household incomes* in development, adaptive reuse and rehabilitation, and redevelopment of residential areas;
- *Inclusionary zoning* to require developers to incorporate a proportion of affordable units in residential projects (and in some jurisdictions, commercial and institutional projects);
- *Community land trusts and housing trust funds* to provide sites and financial support for providing affordable housing;
- *Elimination or mitigation of inequitable impacts of public facility siting* within jurisdictions and across regions, by advance consideration of alternative facilities and locations, potential facility impacts, and provisions for impact minimization and remuneration.

Regional and State Techniques to Support Local Growth Management

Although regional agencies play important roles in growth management and state legislation and although these agencies are highly influential in guiding local development, their direct engagement in managing growth at the local level is focused on a few important initiatives.

- *Collaborative regional planning* (required by many states and federally mandated for transportation planning), which promotes agreements among local governments about long-range plans for regional development, though often with little accountability for strict local adherence to the plans;
- *Administration of regional services* (such as environmental protection, public transit, and waste disposal), provided by a number of regional agencies that recognize the benefits of coordinated service provision across municipal boundaries;
- *Regional accountability measures* (including federally mandated financially constrained transportation programs and air quality protec-

tion), which are required by some states for such programs as fair-share affordable housing (and environmental protection);

- *State and regional reductions of local revenue disparities*, which provide for collection and redistribution of designated tax revenues to recognize disparities among local jurisdictions in wealth and needs (e.g., for education and roads);
- *State requirements for local planning and regulation*, which have transitioned in many states from simply enabling local governments to plan and regulate development to stating detailed requirements for those actions, usually accompanied by state reviews and even approvals of the local acts;
- *State incentives for local actions in support of sustainable development and smart growth principles and interlocal cooperation*, to reward communities for adopting innovative planning and programs, particularly community design and environmental conservation;
- *State agency programs*, especially in departments of transportation, housing, environment, parks and recreation, and economic development, that encourage achievement of local growth management programs.

It is entirely probable that readers will identify more techniques, or important variants of the techniques listed above, especially given the innovations taking place in communities throughout the nation. Nonetheless, the list attempts to call out the principal techniques in use today as an introduction to the fuller descriptions in the following chapters.

A Real-world Perspective from Another Path-breaking Community

The choices and interplay of growth management techniques are illustrated in the experience of Montgomery County, Maryland. This county's blending of various growth management techniques provides a real-world introduction to the practices, successes, and perils of techniques available to many communities.

Montgomery County is an affluent suburban jurisdiction just north of the District of Columbia in the Washington metropolitan region. The county has managed growth through a comprehensive, multifaceted program for almost eighty years and has earned a nationwide reputation for comprehensive, imaginative, and aggressive planning and growth management, using a variety of increasingly complex, interactive techniques.

Populated by 932,000 residents in 2006, Montgomery County adjoins the northwestern boundary of the District of Columbia. Until the 1950s, its pastoral landscape was dotted with rural settlements. Near the District's border at the turn of the twentieth century, a few subdivisions sprang up catering primarily to higher-income families seeking a country-club or semirural setting. However, during the post–World War II decades, from 1950 to 1970, development spilled over the District's boundaries, attracted not only by the county's suburban lifestyle but also by the construction of Interstate 270 and the I-495 beltway through the county.

The pace of growth continued through the 1970s, abetted by the completion of several Metrorail connections. But the nature of growth changed as the county began accruing the commercial and industrial features of an urban center. High-tech and biotech industries were attracted by the presence of the National Institutes of Health and the Bureau of Standards, among several federal agencies with substantial offices in the central and southern parts of the county. In 2007, 491,000 employees work in the county, almost three fifths of whom live within the county. In-commuting to employment centers exceeds out-commuting. Bethesda, Rockville, and Silver Spring, once small-town market centers, have evolved into major business, shopping, and governmental centers focused around Metrorail stations. In the process, the county has become one of the top jurisdictions in the nation in terms of per capita income and percentage of adults with sixteen or more years of schooling. At the same time, the population has become much more diverse: more than a quarter of its residents are foreign born, and one third of the population is Black, Asian, Hispanic, or another race besides white. The county has become a large, affluent urban center.

Strategic and Detailed Planning

The county's planning process began in 1927, when the Maryland General Assembly established the Maryland-National Capital Park and Planning Commission as the planning, zoning, and park acquisition body for Montgomery County and neighboring Prince George's County. Montgomery County adopted a home-rule charter in 1948, instituting a county planning board as part of the Park and Planning Commission, and in 1968 the charter was revised to establish a county executive and a county council, which, unusually, was given authority for planning. Today, the planning board prepares and administers plans and ordinances, the county council appoints most board members and all hearing examiners and officially adopts plans and ordinances, and the county executive appoints some board members; programs facilities in the capital improvement program; prepares water, sewer, and solid waste plans; reviews and comments on other plans; and may veto planning board appointments and budget items, subject to council overrides.

In 1957, the commission adopted the first master plan for the entire two-county area, which was revised in 1969 as the major development policy document for the counties. Entitled *On Wedges and Corridors*, the plan proposed to contain urban sprawl by focusing development within two major transportation corridors, the I-270 corridor in Montgomery County and the State Highway 29 corridor in Prince George's County. Outside the two corridors, large areas of low-density development and open space were to be preserved as mostly rural areas. Although revised and detailed since

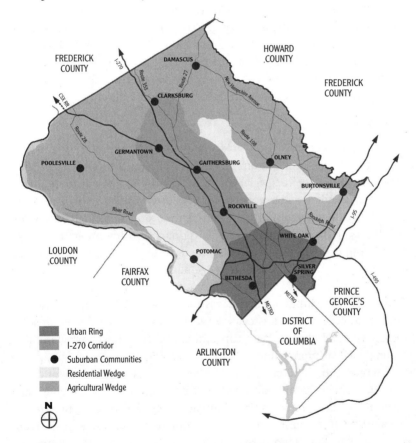

FIGURE 2.1

The County's plan, based on the region's "Wedges and Corridors" concept, illustrates the pattern of urbanized corridors along major highways and transit lines and the residential and agricultural wedges bordering them. (Plan provided by Montgomery County Planning Board.)

then—the latest version was published in 1993—the major concepts in that plan remain the cornerstones of the county's planning efforts.

The plan has been augmented by community and sector plans that apply more detailed land use guidance to specific areas, including plans for business districts and transit station areas. In recent years, the plan has been supplemented by occasional growth policy reports that assess conditions and recommend course corrections. Zoning and subdivision ordinances have expanded in scope and detail to respond to a wide variety of concerns. A capital improvements program is adopted annually to provide facilities in concert with development.

Because Montgomery County's planning program is highly participatory, a number of task forces and special working groups have reviewed the policies of the general plan over the years. In general, the groups have continued to support the basic elements of the plan, reaffirming the concentration of development around existing settlements and the preservation of farmland and open space in the northern part of the county.

Plan Implementation

The county implements the plan through the usual regulatory and programmatic devices, such as zoning, but four programs adopted more than thirty years ago deserve special mention: (1) the use of adequate public facilities measures as a core concept for year-to-year management of development; (2) the agricultural land preservation and transferable development rights (TDR) program; (3) an inclusionary housing program; and (4) the focusing of high-density development around Metrorail stations. All are keys to the county's growth management program that have received nationwide attention.

An adequate facilities ordinance was adopted in 1973 to require as a condition of project approval a review of facility capacities available to serve prospective development. With this ordinance, the county's programming of capital facility improvements (water, sewer, roads, transit, schools, police and fire protection, and health clinics) became an urgent matter for developers. Subsequently, the planning board has employed computer-assisted models to estimate traffic and fiscal impacts of proposed developments.

Since 1986, the county has prepared annual and, in recent years, biennial "growth policy" reports that define guidelines to help determine the facility capacities available for proposed subdivisions throughout the county. In most cases, the key test of adequacy involves road capacities, currently the most vulnerable part of the infrastructure system. The annual report identifies twenty-nine policy areas in which transportation capacities are tracked, including eleven where Metro stations are located. Each subdivision proposal must conduct a "local area" transportation review to determine that capacities of local intersections are adequate to serve traffic demands from the subdivision, taking into account projected construction and allowed congestion levels, which vary within policy areas served by Metro. Developers may propose traffic mitigation programs or intersection improvements to satisfy traffic demands. In addition, the county council may create development districts to fund needed road improvements in areas where substantial development is expected or encouraged.

Over time, the county discovered that the adequate facility requirements were prohibiting further development in the areas planned for higher-density growth, especially around Metrorail stations. The required level of private improvements also was forcing developers to forgo the development of affordable housing. Accordingly, the county revised adequate facility requirements for Metro policy areas in 1994 to permit continued development near Metrorail stations and development of affordable housing. The county also allows payment of impact fees to pay for road improvements.

School capacities are tracked annually for twenty-four high school clusters for five-year periods, not counting relocatable classrooms. In 2004, the clusters provided an adequate capacity for projected demands, except at the high school level, which can be corrected with minor boundary changes. The growth policy also provides adequacy guidelines for water and sewerage facilities and for police, fire, and health services.

Measuring adequate facilities has been complicated by the unpredictable delivery of Capital Improvement Program improvements (which is affected by the usual problems that arise during annual budget decisions). Facility capacities are also influenced by the difficulty of matching incremental demand increases to the timing of major facility construction, by continual changes in consumer demands and expectations for facilities, and by reductions in state and federal funding for capital facilities.

Preservation of agricultural land is a second major policy. In 1980, after several years of studies, the county council adopted a "plan for preservation of agriculture and rural open space," which established a 25-acre minimum lot size for the northern one third of the county—91,000 acres—and proposed the use of TDRs to partially compensate affected property owners. Later, plans identified "receiving areas" to which development rights could be transferred, raising permitted densities in those areas. The TDR program has strongly helped lower the political heat that might be expected from up-county property owners (especially after a judge upholding the program commented that the county legally could have downzoned with-

out resort to TDRs). However, the program ran into considerable controversy in the neighborhoods selected to be "upzoned" by receiving added
development rights. Nevertheless, by mid-2005 (twenty-five years after
program initiation), the TDR program had acquired development rights
from 48,600 acres of agricultural land. In addition, other preservation
efforts by the county, nonprofit groups, and the state had preserved another
16,000 acres. All told, more than 100 square miles of land have been preserved for continued agricultural use in an otherwise urban county, not
counting significant lands acquired for regional and local park purposes.

A third significant program is the county's inclusionary housing program. Adopted in 1973 (long before most similar programs elsewhere), the
program requires developers of fifty or more units of housing (changed in
2002 to thirty-five or more units) to set aside up to 15 percent of the units
for moderate-income housing. In return, developers can obtain an increase
of up to 22 percent in permitted density, fee waivers, and decreased lot area
requirements. Units are dispersed throughout the subdivisions and
designed to blend in with market-rate units. Although builders and developers have grumbled about the program, they have constructed eleven
thousand units of moderately priced housing through the program.
Program requirements have been tweaked from time to time, most recently

FIGURE 2.2
Metro Center, the first major mixed-use project in Bethesda's development as a
regional center, created a landmark cluster of buildings over the underground subway
station and bus terminal.

to recognize the market shift to higher-density forms of housing. The county has also sponsored the production of nearly eleven thousand low- and moderately priced rental housing units through other county-sponsored affordable housing programs.

Reflecting the general plan's call for focusing development along transportation corridors, Montgomery County has aggressively pursued the development of high-density, transit-oriented development around Metrorail stations. Floating zones that permit higher densities subject to design review procedures and developer contributions of amenities have helped focus much development around stations in Friendship Heights, Bethesda, Silver Spring, White Flint, and other county business centers. The county also invested substantial sums in a long-term redevelopment program to transform the area near the Silver Spring station into a mixed-use suburban center. In Bethesda, millions of square feet of office space and hundreds of residential units were developed within three or four blocks of the Metrorail station during the 1980s and 1990s. Developers contributed a wide variety of public art, fountains, landscaping, and other amenities to obtain project approvals, in the process gaining substantial density increases.

Now, in the early years of the twenty-first century, transit-oriented development is moving north, forming around stations along the Metro line, assisted by county investments in a convention center and the Strathmore Music Center and major private investments in office, retail, and residential construction.

Consistency and Longevity

Over eight decades, Montgomery County has steadily evolved an approach to growth management that has generally prevailed over attempts to change its direction and import. Richard Tustian, the county's planning director during the 1970s and 1980s, attributes this progress to four principal factors:

- Montgomery County's status as a chartered county, coupled with attitudes of state courts that generously applied the "fairly debatable" rule, both of which gave the county considerable latitude to develop its own planning approach;
- the outlook and standards of early residents (many of whom came to the Washington area as New Dealers and who respected professionalism in government), and residents' affluence and education, which allowed them to meet their high standards;
- the early personalities who had the vision and political savvy to estab-

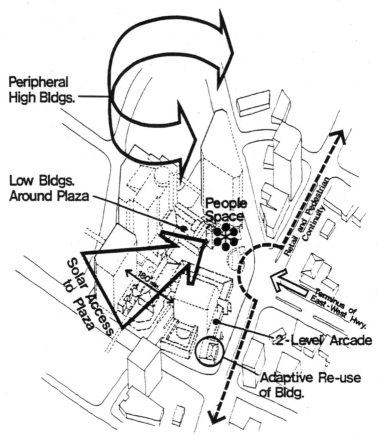

FIGURE 2.3

Metro Center was consciously designed through public/private collaboration to provide an instantly recognizable, central gathering place for residents and visitors, establishing Bethesda as an important activity center for lower Montgomery County.

lish the bicounty planning commission and water and sewer agency to guide growth;

• the long-term strength of the Washington metropolitan economy, which has provided a fairly predictable stream of public and private investment capital to support community development.

The confluence of these factors has tended to shelter the planning function from extremes of political and economic cycles. But innovations in planning, zoning, and implementation programs have not escaped controversy. Neighborhood groups, community coalitions, and even political parties have formed to resist or boost almost every new approach to development management. Particular issues in recent years have focused on traffic congestion, school overcrowding, open space preservation, and rapid changes in redeveloping business districts and growing residential areas. Growth issues are ever present in election campaigns, including one effort to cap growth and others to cut county investments in redevelopment.

Montgomery County's role in the wider regional development scene is also problematic. Washington real estate watchers believe that the county's rigorous development reviews, restrictive agricultural zoning, and developer exactions have driven small developers to less demanding jurisdictions and escalated land and housing prices. Certainly, bordering counties are undergoing real estate booms while Montgomery County is facing a growing shortage of developable land. Yet many of the county's planning woes are products of regional development forces beyond the county's control. Traffic problems, for example, are due more to through traffic pouring in from the growing counties to the north than to local travel. Only a more rational, workable regional planning process (which is unlikely in the Washington area) would begin to overcome this problem.

Looking Forward

Montgomery County's growth management system is continuing to build on the fundamental concepts laid down by the general plan some forty years ago. Since then, the planning board has been refining and improving both the high-level policy area and the nuts-and-bolts technical ends of the system. Today, the county represents a populous, rapidly growing jurisdiction that employs most of the bells and whistles contrived by planners to expand ordinary planning and zoning into full-fledged growth management. Montgomery County's growth management emphasis on ensuring development quality, focusing development along transportation corridors while preserving agricultural and open space lands, and requiring adequate facilities will continue. But a "Planning Framework Report" issued in November 2005 concluded that greenfield development is almost over, that infrastructure expansion, except for transit, is no longer a priority, and that the focus of planning should shift from large-scale planning to neighborhood and other small-scale efforts. Approaching buildout, says the report, the county will add 170,000 jobs and 94,000 housing units by 2030 but will benefit from improving existing commercial centers and producing more affordable housing. The county will continue a transition "to a focus on a more compactly developed, urban future."[6]

This chapter demonstrates that communities can employ a variety of techniques in practicing growth management. The subsequent chapters illustrate in detail how such techniques have been and are being applied in specific circumstances. The final chapter describes how the techniques can be mixed and matched to structure a balanced program that meets community objectives. The use of visioning approaches, collaborative planning, and benchmarking help communities reach that balance.

It is safe to say that growth management has come of age. The concept is now seen as a fundamental means of organizing community efforts to anticipate future development and provide ways to guide that development toward goals that meet community-wide objectives. As the following chapters make clear, the practice of growth management can be complicated, both politically and technically. Techniques and approaches must be carefully tailored to specific community needs and attitudes and constantly adapted to changing circumstances. The evolution of the growth management approaches and techniques described here will continue to open up new possibilities for managing community development.

CHAPTER 3

Managing Community Expansion: Where to Grow

A significant goal of public management of the development process is to establish the most desirable locations and qualities of future development. To accomplish this goal, communities large and small have crafted comprehensive plans and zoning ordinances that spell out public policies to guide development. Typically, they include specifications of the desired types and locations of expected growth and plans for extensions of infrastructure systems to serve urbanizing areas.

Over decades of experience, however, public officials and civic activists gradually realized that comprehensive plans and zoning frequently lack the strategic force (or political backing) required to adequately control the development process. Confusing and sometimes cross-cutting policies and regulations make decision making difficult. Requirements become outdated as market and political interests change. The result in many communities is a continual stream of plan amendments and rezoning actions that erode the predictability of local development policies.

Public officials sought a better way to ensure long-term certainty about where and what growth will take place. The interrelated techniques of delineating specific areas for community expansion (by boundaries or otherwise), directing some growth inward rather than outward, and limiting development outside the boundary provide more powerful strategic guidance over long-term development. Typically, these policy decisions are implemented through zoning that promotes development in some areas and dampens it in other areas.

The county commissioners in Sarasota County, Florida, were concerned with directing growth to certain areas when they established the county's first growth boundary in 1975. The county was just beginning to assume responsibility for providing services to the increasing development occurring outside the three principal towns along the coast, and the commissioners wanted to make a firm statement in spatial terms about the extent of their responsibilities. They chose the centerline of Interstate 75, a north-south highway then being planned, as a convenient cutoff line for urban development. The areas east of the highway were to remain as open space, chiefly agricultural land and wetlands. The county's comprehensive plan indicated that future development would be concentrated west of the highway.

For twenty years, the line held fairly firm, although it was extended east across the highway in one or two areas. Establishing the boundary gave the county government the breathing room needed to organize and implement the infrastructure systems and services necessary to support existing and projected urban development. However, as the county's population continued to increase and developers chose to build at relatively low den-

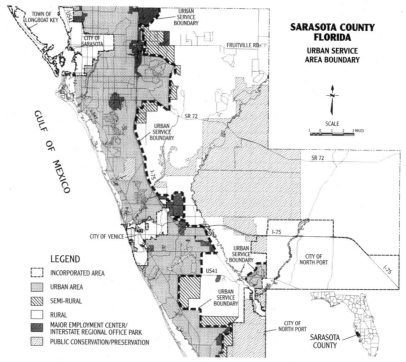

FIGURE 3.1

Sarasota County's growth boundary established in 1975 and indicated in this 1989 plan has continued to demarcate the area in which the county will extend urban services. The boundary has been moved east in several places to accommodate development pressures but much of the rural area remains. (Plan provided by Sarasota County Planning Commission.)

sities, the boundary came under intense pressure for expansion. Each revision of the comprehensive plan, with proposed boundary changes, has been attended by rancorous arguments, including court cases. A study by an Urban Land Institute panel in 1999, noting the policy issue created by the boundary, recommended that the county focus more strongly on infill and redevelopment yet also acknowledged needs for land east of I-75 to serve future growth by planning for a greenway system and clustered development.[1] That has led to county plans to allow limited developments east of the interstate highway and to decisions by at least two cities to promote more intensive infill and redevelopment within their boundaries.

Sarasota County is just one of more than 130 jurisdictions across the nation attempting to contain growth within boundaries or designated growth areas, according to a recent study of "urban containment" programs.[2] The city of Lexington and Fayette County, Kentucky, adopted the first growth boundary in 1958. It limited development to an area of sixty-seven square miles, later expanded to seventy-five square miles. Development outside the boundary was limited to lot sizes of ten acres or more by state requirements for septic tanks. Oregon's 1973 state growth management law required all cities and the urban areas of counties to draw growth boundaries and to restrict land outside those boundaries to rural activities. The regional boundary of Portland, Oregon, is the best-known example. Several other states require local governments to establish growth areas or boundaries, and more and more metropolitan regions and municipalities have also done so. After a long period of allowing, and even promoting, almost unlimited outward expansion, it appears that public policy makers are becoming more concerned with determining "where to grow."

Motivations for Harnessing Growth

During the long evolution of human settlement, people clustered in cities and towns because they needed to be within walking distance or a brief horse ride of one another. Proximity to others had many benefits: it enabled trading in goods and services, manufacture of products, participation in religious rites, attendance at schools, enjoyment of entertainment and simple social contact, and protection from marauding invaders. To gain these benefits, people lived and worked close together in dense settlements and urban centers.

In the United States, from the 1850s onward, the railroad and its urban counterpart, the trolley, began to open up opportunities to live and work in different places. Trolleys (first horse drawn then electrified) began transporting people throughout expanding urban centers, and commuter rail lines snaked into the countryside to bring people from towns miles away from their work. But beginning in the early 1900s, the automobile gave individuals freedom to travel long distances in their daily lives. The dense urban center then became a problem for mobility rather than an opportunity for accessibility, and the countryside beckoned one and all. The automobile loosened the forces that had once pulled people together.

The result was an unprecedented sprawl of urban development into the countryside, especially after World War II, when cars were plentiful, federally backed home mortgages were available, and the economy was on the move. By the 1980s and 1990s, suburbia was a way of life for many Americans. But for many people, the outward explosion of urban growth poses troublesome concerns. The traditional tight-knit fabric of urban living has given way to greater physical and, some believe, social separation among individuals, families, and groups, lending support to "us and them" outlooks. Similar physical separations have taken place among activities essen-

BOX 3.1

The Cost of Sprawl

City planners have long maintained that sprawling suburban development raises capital and operating costs for infrastructure systems. The first major study of these factors, *The Costs of Sprawl*, was commissioned in the early 1970s by the U.S. Department of Housing and Urban Development, the Council on Environmental Quality, and the Environmental Protection Agency.[1] Although its methodology has been criticized, the research found that low-density development required more extensive, and therefore more costly, infrastructure systems than did higher-density development. In a 1989 summary of cost-of-sprawl studies to date, James Frank concluded that capital costs of streets, sewers, water, storm drainage, and schools for a typical subdivision of three houses per acre can be reduced by at least one third by developing near basic public facilities and employment centers and at densities averaging twelve houses per acre (assuming a mix of housing types).[2]

The most recent and comprehensive study—more than six hundred pages long and the product of five years of research—is *Costs of Sprawl—2000*, sponsored by the Federal Transit Administration. Defining sprawl as low-density development that has leaped over other development to outlying, unbounded areas, the study found that sustained sprawl was occurring in 431 counties and projected that 24 percent of all counties would be experiencing significant sprawl from 2000 to 2025, affecting more than 13 million (or 56 percent of all) new households during that period. Under a controlled-growth scenario that shifts a proportion of expected growth from sprawling counties to more developed counties, the study concluded that water and sewer infrastructure costs could be reduced by $12.6 billion over the twenty-five-year projection period and that local road costs could be lowered by $110 billion. About 4 million acres of land would be saved from conversion to urban uses under the controlled-growth scenario.

tial to daily living, such as residence, shopping, and working places, requiring travel that takes time and energy. Thus, although the automobile may widen opportunities for where and how to live and work, these choices also generate social and economic costs not desirable or affordable by everyone.[3]

The trend toward scattered development dependent on automobility raises other concerns as well. One is the cost of extending and expanding infrastructure systems that provide the necessities of daily living—the roads and highways, water and sewer lines, schools and libraries, telephone and power lines, and other common facilities and services. These costs tend to increase for each unit of development as densities of development decrease. Furthermore, as people move out of settled areas to new ones, they leave behind major investments in infrastructure that cannot be properly maintained by the remaining population and require costly investments in constructing new systems of facilities in developing areas.

In addition to raising infrastructure costs, the typical low-density spread of developing areas occupies land that otherwise might be left available for

BOX 3.1

(Continued)

Most such studies assume that all development will be served by urban-type facilities, but much development in rural areas relies on private infrastructure, such as developer-built or unimproved roads, water wells, and septic tanks. However, scattered, low-density development raises the costs of many nonprivate facilities, such as schools (including bussing), fire stations, police protection, and road maintenance. Continued development also often requires substantial investments to replace private with public infrastructure. In addition, the dependence of scattered development on wells and septic tanks almost inevitably leads to maintenance problems and impacts on water quality.

The upshot of analyses to date is that sprawling development increases some infrastructure costs—about 25 percent for local roads, 15 percent for water and sewer systems, and 5 percent for schools.[3] In addition, however, evidence suggests that sprawl development commonly impacts important environmental qualities and generates longer commuter travel. The most conclusive test may be Americans' increasing concern over the amount of open space and environmentally sensitive land being consumed by development.[4]

1. Real Estate Research Corporation, *The Costs of Sprawl: Detailed Cost Analysis* (Washington, D.C.: U.S. Government Printing Office, 1974).
2. James E. Frank, *The Cost of Alternative Development Patterns: A Review of the Literature* (Washington, D.C.: Urban Land Institute, 1989).
3. Robert Burchell, of the Rutgers University Urban Center, and Paul Tischler, of Tischler and Associates, speaking at the American Planning Association's annual conference in Orlando, Florida, and at a Washington-area workshop, both in April 1996.
4. In the immense literature on sprawl, one helpful brief discussion of the nature and effects of sprawl is an article based on a report prepared for the Florida Department of Community Affairs by Reid H. Ewing, "Characteristics, Causes, and Effects of Sprawl: A Literature Review," *Environmental and Urban Issues* 21, no. 2 (Winter 1994): 1–15. The article contains an extensive bibliography on sprawl.

farming, forests, or scenic open space, or be protected from disruption or destruction of environmentally sensitive resources. Much of the development on the edges of metropolitan areas is consuming two or three times as much acreage per person as was the case in earlier decades. Land thus occupied is difficult to develop further as the population grows. People living in urban areas must travel longer distances to reach the open countryside. The dependence on automobile travel for almost every function of daily living aggravates both traffic congestion and air quality throughout urban regions.

Consequently, in place of traditional urban centers with strong commercial, civic, and industrial cores surrounded by pleasant neighborhoods, the contemporary "multinodal" urban pattern generally consists of a declining central city with a belt of aging suburbs surrounded by sprawling suburban residential areas that are punctuated by concentrations of commercial and industrial development. Metropolitan regions are spreading into the countryside, developing scattered retail and employment complexes, some quite extensive yet relatively isolated from the historic center. Joel Garreau describes these areas as "edge cities."[4] And recently, Robert Lang found "edgeless cities"[5] popping up on the outskirts of metropolitan areas, oriented as much to rural areas within the market reach of metropolitan activity as to the urban region.

To control this mode of rather randomly related, nonurban growth, local governments adopt growth boundaries and other means of delineating areas to accommodate future urban development. Indeed, Nelson and Dawkins consider what they call "urban containment" to be the essential framework of growth management plans, because controlling growth "involves clearly separating urban and rural land uses, directing the regional demand for urban development to specific areas, and choreographing infrastructure investments to make this happen."[6] However, such a strategy is not without opposition, given the propensities of property owners to seek opportunities to gain value from growth.

In a study of 131 jurisdictions with adopted urban containment programs, Nelson and Dawkins identify four types of approaches, differentiated by the extent to which they incorporate relatively specific policies to (1) promote accommodation of projected growth within growth areas or boundaries and (2) preserve open space outside those areas or boundaries:[7]

- "weak-restrictive" programs (mostly in California, Colorado, and Maryland), which incorporate relatively ineffective controls over development outside growth limits while doing little to plan and guide development within the limits;

- "weak-accommodating" programs (scattered across the nation), which impose relatively weak controls over development outside growth limits while providing policies promoting accommodation of market demands;
- "strong-restrictive" programs (found mostly in California), which direct growth into designated urban areas but limit population and employment growth;
- "strong-accommodating" programs (mostly on the west coast and in Florida), which are designed to preserve rural and other open spaces outside designated growth areas or boundaries while promoting accommodation of growth within the areas or boundaries.

Of the 131 programs, the researchers placed 21 programs in the first category, 31 in the second, 29 in the third, and 50 in the fourth. The study suggests that about 40 percent of the programs in place when the study was conducted are structured to guide projected growth effectively, another 40 percent are framed to be relatively ineffective in containing development, and about 20 percent of the programs limit both the amount and the location of projected growth (which probably shifts potential development to other, nearby communities). The authors conclude that the strong-accommodating approach is the best compromise for allowing growth while preserving open space, but they also caution that local conditions may call for other choices.[8]

The Land Supply and Housing Cost Issue

Public controls meant to contain growth around communities or metropolitan areas are controversial, to say the least. Many property owners, representatives of the development industry, and organizations with a conservative outlook on public regulatory powers argue that restricting development within specified areas clearly curtails the supply of land for development and thus increases development costs and, especially, housing prices. Ascertaining the effect of regulations on housing prices is an old and continuing research issue that largely stems from the difficulty of distinguishing public regulatory impacts from private market effects on housing prices. Economists have carried out elaborate statistical exercises to "prove" either case.

Defining areas where public policies support development and other areas where policies discourage it automatically reduces the potential availability of land for development in outlying rural areas and small towns.

The price inflation induced by such controls is especially noticeable in regions where households have little recourse to avoid controls by locating in other jurisdictions.

A classic analysis in the early 1990s by John Landis compared the housing price effects of seven "growth control" cities in California (including Petaluma) with similar cities nearby that had not adopted stringent growth controls.[9] The study showed that growth control measures (in these cases, mostly limits on building permits issued per year) only slightly restrained population growth and housing development. As for the effect on housing prices, Landis found that median single-family home prices rose no faster or higher in cities with growth controls than in pro-growth cities. "Indeed," he wrote, "housing was more affordable in some of the growth control cities than in their corresponding comparison cities."[10] He goes on to make the point—significant for all such studies—that controls quite possibly might have affected new homes and existing homes differently, pushed up prices in some neighborhoods but not others, or affected the various housing quality segments differently.

Why did controls not unduly escalate home prices? Landis concludes that (1) the controls as implemented might be ineffective; (2) controlled communities might have caused "spillover" to other nearby, less controlled communities; and (3) the price effects of local growth controls may be quite small in relation to other regionwide forces affecting housing prices. In short, growth management regulations are neither necessarily nor solely to blame for rising housing prices.

Landis updated his 1992 conclusions in 2006 with a new analysis of the effects of growth management on the location of growth, price effects, and population shifts, especially focused on the California experience.[11] He points out that limiting growth by restrictions on building height and bulk is the oldest and most popular form of growth management, followed by capping the issuance of building permits for new homes and placing limits on annexations—all of which seriously reduce the availability of affordable housing for would-be residents. But programs that do not constrain housing production below their communities' shares of regional demand for housing have little effect on raising housing prices. Urban growth boundaries, for example, appear mostly to redistribute development from fringe areas to more central locations or to adjacent communities.

In a 2004 Brookings Institution publication edited by Anthony Downs, *Growth Management and Affordable Housing*, Arthur Nelson and other authors explore the academic evidence for linking growth management with housing affordability. After analyzing dozens of studies, the authors conclude that "both traditional land use regulations and growth management policies can raise the price of housing," either by raising costs of development or by restricting supply relative to demand or both.[12] But such policies, say the authors, can be expected to raise prices since they are intended to confer value on development through improving public facility efficiencies, conserving natural lands, imposing safe and healthy building standards, and addressing other aspects of development. The authors emphasize, however, that "market demand, not land constraints, is the primary determinant of housing prices."[13]

William A. Fischel's commentary on the study points out that although growth management programs may be fashioned to offset regulatory constraints on development outside growth boundaries by promoting higher density within boundaries, that goal may be subverted by exclusionary practices of local governments, thus worsening the housing price inflation effects of growth management.[14] The Nelson and Dawkins study concludes that legitimate concerns exist about the effects of urban growth boundaries on land supply and housing prices: "Few growth management plans with an urban containment framework include a formal analysis of the projected land or housing value impacts of their proposed . . . policies."[15] Of the urban containment plans they subjected to statistical analysis (127 of the 131 jurisdictions studied), only 3 included a detailed examination of the land value impact of the urban growth boundary and only 12 evaluated the housing price effects of such a boundary.

These issues were partially addressed in the state of Washington by "buildable lands" analyses conducted by the state's six largest counties. In 1997, responding to complaints about possible shortages of developable land, the state required such studies to determine the supply of developable land delineated in the counties' planned urban growth areas. Such estimates call for many judgments about basic inputs, from determinations of future household sizes to definitions of underused or undevelopable land, and they require assumptions about such factors as future development densities, water and sewer service extensions, and landowner intentions for development during the planning period. However, after the analytical dust settled, the studies determined that planned growth areas in the six counties contained at least a twenty-year supply of land for projected growth, allowing plenty of time for midcourse corrections, if necessary. But questions remained about the associated commitments of local governments (1) to actually permit promised infill development at relatively higher densities than current development and (2) to find funding to adequately expand infrastructure systems to support growth in designated areas. Local leaders of the real estate industry believed that neither commitment was likely to transpire. Nor was it clear that local affordable housing policies and programs sufficiently accounted for these issues.[16]

That leaves room for considerable uncertainty about the reality of the price effects of constraints on land supply—doubts amplified by studies such as one published by the Reason Institute in 2001. After examining the impacts on housing affordability of state growth management programs in Florida, Oregon, and Washington, the study found that housing prices in these states' metropolitan areas increased faster than personal income and economic growth during the 1990s.[17] (The study did not report on trends in states without state growth management programs.) An analysis entitled "The Effects of Florida's Growth Management Act on Housing Affordability," published in 2003, concluded that growth management in Florida has reduced housing affordability "in a statistically significant manner." However, author Jerry Anthony added that the rapid growth of population, not just the effects of Florida's Growth Management Act, significantly contributed to the state's affordable housing crisis.[18]

We can sum up what we know about the land supply and housing price issue as follows: (1) growth management effects on housing prices may be minor or substantial, depending on local housing market conditions and local governments' willingness to allow higher-density infill and to extend infrastructure to delineated growth areas; and (2) gauging the significance of price effects and possible offsetting benefits remains a perplexing question. A paper presented by Michael Schill in 2004 at a Washington, D.C., conference on regulatory barriers to affordable housing, sponsored by the U.S. Department of Housing and Urban Development, complained that studies of the effects of regulation on housing supply and pricing have been less than satisfactory: "Informed public debate concerning the issue of regulatory barriers to housing development is impeded both by the lack of precision concerning the concept of 'regulatory barriers' and the absence of sophisticated research on the impact of regulations on the supply and cost of housing."[19]

While acknowledging that a wide range of regulations can affect housing supply and costs, Schill remarks that many can be justified as necessary to promote public health and safety and that others, by generating amenities, actually increase housing value and demand. Current studies, he says, "either ignore entire categories of relevant rules or employ methodologies that are not well designed to separate out the independent effects on demand and supply."[20]

The remainder of this chapter focuses on measures used in three major approaches to controlling the spread of urban growth: (1) containing the expansion of developing areas, (2) redirecting growth to existing urban or urbanizing areas, and (3) managing growth beyond local jurisdictions' boundaries.

Approaches to Controlling Urban Expansion: Urban Service Limits, Boundaries, and Growth-area Designations

Local governments adopt urban service limits, urban limit lines, urban growth boundaries, and similarly legislated plans and policies to define the desired extent of the jurisdictions' development over a stated period of time, typically twenty years. Other terms sometimes used to describe these intentions are *urban/rural limits, designated growth areas,* and *development policy areas* (or "tiers"). Such measures are intended to contain or concentrate urban development to areas within or adjoining established communities—a time-honored principle of city planning and one supported by advocates of new urbanism and smart growth.

One common approach to controlling the location of urban development is establishing *urban service limits* for areas in which urban service extensions are planned. For example, Sioux Falls, South Dakota, delineates seven districts contiguous to municipal boundaries for which the city has planned extensions of infrastructure systems. The phasing of infrastructure improvements directs the timing and location of future growth in Sioux Falls. Lincoln, Nebraska, has followed a similar approach for decades, as described more fully later in this chapter. This approach to growth management allows local governments as well as agencies that provide specific services, such as water supply and sewerage, to improve the scheduling and cost-effectiveness of infrastructure services in coordination with planned growth. Identifying service areas and preparing phasing plans for future system expansion is especially important in states that require local governments to provide urban services within annexed areas.

In Sioux Falls and Lincoln, urban service limits function much as growth boundaries do. Limits on expansions of urban services can be particularly effective if owners of properties outside the limits either require or desire urban services to support development. For example, Lexington–Fayette County was able to minimize development outside its boundary because of soil characteristics that prohibited individual septic systems for lots under ten acres. The Metropolitan Council of the Twin Cities (Minneapolis and St. Paul) in Minnesota defines a metropolitan urban service area within which it provides regional sewerage service.

Development outside the service area is supposed to be limited to densities appropriate for individual septic systems—densities that are generally quite low because of the poor soils in much of the urbanizing area. However, both the Lexington–Fayette County and Twin Cities regions have experienced substantial leapfrog development to outlying areas that can sustain septic systems or to communities outside the region that can provide sewerage service. While the urban service limits provide some protection against urban development close to the service boundary, the limits are unable to control development in more remote areas that may still be within commuting distance of the metropolitan centers.

Another issue is the possibility of unilateral action by an uncooperative authority or agency whose infrastructure extension policies are not controlled by the local government. Commonly, water and sewer agencies, for example, act like enterprising businesses in expanding service without regard to local development policies. This scenario has presented an ongoing problem in the Seattle area, for example. In King County, Washington, county officials have spent decades attempting to reach agreement with the regional sewer agency to limit sewer extensions to planned growth areas. As of 2007, this issue still has not been fully resolved.

To establish urban limit lines, engineering studies are conducted in coordination with other planning studies to determine the areas that can be served efficiently by extending existing infrastructure systems or where topographic and other conditions will allow low-cost construction of new facilities. Sewer and water lines, for example, are most easily and inexpensively extended throughout a watershed; major roads must link to the regional road network; and other service areas will be constrained by geographic features or jurisdictional limits.

Generally, such system plans are prepared for implementation over five- or ten-year periods, although major facilities, such as dams, long-distance sewage interceptors, and major highways, may need longer lead times for design and construction.

Variations on the theme of urban service limits are numerous. The city of Virginia Beach, Virginia, established a "green line" to delineate its urban service boundary, and Boulder, Colorado, imposed a "blue line" in 1959 to identify the limit of water supply services to development on the surrounding mountainsides. In 1977, Boulder joined with the county to adopt a formal growth boundary to stop urban sprawl.

The establishment of *growth boundaries* for urban development in general occurred infrequently until the 1990s, but today the concept is increasingly employed by municipalities, counties, and, to a lesser extent, metropolitan areas. Best known are the Oregon state requirements adopted in 1973, which mandated the establishment of urban growth boundaries by all municipalities; the necessity of intergovernmental collaboration in drawing a boundary around the Portland metropolitan area gave birth to a regional boundary established by the Metro regional organization for twenty-four cities and parts of three counties. Ten years after Sarasota County, Florida, established an urban growth boundary, Florida's 1985 growth management law encouraged local governments to contain urban growth and prompted many local governments in that state to establish various forms of boundaries.

The states of Washington (in 1991, for most counties) and Tennessee (1998) require local governments to define *urban growth areas* rather than continuous boundaries. For example, Washington's act required Whatcom County to negotiate with several municipalities to establish properly located and sized areas for future growth at densities of at least four units per acre. Similarly, in Tennessee, the city of Maryville exchanged proposals with Blount County to define its future growth area, with the county reaching a final decision. In both cases, the delineated growth areas adjoining cities are understood to be slated for eventual extension of urban services and annexation.

In a variation on the concept of designated growth areas, Maryland enacted a "smart growth" statute in 1997 that requires local governments to identify areas to be given priority for state funding to support growth. The comprehensive plan for Charles County illustrates the concept: it designates about one third of the county for urban development, anticipating that about 75 percent of its future growth will take place in that area. Within that area, the plan gives funding priority to areas served by water and sewer.

But even without state urging, many local governments have enacted various forms of growth boundaries, especially in the fast-growing West. San Jose, the third-largest city in California, adopted a "greenline/urban growth boundary" to focus development within the urban service area and to retain land outside the boundary (under Santa Clara County jurisdiction) in uses of rural character. San Luis Obispo (partway up the coast from Los Angeles toward San Jose) established an "urban reserve line" within its urban fringe that allows future development within the line and discourages development outside the line. Development within the urban reserve can occur only after adoption of a specific plan prepared for that purpose, which is contingent on the availability of funding for needed infrastructure.

Another variation on growth boundaries is the establishment of *distinct areas* (or "tiers") in which development policies vary. The tiers function as policy areas or overlay zoning districts, providing for gradations of development. One well-known example is San Diego's tier system. Adopted in 1979, it defines urban, urbanizing, and urban reserve areas, each with its own set of development standards. The city also tied its infrastructure funding policy to the areas, levying impact fees in urbanizing areas but waiving them in urban areas to stimulate the redevelopment of older areas.

Kane County, Illinois, a county in Chicago's suburban ring, adopted a comprehensive plan in 1996 that divided the county into three sections from east to west: urban, suburban, and future urban. The urban section incorporates the older towns and cities along the Fox River corridor, while the suburban section comprises areas undergoing development. The future urban section, almost entirely agricultural, will be protected from development until the suburban section is mostly developed. The county works closely with the cities and rural towns to promote infill and redevelopment in the older developed areas and to maintain a viable agricultural economy. In 2007, the county was considering adoption of the 2030 Land Resource Management Plan, which builds on the 1996 plan.[21] Palm Beach County, Florida, also adopted growth tiers—urban service areas, a limited urban service area, and a rural service area. The thirty-nine municipalities are expected to shoulder much of the responsibility for development in urban service areas.

Establishing and Administering Boundaries

The concept of drawing lines around communities or growth areas to contain urban development is appealing in its simplicity and directness. It is also highly marketable to voters upset by growth and to environmentalists concerned with protecting rural areas from suburban sprawl. A boundary suggests order, organization, discipline, and rationality. Nevertheless, boundaries present complex technical, political, and legal issues that have generated controversies and conflicts.

The *technical* problem is how to define a rationale for designating growth limits or areas—that is, where should the lines be drawn? This task is not necessarily more difficult than delineating appropriate areas of land use on a comprehensive plan map, but it is perhaps more potent in the implications of the defined boundary or areas. If the boundary is to designate the area within which a jurisdiction intends to deliver urban services, the potential extent of the major systems must be determined. This analysis will include projections of expected types of development and judgments about standards or levels of service and the most efficient areas for delivering those services. If the growth limits are to incorporate areas large enough to accommodate projected future development (including areas to

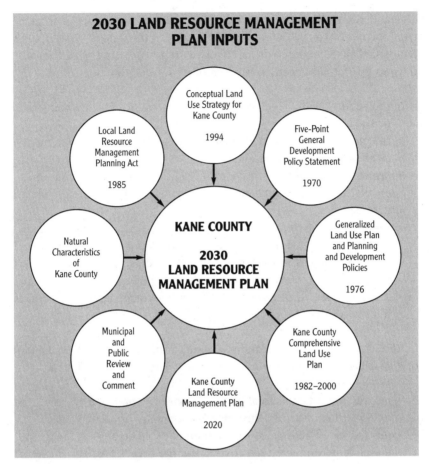

FIGURE 3.2

Kane County, Illinois's 2030 Land Resource Management Plan was shaped by a series of planning activities stretching back to 1970. Over the years the county planning office has formulated plans and policies, based on three tiers of development from urban and developing areas to rural protection areas.

be served by expanded urban infrastructure), then the amount and location of developable land required for future growth must be calculated and mapped. Usually, planning agencies will expect to incorporate enough land to accommodate about twenty years' growth, which provides a considerable range of choice in the property market and is the traditional planning period for comprehensive plans. The theory proposes that periodic boundary revisions will maintain that twenty-year supply of developable land within the boundary.

The determination of future land needs calls for a number of substantive judgments. The guidelines issued in 2000 for the state of Washington's Buildable Lands Program outline the basic steps. First is a series of calculations to project land needs to accommodate future growth:

- projection of probable population increases during the twenty-year period;
- calculation of the related increase in housing units based on the anticipated average household size;
- projection of the net acreage of residential land needs based on the estimated net density per acre of new housing during the projection period;
- a similar set of calculations to estimate the acreage increase needed for net employment land, generated by the number of projected employees, the average building square footage per employee, and floor-area ratios of expected business development; and
- the combination of residential and employment land needs equals total needs over the projection period.

The second series of calculations is aimed at determining the availability of *developable* land in areas considered appropriate for future urban growth:

- measurement of the total gross acreage of vacant, partly used, and underused land within the potential boundary or growth areas;
- subtraction of acreage considered unbuildable because of topographic, soil, environmental sensitivity, or other conditions;
- subtraction of land unserviceable by water and sewer infrastructure within the planning period;
- subtraction of land required for public facilities and purposes; and
- subtraction of land estimated to be unavailable for development during the planning period (such as prospering farmers).

Adjustments in lands considered for growth are made until the amount of developable land available for growth corresponds with projected land needs.

Of course, *political issues and decisions* can alter technical findings, beginning with determinations of types of future development to be accommodated and the specific areas to be included within growth limits. Public decisions about acceptable development densities to be achieved and changes in use designations can greatly affect projected land needs. Judgments about desirable redevelopment and more intensive development of underutilized land can reduce needs for use of undeveloped land. Other considerations include the amount of developable land within current jurisdictional boundaries, annexation policies, and other political constraints.

One danger is that such decisions can devolve into a wishing game. Jurisdictions wishing to expand employment to strengthen their economic base can project land needs for such development that represent desirable targets rather than likely trends. Jurisdictions hoping to slow the pace of growth can reduce population projections and hence the supply of developable land despite expectations for regional growth.

For many local governments interested in establishing boundaries, the key political issue is reducing development opportunities outside the boundary. Zoning for these outer areas usually establishes minimum lot sizes large enough to discourage residential development—for example, at least 10 acres outside the Lexington–Fayette County boundary, 10 to 20 acres outside Portland's, and 40 acres in lands designated for agriculture outside the Twin City urban service area. McHenry County, Illinois, set a 160-acre minimum lot size for its agricultural area. Zoning for these areas usually permits only activities associated with rural areas—various types of farming, forestry, and so forth—although it may allow for limited development in existing rural towns and settlements. (A detailed discussion of techniques for protecting open space, agricultural areas, and other rural areas from development is found in chapter 4.)

Restrictive zoning outside the boundary, however, results in property values and development dreams of landowners in that area being put on hold until the boundary is shifted. Landowners frequently view such constraints as a public taking of their properties without compensation. (In fact, this is what caused the approval by voters in Oregon in 2004 of Measure 37, which required public remuneration for any zoning that reduces property values— a controversial undercutting of the whole concept of zoning.)

Some communities soften impacts on property owners outside boundaries by defining an "urban reserve" area outside the boundary, implying that development is being phased over time and will occur at a future date. Other local governments establish programs to promote purchase of development rights in these areas, with or without the possibility of transferring such rights to urbanizing areas. Both techniques (discussed further in chapter 4) provide some compensation to rural landowners unable to profit from development. Still other communities make the case that agriculture and natural resources, such as forests, are significant economic resources that should be protected from potential impacts of scattered development. For example, the rationale for the statutes requiring Oregon's urban growth boundaries and Washington's urban growth areas centered on the immense value to the states' economies of the rich croplands and forests to be conserved through limits on urban development.

The 2040 regional plan adopted in 1994 by Portland's Metro organization defined the future boundary for metropolitan development, establishing its future urban form as a compact urban area. In defining the boundary, planners evaluated four alternative concepts: (1) the results of existing trends, (2) a more compact form, (3) a highly concentrated form that assumed no boundary expansion, and (4) an assumption that one third of future growth would take place in satellite cities. The plan selected by the Metro council, a regional elected body, called for only minor changes in the existing boundary, drawn in the 1970s, and emphasized intensive development and redevelopment in and around existing urban nodes.

Another example concerns the Sarasota County urban boundary described at the beginning of this chapter. The county's 1981 comprehensive plan made only modest changes in the original boundary set in 1975. To reduce pressure on the boundary, planners proposed higher-density centers and optional high-density residential development areas. In fact, by 1989, development densities had decreased rather than increased. Opposition to high-density development from NIMBY (Not In My Back Yard) project neighbors persuaded county officials to turn down such projects, undercutting the density policy and necessitating a significant expansion of the boundary. The proposed boundary changes, however, set up a storm of complaints by environmental groups and civic activists. Conflict over the boundary continues to this day.

This reaction to boundary changes has occurred in many communities that have established growth boundaries, belying Robert Frost's principle that "good fences make good neighbors." It appears that boundaries, once set, may generate conflict over growth rather than resolve it; they become political lightning rods for controversies over future development. San Diego's experience provides a dramatic example. Its "urban reserve" was intended to be opened up for development as urbanizing areas became fully developed. Instead, for many San Diego citizens, the twelve thousand acres took on a new significance as the last vestige of the city's once-plentiful open space. After several attempts by developers to redesignate the area for development, a citizen's initiative was approved that requires a public vote to approve any change in the reserve. Meanwhile, developers took advantage of the option that allowed clustered development to build golf course communities. And development long ago jumped over the urban reserve to fuel growth in other rapidly growing communities in San Diego County.

The *legal* issues in setting boundaries or designating growth areas usually are less onerous than the political factors. Courts generally have allowed local governments to restrict development if the public purpose is clearly defined. Regulations that merely reduce property values or dampen their potential increase are seldom held to be a public taking of property without compensation. To protect themselves against a takings suit, however, local governments should carefully establish the purposes and benefits of imposing restrictions on the location of urban growth. Studies that demonstrate the value of retaining farmland or natural resources, and detailed programs that indicate the orderly expansion of infrastructure systems to developing areas, help to make the case. In addition, allowing some development to take place in areas outside boundaries, such as one-family homes that are accessory to farms, and provision of appeals processes that consider hardships demonstrate the government's good faith in restricting development.

Unexpected Consequences

Market forces, of course, may not cooperate with public policies. After decades of community experience with regulating development in and out of designated growth areas, two concerns arise about the effectiveness of boundaries in guiding community expansion. One is the problem of generating increased development *within* the boundary, an objective usually linked hand in hand with growth restrictions. Many communities that have adopted some type of growth boundary have not succeeded in promoting truly compact development within existing urbanized or urbanizing areas. The example of Sarasota County described above, where continued low-density development within the boundary has generated constant pressures to expand the boundary, is typical rather than unusual. Planners at the Metropolitan Council in Minneapolis–St. Paul acknowledge that development in most of the area within the decades-old regional boundary can be characterized as urban sprawl. Only the extensive amount of land within the original boundary and the relatively moderate pace of regional growth have limited needs for expanding the boundary.

The trend toward sprawl within boundaries is being reduced to some extent by the recent increase of market interest in center-city and inner-suburban infill and redevelopment. However, as explained in the following section, the revival of development in existing urbanized areas represents a fairly limited proportion of growth in most communities, and low-density development continues to dominate the real estate markets.

The Metro regional organization in Portland, Oregon, addressed the problem of sprawl within the boundary by legislating minimum-density targets for all communities in the region. Normally, zoning establishes maximum densities that proposed development should not exceed. Portland-area communities were urged to achieve threshold densities that development should reach or exceed, as a means of ensuring compact development and producing affordable housing. Within the metropolitan growth boundary, that goal has been effective in raising the general density of development. (More discussion of Metro's program can be found in chapter 8.)

The second question about the effectiveness of growth boundaries is the extent to which development is "leaking" *outside* the boundary line. A 1991 study of Oregon communities' experience with growth boundaries found that a considerable amount of development was occurring outside the mandated boundaries.[22] In one small town, more development had taken place outside than inside its boundary. Such development was taking place on lots recorded prior to the establishment of the boundary or on "exception" lands determined to have low value for agricultural or forestry use. About 1 million acres of Oregon land were categorized as exception land.[23]

Portland's growth boundary has held relatively firm for more than thirty years (including a decade or so of almost no population growth). But thousands of lots have been developed outside the official urban growth boundary—about 9 percent of the region's new housing units. In fact, Metro's projections of future land needs within the boundary for the 2040 plan assumed that about one third of the regional household growth would take place outside the boundary, hopefully in satellite cities. In past years, much Portland-generated growth has occurred in the state of Washington, just across the Columbia River, but a considerable amount has taken place in rural lands outside the Metro boundary. Local residents call the rural homes "hobby" or "martini" farms because their owners purchased large lots while declaring their intention of using most of the lot for raising horses or planting gardens. (These are the low-density developments that plague planners attempting to expand the Portland boundary.)

Other growth boundary jurisdictions have experienced similar leakage or leapfrogging. Developers and builders kept out of San Diego's urban reserve are building instead in the booming towns and cities in the northern part of the county. Lexington–Fayette County's urban limit line has protected the horse farms outside its boundary, but a considerable amount of development, including significant employment growth, has occurred north and west of the city in other jurisdictions. This experience emphasizes the reality that a growth boundary is fully effective only if it controls the amount and timing of development in most of the region's highly desirable, developable land.

Urban limit lines have their limitations. They tend to become political pawns, symbols of broader community conflicts over development. They may curb urban sprawl but in themselves will not provide a cure-all for urban development ills. If not managed as part of a more comprehensive strategy for handling growth, boundaries can create exclusionary effects. Finally, boundaries alone cannot control development in outlying areas.

Communities evaluating the concept might consider the following guidelines:

- Growth boundaries should build on and logically link to comprehensive planning policies, zoning requirements, and infrastructure programs; they should not be regarded as a substitute for adequate planning.
- Growth boundaries should be based on realistic projections of growth and the types of activities to be accommodated.
- Calculations of future land requirements should consider not only amounts and densities of various land uses but also conditions of land ownership, site development, geographic constraints, and other potential restrictions on the supply of land for development.
- Boundary proposals should include procedures for periodic review and adjustment of boundaries, with specific provisions for maintaining an adequate supply of developable land within the boundaries.

Approaches for Redirecting Growth to Existing Urban and Urbanizing Areas

Many communities' growth management programs propose to offset restrictions on rural-area development by accommodating a substantial amount of expected growth in existing urban and urbanizing areas. For decades, this policy was a daring but mostly forlorn hope. Cities across America had endeavored through much of the twentieth century to halt the debilitating loss of housing and jobs to expanding suburbs. Civic leaders launched ambitious programs to replace teeming tenements with new housing projects; cities sought to wipe out crumbling industrial areas and clean up depressingly shoddy downtowns. Many rebuilding initiatives tore down large tracts of housing, dislocating their residents and disrupting neighborhoods.

Some of these efforts succeeded in attracting shiny new projects and erecting imposing civic facilities in choice locations. But despite the remarkable revival of many cities' commercial cores during the 1980s and 1990s, many inner neighborhoods continued to empty out. Many first-tier suburbs also began to feel the pinch of declining demands for central locations, leading to signs of wear and tear among shopping strips and residential areas. The century-long shift of people and jobs out of cities to outlying locations left abandoned and obsolete buildings, acres of vacant lots and contaminated sites, and numerous tax-delinquent properties. Attracting market attention to in-city development was a planners' pipe dream. Instead, developers' attentions were almost totally focused on opportunities in suburban greenfields, where land was cheap and regulations were light. The often disastrous attempts of public redevelopment authorities to stimulate urban renewal only heightened developers' aversion to building in existing neighborhoods.

Viewed another way, however, the underused or vacant buildings and lands represented a valuable resource: structures (many of them architecturally distinctive) awaiting reuse and vacant sites available for new development, all within areas already served by basic infrastructure and many near employment centers. Recognition of these opportunities began in the closing years of the twentieth century with the confluence of several trends—the aging of the baby boomer generation, the increased diversity of consumer households, and the strengthened position of urban cores as employment, cultural, and entertainment centers. Today, a rebirth of interest in centrally located jobs, housing, and amenities is fueling infill and redevelopment in many cities and inner suburbs. Historic buildings are being adapted for new uses, ramshackle housing is being replaced or restored, and disused business centers are being reconfigured. Empty spots in the urban fabric are being filled. Contaminated old industrial sites are being cleaned up for new development.

Profound demographic changes underlie the renewal of interest in urban infill and redevelopment. Traditional families of two adults and children represent less than a quarter of the demand for today's housing. The dominance of less traditional households—single persons, childless couples, unrelated adults, empty nesters, and single parents—is growing. Their interest in urban environments and amenities (and shorter commutes) is increasing. New consumer trends and global economic shifts have transformed markets for nonresidential development as well, generating mixed-use developments and remakes of older commercial centers in cities and first-ring suburbs. Ever keen to discover a new niche market, developers have sniffed the trend and come running. Adaptive reuse of buildings, infill development, and redevelopment within cities and inner suburbs have become thriving industries.

The spread of interest in sustainable development and smart growth has both paralleled and encouraged the groundswell of market interest in urban infill and redevelopment opportunities. These visions of better ways to grow emphasize the benefits of conserving and reusing existing urban resources— land, buildings, infrastructure—and call attention to the value of urban qualities of life. They help to establish the necessary political backing for zoning changes and capital spending to support reinvestment in urban neighborhoods. And the growing enthusiasm for traditional neighborhood, new urbanist, and transit-oriented designs, while focused primarily on reshaping suburban forms of development, is helping to win consumer and political approval for intensive developments in urban areas as well.

Adaptive Reuse

As suburban development flourished, many people, including developers, perceived old and historic buildings as obsolescent structures with unstylish architecture. They were thought to be expensive to renovate and unappealing to potential buyers or renters. Increasingly, however, developers have found that recycling old buildings has become a respectable market niche in many cities and older suburbs. Restoration and reuse of "structures with a past" often achieves the pragmatic goal of profitable development. Consumers and developers have been especially attracted to historic areas and buildings that offer uniquely interesting spaces and appearances.

FIGURE 3.3
Tacoma, Washington, is enjoying a rebirth of its central area, including new apartments and civic buildings and a rather classy bridge at the gateway to downtown.
(Photo used by permission of Rita Robison, a planner in the state growth management office.)

The ambience of old neighborhoods, with their storied pasts and unique design features, provides a special living environment for people seeking something different from suburban lifestyles. Often, such neighborhoods are located close to downtown employment and cultural institutions and offer convenient access to retail shops and services as well.

Old industrial buildings, in particular, commonly possess intricately designed facades, and their extensive floor spaces and large expanses of glass make them adaptable for any number of uses. Consequently, developers have seized opportunities to put new life in old places—for example, in locations as varied as Tucson's warehouse district, Wichita's railroad industrial corridor, Denver's Lowertown, Portland's River District, Chicago's West End, and Philadelphia's Old City. These historic areas, once almost wastelands, are being reborn as in-town residential, entertainment, and mixed-use areas.

Numerous successful projects testify to the attractions of historic industrial buildings. An admirable example is West Village in Durham, North Carolina, which demonstrates the serendipitous matching of growing market interest in in-town living and the availability of centrally located, adaptable structures in a thriving region. A local development partnership, Blue Devil Ventures, recycled five historic tobacco warehouses located in the city's once-declining core to create 241 loft apartments and thirty-six thousand square feet of office and retail space. The five red-brick structures, built from 1900 to 1926, feature the high ceilings and large windows of older industrial buildings, and the exteriors of two are adorned with decorative window frames, cornices, and ornate chimneys. The developers carefully targeted a market that included twenty thousand faculty and staff members at the nearby Duke University campuses and Medical Center, thirty-eight thousand workers at Research Triangle Park, and additional thousands of employees in downtown Durham, a few blocks east of the site. Every phase of the $40 million project has been well received in the marketplace. The project has combined with other adaptive reuse projects and city investments in a new civic center, a restored theatre, and a new park to renew the vitality of Durham's historic center.

The success of West Village stimulated Blue Devil Ventures to expand the development to include the seven remaining buildings in the former Liggett and Myers complex. In 2006, they began renovations to create an additional 375 loft-style apartments, 164,000 square feet of office/lab space, and 58,000 square feet of retail space. Altogether, about a thousand residents and one thousand employees will live and work at West Village. The Village also will become transit oriented: plans call for a new Amtrak station on the site, Durham's downtown regional rail station on an adjoining site, and a new bus terminal only a few blocks away.

Another former factory, the former Ford Model T manufacturing plant in Cincinnati, was classified as a historic building but abandoned in 1998, sadly dilapidated and covered with graffiti. The 1915 brick-and-concrete structure, highly visible from Interstate 71, was likely designed by Albert Kahn, a famous industrial architect. Four real estate developers and investors, three based in Cincinnati, teamed up in 2001 to purchase and reclaim the landmark structure for loft office space. Financing included historic tax credits, which required preservation of the building's historic features. Renovation costs included repair and replacement of the huge windows and removal of two hundred tons of debris. But the renovation yielded 120,000 square feet of office space on three floors, a conference room in the original automobile showroom space, and indoor parking. The high visibility of the building, its unique design features, and its spacious interior proved attractive to tenants. Construction was completed in late 2003, and the building was fully occupied within a year.

Adaptive reuse of old and historic buildings usually takes extra time, effort, and imaginative thinking by developers. Often, they are working with one-of-a-kind structures with many possibilities for hidden faults. Critical aspects of construction may not meet current building codes. Zoning changes or special permits may be needed to allow new uses in old buildings. Renovations of historic buildings, in particular, can cause many headaches. For example, the restoration of a former Atlanta high school to create Bass Lofts, a residential development including 103 luxury loft apartments plus 30 new units, required special treatment for the ten-foot-high windows. Retaining the existing frames and sashes required a double reglazing. Workers discovered asbestos in the window caulk and more lead-based paint than expected on the frames, both necessitating careful and costly removal. Abatement of environmental hazards for the Bass Lofts project ultimately cost twice the original estimate.

The restoration of historic buildings, therefore, especially those that will use preservation tax credits, demands careful preparation. Some fundamental principles for success are detailed by Donovan D. Rypkema, a real estate economist who specializes in renovated buildings:

- Employ architects and building contractors who have successfully completed renovations of old buildings and, for a tax-certified historic rehabilitation project, who have done so for projects that meet U.S. Department of Interior standards for historic preservation.

- Expect to take more time to complete the project than normally required—rehabilitation almost always encounters structural and regulatory surprises.
- At the outset of the project, before signing the option agreement, discuss requirements that will affect project feasibility with local building officials and, for tax-credit projects, with representatives of the state historic preservation office.
- Conduct physical and environmental analyses and prepare cost estimates to cure structural problems, remove lead paint, or abate asbestos before property acquisition.
- Make use of the peculiar features of the building to lure tenants, who often view the individual character of old and historic buildings as the principal attraction.
- Look for allies in local preservation groups who can supply valuable information about a building's history and possibly provide access to financial resources and political support.
- Be prepared to obtain multiple sources of financing, including public sources of subordinated funding.[24]

Despite the difficulties, the many success stories of adaptive reuse demonstrate that renovations of existing buildings can turn a profit, even with extra costs for preserving historic features. Renovation costs for buildings qualifying for historic tax credits may be 60 percent or lower than the cost of comparable new construction. The expense of a complete rehabilitation, including exterior repairs and replacement of all systems and the roof, may cost more than equivalent new construction, but the distinctive quality of the completed building generally makes up for the extra cost. Renovations of nonhistoric buildings usually can be accomplished at considerably less expense. Indeed, renovating older housing properties to retain housing affordability, for example, keeps costs down, according to Hunter Johnson of LINC Housing in Long Beach, California. With projects such as Beechwood Manor, a one-hundred-unit existing housing project in Lancaster, California, says Johnson, "it is possible to acquire and refurbish units for between one-half and two-thirds of the cost of developing the same complex from the ground up."[25] The additional costs of land for a new development and the design, entitlement, and finance process easily raise project costs to levels that defeat the goal of affordability.

It is not as difficult as might be imagined to convert old buildings to new uses. Adaptive reuse may require skillful redesign, but the results can attract tenants interested in unique spaces and great locations. Expansive floor spaces are not a requirement of many tenants, especially in downtown areas. In most cities, in fact, the majority of office tenants have fewer than twenty employees.

In short, adaptive reuse of old buildings, whether historic landmarks or not, can pay off with the production of individualistic projects that are highly attractive in the marketplace.

Infill Development

Infill implies a "shoehorn approach" to developing in existing urban and urbanizing areas—for example, inserting small projects into a few leftover acres or undeveloped lots within a built-up environment. Infill, however, comes in all sizes. Some infill projects involve a few lots or acres, whereas others take advantage of larger parcels that become available as former uses decline or vanish. Sites may include skipped-over or underutilized parcels, parking areas in downtowns and around transit stations, lands formerly used for industries that have closed down, and lots left when abandoned housing is demolished. Some infill projects gain from proximity to downtown or upscale neighborhoods. Many focus on residential development, while others involve development of retail and entertainment complexes, office buildings, and mixed-use projects.

The development of infill sites can help upgrade the quality of neighborhoods and commercial centers, possibly stimulating market interest in such areas. A superb example of this effect is Millennium Place in Boston, a pioneering mixed-use project sited in the so-called "Combat Zone" of downtown Boston. On three acres of former parking lots, Millennium Place provides 1.8 million square feet of gross building area for offices, 304 apartments, a 200-room hotel, and parking for 850 cars. Its location in a notoriously rundown neighborhood next to Boston Common made it an instant landmark and transformed the area. The Congress for New Urbanism presented it with its 2002 Charter Award, calling Millennium Place a "critical mass for an economically sustainable mixed-use neighborhood." The high-density development also won a 2003 ULI Award for Excellence.[26]

At the other end of the scale, smaller, less intensive projects can spark new life in residential neighborhoods. For example, a 2.76-acre brownfield site in Houston that once housed a greenhouse and used car lot was acquired by the nonprofit Avenue Community Development Corporation, cleaned up by a concerted effort of the city's Brownfields Redevelopment Program working with federal and state agencies, and developed by private-sector developers. The seventy-four-unit, mixed-income apartment complex, Washington Courtyards, opened in 2000 and is credited with giving the low-income neighborhood "a financial and psychic boost."[27]

In another example, the Town of Breckenridge, Colorado, reclaimed twenty-two acres of an eighty-five-acre contaminated mining site to allow the development of Wellington Neighborhood, a traditionally designed cluster of 122 homes affordable to working families, with another twenty acres preserved for parks and open space. Eighty percent of the 122 homes are reserved for purchase by people who work in Summit County, many of whom otherwise could afford a home only on the other side of Hoosier Pass, a forty-five-minute commute. Covenants keep the homes affordable for future generations. The success of the project has generated plans for developing an additional 128 affordable homes.[28]

Retail developers are also finding infill sites in older, first-ring suburbs. Expanding on the substantial office and retail development that has occurred over the past twenty years around Bethesda's Metrorail station, Federal Realty Investment Trust began developing Bethesda Row in 1995 as a multiphase mixed-use district. The developer has rehabilitated former light industrial buildings and infilled vacant lots with new construction, all centered around a one-thousand-car county parking garage and adjoining a cluster of recently built high-rise apartments and densely designed townhomes. The project created shopping streets with brick sidewalks, trees, fountains, plazas, and outdoor seating that encourage residents and visitors to walk around the mix of local, regional, and national retailers and restaurants. As of 2007, the final phase, a residential project, was under construction.

The development of infill sites can encounter difficulties, however. The availability of well-located sites is limited, and land costs may be prohibitive. Working with multiple property owners to assemble a developable site can be frustrating and can heighten risk and costs. Undeveloped land in otherwise-built-up areas may be burdened with physical or legal issues, such as rough topography, toxic contamination, or cloudy ownership titles. Also, in residential areas, neighboring property owners accustomed to the open space created by vacant lots may oppose the development and resent building designs that appear to crowd their property lines or overshadow their buildings. Developers may find that they spend as much time and effort pushing small projects through the permit pipeline as are necessary for larger, more profitable projects. (For example, the developer and designers of Wellington Neighborhood in Breckenridge spent three years convincing city officials that the site's zoning density should be upgraded to permit traditional neighborhood design.) However, some developers and builders succeed in finding and developing leftover land, turning overgrown, trash-strewn lots into attractive, value-enhancing additions to a neighborhood.

Redevelopment

The term *redevelopment*—also called "urban renewal"—conjures up images of rundown neighborhoods being torn up in the 1960s, and their inhabitants scattered, to create sites for new development. Often, it seems, the areas lay dormant for years, waiting for private investments that seldom arrived in sufficient quantity and quality. For many communities, the whole idea of redevelopment became anathema, and federal dollars to underwrite programs declined precipitously.

That was then—and smarter redevelopment is now. Smarter, because local governments have learned how to target renewal where it can take advantage of rising market interest in central-city and inner suburban locations. Smarter, too, because developers and their architects have recognized the opportunities inherent in mixed-use, high-quality designs that integrate public and private interests in the finished product.

Since the demise of the federal urban renewal funding, many local governments have reinvented programs to accomplish redevelopment by

FIGURE 3.4
The city of Breckridge reclaimed 22 acres of a former mining area to develop 122 affordable homes with 20 acres of parks and open space - a boon to residents of this somewhat isolated skiing area.

establishing strategic goals and applying them in carefully selected areas. In general, local public officials seek to leverage opportunities for developing leftover redevelopment areas, former military bases, abandoned railroad yards and industrial properties, and aggregations of public properties. Typically they assign the city's redevelopment agency the responsibility of determining and administering appropriate development.

In the past ten years, the Village of Arlington Heights, Illinois, has based much of its town center redevelopment strategy on recycling land resources originally acquired for commuter parking around a Metra rail transit station. Located about twenty-four miles northwest of downtown Chicago, the village of seventy-seven thousand residents has undertaken a series of highly successful public-private projects, beginning with two residential developments in the late 1980s. Ten years later, sensing the advent of new real estate markets, the Village issued a request for proposals to develop a 3.75-acre site, 40 percent of which was owned by the Village and mostly used for surface parking. A developer who had acquired most of the remaining properties was selected to construct Arlington Town Square, consisting of a six-screen movie theater, retail shops with office space above, ninety-four condominiums in a thirteen-story tower, an urban plaza, and underground parking. In the following year or two, the Village approved development of three more condominium buildings and a performing arts center, mostly on publicly owned sites once used for commuter parking. An 816-space public parking garage provides parking space for both the Metropolis project and park-and-ride commuters. The number of housing units in downtown has zoomed from 150 in 1980 to 1,160 in 2005, with another 300 units planned for the near future. Best of all, downtown Arlington Heights has been re-created to offer village residents a walkable, attractive, busy town center.

Another example is East Pointe in Milwaukee, a $57 million project sited on nine blocks of land cleared in the 1960s for a freeway that was never built. Located just north of downtown Milwaukee, the seventeen-acre site became officially available for redevelopment in the mid-1980s. Redevelopment was managed by the Milwaukee Redevelopment Corporation, which formed a partnership with Barry Mandel, a local developer, to plan and construct the project. The final plan for East Pointe was decidedly urban in design, calling for 438 units of market-rate rental apartments and condominium townhomes and a neighborhood retail center on only half the site. To support that density, most residences have underground parking. Development is clustered to conserve almost half the site in open space. Ground breaking occurred in late 1990, and the last of the five phases was completed in 2000. Residential units rented quickly, and the retail center almost doubled expected sales. Because streets were designed to attract pedestrians and join with those in the surrounding neighborhood, about one third of the commercial center's patrons walk to the stores.

The city-county development and housing agency in Nashville, Tennessee, followed a more traditional route to redevelopment for the thirty-four-acre Rolling Hill area, located next to downtown on a bluff overlooking the Cumberland River. Much of the site, once mostly residential, was a wasteland of parking lots and disused buildings, including a historic hospital complex. The agency had acquired most of the properties over a number of years and hoped that successful redevelopment would expand the supply of in-town housing and spark future improvement efforts in the adjoining neighborhood.

After sponsoring a public planning process that produced a detailed plan in 2004, the agency prepared plans and began construction of a new street system, underground wiring, sewer and stormwater systems, site grading, greenways, and streetscapes to provide "pad-ready" sites for developers. In 2005, two development firms were selected for construction of the first two phases of development.

FIGURE 3.5
Crawford Square is a mixed-income residential development built on a long-vacant urban renewal site next to downtown Pittsburgh. The plan and housing designs were prepared with the intensive involvement of local residents and neighborhood leaders.

Military base closings and former airports typically offer opportunities for large-scale redevelopment. Denver is implementing major redevelopment programs in both the 1,866-acre Lowry air force base, which was declared redundant in 1991, and Denver's 4,700-acre Stapleton Airport, replaced by Denver International Airport and closed in 1995. Plans for each are wedded to sustainable development principles and involve considerable site cleanup and recycling of buildings and materials. Lowry, which is being redeveloped by an intergovernmental agency formed by the cities of Aurora and Denver, got a head start, but Stapleton's rebuilding, administered by the city in partnership with the Stapleton Redevelopment Foundation, enthusiastically embraced green building and new urbanist design ideas in its adopted "Green Book" framework plan. The plan declared the goal of developing "a network of urban villages, employment centers and significant open space, all linked by a commitment to the protection of natural resources and the development of human resources."[29] In 1999, the Forest City development company was selected as master developer to manage the redevelopment process, and by fall 2001, construction was under way on the first of twelve thousand planned homes, an extensive green infrastructure system, and schools and other public facilities. An array of retail shops in five town centers and 10 million square feet of office space are planned to generate thirty-five thousand employees. Two schools and the first town center opened in 2003; by 2005, Stapleton had four thousand residents; and in 2006, the first phase of its Central Park opened.

A Little Help from the City

The sites for all of the examples of adaptive reuse, infill, and redevelopment described above could have remained derelict without imaginative design approaches that responded to new opportunities in the real estate marketplace. But local leadership was a necessary ingredient as well. Developing in already urbanized areas benefits from—and frequently necessitates—assistance from public agencies and programs. A twelve-city survey of programs to stimulate urban housing reinvestment found a variety of programs intended to assist developers and property owners in accomplishing these aims:

- city assemblage and cost write-downs of development sites, often involving the acquiring and packaging of tax-delinquent and abandoned properties plus unneeded publicly owned properties (such sites often also require cleanup of contaminated brownfields);

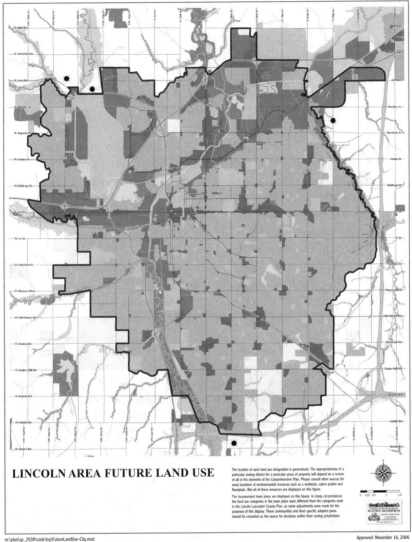

LINCOLN AREA FUTURE LAND USE

m:\plan\cp_2030\code\lrq\FutureLandUse-City.mxd

Approved: November 16, 2006

FIGURE 3.6
Lincoln-Lancaster County's future land use plan identifies the urban service line around the urbanized area and close-in areas designated for development.

- assistance in financing development by grants, loans, tax abatements, reductions of mortgage interest, and city contributions to infrastructure costs;
- education and information campaigns to stimulate market interest,

including mayoral "summits" to attract wide attention to rebuilding needs and programs;

- relief of regulatory obstacles by reorganizing agencies and streamlining regulatory processes; and
- neighborhood conservation programs that combine a multitude of improvement programs to generate visible upgrading and establish a supportive development environment.[30]

Cities and inner suburbs undertake these initiatives with the aim of creating a market position that is competitive with sites in outlying suburban jurisdictions. They also hope to win support from urban residents who might otherwise resist change. The combination of tangible contributions for improving development feasibility and proactive marketing of in-city development opportunities has helped to capitalize on the rising interest in urban and inner-suburban locations.

The development of RiverStation I in Minneapolis, Minnesota, offers an example of the lengths to which city administrations can go in supporting revitalization. The city's Community Development Authority had been laboring since the 1970s to revive activity in the virtually abandoned ware-

BOX 3.2

A Note about Redevelopment and Eminent Domain

Successful redevelopment programs in many communities may be threatened by the public uproar over the 2005 U.S. Supreme Court decision in *Kelo v. City of New London* (545 U.S. 469 [2005]). At last count, some twenty-seven states were preparing legislation restricting local governments' use of eminent domain to assemble sites for redevelopment. The suit arose from the use of eminent domain powers (sometimes called "condemnation") by New London, Connecticut, to acquire privately owned properties over the objections of their owners.

The issue centered on whether New London proposed to use the property for a "public purpose," which the courts have allowed for centuries. Public jurisdictions frequently use eminent domain to acquire land to build a road or construct a school, for example, and many times have employed it to promote economic development of a blighted or declining area—a condition New London had not asserted. So this appeared to be an extreme case of a city forcibly acquiring properties, including occupied residences, to permit redevelopment of the waterfront for commercial uses that public officials claimed would benefit the city.

The Supreme Court decided, to the surprise of many, that New London had acted properly to pursue a public purpose—that eminent domain was a legal course of action in this case. Unfortunately, negative reactions to that decision leading to major restrictions on the use of eminent domain, thereby increasing the difficulty of assembling sites for desired development, may throw a monkey wrench in many cities' redevelopment programs.

house district north of downtown. It had helped to clean up pollution in the nearby Mississippi River and had constructed an inviting parkway along the riverfront. It worked with developers to build several small residential developments, but most of the area remained vacant. Then, in 1996, the Authority was approached by the two principals of Heritage Renovations LLC, who proposed to redevelop a 9.25-acre parcel for 348 condominium apartments and townhouses, to be priced for middle-income households. At the time, the proposal would create the largest owner-occupied housing development for middle-income purchasers in the city's history.

However, the developer needed the Authority's help in making the property available for development—specifically, to acquire the former railroad property, remediate site contamination, and then sell the property to the developers in phases to reduce the developer's holding costs. Eager to spark development in this neglected area, the Authority agreed to the developer's conditions and to convey the site for one dollar, to provide partial financing for landscaping and street improvements, and to offer financial aid for prospective home owners. The developers then sought and obtained an equity investment by Fannie Mae's American Community Fund that helped secure other financial commitments to support later phases of development.

The proposed development was to consist of ten four-story buildings of about 86 units each, with two-story townhouses topped by two stories of apartment units. Elevators and underground parking were featured. Development got under way in early 1998, the first phase sold out by the end of that year, and the project was completed in 2003. (The same developers also built a 229-unit rental project on part of the site. The project was completed in 2000, with 20 percent of the units reserved for moderate-income households.)

The experience in RiverStation and the other projects described above demonstrates the resilience of cities in shaping workable and politically savvy redevelopment programs with little assistance from federal agencies. They have succeeded in accommodating an important segment of regional growth that is reestablishing activity in older urban and first-ring suburbs, offering new choices of living and working environments, and reducing outward pressures for greenfield development.

Controlling Development beyond the Jurisdiction

Controlling urban expansion by use of growth boundaries and similar techniques is a relatively straightforward process if the boundary is entirely within the jurisdiction exercising control. Many of the examples described in the preceding section consist of regional agencies or large counties that have plenty of space to allow both urban development and protected rural lands. Most local governments, however, must cope with the fact that much of their growth may develop outside their jurisdictional boundaries. Their ability to influence the location and quality of this development may be critical to the economic and social viability of the community.

Recognizing this problem, many states have given cities and towns tools to manage, at least to some degree, development occurring outside their borders. These measures include extraterritorial jurisdiction, annexation, extension of urban services, and intergovernmental agreements.

Extraterritorial Jurisdiction

Municipalities in many states are given powers to manage or influence planning and zoning for development in a circumscribed area around their boundaries. These powers vary widely from state to state, ranging from total control for establishing development standards to the right to review and comment on rezoning and subdivision proposals or to prepare plans for the areas involved. North Carolina gives local governments planning and zoning jurisdiction over areas up to three miles outside their boundaries. The City of Raleigh, for example, has used this power for many years to establish development standards for urbanizing areas outside the city. In addition, the state gives municipalities the power to annex developing land as densities reach urban levels. In 1988, the state authorized cities such as Raleigh to negotiate interlocal agreements with other municipalities to establish "spheres of influence," or boundaries for future annexation. With these powers, Raleigh can exert a considerable amount of control over development on its fringes.

California and Idaho cities also can establish spheres of influence over urban expansion that ultimately may be annexed to the growing city. Cities can plan for extending infrastructure systems to these areas and can establish standards for the type of development that will be allowed. Fresno, California, as an illustration, adopted an ordinance designating an "urban growth management area" outside its corporate limits. The area is anticipated to become urbanized over a twenty-year period. Following California law, Fresno prepares plans for infrastructure systems in the growth management area, and as development takes place, it annexes territory in which it provides urban services.

At a smaller scale, Maryville, Tennessee, is allowed to annex territory after it has prepared plans for extending urban services into its designated urban growth area, now within the jurisdiction of Blount County. As an indication of the typical complexities of extraterritorial powers, Maryville is allowed to exercise subdivision regulations but not zoning powers over development in the urban growth area until it annexes it. Perhaps the most significant control over future development is exerted by New Mexico municipalities, which are authorized to control zoning in a five-mile area outside their boundaries.

However, many states in New England, the Mid-Atlantic, and the Midwest do not authorize extraterritorial jurisdiction. States such as Massachusetts, New Jersey, and Michigan have divided their entire area into towns, townships, or municipalities that individually can exercise planning and zoning powers. In other states, such as Maryland and Virginia, powerful counties can control growth management in unincorporated areas, acting much like supermunicipalities.

To sum up, states differ greatly in granting extraterritorial powers to local governments; in some states, local jurisdictions possess significant control over developing areas beyond their corporate boundaries, while in others they are dependent on annexation, which may be relatively simple or prohibitively difficult.

Annexation

Most states authorize their municipalities to annex territory to retain some control over growth in developing areas. As indicated above, however, the political likelihood of successfully exercising this power varies greatly from state to state. Some states, such as North Carolina and Texas, require only that the city provide or commit to providing urban services in the area annexed. A number of states require reviews of annexation proposals by courts, special quasi-legislative bodies, or even the state legislature. Other states have established elaborate annexation procedures that require affirmative votes from residents of the annexing jurisdiction, the public officials of the jurisdiction losing territory, and the residents of areas to be annexed—a difficult test to pass.

Where annexation is feasible, some local governments prepare detailed plans and appropriate zoning that becomes applicable when annexation takes place. San Jose, California, is one of a number of California cities that take advantages of the "specific plan" process permitted by state law. San Jose officials worked with Santa Clara County officials, as well as with local landowners and developers, to prepare detailed plans, including infrastructure needs, for developing areas as a condition of annexation.

In many states, unfortunately, the primary way individual municipalities can control their growth is through negotiating annexation agreements with developers. Typically, a deal is struck for zoning more permissive than that proposed by a competing municipality or in county territory. Illinois towns, for instance, routinely compete for annexations of proposed developments, especially commercial and business developments that promise to increase tax bases. That type of negotiation—in effect, zoning for sale—virtually eliminates opportunities for growing cities to retain control over the quality of future development.

Cities forgo annexation opportunities at the risk of losing control over future development. City officials in Blacksburg, Virginia, a university town in western Virginia, decided not to annex a developing area along the principal highway. Within a few years, the area had developed with a hodge-podge of uses and inadequate public facilities, creating a tacky entrance to the community and congesting the highway. Once developed, of course, the area resisted the idea of annexation. When officials in the cities of Sarasota and Venice, Florida, declined to annex developing areas in the 1970s, the county was forced to play catch up in developing the administrative skills, funding sources, and infrastructure systems needed to support urban growth. Thus cities and towns can view annexation as either an opportunity or as an unwanted responsibility.

Annexation processes are further complicated by the degree to which the state encourages the incorporation of new municipalities and the organization of special taxing districts. In such states as Oregon, Arizona, and Illinois, residents of developing areas can incorporate new municipalities rather easily, providing a potentially desirable alternative to being annexed by the city next door. Residents of two urbanizing areas in the Portland, Oregon, region, for example, voted to incorporate, primarily to prevent potential development of multifamily housing in their areas. Developers and residents of urbanizing areas in many states can also form special taxing districts to provide essential services, thus removing a major incentive for annexation to adjoining cities. (See the discussion of special districts in chapter 6 for more details on this process.)

Service Extensions

Local governments that operate essential public facilities—police and fire protection, road construction and maintenance, sewage collection and treatment, water treatment and distribution, and libraries—have discovered the value of controlling service extensions to influence the character of development in urbanizing areas. Some of these services may be provided in other ways: volunteers may organize fire stations, for example, and some services may be provided selectively by other levels of governments, private companies, or special districts formed for that purpose.

But local governments can employ service extensions as a way to manage growth if they provide desirable services unavailable from other service deliverers. The earlier description of regional agencies in Portland, Oregon, and the Twin Cities in Minnesota described how they relied on metropolitan sewer service as one means of managing regional growth. In most cases, growth boundaries are employed in concert with policies for extending urban services to determine the location and quality of future development. As demonstrated by Raleigh's experience, using extraterritorial jurisdiction and annexation powers effectively depends on capabilities for extending desired urban services to developing areas.

This approach to growth management is undercut when local managers of semiautonomous urban service agencies act like private enterprises more interested in maximizing their service areas than adhering to growth management policies. In other cases, state laws or court decisions have limited the ability of local governments to direct services to selected areas. The intentions of Boulder, Colorado, to limit expansion of water and sewer service outside its borders as part of its growth policy were dashed by a Colorado Supreme Court decision declaring that such services were public utility enterprises that should not be constrained by other policy concerns of the city.[31]

Interlocal Agreements

As indicated in the preceding sections, interlocal agreements can play an important role in securing guidance over development outside jurisdictional boundaries. Although specific forms of such agreements vary from state to state, most empower local governments to enter into cooperative agreements with other local governments, state agencies, and special taxing districts regarding service policies. In general, agreements can commit the signatories to undertake cooperative actions that they are permitted to conduct individually. Interlocal agreements may be made informally, resulting from collaborative discussions by public officials or deliberations by advisory groups, or by formal, signed compacts or memorandums of agreement or understanding, or by contractual agreements for specified services. Interlocal agreements to manage development outside local governmental boundaries are fairly common; the experience of Raleigh described above is typical.

Another example is Boulder's long-standing agreement with Boulder County for managing growth outside the city. The city and county adopted a jointly sponsored comprehensive plan for Boulder Valley in 1970, followed in 1977 by an intergovernmental agreement to approve a new Boulder Valley Comprehensive Plan, which has since received five major updates, the most recent in 2005. The plan concentrates urban development in the city, defines the urban service and annexation area, and preserves the rural character of lands outside the city's urban service area. It also delineates a reserve area for potential development beyond the fifteen-year planning period. The city maintains planning and zoning powers within the municipal boundaries, and the county administers zoning in the remainder of the planning area.

Another nearby example is Fort Collins, which executed an agreement in 1980 with Larimer County and Loveland, a city to the south, to define an urban service boundary. The agreement established the policy that Fort Collins could annex developing areas within the boundary and set urban standards for interim development of those areas prior to annexation, including a minimum-density requirement. Over the years, the agreement has been amended (most recently in 2000) to coordinate Fort Collins and Larimer County plans through establishing an urban growth management area, delineated by the county as an overlay zoning district. The city-county agreement requires that areas outside the growth management area will not be provided public services and facilities at urban levels. A city-county board was established to recommend decisions on development applications within the growth management area to the county board of commissioners, which retains final authority for approval or disapproval of development proposals.[32]

A number of cities and counties have entered into interlocal agreements to form joint planning and zoning commissions as a way to coordinate development across city boundaries. Among them is Lincoln–Lancaster County, Nebraska, whose growth management program is founded on the skillful combination of many of the growth management approaches discussed above.

Putting It All Together: Growth Management Strategy of Lincoln, Nebraska[33]

Lying about 40 miles southwest of Omaha, Lincoln is the last city west of the Missouri River until Denver, some 450 miles away. Founded in 1867 as the state capital, Lincoln is a white-collar town, the state's center of government and home of the state university. With a population approaching 225,000 in 2000, Lincoln's growth has been slow but steady for decades. Its substantial cadre of professional and civic leaders has a long-standing commitment to "good government" and forward-looking policies.

Lincoln has a rich history of planning endeavors, made more significant by its relative isolation in the farmlands of the plains states. A municipal plan commission proposed preparation of the first city plan as early as 1912. Although the plan was not adopted, in 1924 the city succeeded in adopting a zoning code, and in 1929, responding to local leaders' concerns for controlling future development, the state legislature gave the city zoning jurisdiction over a three-mile area outside the city borders. The city's first comprehensive plan was developed and adopted between 1948 and 1952. A joint city-county planning commission was formed with Lancaster County in 1959 and adopted a regional comprehensive plan in 1961. City-county plans were updated in 1977, 1985, 1994, 2002, and 2006.

The Comprehensive Plan

The cornerstone of Lincoln's growth management program is the city-county comprehensive plan, which outlines planning goals, establishes growth patterns, and provides a policy framework for such implementation tools as zoning, capital and transportation improvement programs, design standards, and protection of the natural environment. Versions of the plan through the years have emphasized several policy areas of particular concern to Lincoln citizens. One is guiding the physical pattern of growth—specifically, attempting to contain growth within a generally concentric pattern outward from the established core of the city. Each plan has emphasized the importance of contiguous development as a means of retaining a vibrant community and the provision of efficient urban services by imposing an urban services boundary. As of 2006, this double-edged policy has been reaffirmed in adoption of a 2030 plan. Allied with this interest are other concerns for maintaining and revitalizing the downtown area as the center of state interest and maintaining the quality of life and physical condition in older neighborhoods, a direct result of the city's interest in containing development.

In the 1990s, the city's attempts to encourage a steady pattern of concentric growth ran athwart of market forces, which favored development toward the southeast—toward Omaha—even as the city desired to retain a balanced pattern by promoting more growth to the west. The failure of a city-backed, large-scale project in the west roiled the political waters, and today, although some western growth has materialized, developers continue to press for expanding the service boundary to the southeast. There is even talk of establishing a corridor development plan between Lincoln and Omaha.

Nevertheless, aided by its strong annexation powers, Lincoln has assimilated new growth as it occurs. Lincoln continues to incorporate 90 percent of the county's population, and nearly all of the county's population increase has been within the city's boundaries. The current comprehensive plan is still predicated on maintaining a pattern of urban expansion that keeps new development contiguous to the existing urban edge.

Control over Future Development Areas

Significant state and local legislation forms the structural basis for successful implementation of Lincoln's comprehensive plan. First, as indicated earlier, the state authorized the city to maintain zoning powers over development in the area three miles beyond the city limits. Second, state laws also prohibit the incorporation of municipalities within five miles of the city limits without the city's consent and establish a relatively easy annexation procedure. Third, through an intergovernmental agreement, many city and county functions are combined, including the departments of planning, health, employment, and human services. Finally, the municipality controls water, sewer, and electric services. Connection to Lincoln's water supply, in particular, is a necessity for development in a water-scarce area. The city ties the extension of services to a six-year schedule of capital improvements and the designation of an urban service area (although the city extends electric power services outside the city).

These powers, which many American cities lack, give Lincoln almost total control over the development of its urbanizing fringe. Lincoln has taken utmost advantage of these powers to direct development by tying the extension of urban services to the annexation of urbanizing areas. Marvin Krout, the current planning director, indicates that the city is not imposing a boundary in order to constrain development. Rather, he says, it employs the urban service boundary, annexation process, and capital improvements program as a means of keeping up with needs for extending infrastructure to urbanizing areas. Over the years, the process has worked well to provide services as needed, especially with regard to the water, sewer, and electric power services funded through fees and charges. The city's particular concern at the moment is finding funds for major road improvements to serve new development, after depending for years on the existing road system. Lincoln's decision to adopt road impact fees for this purpose have generated controversy (the issues raised by impact fees are described in chapter 5).

Intergovernmental Coordination

In addition to city controls over development outside its boundaries, the city and Lancaster County have worked together for years to coordinate development policies. In 1959, a joint city-county planning commission was formed. Since then, city and county have worked closely in formulating the series of joint comprehensive plans. The 1994 plan included, for the first time, a unified land use plan illustrated on a single map, a practice that continues. The joint planning process allows the city-county plan to recognize the relationships between urban and rural areas, the needs for protecting natural features, and the concerns for maintaining the vitality of the twelve municipalities and rural settlements outside the city.

Citizen Participation

A well-educated, professionally employed polity has helped ensure well-informed community involvement in planning and implementation processes. The latest comprehensive plan, adopted in 2002 and updated every year since, evolved through a series of task force meetings and extended discussions with the city and county officials. The planning department provides an annual review that recommends amendments and provides information pertaining to a series of previously defined indicators, such as the rate of population and employment growth compared to targets. The city also completed and adopted a new downtown plan in 2005 and in 2006 launched an eighteen-month updating of the city-county transportation plan.

City-county policies and state legislation have established a solid track record in Lincoln's management of development. Growth remains orderly, without the leapfrogging that places inordinate demands on service delivery. City boundaries have kept pace with development and stayed within the existing watershed. Lincoln's downtown has remained as vital as can be found in any city its size. In addition, the quality of commercial development is high and the municipal services are considered excellent.

Limits on Growth: Stopping or Slowing Expansion

The growth management concept gained widespread attention during the early 1970s when towns and cities began imposing limits on the amount or pace of development. Even today, some people associate growth management with those early efforts to curb growth rather than accommodate it. Some communities even continue to limit development. Although the City of San Diego dropped limits after a brief period, most of the seventeen other cities and towns in San Diego County have adopted caps on annual development. In the Denver area, at least four cities (Boulder, Golden, Louisville, and Westminster) limit the amount of annual growth or are considering limits. California and Colorado communities are more apt to impose limits than communities in other states; in fact, these two states probably account for more local growth-limiting programs than all other states combined. The combination of residents' reactions to long-term rapid growth, legal restraints on raising revenues for infrastructure, and permissive local and state laws appears to stimulate this type of approach to growth management.

Approaches and Techniques

Growth limits take several forms. The most common is setting a limit on the annual number of residential building permits that the local government may issue. Typically, the limit is based on average growth rates prior to the most recent surge of construction activity. Boulder limited development to a rate of 1.5 percent, or about 450 units a year, after several years of 5 to 10 percent annual growth. Westminster, Colorado, employs a variation based on its rationale for growth control: the available water supply. It limits annual water service connections for residential development. Carlsbad, California, determined the number of units that would ultimately "build out" the community, related that number to a schedule of facility construction, and arrived at an annual average number of housing units it would approve.

Other communities find other ways to limit growth. Perhaps the most prevalent means is community enactment of an adequate public facilities requirement followed by a slowdown or lapse in scheduling public facility construction at a rate that will keep up with growth. Developers across the nation complain about this unspoken method for slowing growth. A number of California cities, including Santa Barbara, have refused to plan and fund increases in water supply, thus instituting a de facto limit on growth. At one time, many of the towns around Boston were issuing no new sewer hookups unless developers paid for expensive system improvements. In addition, many growing suburban communities react to growth by restricting development of multifamily housing or rezoning large areas for very-low-density development, thus reducing growth rates, if not the root causes of growth problems.

Communities that impose official growth limits must determine a way to select projects to receive the go-ahead for development, assuming that more requests for approval will be submitted than permitted by the limit.

Petaluma and Boulder both instituted "point" or "merit" systems for that purpose. The systems were used to rate proposed projects according to stated criteria, such as the availability of public services to provide for the needs of project residents, the quality of architectural and site design, and the provision of amenities, such as bicycle paths and footpaths. The systems encouraged developers to "donate" facilities and amenities to win more points. Petaluma's system was applied to all applicants; Boulder's went into effect when the semiannual allocation of permits was exceeded. Ironically, because growth rates in both cities remained generally lower than the limits, the systems were discarded as a means of allocating permits, although Boulder still uses its system to evaluate projects.

Other communities use existing subdivision regulations to evaluate projects but still must determine whether to award permits on a "first-come, first-served" basis or by prorating available permits among all applicants. Most communities also set up special quotas for types of housing considered especially desirable, such as low-cost housing or infill development. Administration of such processes can become quite complicated. Tracy, California, discovered that its permit award system resulted in certain developers of large subdivisions acquiring most of the allowable permits, creating monopoly conditions and opening the door to sale of permits among developers.

Growth limits can also be applied to specific areas. In applying adequate facilities requirements (as detailed in chapter 6), for example, inadequate facility capacities can lead to de facto limits or moratoriums in certain areas until facility capacities are increased to allow continued development. In addition, a number of local governments instituted limits on the development of downtown office buildings in the development boom of the late 1970s to mid-1980s. Seeing huge developments changing the face of their central business districts, local residents pressed for slowing development and making it more compatible with the existing downtown environment. San Francisco's program was best known. It limited office development to 475,000 square feet per year and required special attention to design details and amenities. Seattle adopted similar restrictions and requirements. (Both of these cities and others also adopted "linkage" programs, described in chapter 6, that required downtown developers to contribute to housing programs.) These downtown growth limits are practically irrelevant in today's market, although they are still on the books.

Limits on growth also have been considered for metropolitan areas rather than for individual communities. In both the San Diego and Portland regions, some citizens' groups were concerned enough about

rapid growth to press for slowing it down. After studies pointed out the difficulties and potential consequences of actions that would cause development to decline, the notion was dropped as a viable strategy.[34]

Moratoriums

Development moratoriums are temporary growth limits that usually halt all
further issuances of building permits for a specified period of time. A moratorium can postpone all development or development only of a particular
type or in a particular area, such as any residential construction, commercial construction along a congested highway segment, or development in a
certain school district. It can be a few months or several years in duration.

Communities adopt moratoriums to allow a catch-up period for
responding to critical problems, such as mounting concerns about critical
public facilities or failing development policies. Calvert County, Maryland,
adopted a six-month moratorium in 1995 on issuing permits in three anti-
quated subdivisions that suddenly were attracting hundreds of new families with children, quickly overloading available school capacity. The unex-
pected spurt of students was one problem; the other was that the county's
impact fee did not apply to these subdivisions, which had been platted
some thirty years earlier. In the boom development days of the mid-1980s,
Nashua, New Hampshire, imposed a one-year moratorium on further commercial development on a major highway to prepare plans that would alleviate traffic congestion. San Diego adopted an eighteen-month "interim
growth control ordinance" that allowed substantially fewer permits for residential construction than the previous rate of issuance while the city's
planning and growth management policies were reconsidered.

The legality of moratoriums has been well established in the courts.
Generally, moratoriums are considered within the rights of local governments if they

- are intended to deal with a defined problem that will be created or
  worsened by development; and
- extend for a reasonable time during which local officials take steps to
  find solutions to the problems triggering the moratoriums.

Local governments, in other words, must demonstrate a health, safety,
or welfare basis for halting development and then move to determine a
solution that will permit development to resume. Daniel Mandelker, one
of the nation's foremost land use attorneys, comments that courts usually "take into account the purposes served by the interim control and

the restrictions it imposes. The courts will strike down interim controls that clearly serve improper regulatory purposes." The courts, he states, "view the interim control as a necessary measure to protect the municipality from development" that might be inconsistent with new policies and ordinances.[35]

Moratoriums have their downsides, however. Most significantly, short-term moratoriums seldom affect the current pace of development. In most communities, enough development has received permits or commitments (by subdivision plat approval, for example) to keep the development pipeline flowing for some time. That problem is heightened by the permit rush that typically occurs when builders learn that local officials are considering a moratorium. In Calvert County, for example, builders obtained hundreds of permits just before the moratorium took effect. Although many of those permits were not translated into construction, the development process was thrown into disarray.

Long-term moratoriums create other problems by disrupting the development process, generating political conflict and often litigation, and allowing monopoly conditions to inflate land and housing prices. Furthermore, one commentator observes that "if jurisdictions merely pause without seriously reconsidering and reforming their approach to land use regulation and growth management, moratoriums may do more harm than good. They can disrupt local economies, increase unemployment, and inflate real estate prices, possibly with effects that persist and outlast the term of the moratorium."[36]

In addition, moratoriums are a visible reminder that the local government has not kept pace with growth, that its past actions have been too little and too late. A moratorium is an admission of failure on the part of government officials. Eric Kelly, a noted land use attorney, observes that "a moratorium is a worst-case result for all parties."[37] Not only are developers stopped from pursuing plans that may have received approval and in which substantial investments have been made, but city officials are forced to forgo potential revenues from that development. Kelly cites the instance of Westminster, Colorado, which found in 1978 that it had approved far more development than its water and sewer system could serve. However, the city needed connection fees from new development to amortize bonds issued to pay for existing utility lines. The brief moratorium it imposed caused headaches for both developers and city officials, something that might have been avoided by "planning ahead."[38] Politically, however, citizens upset by development trends find moratoriums a satisfying response to current crises, if not long-term solutions.

Techniques that allow communities to influence the location of growth offer some of the most potent regulatory approaches in the arsenal of public policies governing development. Growth boundaries and similar methods establish strong guidelines for the development process, providing a policy framework for zoning and other regulatory actions as well as affecting private development decisions. Proactive efforts to redirect growth inward by promoting adaptive reuse, infill, and redevelopment legitimize and strengthen the containment policy.

Similarly, local powers to control growth in developing areas outside existing jurisdictional boundaries are essential to managing community development. Without those powers, communities are unable to guide their destinies and are vulnerable to the potentially damaging effects of development decisions outside their control. In combination, as we see in the experience of Lincoln, Nebraska, these growth management tools can provide highly effective approaches to responsible growth management.

CHAPTER 4
Protecting Environmental and Natural Resources: Where Not to Grow

Communities can manage growth as much by deciding where *not* to grow as by determining where to grow. The previous chapter explains that designations of urban growth areas, to be most effective, should be accompanied by programs to protect rural and natural areas adjoining urban and urbanizing places. In addition, advocates of sustainable development, smart growth, and green infrastructure urge that natural systems be sustained within urban areas by strategically protecting some from development or even creating new green spaces in and around urban areas. This chapter describes principles and practices for preserving ecosystems and nature's resources that support all life on the planet.

The Value of "Green Space"

The term *green space* is perhaps more apt than *open space*, which implies an absence—rather than an abundance—of features and qualities. Green space encompasses many forms of urban, rural, and natural spaces, from parks and playgrounds to farmlands, stream valleys, and scenic swaths of forests and mountains. Formal urban squares and plazas in built-up areas also qualify (these are discussed in chapter 6). This chapter focuses on preservation of the natural systems and resources that undergird and surround human settlements—and that add value to the human experience in many ways.

Foremost is these systems' utility in sustaining a livable and healthful environment. Wetlands, for example, are among the most biologically productive and diverse natural systems. They provide wildlife habitats, reduce flooding, improve water quality by absorbing pollutants, absorb wave action that might otherwise erode coastal areas, and offer spawning grounds and shelter for fish, shellfish, and birds. Forests and clusters of trees calm stormwater runoff, shelter wildlife, and cleanse and cool the air.

These resources are also valued for the enjoyment they offer residents of urban areas. People yearn for natural open spaces and for the recreational opportunities offered by parks, trails, and waterways. They enjoy views of the farmlands and forests that also function as economic resources. In these open spaces, they find respite from busy urban activities.

Green space, in other words, is not simply a commodity awaiting development. Stream valleys are not just handy places to dump trash. Prime agricultural land is a finite resource that should not be indiscriminately covered with rooftops and concrete. Even marshes and floodplains perform valuable functions for human benefit as well as for the natural order.

However, unguided urban growth threatens and often engulfs green spaces. Growing metropolitan areas are converting more land to urban uses than ever before. Some, such as Cleveland and Detroit, are expanding into the countryside even while their regional populations are declining.

How, then, to preserve the multiple values of green space for future generations? We can begin by acknowledging the interdependence of human and natural systems. The goal for sustainable communities is to improve what Dan Perlman and Jeff Milder call "the ecological integrity of human-influenced landscapes" while ensuring that humans benefit from and are not endangered by those landscapes.[1]

Integrating Natural and Built Environments

In his most famous work, *Design with Nature*, Ian McHarg writes of the interaction of man and nature:

> A single drop of water in the uplands of a watershed may appear and reappear as cloud, precipitation, surface water in creek and river, lake and pond or groundwater; it can participate in plant and animal metabolism, transpiration, condensation, decomposition, combustion, respiration and evaporation. This same drop of water may appear in considerations of climate and microclimate, water supply, flood, drought and erosion control, industry, commerce, agriculture, forestry, reaction, scenic beauty, in cloud, snow, stream, river and sea. We conclude that nature is a single interacting system and that changes to any part will affect the operation of the whole.[2]

McHarg makes us aware that human and natural systems are intricately bound. Cities, he believes, exist in natural settings whose qualities are essential to maintaining life in all its forms.

The concept of sustainable development builds on McHarg's ideas. It calls for maintaining the integrity of complex ecological systems while promoting the economic viability and social equity of human settlements. Development is necessary to further economic and social ends. But the principles of sustainability call for development to be undertaken in ways that limit its impacts on the natural functions of landscapes, hydrologic systems, and habitats. It is seldom possible to sharply demarcate natural preserves to make them off-limits to people, even in the high Himalayas or the coral reefs of Tahiti. Instead, we look for ways to retain natural functions in the presence of human settlements. As Perlman and Milder put it in their book on ecosystem practices: "The challenge is to integrate humans and nature more beneficially by retaining ecological values in largely domesticated landscapes."[3] Urban historians Christine Rosen and Joel Tarr write that "the natural and built environments evolved in dialectical interdependence and tension," in which the built environment, "through its effects upon and interaction with the natural environment, is a part of the earth's environmental history."[4]

However, the goal of integrating built and natural environments presents a conundrum: how strictly should natural areas and systems be preserved within developing cities and suburbs? Protecting natural settings by limiting development generally results in low-density living and working environments, spreading urban growth across a large area. Typical large-lot subdivisions offer a perverse example of this approach, as they "preserve" denatured lawns and land covered with rooftops and roads. Conservation subdivisions that cluster development within conserved natural or agricultural areas do a better job of preserving natural qualities. But an extensive landscape of conservation subdivisions in rural and natural areas still raises concerns about damaging natural systems as well as the inefficiencies of low-intensity suburbanization.

By contrast, great cities and growing suburbs that are developing more densely face limited opportunities for preserving natural qualities within developed areas. Trading excitement and activity for the wide-open spaces of rural areas, urban places cover a high proportion of land with rooftops and pavements; streams are closely bounded by development, and rivers may be constrained by walls and dams. Stormwater and sewage flows are collected in mains, and discharges encourage downstream erosion; vegetation and wildlife habitats are disrupted. Only highly regarded natural features are protected in parks and recreation areas.

Two strategies can mitigate these problems. Ideally, the rural lands saved when urban areas develop compactly can be conserved through regional programs to offset environmental losses that occur in built-up areas. In addition, "green" techniques for softening the effects of urban construction—such as permeable pavements and other runoff-relief methods—can reduce urban impacts on sensitive environmental qualities.

In any case, McHarg's vision in 1969 of the intrinsic values of regional landscapes in shaping and supporting human settlements remains a powerful force in managing community growth. The concepts inherent in his phrase "design with nature" are embodied in countless planning policies, zoning and subdivision provisions, and growth management techniques in use today.

Communities determine "where not to grow" by identifying significant natural areas and resources and planning for their protection. Then, to imple-

BOX 4.1
Major Federal Environmental Laws

Clean Air Act. Adopted in 1963 and administered by the Environmental Protection Agency (EPA), the act seeks to prevent and control air pollution by requiring conformance with clean air standards within metropolitan areas. EPA sets emission standards for major pollutants emitted by stationary sources, such as industries and utilities, and by mobile sources, such as vehicles. Deadlines set by Congress for attaining standards have been reset time after time; in 1990, Congress mandated a system of graduated controls and staggered deadlines for compliance. In addition to requirements for reducing pollution from power plants, industries, and other sources, proposals for achieving standards include reductions in urban sprawl and greater use of transit and other alternatives to single-occupancy vehicles.

National Environmental Policy Act. The overarching environmental act, passed in 1970, the National Environmental Policy Act requires federal agencies to consider the potential environmental effects of "major actions" by preparing environmental impact statements (EISs) for "all federal actions significantly affecting the quality of the human environment," including highway construction, subsidized housing, and other assistance in development projects. Statements must analyze potential environmental effects, identify unavoidable adverse impacts, evaluate a reasonable spectrum of alternatives, and define measures to mitigate these effects. Many states have adopted similar requirements governing state actions, including the permitting of private-sector projects.

Clean Water Act. Intended to "restore and maintain the chemical, physical, and biological integrity of the nation's waters," this 1972 act establishes procedures to reduce or eliminate discharge of pollutants into navigable waters and to protect fish, shellfish, and wildlife. Perhaps the best-known section pertaining to development is section 404, which requires permits for filling or dredging in wetlands. The permits are issued by the U.S. Army Corps of Engineers, but the EPA may review Corps decisions and veto them, if appropriate. Current policy gives priority

ment green space policies, they deploy a variety of regulatory, funding, and programmatic approaches to guide or restrict development in natural areas, buttressed by federal and state requirements for environmental protection.

The Framework of Federal Laws and Programs

Beginning in the 1960s, environmental activists backed by a broad constituency of concerned citizens persuaded the U.S. Congress to enact many ambitious laws and programs to protect vital environmental qualities. (Not coincidentally, they relate to McHarg's eight important features of the regional landscape, described later in this chapter.) The principal laws, listed by date of enactment, are described in box 4.1.

In addition to the federal laws, many states also enacted environmental laws, including acts modeled after the National Environmental Policy Act

BOX 4.1

(Continued)

to avoiding any development of wetlands but allows some use of wetlands if mitigation measures are taken to avoid any "net loss" in wetland resources.

Coastal Zone Management Act. Also enacted in 1972, this legislation encourages wise management of coastal areas by offering federal financial assistance to states that voluntarily agree to participate in conserving coastal resources. State programs coordinate and guide actions of federal, state, and local governments that affect coastal areas.

Endangered Species Act. This 1973 law protects species of fish, wildlife, and plants threatened with extinction. Species listed as endangered by the U.S. Department of Interior and U.S. Department of Commerce are protected from any action that would harm them, including a loss of habitat. However, the "taking" of endangered species may be permitted through federal agency consultation with the wildlife agency or the preparation of a habitat conservation plan that provides commitments to habitat preservation and mitigation.

Resource Conservation and Recovery Act. This 1977 act promotes improved management of solid waste by state and local governments. It promotes recycling, prohibits open dumping of solid waste, and controls the generation and management of hazardous wastes.

Superfund Act. Officially entitled the "Comprehensive Environmental Response, Compensation, and Liability Act of 1980," this act provides for determining liability, compensation, cleanup, and emergency response for hazardous substances released into the environment and the cleanup of inactive hazardous waste disposal sites.

Coastal Barrier Resources Act. Intended to preserve the barrier islands lying off the continental coastlines, this 1982 act prohibits federal expenditures for flood insurance, bridges, airports, sewers, roads, and other grants and loans for facilities in undeveloped coastal areas.

(NEPA). Most of these statutes parallel NEPA by requiring evaluations of the environmental impacts caused by state actions and, in some cases, by major private development projects. In general, the environmental protection laws require federal and state agencies to determine that proposed projects will have little or no impact on environmental qualities or that actions will be taken to avoid, reduce, or compensate for impacts before permits can be issued. In addition, the NEPA process provides opportunities for public review and comment on proposals and for litigation on both the substance and procedures of environmental impact reviews.

In two significant ways, however, the federal and state environmental laws fail to respond to McHarg's call for respecting nature. First, permitting procedures generally deal with individual project applications rather than areawide environmental concerns. The possible cumulative effects of many projects over time are not evaluated. Relationships between permits for different purposes are seldom established. In many cases, opportunities are missed for reconciling competing objectives or making trade-offs for securing better conservation.

Second, federal permitting procedures operate virtually independently of regional and local planning processes. Federal agencies view their role as regulators, administering laws and rules in a top-down manner. They make little attempt to ensure that permits make sense in the context of local planning and policies. A report by the Maryland Office of Planning observes: "The regulations may treat matters in isolation but nature does not." The report makes the point that "a more ecological approach to regulation, one that looks at the relationship of all the pieces, would prevent some of the defects in the present system."[5]

Nevertheless, NEPA and other federal and state environmental laws have nurtured Americans' awareness and appreciation of natural systems as vital aspects of our cities, economy, and society. The following sections explore how public and private initiatives are preserving valued natural qualities and features for future generations.

Planning for Conservation

Determining "where not to grow" requires identifying what and where significant environmental and natural resources exist and preparing strategies and plans for conserving them. Urban and environmental planners expend much time and effort to determine the location and characteristics of specific resources in the path of future development. Planners usually begin their projections of future development patterns by identifying significant natural features that ought to be conserved, both within urban areas and outside them. In *Design with Nature*, McHarg identified eight important features of the regional landscape: surface water, marshes, floodplains, aquifers, aquifer recharge areas, steep lands, prime agricultural land, and forests and woodlands. These landscape and water qualities, he taught, form natural systems that are an essential component of our living environment.

Based on that perspective, community development policies are increasingly recognizing the value of natural functions. For example, local comprehensive plans in Florida are required to incorporate a conservation section that addresses needs for "the conservation, use, and protection of natural resources in the area, including air, water, water recharge areas, wetlands, waterwells, estuarine marshes, soils, beaches, shores, flood plains, rivers, bays, lakes, harbors, forests, fisheries and wildlife, marine habitat, minerals, and other natural and environmental resources."[6]

In addition, subdivision regulations now routinely require stormwater retention measures to control erosion, setbacks to buffer stream valleys, and protection of floodplains, among other measures to preserve environmental qualities. Zoning ordinances frequently incorporate conservation, agricultural, and open space districts to protect valuable natural areas.

In many cases, analysts employ a McHargian technique of overlaying resource maps to define areas that are of greatest value for natural conservation. This process has been aided by the increasing use of geographic information systems (GIS) to record and relate mapped data. The information also allows analysts to undertake a "carrying capacity" analysis, another McHargian-inspired technique, to determine areas (such as floodplains, steep slopes, and prime farmlands) that should not be developed, areas that may be developed with special care to avoid erosion and other adverse impacts, and areas suitable for development. The capabilities of underlying geology and soil conditions to sustain development also can be evaluated, particularly if the use of septic tanks is being evaluated. In such an expansive approach to conservation planning, planners may identify significant ecosystems that have particular attributes for supporting plant, aquatic, and animal life—rivers, wetlands, ponds, and forests, for example—that help to maintain biodiversity.

A carrying capacity analysis does not provide an absolute measure of land to be conserved—that is, a specific level of development that cannot be exceeded without grave environmental impacts. Other factors can influence that determination, such as the feasibility of applying technical practices to allow some development while protecting the resource. For example, the widely used standard that prohibits development on slopes of more than a

15 percent incline makes sense for certain types of development but not for others, such as apartment buildings, which can take advantage of hillside scenic views while employing design and construction techniques to minimize adverse effects on steep slopes. In the right circumstances, siting a one-hundred-unit apartment building on a hillside may be more desirable than allowing fifty single-family houses with associated streets and driveways to sprawl over two or three times as much land. Carrying capacity, in other words, may not indicate absolute restrictions on development but can be a useful initial measure of potential constraints that might be employed.[7]

Green Infrastructure: Interrelating Natural Systems

Reflecting McHarg's concerns for considering all aspects of natural systems, the concept of green infrastructure is attracting attention for its emphasis on incorporating and interconnecting a wide variety of green spaces. The term describes networks of natural areas—wetlands, waterways, woodlands, and wildlife habitats, for example—which, together with parks, recreation areas, farmlands and woodlands, are connected by trail systems and natural corridors. Advocates speak of "links" and "hubs" in such networks. (Greenways can be composed of similar components but sometimes focus more particularly on trails and corridors.) The notion of combining these green spaces and corridors as green infrastructure systems generates three immediate benefits:

- Structuring the relationships among green spaces reduces the fragmentation of natural systems that commonly occurs as cities develop.
- Fashioning green networks as infrastructure systems reinforces their significance as necessary components of urban areas.
- Plans for green infrastructure systems create recognizable frameworks that help to ensure preservation of nature-based resources.

A green infrastructure strategy, according to some advocates, should be regarded as an overall framework for community and regional conservation and development. Protecting green infrastructure in advance of development ensures that existing green spaces are valued as essential community assets.[8] The concept of preserving green infrastructure systems also provides a rationale for connecting natural systems in rural areas.

Planning for green infrastructure systems involves tasks similar to most conservation planning efforts: (1) setting goals, (2) determining criteria to identify and analyze natural features and their interrelationships, (3) analyzing resource values and vulnerabilities, (4) determining a planned system, and (5) creating strategies for implementation. Plans should indicate how green infrastructure systems are integrated with patterns of urban development, and strategies should include determinations of preservation priorities, protection measures to be employed, and funding mechanisms. As described in the following sections, these aspects of planning for green infrastructure systems are increasingly applied in entire watersheds, multi-

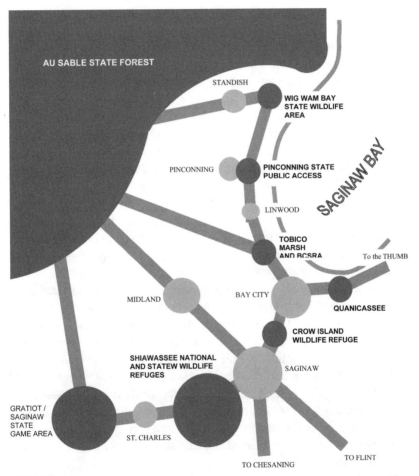

FIGURE 4.1
The Saginaw Bay Greenways Collaborative, with the assistance of the Conservation Fund, assembled representatives of conservation agencies and organizations to formulate a green infrastructure plan for the Saginaw Bay area. The plan, which identifies hubs of green space connected by greenway corridors, provides a vision to guide future conservation actions in the area. (Plan provided courtesy of the Greenways Collaborative and the Conservation Fund.)

state and multicounty regions, metropolitan areas and individual communities, and specific development projects. Depending on the affected area, the planning process may involve many levels of government, nonprofit organizations, citizens' groups, and property owners and developers as well.

Federal and State Planning for Conservation

Federal and state agencies responsible for managing land and water resources in green spaces—for example, national and state parks, forests, and wildlife conservation areas—draw up plans for conserving natural resources in those areas. Special planning efforts include the special area management plans (SAMPs) prepared by the U.S. Army Corps of Engineers in accordance with the Coastal Zone Management Act. The plans, undertaken in conjunction with federal, state, and local resource agencies, provide for both natural resource protection and reasonable coastal-dependent development in designated areas. The Endangered Species Act allows landowners, government agencies, and environmental groups to collaborate in preparing habitat conservation plans (HCPs) to identify habitats to be conserved as well as areas that may be developed. The U.S. Environmental Protection Agency (EPA) and the Corps also carry out studies to provide "advanced designation" of wetlands to reduce conflicts between landowners and the agencies over section 404 permits. These federal planning efforts typically involve state and local agencies as well as nongovernmental organizations.

Many states encourage conservation planning in key areas by designating or requiring local designation of *critical areas* threatened by development. For example, the Washington State Growth Management Act requires county and city comprehensive plans to designate critical areas, defined as wetlands, aquifer recharge areas, fish and wildlife habitats, frequently flooded areas, and geologically hazardous areas. Critical areas, as well as lands that have long-term significance for agriculture, forests, and mineral resources, are to be protected from urban development.[9] A state agency evaluates local comprehensive plans to determine that critical areas are properly defined and protected and may suggest additional measures to accomplish those ends.

The California Natural Community Conservation Planning (NCCP) program, enacted in 1991, provides a broad-based ecosystem approach to planning for the protection of biological diversity while accommodating compatible economic activity. The program provides leadership and funding assistance for regional and local collaborative planning to protect wildlife species. It seeks to anticipate and prevent the controversies arising from the listing of endangered species in developing areas by focusing on establishing the long-term stability of wildlife and plant communities while designating developable areas.

The initial effort concerned the coastal sage scrub habitat in more than six thousand square miles in five counties of Southern California. The ecosystem is home to about a hundred potentially threatened or endangered species in an area that has been growing rapidly for decades. Counties and cities within this area have been working with state and federal agencies and landowners to identify key habitat areas and corridors, characterized by a range of soils, terrain, slopes, and other landscape features, that will accommodate a wide variety of species. Just a few years into the program, more than half of the scrub habitat has been protected by voluntary commitments of thirty-one local governments and thirty-seven private landowners and developers. The planning process also has identified developable lands outside habitats for future urban growth.[10] As of 2006, NCCP programs have also been initiated outside of Southern California in two counties and are being considered in four other counties. Typically, the plans involve a broad range of conservation and funding mechanisms.

The Highlands Coalition, a northeastern multistate organization established in 1988, was formed to encourage conservation of the broad band of mountain landscape stretching from eastern Pennsylvania through northern New Jersey and eastern New York state into Connecticut.[11] The Coalition brings together one hundred conservation organizations and four state governments to protect 3 million acres of forests, scenic ridges, waterways, and productive farmlands from the intense pressure of poorly planned development. More than 14 million people visit the Highlands annually to enjoy historic towns and sites, scenic views, and close to half a million acres of public recreational lands. Nearly 55 percent of the Highlands in New York and New Jersey provide habitat for 247 rare, threatened, or endangered species of plants and animals. Highlands forests supply clean drinking water for more than 15 million people. Yet only 14 percent of the four-state region is permanently protected from development.

The Coalition has been vital in encouraging research to identify key resources and in gathering support for conservation actions. The U.S. Forest Service updated its 1993 study in 2002 to assess the region's natural resources and recent land use trends and to project potential impacts of continued development. The assessment built on analyses previously completed by the Regional Plan Association. The Coalition identified "treasures" of historic buildings and towns, scenic areas, and special natural features in each state. The Coalition also succeeded in having the U.S. Congress pass the Highlands Conservation Act, which recognizes the importance of the region and authorized $100 million over ten years for acquiring land for conservation and $10 million over ten years for additional studies and other assistance by the Forest Service to achieve conservation goals. In 2004, the New Jersey Legislature enacted the Highlands Water Protection and Planning Act, which authorized measures resembling the 1979 act for the New Jersey Pinelands region (described in chapter 8): establishing a council to develop a regional master plan and implementing regulations to identify where "development shall not occur." The Coalition is pursuing similar legislation in the other states.

In another multistate program, the states of Maryland, Pennsylvania, and Virginia, together with the District of Columbia and the U.S. EPA, signed the Chesapeake Bay Agreement in 1983 (renewed in 1987 and 2000), which committed each party to take immediate, substantial measures to restore and protect the bay. The largest estuary in the United States, the Chesapeake Bay stretches some 195 miles from north to south and drains an area of 64,000 square miles in six states and the District of Columbia. The watershed is rich in wetlands, of which 1.2 million acres remain. The impacts of population increases in the Bay region began to cause dramatic declines in fisheries, waterfowl population, and general water quality as well as submerged aquatic vegetation.

A seven-year EPA study completed in 1983 identified point and non-point sources of pollution that increased nutrient and sediment loading of bay waters. Following the agreement, Maryland made a dramatic commitment to bay conservation. The Maryland Chesapeake Bay Critical Areas Law, approved in 1984, defined a critical area consisting of the water of the bay, tidal wetlands and tributaries, lands under these waters, and one thousand feet of upland adjoining the water boundary. A twenty-five-member commission established criteria (enacted into law in 1986) to guide the plans and actions of the sixteen counties and forty-five municipal governments within the critical area. To minimize adverse impacts of pollutants on water quality and to conserve fish, wildlife, and plant habitat, the statute established land use policies that would accommodate growth but control growth-related pollution by limiting growth in undeveloped areas and defining standards for reducing pollution in areas designated for future development. Grandfathering provisions accommodated existing projects and allowed development of approved plans and intrafamily land transfers. Other criteria were spelled out for specific types of activities and areas, such as shore erosion works, forests and woodlands, wetlands, and agriculture.

The commission required local governments to prepare plans responding to the approved criteria and submit them for commission approval. Planning funds were provided, and over an eighteen-month period, commission staff worked with counties, cities, and towns to secure approval of plans. Eventually, all local plans were approved, although not before delays and conflicts over the commission's requirements. Nevertheless, the commission succeeded in prompting local jurisdictions to account for environmental factors in planning for development, and substantial preservation efforts are now in place on the shores and waters of the bay.[12]

These examples of state and multistate initiatives to promote environmental preservation only hint at the range and number of state efforts. Especially during and after the 1990s, state interest in preserving green space has blossomed into dozens of programs that provide funding, encourage planning, and enable the use of specific approaches for preservation of green space.

Regional Planning for Green Space

Regional concerns for protection of green space are growing in importance as the pace of metropolitan expansion steps up the development of open lands. Planning for saving regional green space may embrace entire metropolitan areas or focus within only a county or two, and it may be conducted by public agencies or nongovernmental organizations or both. A regional outlook enables the identification of significant green spaces well ahead of spreading development and, given effective leadership, provides access to a wide spectrum of public and private resources for preserving them. The well-known Santa Monica Mountains Conservancy, for example, has helped to preserve more than fifty-five thousand acres of parklands, improve recreation areas, and preserve conservation areas in several mountain chains around Los Angeles. Established by the California legislature in 1980, the Conservancy prepared a strategic plan to guide its actions and those of local governments. As an independent government agency, it draws on state funding and private contributions and works closely with local governments and nonprofit groups to protect green space.

The Conservancy's central mission is to acquire, preserve, and restore lands "to form an interlinking system of urban, rural, and river parks, open space, trails, and wildlife habitats that are easily accessible to the general public"—a description of what are now known as "green infrastructure systems," or greenways. In fact, many regional organizations are championing preservation of green space corridors that connect natural spaces and systems across municipal boundaries.

Some greenways focus primarily on trails, which can be quite lengthy:

the Appalachian Trail, the granddaddy of them all in age and length, extends for 2,167 miles. The 215-mile San Francisco Bay Trail links the Bay Area's urban waterfronts to more than 130 parks and environmental preserves in nine counties and forty-seven cities; ultimately, it will be 400 miles long. The 790-mile Arizona Trail connects three national parks and four national forests.[13]

Many greenways have been established along disused railroad rights-of-way, helped in many cases by the Rail-to-Trails Conservancy. The Western Maryland Rail Trail, for example, runs for twenty miles along the abandoned rail bed of the Western Maryland Railway, paralleling the historic Chesapeake and Ohio Canal beside the Potomac River. Beginning at Fort Frederick State Park (a Revolutionary War fortress), the route passes through the historic town of Hancock and a series of Appalachian ridges. In addition to canal locks and aqueducts, the paved trail offers access to river views, boat launch ramps, an information center and museum, campsites, and commercial services.

Other greenways are being assembled by strategic acquisitions of paths, lands, vacated streets, and other properties that provide connections to existing green spaces. Numerous cities—including Hartford, Connecticut, and Chattanooga, Tennessee—have recovered former industrial areas along urban waterfronts to create attractive greenways.

The City of St. Louis, Missouri, along with St. Louis and St. Charles counties, has undertaken an ambitious project to build the "River Ring," a more-than-600-mile web of forty-five greenways along the Missouri, Mississippi, Meramec, and Cuivre rivers. A voter-approved Great Rivers Greenway District is collecting a one-tenth-of-one-cent sales tax increment and working with local governments and private donors to piece the "ring" together. It will link as well to trail and greenway projects developed by Madison and St. Clair counties in Illinois.

Yet another example is the forty-nine-mile trail on an abandoned railroad corridor between Palatka and Lake Butler in northeastern Florida. Acquired by the Florida Department of Environmental Protection's Office of Greenways and Trails, it will connect eleven towns and cities in four counties and provide a pathway for biking, hiking, skating, strolling, and riding horseback.

Local Planning for Green Space

Many of the most intensively used green spaces are located in cities and suburbs, created through planning efforts of local governments working in partnership with private developers. For example, the Maricopa Association of Governments prepared a Desert Spaces Management Plan for the

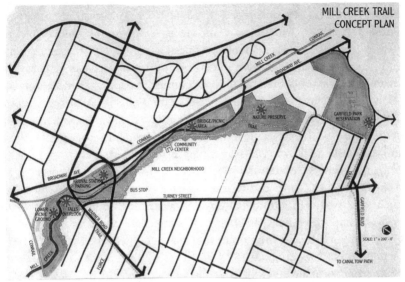

FIGURE 4.2
The Mill Creek Trail in Cleveland, Ohio, located along a stream valley, provides a recreational trail along a stream valley through a built up neighborhood. The greenway also borders a development of affordable housing on an adjacent site.

Phoenix area in Maricopa County, Arizona. The plan is notable for identifying and defining priorities for lands worthy of protection, thus providing a guide for future actions of governments, landowners, and conservation organizations in the area. The plan indicates three classes of open lands:

- public and private lands with outstanding open-space values that should be protected from development;
- public and private lands with high open space values whose environmental features should be retained through sensitive development; and
- existing or designated parks, wilderness areas, and wildlife areas.

The plan recommends acquiring the first category of lands, some 1.5 million acres, through a combination of regulatory restrictions, reservations through the subdivision exaction process, donations by individuals and conservation groups, purchase of easements, and acquisition. The second category, about 2.2 million acres, is expected to be managed through zoning and subdivision approval processes that could secure reservations of important natural features in development plans.

The Association of Governments adopted the Desert Spaces plan in

1995 as an advisory document to guide local conservation initiatives. Maricopa County, which has planning jurisdiction for unincorporated areas within the region, adopted a master plan in 2001 that includes an open space plan identifying dedicated and proposed open spaces. Its centerpiece was a planned trail system connecting county parks and recreational areas. The county formed a Trail Commission in 2000, which completed a plan in 2002 that delineates 240 miles of trails, 72 percent within land owned by the U.S. Bureau of Land Management, other public agencies, and utility systems. Trails crossing private properties are to be dedicated by the owners through the subdivision approval process. Typically, the commission negotiates dedication of a thirty-foot pathway, which frequently is part of a considerably wider swath of unbuildable washes or arroyos that will remain in a natural state. Trail manager Christopher Coover predicts that at the current rate of area growth, the trail system will be fully in place by about 2015.[14]

Another local jurisdiction that has chosen to implement the Desert Spaces Management Plan is Peoria, Arizona, a city of about 140,000 residents. It adopted a Desert Lands Conservation Master Plan in 1999 and has negotiated the acquisition of more than 3,600 acres of open space, mountain preserves, and parks; it followed that up with a conservation ordinance in 2005, which calls for developing a trail along both sides of the Agua Fria River, which, with tributaries, winds through much of the city's territory. As development projects are submitted for subdivision approval, project designers are encouraged to minimize impacts on habitats, trees, and vegetative buffers along the stream beds and provide trails that will link into a citywide trail system.

In San Diego County, California, the San Diego Association of Governments (SANDAG) took a bold step to preserve the remaining coastal sage scrub ecosystem (as part of the state NCCP program described in the regional discussion earlier in this chapter). SANDAG cooperated with several constituent jurisdictions and key organizations to undertake a series of habitat protection studies to identify, in advance of development, major habitat conservation needs throughout the county. One product is the Multi-Species Comprehensive Plan (MSCP) for the southern part of San Diego County, a remarkable effort to proactively reconcile habitat protection with future development, thereby improving the certainty of the development approval process in the fast-growing area. The plan calls for conservation of about 85 percent of the 109,000 acres of privately owned habitat and 96 percent of the 75,000 acres of publicly owned habitat in the study area.

An economic impact analysis of the plan demonstrated that the multi-

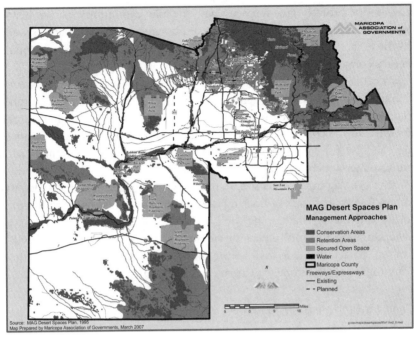

FIGURE 4.3
The Maricopa Association of Governments oversaw preparation of a Desert Spaces
Plan to guide conservation actions of the county and many local governments in the
region. It depicts appropriate management approaches to conservation of important
open space resources.

species protection approach will produce measurable economic benefits in
comparison to "business as usual," project-by-project habitat protection
efforts that sow discord and extend the development approval process.
Such disruptions could result in fewer jobs and lower resident incomes.
The study estimated that the MSCP plan would generate additional jobs,
lower the unemployment rate, and increase personal income in the region.
On the cost side, even the high-acquisition alternative (requiring major
public outlays for habitat purchase) would require only about $15 to $20
per household per year.[15]

Developers commonly contribute to preservation of green space as part
of their developments, either in adherence to regulatory requirements or
as good development practice that clearly boosts the value of the resulting
product. In Denver, for example, the redevelopment plan for the city's former Stapleton Airport (described in chapter 3) calls for 1,100 acres of green
space, nearly a quarter of the total acreage. Designed as an integral part of

the entire project, green spaces will include community parks, play-grounds, and nature preserves connected by greenways and trails, as well as the 80-acre Central Park, a community gathering place and recreational mecca completed in 2006.

Another example, this one less extensive, is the restoration of green infrastructure for the 240-acre Summerset at Frick Park in Pittsburgh. Summerset was designed to provide sites for 710 homes to be built on a brownfield site composed of slag from the steel mill operations of decades ago. One of the first design issues concerned treatment of the Nine Mile Run ravine, which transected the site. Rather than bury the Run by bull-dozing the slag into a level site, the designers, LaQuatra Bonci, decided to retain it and plan rows of housing that could take advantage of the scenic views offered by the sloping terrain. Nine Mile Run was restored as a "working" stream, and 105 acres were planted as green open spaces provid-ing an attractive residential setting and connecting the venerable Frick Park higher up the slopes to the riverfront below.

Tools for Protecting Green Spaces

The large- and smaller-scale planning efforts described above indicate the range of concerns being addressed and approaches being employed across the nation to preserve green space. The examples demonstrate that green space is respected as a valuable adjunct to urban development and as a last-ing contribution to a sustainable environment. To achieve those goals, public agencies, nongovernmental organizations, and private developers use a variety of techniques and tools for preserving green spaces, including several forms of property acquisition, public regulations, incentives and partnerships, and development designs.

Land Acquisition

Acquiring land is the most certain means of preserving its environmental and open space attributes for future generations. Traditionally, local, state, and federal governments and special public agencies acquired land for this purpose. Spending by public agencies, however, has not kept up with mounting demand. With aging baby boomers able to spend more time enjoying the outdoors, the increased participation in sports and such activ-ities as hiking and biking, and a growing interest in ecotourism, the needs for more land and facilities are climbing rapidly. Federal and state pro-grams to fund land purchases, including the federal Land and Water Conservation Fund, have been unpredictable. Property tax revolts in the

FIGURE 4.4
Summerset, being developed for up-scale housing on a former slag heap in
Pittsburgh, restored the stream running through the property and extensively landscaped the hillsides flanking the residential areas. The on-site green spaces link into a
major park on the north and a riverside trail system on the south.

1970s curtailed municipal spending on green space. However, a spate of
voter-approved ballot measures since the mid-1990s have expanded state
and local investments in green spaces; in 2005, the Trust for Public Land
reported that voters in twenty-two states approved 106 such measures that
will generate more than $1.7 billion in new funding for conservation.[16]
But public agencies are still struggling to keep up with demand, especially
as land prices continue to rise.

The most direct and often used means of land acquisition for conservation purposes is outright purchase of "fee simple" ownership by governments or by nonprofit groups that will hold the land in trust. Federal and
state parks, wildlife refuges, wilderness areas, forests, and similar areas are
acquired in this manner. Land acquisition by public jurisdictions often is
augmented by lands purchased by environmental organizations such as
land trusts—nonprofit organizations that work to conserve open lands by
acquiring or helping to acquire land or conservation easements and frequently managing conservation resources as well. They accept donations
or bequests of land or land acquisition funds from landowners interested
in protecting open space, and they work with governmental agencies to

leverage public acquisitions. Land trusts can act quickly to purchase options, obtain appraisals, and acquire properties in advance of governments' financial abilities. More than two thousand land trusts have been formed throughout the nation to hold donated or purchased land and easements for conservation purposes.

Perhaps the best known organization promoting land acquisition by land trusts, as well as other types of partnerships, is The Nature Conservancy, an international nonprofit group that works in twenty-seven countries and has protected 15 million acres in the United States alone, many of them preserved in cooperation with federal, state, and local government agencies. The Conservation Fund has joined with a variety of agencies and organizations to protect more than 5 million acres of wildlife habitat, wetlands, community open space, and other open lands. The Trust for Public Land has helped public agencies and communities protect 2 million acres, and the Land Trust Alliance has helped form (and provides technical information to) more than 1,600 land trusts across the nation.

Such organizations often act as third-party "facilitators" of property acquisition for conservation. For example, the Conservation Fund acquired the land and water rights for 2,800 acres of converted farmland in La Paz County, Arizona, from a drainage and irrigation district. The property is in the floodplain of the Colorado River adjacent to the Cibola National Wildlife Refuge. As a component of the Lower Colorado River Multi-Species Conservation Plan, the land will be restored to native riparian, wetland, and aquatic habitat to benefit more than a hundred federal or state-listed wildlife species. The property will be managed by the U.S. Bureau of Reclamation and the U.S. Fish and Wildlife Service.

Local governments commonly adopt programs to acquire land and pursue conservation strategies as part of their growth management efforts. Citizens in Boulder, Colorado, for example, voted in 1967 to levy a special sales tax of 0.4 percent to acquire mountain land around the city, hoping to retain the city's distinctive setting. By 1992, the city had acquired more than twenty-two thousand acres of open space with $59 million in revenues from bond issues secured by the tax. Some of the land is used for recreation and adjoins mountain parks owned by the city and county. Other land is leased to farmers. All together, the open space acquisition program, combined with Boulder's "blue line" limit on development above a certain elevation, has created a virtual greenbelt around the city. The city's experience testifies to the power of a long-term acquisition program based on a relatively small tax.

Sarasota County, Florida, whose establishment of a growth boundary was described in chapter 3, reinforced its constraints on rural development out-side the boundary by acquiring thousands of acres to protect its major water supply aquifer. These lands, added to a state-owned park of nineteen thou-sand acres, ensure preservation of a large amount of the county's green space

Scottsdale, Arizona, is playing an important role in implementing the Desert Spaces Management Plan adopted by the Maricopa Association of Governments. Mayor Mary Manross, in her 2005 "State of the City" address, reminded residents that the city had determined to preserve one third of the city's area in open space, including the sections of the McDowell Mountains and the Sonoran Desert within the city boundaries. To that end, she said, a citizens' task force recommended establishment of the McDowell Sonoran Preserve. A 1994 resolution for that purpose was followed in 1995 by a city-wide vote to increase the local sales tax from 1.2 to 1.4 percent to raise funds for acquiring 4,000 acres of open space land in the preserve. Overall, the city has acquired 13,485 acres of open land. In 2005, it opened two new trails and trailheads giving access to the open lands and expects to create at least one new access point in each of the next three years.[17]

Local governments in most states can also establish special authorities with their own taxing powers to acquire and manage parks and other open spaces. The extensive forest preserve system in the Chicago region, for example, is managed by county authorities in Cooke and its surrounding counties. The authorities use earmarked increments of property taxes to acquire open lands and manage them for recreational and conservation purposes. Montgomery County, Maryland, is part of the bicounty Maryland-National Capital Park and Planning Commission, which is charged with expanding and operating all types of parks and recreational spaces. The commission has aggressively pursued an acquisition program to preserve large acreages for parks, wildlife refuges, and similar open spaces in the northern part of the county to help preserve its rural charac-ter. Montgomery County also participated in Maryland's Rural Legacy pro-gram, which provided state funding for acquiring lands that would link existing conservation areas into green infrastructure systems.

The *Wall Street Journal* reported in 2006 that cities across the nation are spending hundreds of millions of dollars to purchase land to preserve drink-ing water supplies. The cities recognize that this strategy provides a cheaper alternative than building treatment plants. For example, the cities of Austin and San Antonio, in Texas, are competing to buy lands over the Edwards Aquifer, which is particularly vulnerable to contamination because it is com-posed of porous limestone. The aquifer supplies nearly all of San Antonio's drinking water as well as 5 percent of Austin's, and it holds enough water to continue supplying San Antonio alone for more than one hundred years. San Antonio has spent about $45 million to purchase seven thousand acres of land to prevent further sprawling development that might endanger the water source. In May 2005, city voters approved a $90 million tax measure to purchase thousands more acres. Austin has raised $80 million in bonds since 1998 to buy twenty thousand acres of land and may ask voters to approve a $100 million bond measure for additional property acquisition. But the policy has its opponents, mainly land developers and local land holders who say the policy depreciates the value of their properties.

Land is also acquired to prevent the impacts of stormwater runoff on water quality. Massachusetts has spent $120 million since 1985 to purchase about twenty thousand acres of land around two reservoirs that supply Boston, while New York City has bought about seventy thousand acres adjoining stream and rivers in the Catskills that feed into reservoirs that supply the city.[18]

Conservation Easements

Because outright acquisition of conservation land can be expensive, some-times only certain rights are acquired, at a considerably lower cost than if all rights were acquired. Especially since the early 1980s, after the U.S. Congress enacted permanent tax subsidies for donations of conservation easements, such easements are increasingly used to conserve natural qual-ities and resources. Government agencies or land trusts may purchase and hold easements to allow the public use of property for specific, limited pur-poses, such as hiking trails, scenic enjoyment, or picnicking, while the property owner can continue ranching, farming, or other uses compatible with conserving the property's natural qualities. Land trust organizations sometimes work out agreements with property owners for long-term leases or rights to manage land for certain purposes. Because conservation ease-ments are dedicated to a public purpose, almost every state has adopted enabling legislation allowing acquisition of conservation easements.

One example of the use of conservation easements is the Conservation Fund's application of the concept along a 13.5-mile section of interstate highway between Castle Rock and Colorado Springs, Colorado. The ease-ment limited development along bordering land to preserve agricultural land, scenic qualities, and rare wildlife habitats.[19]

Usually, conservation easements also mandate against development to retain land in its natural state. Based on the legal concept of property own-ership as a bundle of rights, purchase of a property's development rights permanently removes the right to develop it.

As an example, Anne Arundel County, Maryland, initiated a program to compensate farmers for restricting development by purchasing the development rights of their property. Farmers are allowed to continue farming and may add a home or two for family members but may not otherwise develop the property. The county's program supplements a statewide rights-purchase program funded by a state tax on property transfers. The state program provides annual grants to counties for the purchase of development rights in areas designated for conservation or agricultural preservation. (A similar approach—transferable development rights—is described later in this chapter.)

Environmental organizations and land trusts can negotiate beneficial tax positions as incentives for donations of easements or other restrictions on land development. For that reason, developers increasingly are using conservation easements in "conservation subdivisions" (described more fully below) to create attractive natural settings for a limited amount of development. The amenity value of the conserved land generates high prices for new development—typically primary residences or second homes.

A Lincoln Institute of Land Policy report describes the boom in these uses of conservation easements as "the perception that conservation easements are a win-win strategy in land protection, by which willing landowners work with private land trusts or government agencies to provide lasting protection of the landscape."[20] However, the report observes that the terms of conservation easements are "infinitely variable," that legal standards and public oversight are lacking, and that easement cost-benefit values are uncertain at best. Recent nationwide publicity about claims of excessive property values and tax deductions, as well as insider investors, has intensified uneasiness about the unregulated character of conservation easements, potentially leading to future actions by the U.S. Congress and Internal Revenue Service.

Clustering Development

For decades, planners, builders, and developers have united in promoting clustered development as a way to conserve natural resources as well as reduce infrastructure costs. Clustered development allows developers to plat smaller-than-standard lots on one part of a site to save the remainder of the site for permanent open space. The conserved area then may be used for common recreation space or for protecting environmentally sensitive lands or agricultural uses. Clustered development can be permitted through zoning provisions, subdivision regulations, or special ordinances. Generally, standards and procedures for designing clustered development are written to allow the overall amount of development permitted on the entire tract to be concentrated in one area. In addition, clustering provisions often allow mixtures of housing types and, in some cases, larger numbers of housing units than do standard subdivisions.

Clustering has acquired a negative reputation in some communities that have suffered from poorly designed groupings of homes that devalue neighborhoods. Some people also object to small yards as being virtually "un-American"; clustering in many communities is opposed by residents fearful of any form of development other than single-family, detached houses on large lots.

Because of the need to carefully review clustered housing design, the approval process is less certain than for conventional subdivisions and can be quite lengthy, both conditions that increase development costs. In addition, many communities have not taken pains to connect the green spaces preserved in individual projects into a green infrastructure system that can optimize conservation and recreational benefits. Thus the individual reservations of green spaces contribute less to environmental conservation than they otherwise might and also may be poorly managed by the community associations responsible for them.

Lincoln, Massachusetts, has implemented clustered development as part of a well-managed approach to preserving open lands. The town has taken a proactive role by working out agreements with landowners to either preserve entire tracts or promote clustered development. When a 109-acre, colonial-era farm went on the market in 1966, town officials realized that they lacked the $300,000 purchase price to retain it as open space. Several citizens saved the day by forming the Rural Land Foundation, which purchased the property with a large bank loan (secured by $10,000 guarantees from thirty residents). The Foundation commissioned a development plan designed to preserve half the property and then sold two existing houses and eight additional lots, deeded 56 acres to the local land trust, and cleared $40,000 to be used in future endeavors.

In 1971, the town adopted an Open Space Residential District, which provided a two-for-one density bonus if a property owner left at least 70 percent of a property undeveloped. The bylaw enabled the owner of a 100-acre tract originally planned for forty single-family homes to build eighty condominium units on only 24 acres. A year later, another property received an even larger density bonus in return for an assurance that half the units would be set aside for low- and moderate-income families. Part of the open space preserved on that tract is now a working farm managed by a civic organization.[21] The town's conservation plan adopted in 1976

FIGURE 4.5
Clustering houses in one section of a site to conserve suburban green space in the remainder is a tried-and-true solution for development in areas where natural features are valued. In The Fields of St. Croix in Lake Elmo, Minnesota, the developer set aside farming areas, woodlands, and other green space, all enjoyed by the residents.

guided these efforts, which has resulted in a network of more than 2,200 acres of connected lands that provide for ecosystem and farmland conservation as well as recreational needs.

Calvert County, Maryland, mandates clustering in much of the county. In areas designated as Resource Preservation districts and Farm Community districts, 80 percent and 60 percent, respectively, of sites proposed for development must be set aside as preserved open space, with clustered development permitted on the remainder.

The clustering concept has been reinvigorated in recent years by proponents of traditional neighborhood development and new urbanism. Such urban designers as Andrés Duany and Peter Calthorpe have attracted widespread attention with their designs for building compactly developed urban villages and new towns in suburban areas (described in chapter 6). In turn, environmentally minded land planners and designers have folded the urban designers' concepts in to the conservation-minded designs described below.

Conservation Subdivisions

Joel Garreau once observed that developers named new projects to highlight natural features that the development had usually obliterated. Developers of conservation subdivisions appear to do better by keeping these qualities intact or even enhancing them. Embracing the principles of sustainable

development and smart growth, conservation subdivisions cluster development to expand opportunities for conserving natural qualities and features.
The term *conservation subdivision* has been popularized by Randall Arendt,
among others.[22] Such subdivisions commonly are planned as showcases of
conservation, incorporating restored streams and wetlands, working farms,
areas of native vegetation, wildlife habitats, and scenic features, as well as
parks, trails, and recreational facilities. Development costs for streets and
utilities may be reduced by grouping developed areas and using innovative
natural systems for drainage and other purposes. In the right housing market, the natural amenities add significant value to the new homes.

An award-winning example is Coffee Creek Center, located fifty miles
southeast of downtown Chicago in the Indiana dunes country. The plan
calls for 1,200 housing units in a mix of single-family, townhouse, and
apartment styles, developed in pedestrian-friendly clusters around a 240-
acre park centered on the restored Coffee Creek. Retail, office, and commercial space amounting to 2.6 million square feet is also planned.
Buildings use advanced materials, equipment, daylighting, and energy-sav-
ing techniques.

Another example is the conservation subdivision built by Bielinski
Homes in Germantown, Wisconsin, on farmland with partially degraded
wetlands. The design for the thirty-nine-acre Prairie Glen restored the wetland as part of a stormwater treatment system, producing an attractive
green space amenity. The builder calculates saving in infrastructure costs of
15 to 25 percent as well as adding to homesite values.

Designers and builders view conservation subdivisions as superior alternatives to conventional subdivisions that offer lots with generous setbacks,
side yards, and rear yards. Conventional designs rarely respect existing
landscape features and require lengthy streets and utility lines to serve
building lots. Yet the typical patterns of lots and streets is familiar to much of
the population, well understood in the building industry, and thoroughly
ensconced in local zoning and subdivision regulations. Nevertheless, conservation subdivision designs, when done right, offer tremendous advantages over conventional plans in preserving green spaces and systems.

Typically, conservation subdivisions provide superior alternatives to
conventional subdivisions in suburban greenfield areas. However, they are
not necessarily a cure for urban sprawl. Conservation designs commonly
produce subdivisions with overall densities of less than two housing units
per acre. Coffee Creek Center is planned for 1.8 units per acre; Prairie Glen,
which boasts that 60 percent of the site is preserved in open space, yields
fewer than 0.8 housing units per acre. Both are more or less equivalent in

overall density to conventional suburban developments, falling well short of the kind of compact development that achieves the aims of sustainable development and smart growth. At the regional level, extended areas of conservation subdivisions would convert as much rural land as typical subdivisions do. And typical subdivision procedures usually provide no guarantee that the natural features within individual projects are linked into natural systems of green infrastructure.

Regulatory Approaches

Communities have enacted a variety of regulatory measures to forestall urban development or reduce impacts of development in designated areas of green space. Regulatory approaches include zoning and subdivision requirements for preserving green spaces, incentives for clustering and limited development, programs for transferring development rights, and mitigation banks.

Zoning for Preservation of Green Space

Many communities establish zoning districts or overlays to protect green spaces and specific natural features. Zoning districts have been fashioned to regulate or restrict development within forests and woodlands, areas of steep slopes, mountain tops and ridgelines, floodplains and stream valleys, agricultural areas, and other natural areas. For example, cities and counties in the states of Washington and Oregon must adopt zoning to restrict development in forests and agricultural areas, allowing only types of development that support or are associated with such uses.

Local governments also adopt natural or resource conservation zoning districts that protect a variety of natural features. Frederick County, Maryland, for example, created a Resource Conservation Zoning District, which allows "low intensity uses and activities which are compatible with the goal of resource conservation to be located within mountain and rural wooded areas. Areas within this district include mountain areas, rural woodlands, and cultural, scenic, and recreation resource areas. Environmentally sensitive areas within the resource conservation zone, including steep slopes, wetlands and the habitats of threatened and endangered species, will be protected from development."[23]

The hillside protection ordinance of Scottsdale, Arizona, provides another example. The city enacted the ordinance in 1977 to prevent development of the higher parts of the McDowell chain of mountains, a much-revered natural feature threatened by the city's expansion. In 1988, after landowners sued the city, the Arizona Supreme Court ruled that landowners in the hillside district must be allowed some use of their properties. Subsequently, the city enacted the Environmentally Sensitive Lands Ordinance in 1991 (amended in 2001, 2003, and 2004). The ordinance established an overlay district for a 134-square-mile area in northern Scottsdale. The zoning provisions impose a sliding scale of development densities: one home per five acres on hillside slopes of less than 24 percent; one home per twenty acres on slopes of 25 to 35 percent; and one home per forty acres on slopes greater than 35 percent. In addition, the regulations require set-asides of open space, ranging from 20 percent on relatively flat terrain up to 80 percent on steep hillsides and even 95 percent on unstable slopes. The ordinance provides incentives to locate development in the more suitable lower slopes, including density transfers and clustering allowances to retain open space. To avoid eliminating the value of existing lots, owners are entitled to build at least one single-family home.

A somewhat different approach to green space conservation is zoning that requires lots large enough to discourage development, accompanied by provisions that permit only rural and conservation uses. To provide a sufficient deterrent to development, minimum lot sizes must make their purchase for residential use unreasonably expensive. Because land prices depend on local land markets and pressures for development, the appropriate minimum lot size will vary from place to place. Outside Portland, Oregon, for example, minimum lots sizes are five or more acres. Lexington–Fayette County, Kentucky, precludes most development to preserve the world-famous horse farms by requiring minimum lots of ten acres.

Several counties in Maryland use this technique to preserve agricultural lands. Montgomery County, for example, established an Agricultural Preserve in 1980 that raised the minimum lot size requirement in the northern third of the county from five to twenty-five acres. Lots of this size, while discouraging development, may have encouraged property owners to establish conservation easements that promised tax relief or sale of development rights. Four easement programs (including the transferable development rights program described later in this chapter) have permanently restricted development on close to forty-eight thousand acres; another twenty thousand acres within the reserve has been acquired for public parkland.

Less ambitious approaches—such as expecting one- to five-acre lots to preserve natural features—are unlikely to be effective. Midsize lots, in the two- to five-acre range, are viewed by many home buyers as very desirable. In most housing markets, lots smaller than ten or so acres carry attractive prices geared to low development costs and frequently promote, rather than discourage, sprawling development. Buyers tend to believe that such lots preserve environmental values, although the long-term prognosis for that objective is not good.

To justify zoning restrictions for preserving green space, local governments apply the typical zoning standards of health, safety, and welfare. Conserving environmental qualities that sustain life; protecting against such dangers as floods, landslides, and air and water pollution; and promoting economic activity all provide rationales for conserving open lands and natural areas.

Subdivision Provisions for Preserving Green Space

Probably the most used regulatory approaches to preserving green space are requirements or incentives for conservation incorporated into subdivision regulations. Generally, these provisions require developers to set aside or dedicate sensitive lands and features, such as stream valleys, steep hillsides, wetlands, and floodplains. Typical provisions, for example, can require developed land to retain a setback (or buffer) from a stream bank or wetlands or to prohibit development on hillside slopes that exceed 15 percent. Sometimes developers are allowed to build higher densities in return for set-asides, sometimes not. The reserved lands usually are assigned for management by a community association or dedicated to the jurisdiction.

If conservation lands are required to be dedicated for public use, key issues can arise concerning the magnitude of the lands involved or their intended public use. Developers can claim that they are unfairly burdened by such requirements, as evidenced by the many "takings" cases that have won attention in recent years (see chapter 1 for a discussion of these legal issues). However, requirements for set-asides that are clearly specified in subdivision regulations forewarn developers of their potential effect on site development. Problems usually arise in situations when standards are not established or are being revised, or when developer contributions of green space are negotiated during subdivision approval processes. Nevertheless, developer contributions to preserving green spaces nearly always add value to their projects and frequently are highlighted in marketing the completed development.

Subdivision regulations also may include incentives for conservation of green space by allowing designs for planned unit developments, clustered or conservation subdivisions, or other innovative variations on conventional subdivisions. For example, Genoa Township in Delaware County, Ohio, enacted a Planned Rural Residential Conservation District as an overlay zoning district. It provides for waiving the underlying zoning requirements for subdivisions designed to preserve steep slopes, wetlands, watercourses, ridgelines, native vegetation, and other natural features.

Subdivision regulations may also require payment of *impact fees* for parks and recreation facilities or open space conservation. Usually, such fees are intended to fund acquisition or improvements of green spaces outside the specific development site, such as large community parks and recreational facilities that would not be appropriate to locate within a specific development. A few jurisdictions are levying impact fees to acquire conservation lands. Riverside County, California, for example, levies an impact fee on all development to provide funds for acquiring wildlife habitats. (Impact fees are more fully explained in chapter 5.)

Unfortunately, midsize lots of one to five acres are viewed by many people as a very desirable residential lot size. In a highly contentious clamor over growth during the mid-1990s, for example, residents of communities in the fast-growing northern sector of the Phoenix, Arizona, metropolitan area demanded the retention of one acre and larger minimum lot sizes to "preserve the desert environment" from more concentrated developments proposed by developers. Such low-density development clearly would inflict greater damage on the desert environment than would compact development, but citizen opponents of the development appeared more interested in preserving what they regarded as a desirable way of life than in conserving the desert environment.

Concentrating Rural Development

Another means of conserving rural lands—whether for agriculture, environmental protection, or simply open space—is by taking steps to concentrate future development in and around existing settlements. Crossroads communities, villages, and even small towns can coexist within conservation areas if they are properly planned and developed. Some local governments have adopted plans and zoning that encourage any development in rural areas to locate in areas adjoining already built up areas. This policy has the double effect of reducing development impacts on conservation areas and improving the critical mass of development in some areas to make some urban services, such as transit, feasible. Adherents of neo-traditional development strongly support this type of development because it closely corresponds to their concept of compact urban development.

Loudoun County, Virginia, for example, adopted a comprehensive plan in 1991 that called for retaining rural qualities in much of the county.[24] Plan policies discourage the extension of water and sewer lines to rural areas and promotes clustered residential development in rural villages and hamlets. These policies are to be implemented through the application of rural design guidelines, rural subdivision options that encourage clustering, the acquisition of open space easements, density transfers, and use-value assessments for farmland. Rural villages with a minimum area of three hundred acres, for example, can be developed for one hundred to three hundred dwelling units, plus some community-oriented retail and office space, on 20 percent of the area, leaving the remainder in an open space conservancy. The county subsequently adopted new zoning provisions permitting neo-traditional development districts, use of performance standards, and overlay districts to protect natural resources. However, although some use has been made of these policies and provisions, most development continues to follow conventional designs and densities.

The principal problem confronted by public officials in promoting concentrations of development in rural areas is that it restricts the potential development of most properties in rural areas while rewarding the owners of property in and adjoining existing settlements. Compensatory techniques, discussed below, can help to overcome that obstacle.

Transfer of Development Rights

Programs that promote the transfer of development rights (TDR) from one area or building to another have been employed in a number of communities. By allowing the sale and transfer to other properties of valuable development rights, the practice provides a way to compensate owners for regulatory restrictions that reduce property values. First used to preserve historic properties in central business districts, the concept allows developers to purchase development rights from a property owner and move them to another building or site. One well-known U.S. Supreme Court case, *Penn Central Transportation Co. v. City of New York* (438 U.S. 104, 124 [1978]), which up–held the City of New York's disapproval of construction of an office tower over Grand Central Terminal, hinged at least in part on the city's permission for the developer to transfer unused air rights to other properties.

For decades, the TDR technique has been recognized as a potential tool for preserving green spaces by allowing the transfer of development rights from areas to be preserved to urbanizing areas. But while the TDR concept was popular with planners, its use had to overcome political resistance to limiting development in preservation areas and required a robust market to stimulate developers to acquire and transfer development rights. Robert H. Freilich, a noted land use attorney, phrased it well: "The TDR approach has commonly been viewed as a conceptual all-star but a practical loser."[25] Nevertheless, applications of the TDR concept have spread; as of 2002, 134 communities had adopted some form of TDR program, although many have been less successful than hoped.

The usual TDR approach requires the designation of "sending" areas—those in which property owners may sell development rights—and "receiving areas"—areas to which development rights may be transferred. As a result of transferring rights, property owners in receiving areas can increase densities of development on their properties. Thus the sale and transfer of development rights becomes a market transaction promoted and supported by a regulatory program. The sale of rights is recorded in property deeds, and the transfer is recorded through a certification by the local jurisdiction.

TDR programs have also been used to protect the purity of Lake Tahoe in California and Nevada, by transferring rights from hillside second-home lots to in-town commercial development, as well as to protect fragile ecosystems in the New Jersey Pine Barrens, by transferring rights from conservation areas to in-town properties (see chapter 8 for discussions of these regional programs). Some local governments in Florida and other places have also adopted TDR programs.

A variation on transfer of development rights calls for the *transfer of conservation rights* from developing properties to conservation areas. Currently used in Dade and Broward counties in Florida, the technique imposes a conservation requirement on every development. The requirement can be transferred to conservation areas elsewhere that are considered more suitable for conservation. The South Florida Water Management District operates the program. This approach is not unlike provisions in many communities' subdivision regulations that require or allow payment of fees in lieu of reserving parklands within a subdivision site. The park fees are pooled by local governments to provide funds for acquiring properties in more suitable park locations. In many respects, the concept also parallels the concept of mitigation banks, discussed in the following section.

Another variation on the TDR concept allows density transfers among adjoining properties either to provide more flexibility in planning development for specific sites or to promote the clustering of development in rural areas.

Mitigation Banks

When development adversely affects environmentally sensitive land (particularly wetlands but also, in some cases, wildlife habitats), government agencies commonly require mitigation of those impacts either on or off the site. Mitigation, as defined by the Council of Environmental Quality, includes avoiding or minimizing development impacts, repairing impacts, reducing or eliminating adverse effects over time, or compensating for impacts by replacing them elsewhere. In the latter case, it quickly became clear that finding, financing, perhaps improving or restoring, and managing replaced resources was time-consuming and expensive for individual project developers, whether public or private. A common "bank" of land that could pool a number of project mitigation needs was a more efficient and even more environmentally effective way to satisfy such requirements.

Typically, mitigation banks are formed by public agencies and large corporations whose operations require occasional intrusions on environmentally sensitive lands. (State transportation agencies, for example, are common users.) They identify and acquire a large site with characteristics similar to those being threatened in other areas—an existing wetlands, for example, especially one already threatened and requiring protection and restoration. The wetland is restored, and a management and maintenance program is put in place. The values of the restored wetland are quantified as "credits" that can later be withdrawn, at a price, to compensate for unavoidable wetland losses elsewhere.

Two variations on this scenario include entrepreneurial banks established by private landowners or investors to sell market credits to whomever needs them and joint projects formed by groups of developers who need to compensate for wetland or habitat losses on their project sites.

The mitigation bank idea is one that could be applied, as in Miami and Dade counties, to regional open space and conservation needs. Developers would pay "in-lieu" fees to compensate for using open space in designated growth areas, which would then be used to acquire development rights in areas to be conserved. Such a process could be established by a county, regional agency, recreation district, or other entity with jurisdiction over a fairly large area in which both urbanization and conservation are desirable.

Defining "where not to grow" is an essential element of growth management. In addition to protecting valuable natural resources that might be adversely affected by development, conservation techniques prevent premature development in rural areas and reinforce policies for directing growth to desirable development areas that can be efficiently served by public infrastructure.

An important initial step in conservation efforts is identifying existing resources and evaluating their significance for sustaining community ecosystems, based on generally agreed upon criteria. Some of these criteria are established by federal and state environmental laws; others reflect local attitudes and desires, as evidenced in the Scottsdale, Arizona, program for hillside preservation. The value of understanding and carefully shaping conservation objectives is demonstrated in the experiences of Lincoln,

Massachusetts; Maricopa County, Arizona; and the Chesapeake Bay Commission of Maryland.

At some point, conservation objectives must be considered in relation to economic and social objectives, which may require trade-offs and compromises. The planning process for determining development in keeping with protection of wildlife habitats in Carlsbad, California, provides an example of multistakeholder consensus building that is being widely applied elsewhere as well. (Other processes for reaching agreement on multiple objectives are described in chapter 9.)

After the goals of conservation efforts have been defined, a battery of potential approaches to protecting resources can be employed. Some of the community and regional experiences recounted in this chapter demonstrate how a variety—and usually a combination—of acquisition and regulatory techniques has been effective in many areas.

To underscore the related private and public interests in conserving green spaces, here are a few words from Aldo Leopold, writing in 1934:

> Conservation will ultimately boil down to rewarding the private landowner who conserves the public interest. It asserts the new premise that if he fails to do so, his neighbors must ultimately pay the bill. It pleads that our jurists and economists anticipate the need for workable vehicles to carry that reward. It challenges the efficacy of single-track land laws, and the economy of buying wrecks instead of preventing them. It advances all these things . . . out of a profound conviction that the public is at last ready to do something about the land problem.[26]

CHAPTER 5

Supporting Growth
by Managing Infrastructure Development

Infrastructure issues lie at the heart of most local governments' growth management programs. Local officials know that growth issues most often surface in the public consciousness as shortfalls in public facilities and services—congested streets and highways, overcrowded schools, deficient water supplies, failing sewage treatment plants. These problems directly affect the daily lives of citizens, who clamor for instant solutions that can be difficult to deliver. Often, such problems provoke interest in establishing growth limits, growth boundaries, restrictions on rural development, and other methods of controlling growth. Infrastructure issues loom large on the public agendas of most communities.

For decades, the county commissioners of Sarasota County, Florida, paid little attention to growth issues and related infrastructure needs. Although rapid development was taking place along the coast, most of it was centered in the barrier islands and the two principal towns, Sarasota and Venice. The county government, dominated by rural interests, steadfastly refused to enter into the infrastructure business, hoping that the low capacity of public facilities would discourage development. However, in the 1970s, development began spilling over town boundaries into unincorporated areas of the county, promoted in part by the towns' announced opposition to further annexation. By the early 1980s, in piecemeal responses to growing pressures for providing infrastructure, the county had granted franchises for 49 water supply systems and 115 separate wastewater treatment plants, issued permits for more than forty-five thousand septic tanks, and approved the establishment of drainage districts that constructed more than eight hundred miles of drainage canals.

At that point, the county commissioners decided to take a more proactive interest in providing public facilities. During the rest of the decade, the county took impressive steps to improve its management of infrastructure systems, including:

- acquiring existing wastewater treatment systems and uniting them into a workable regional system, phasing out over-aged treatment plants, and building two regional plants;
- establishing five solid waste service districts to finance waste collection and disposal and acquiring land for landfill sites;
- purchasing a large tract to protect potential water production sites and extending a water supply system throughout the southern part of the county;
- receiving voter authorization in 1989 for a one-cent sales tax to overcome existing deficiencies on county roads and other facilities;
- preparing a stormwater management plan to reduce runoff and improve its quality and establishing a stormwater utility to raise revenues to implement the plan; and
- consolidating existing Sarasota and Venice parks and recreation areas into a countywide park system, including stepped-up acquisition of park lands.

In addition, the county began, in 1981, to prepare and follow five-year capital improvement programs that identified future needs, determined priorities and scheduling, and defined expected funding sources. Beginning in 1989, in response to the 1985 state growth management act, the capital improvement program became a vital part of the county's growth management efforts. It keyed public investments in infrastructure to requirements for adequate facilities to support expected growth. In just a few years, the county government had assumed a powerful role in the local development process, which it still holds today.

Sarasota County's experience is not unique. Citizens and public officials in many growing communities have failed to recognize the consequences of growth until the consequences have overtaken them. Like Sarasota County, they hope to avoid the responsibilities for planning and financing costly infrastructure systems. They play for time, believing that the issue might fade away. Only after a long period of temporizing with incremental "fixes" to tide them over until the next crisis do they accept the responsibility for supporting growth with adequate, efficient systems of basic facilities.

Once officials in Sarasota County accepted that responsibility, however, they moved with admirable firmness to put their house in order. Led by county officials armed with detailed plans, citizens voted one bond issue after another to retrofit existing development with new sewer, water, and road systems capable of extensions to serve new development. The commissioners reorganized county government to systematically plan and deliver public services. They made the capital facilities program, based on the comprehensive plan, the keystone of the county's budgeting for capital investments. Within a decade, they brought order to chaos and established a management process capable of supporting development well into the next century. Currently, county officials still must deal with fractious infrastructure issues in a growing and changing development climate, as well as bicker annually over the next improvement funding priorities, but they continue to work within an established framework of policies and procedures.

A Complexity of Responsibilities for Service Delivery

Over centuries of experience, public officials have invented many approaches to supplying public facilities. Grappling with a wide variety of locational demands and physical facility characteristics as well as multiple means of funding and service delivery, officials and administrators must determine specific responsibilities for planning, financing, and managing public services that establish fundamental qualities of urban life. Their decisions reflect several considerations:

- the significance of the facility for sustaining the health, safety, and welfare of community residents and workers (e.g., public education is usually viewed as a fundamental necessity, while public golf courses may be considered an optional amenity);
- the efficiency of service delivery through large linked systems (e.g., sewer and water systems) common to all or through individual facilities (e.g., libraries and airports) more customized for individual area needs;
- the ability to assign service costs directly to users, such as by metered water use, or as a common financial responsibility, such as a city hall building or a zoo; and
- the size and complexity of the facility or system, which may require lengthy periods for design and construction (e.g., a sewage treatment plant) or be readily available on demand (e.g., a police car).

Various entities charged with delivering specific services may include local public works agencies (that build and maintain roads, for example), special authorities functioning as arms of local governments (that manage water and sewer systems, for example), independent authorities or districts operating within one jurisdiction or across many (such as school adminis-trations or airport authorities), and state agencies (such as transportation and health departments) that plan, fund, or regulate facility development. Some services may be privately owned and administered, such as home-owners' septic tanks and playgrounds operated by community associations.

Depending on the choices made, community residents may obtain water through individual wells, small community-scale treatment and dis-tribution systems, or regional systems that may encompass remote dams and reservoirs and lengthy pipelines. Citizens may drive on local roads built almost entirely by developers, on higher-volume highways built by state and local governments, on high-speed highways financed mostly by the federal government, or on toll roads constructed and managed by public authorities or even private companies. Residents may send their children to nearby public schools, have them bussed long distances to consolidated schools, enroll them in private schools, or send them away to public or private institutions.

The complexity of service delivery stems from the different assignments made for planning to meet future needs, securing financing, constructing facilities, and managing operations. Responsibilities may be split among local, state, and federal governments, special authorities, and private companies, and the relative sharing of responsibilities is constantly shifting. The relative roles of public and private sectors in providing infrastructure have changed considerably over the years. At one time, it was not unusual for private com-panies to build toll roads and bridges or to operate water supply systems. Now, major road systems are almost entirely a governmental responsibility. Before World War II, many local governments assumed the responsibility for financ-ing roads, sidewalks, and other facilities in new subdivisions. Since the war, developers have been increasingly required to provide basic facilities in new subdivisions and often special amenities as well. Water and sewer authorities that once readily extended service to developing areas as an opportunity to broaden their markets now charge fees to pay for construction.

As these relationships evolve over time, every community acquires a distinctive approach to providing services that influences its approach and ability to manage growth.

Managing Growth by Managing Infrastructure

For local governments to manage growth, they must possess substantial control over the supply of public facilities and services to their residents. As the commissioners of Sarasota County learned, the location, quality,

BOX 5.1

Fiscal Issues in Managing Growth

Paul S. Tischler, TischlerBise, Fiscal, Economic & Planning Consultants, Bethesda, Maryland

Fiscal analysis techniques can evaluate the fiscal implications of various land use plans and other managed growth scenarios. The bottom line for fiscal impact analyses[*] is the positive or negative cash flow to the public sector based on projected revenues, capital costs, and operating costs from prospective development. These factors often vary according to the location and characteristics of expected development.

Probably the most important component of fiscal analyses is revenues. Depending on specific state and local revenue mechanisms, it is possible that lower-density, high-value market values will generate higher net revenues to a local government than more compact development, even after accounting for higher capital and/or operating expenses. Growing jurisdictions in Maryland, for example, generate most of their revenues from property and income taxes and transfer fees, all related to the market value of development. Residential market values generally increase as densities decrease. These kinds of findings must be understood as part of the decision-making process for managing growth. They may add significance to the nonfiscal impacts of growth on the environment, quality of life, and other aspects of community life.

Unfortunately, fiscal analyses too often consider only potential capital costs, which can lead to erroneous conclusions. Urban sprawl costs more than concentrated development in almost all cases when only capital facility costs are considered. Longer lengths of pipes and roadways, as well as school bus routes, make low-density development more expensive to serve with urban facilities. However, capital costs make up only 10 to 20 percent of most jurisdictions' budgets, making operating costs a major consideration. For some services operating costs may not vary significantly due to development patterns. For others, such as fire protection, marginal-cost fiscal impacts based on case studies usually indicate significant operating cost variations. For that reason, infill and continuous new development are likely to produce lower fire protection costs than for "leap-frog" development.

Other fiscal factors pertain to the timing and geographic distribution of projected development. Once facilities and services have been extended to urbanizing areas, rapid development of those areas usually produces the best fiscal results. Debt service and other costs for new facilities benefit from steep increases in revenues from new development. Similarly, understanding fiscal implications of development in various parts of an urbanizing area can assist planners in optimizing both the geographic location and timing of future development. A candid assessment of fiscal impacts of different development scenarios will lead to a more realistic, fundable, implementable growth management program.

[*] Fiscal impact analysis should not be confused with economic impact analysis. The latter shows how increases in employment and development generate income in the economy and, when shown, generates increases in public sector revenues. Costs are not considered.

and timing of public facility construction strongly shapes the direction and character of community development. The popular view that new roads and sewers stimulate development is not far from the truth:

frequently, communities open up new territories for development simply by extending key facilities. For homebuilders looking for desirable building sites or for commercial developers selecting locations for shopping centers, available capacity in public facilities is a strong attraction.

The quality of facilities is also a factor. Sarasota County's officials understood that 115 sewage treatment plants and 45,000 septic tanks in a region with a high water table could not sustain desirable development. Parents of schoolchildren know that a school system known for quality can boost home prices. Developers planning residential projects can calculate in advance the price premiums they can demand for property near conservation areas, parks, and recreational amenities. The quantity and quality of water supply can serve as a strong attraction for certain types of industries.

It is not surprising, then, that local governments seeking to manage future development are vitally concerned with ensuring the supply and quality of infrastructure systems. In formulating comprehensive plans, they make decisions about future directions of development that will affect where infrastructure systems need to be extended. More detailed functional plans may be drawn up for specific types of infrastructure, such as transportation and water and sewer systems, that establish standards for the amount and quality of desired facilities and define existing and future infrastructure capacities. Local officials rely on this information to lay out multiyear capital improvement programs to schedule the timing and sequencing of facility construction and improvements, estimate costs, and determine sources of revenues to pay for improvements.

To implement long-range plans, local governments set standards for local roads and assert their interests in state and regional decisions on highway improvements. They operate water and sewer systems, often through special authorities controlled by local elected officials, or insist on approval of water and sewer development plans proposed by separate special districts. They require developers to abide by standards and plans for all of the infrastructure placed in new developments. In these ways, local governments fashion a fundamental plan of action for infrastructure development and a process by which to track needs and accomplishments.

Linking Development to Infrastructure Capacity

One of the most commonly used growth management techniques makes development approvals contingent on the availability of facilities adequate to serve the proposed development. Adequate public facilities (APF) provisions require that capacities of public facilities are adequate to serve proposed developments before subdivision plats are approved or building permits are issued. APF requirements usually assume that developers will supply the basic on-site infrastructure to serve proposed development—such as local roadways, sewer and water systems, parks and recreation areas, and drainage—and also reach further to evaluate the impacts of development projects on the capacities of off-site or community-wide infrastructure systems. Local governments spell out APF provisions in policy statements, as separate ordinances, or as conditions of subdivision approval or issuance of building permits.

Such requirements are spreading throughout the United States and are especially common in certain fast-growing states. As long ago as 1991, a League of California Cities survey indicated that almost one third of all California communities had adopted APF provisions, and that proportion has undoubtedly increased since then.[1] APF requirements are also common in Colorado communities. A 2005 survey of Maryland's local jurisdictions showed that thirteen counties and twelve municipalities are administering APF regulations.[2] Even in states with conservative outlooks on land use regulations, many communities find ways during subdivision review procedures to negotiate agreements with developers to upgrade inadequate infrastructure systems. Indeed, based on anecdotal data, it appears that many local governments use such requirements as their principal technique for managing growth.

The concept of adequate facilities provisions was first suggested as early as 1955, when Henry Fagin, president of the Regional Plan Association of New York, described a system of regulating the timing of growth based on innovative regulations in several small New York towns. Writing in the Duke University journal *Law and Contemporary Problems*, he advocated tying development permits to a schedule of infrastructure improvements, thus guaranteeing that public facility capacities would be adequate to serve new development.[3]

This regulatory approach received legal support in 1971, when New York's highest court upheld the innovative zoning amendments adopted by the town of Ramapo, New York (as described in chapter 2). The ordinance was invalidated by the trial court but upheld on appeal by a split decision (in *Golden v. Planning Board of Town of Ramapo*, 324 N.Y.S.2d 178 [N.Y. 1971]). Although the decision was controversial, the case established the use of adequate facilities requirements as a proper exercise of the police power.

Ramapo adopted zoning amendments that set up a rating system by which each project was required to demonstrate the adequacy of key components of public infrastructure. An eighteen-year schedule of public improvements linked to development phasing was also established. Unfortunately, the phasing system depended on the construction of several types of public facilities (such as sewers and roads) by other jurisdictions and agencies, over which the town had little control. In addition, the town never adhered to its schedule of improvements. Without improvements, further development virtually stopped; a decade and a half later, citing a long decline in the town's fortunes, town officials voted to dismantle the system in favor of a program to stimulate economic development.

Ramapo-type provisions are still the norm in many communities. However, some local governments have broadened APF requirements by establishing "thresholds," or performance standards, for facility capacities, environmental qualities, and other elements of community development. Examples are level-of-service standards for public facilities and services or water and air quality standards for the community and region. A proposed project that fails to meet one or more of the thresholds can be rejected or required to mitigate its impacts to earn approval.

The city of Chula Vista, California, south of San Diego, formulated threshold standards in 1987 that the city used in evaluating its general plan scenarios as well as individual proposals for development. The standards addressed eleven topics, including air quality, fiscal impacts, and nine public services. Annual evaluations determine the cumulative impacts of development on the standards.[4]

The states of Florida and Washington have adopted state growth management laws (as described in chapter 8) that prohibit local governments from issuing development permits unless adequate infrastructure is available concurrently with development—the *concurrency rule*. All local governments in those states are bound by such provisions, although in both states the strictness of concurrency requirements has varied over time.

Procedures and Methods

Although eminently sensible on their face, APF requirements can lead to difficult administrative and political problems. A substantial number of communities apply APF regulations to the full range of public facilities, although most jurisdictions using APF requirements address needs for only one or two types of facilities that are viewed as critical community concerns, such as roads and schools.

Ideally, facility capacity standards are keyed to communities' adoption of annual capital improvements programs (CIPs) that define a schedule of public facility construction for a multiyear period. Such programs supposedly define the local government's fiscal capacity to meet infrastructure needs in a responsible manner, so development proposed for areas not adequately served by existing or programmed infrastructure can be presumed to conflict with publicly announced responsibilities for supporting growth. Communities usually will allow development if facility improvements scheduled in the CIP will provide the necessary capacities, although some communities base the decision on the availability of improvements within two or three years of the program—a near-term period in which improvements are considered more likely to be achieved. Some communities, however, allow approval of development only if funding for specific improvements has been authorized or appropriated in the annual budget.

Typically, facility capacity to support proposed projects is evaluated during the subdivision approval process. If, for example, the amount of traffic generated from a proposed project will decrease the level of service of a nearby road intersection below the established standard, the development must be postponed until (1) public programs are scheduled or funded to improve the intersection's capacity, (2) the developer promises to institute traffic management programs to reduce traffic generation to desired levels, or (3) the developer commits to funding or constructing capacity improvements to meet the standards. Until agreement is reached on solutions to the congestion problem, the proposal is put on hold. If a large project or cluster of projects will create a capacity problem, a de facto moratorium on further development in the area may be established until a capacity solution is reached. In communities where voters are opposing further development or where capacity solutions are extremely costly, projects may be delayed for years.

However, public officials and developers in communities committed to accommodating development struggle to avoid moratoriums, either by cobbling together developer contributions and "emergency" public funding to undertake the needed improvements or by reducing standards or waiving their application for projects that contribute to community needs. Most adequate facilities requirements include waiver clauses for selected types of development deemed to be highly desirable (such as affordable housing) and to allow developers to "advance" the official schedule of improvements by contributing funds or undertaking construction of facilities. Since many communities fail to schedule improvements and authorize sufficient funding to keep up with development needs, developers often use the waiver provision.

Some communities have been particularly successful in linking together their comprehensive plans, facility improvement programs, and APF requirements to manage growth. One is Carlsbad, California, up the coast from San Diego.[5] Caught by a surge of growth in the 1980s that quickly overwhelmed existing infrastructure systems, Carlsbad's city council passed one interim growth control measure after another—six in less than a year. In 1985, city officials began working on a growth management program that was enacted a year later and subsequently ratified by voters.

Carlsbad's growth management program unequivocally requires that development can take place only when adequate facilities are available concurrently with development. Of the eight purposes of the growth management program spelled out in the adopted ordinance, five refer to the need to link development to the orderly provision of public facilities and services. The program specified the content of a citywide facilities plan and local zone plans and outlined a three-tiered procedure for their preparation, review, and approval (table 5.1).

The Citywide Facilities and Improvement Plan was adopted just two months after the growth management program was enacted. It defined the existing and future level of development in the city, specified eleven public facilities to be evaluated for adequacy and spelled out performance standards for each one, and identified the existing supply of facilities and future needs to accommodate existing and buildout demands. The city

TABLE 5.1

Carlsbad's Three-tiered Growth Management Program

	Citywide Facilities Improvement Plan	Zone Plans	Individual Development Applications
Performance Standards	Establishes standards	Shows how standards will be complied with as development occurs	Must demonstrate that standards will be maintained
Provisions of Facilities	Shows existing inventory and future buildout needs	Shows how and when new facilities will be funded and constructed to accommodate growth	All conditions of approval must be complied with, and specific facilities must be constructed concurrent with development
Funding of Facilities	Outlines various funding options	Proposes specific financing mechanisms for each facility	Funding must be provided prior to final map approval, grading permit, or building permit, whichever occurs first

also delineated twenty-five zones for which more detailed plans for public facilities and financing approaches were to be completed before further development could take place within the zone. Six zone plans for mostly developed areas were prepared by the city, but other plans were prepared by the property owners, guided by city staff.

The buildout of developable land in Carlsbad was projected to occur by 2015, based on estimated development of about 54,600 dwelling units, representing a 160 percent increase over the units existing in 1986. Similar projections were made for commercial and industrial uses. As zone plans were completed, these estimates were revised downward based on more complete assessment of existing development, undevelopable acreage, and other constraints on development. Also, the estimated unit count has been lowered as larger homes have become more popular.

The plan specified performance standards for each type of facility (table 5.2). The city also estimated thresholds of development at which facilities would require improvement to continue meeting performance standards. The combination of standards, thresholds, and detailed zone plans provided an overall management plan for ensuring timely infrastructure improvements concurrent with development.

In addition to the citywide and zone plans, finer-grained analyses of facility requirements are conducted for projects under consideration for approval. The analysis allows consideration of potential facility impacts of specific types of proposed development and evaluation of any special features of the site or existing facility systems. It also provides an opportunity to attach conditions for implementing the zone plan.

Carlsbad's focus on staging development in line with the adequacy of facilities was highly regarded by many local developers and builders, who praised the predictability of the process, especially in comparison to some other communities in the region that were ill-prepared to provide the infrastructure systems necessary to support growth.

Montgomery County, Maryland, adopted a somewhat different approach. The Planning Board tests proposed facility needs of new subdivisions against capacities of transportation; schools; water and sewage facilities; and police, fire, and health services. After enacting APF requirements in 1973, county officials and planning staff gradually elaborated the process of determining existing and future facility capacities and evaluating potential project impacts on capacities. For example, the planning staff has been using complex computer models to estimate traffic and fiscal impacts of proposed developments. In 1986, the county began publishing an annual accounting of available facility capacities for new housing and employment in eighteen

TABLE 5.2

Carlsbad's Performance Standards

City Administrative Facilities	One thousand five hundred square feet per one thousand in population must be scheduled for construction within a five-year period.
Library	Eight hundred square feet per one thousand in population must be scheduled for construction within a five-year period.
Wastewater Treatment Capacity	Wastewater treatment capacity is adequate for at least a five-year period.
Parks	Three acres of community park or special use area per one thousand in population within the park district must be scheduled for construction within a five-year period.
Drainage	Drainage facilities as required by the city must be provided concurrent with development.
Circulation	No road segment or intersection in the zone nor any segment or intersection out of the zone impacted by development in the zone shall be projected to exceed service level C during off-peak hours, nor service level D during peak hours. "Impacted" means where 20 percent or more of the traffic generated by the zone will use the road segment or intersection.
Fire	No more than 1,500 dwelling units outside of a five-minute response time.
Open Space	Fifteen percent of the total land area in the zone, exclusive of environmentally constrained nondevelopable land, must be set aside for permanent open space and must be available concurrent with development.
Schools	School capacity to meet projected enrollment within the zone as determined by the appropriate school district must be provided prior to projected occupancy.
Sewer Collection System	Trunk line capacity to meet demand as determined by the appropriate sewer district must be provided concurrent with development.
Water Distribution System	(1) Line capacity to meet demand as determined by the appropriate water district must be provided concurrent with development. (2) A minimum ten-day average storage capacity must be provided prior to any development.

policy areas. The "Growth Policy Report" (now issued biennially) defines the current capacity of each policy area for further development, thus putting landowners and developers on notice about areas in which development could be approved. The capacity ratings are tied to the annual capital improvement program, so that as improvements are made capacities are revised. In addition, each proposed project is also subject to a local-area transportation review. Overall, the key test of adequacy has been road capacities, although in some cases school capacities have been critical.

The county's ability to project facility capacities has been complicated by the unpredictable funding for improvements promised in the CIP, by the difficulty of matching incremental demand increases to the timing of major facility construction, by changes in state and federal funding, and by continual changes in consumer demands and expectations for facilities. With the slowdown in public funding during the 1970s and 1980s, developers were forced to "contribute" more funding to overcome capacity shortfalls, especially for road improvements. The county also instituted an aggressive traffic demand management program to reduce traffic by such measures as carpools, van pools, and transit subsidies. In addition, as congestion in transit-station areas increased to levels that prohibited further development according to APF traffic standards, the county adopted a policy to permit greater congestion in policy areas with greater transit accessibility and usage.

The experiences in Carlsbad and Montgomery County demonstrate how APF regulations can become the centerpiece of local growth management programs. They also suggest some of the administrative and technical complexities introduced by this relatively simple concept, including issues of standards and public roles in supplying infrastructure.

The Issue of Standards

Adequate facilities provisions immediately raise issues about the technical procedures for determining facility adequacy. Two types of analyses are required: one to determine the capacity of *existing and planned* infrastructure to accommodate additional demands, and the second to determine the *potential impacts* of proposed projects on that available or planned capacity.

The capacity of existing facilities and the expanded capacity that will be available within a reasonable period after approval of the proposed project are measured according to capacity standards established by local officials. Carlsbad's standards and Chula Vista's threshold standards, for example, both set a target of providing three acres of neighborhood and community parkland for each one thousand residents. Level-of-service (LOS) standards for road and highway capacities are perhaps the best-known measure of adequacy, widely applied and well-known to public officials and citizen activists. Promulgated by the Institute of Transportation Engineers, the standards rate traffic delays caused by congestion at intersections or on lengths of highways. Ratings are determined by traffic counts at selected hours, usually peak commuting hours, and range from "A" to "F," with level F defined as a delay greater than the wait for one signal change. Many urban roads and highways operate at levels of C or D.

Other types of capital facilities demand different measures of adequacy, some more technically based than others. Standards of water supply, for example, must consider peak flows, fire fighting needs, water quality issues (from overused wells, for example), and availability of adequately sized pipes. Sewer systems demand measures of effluent quality as well as the effectiveness of collection systems. Fire protection measures usually adopt standards of fire insurance companies that define maximum distances from stations. Park and recreation standards can be based on a wide range of published standards relating acres of parkland to population. Air quality standards are set by federal rules and are continuously monitored.

Capacity standards, however, although based to some extent on scientific data, are affected by local experience. Transportation engineers, for example, understand that LOS standards are only crude measures of actual congestion. For example, an F level at one intersection may be a nuisance rather than a crisis. A sprinkling of F-level intersections throughout a street network that affords many optional routes similarly may not pose grave congestion problems. In addition, LOS ratings usually are determined during peak commuting hours and thus do not reflect general traffic conditions. Selection of an appropriate level to be used as the standard is basically a political decision based on citizens' toleration of congestion. Residents of Chicago are likely to have a different view of traffic congestion than will residents in Manchester, Vermont. "Rush hour" in small towns, while momentarily frustrating, may last only five minutes. The worst traffic in many suburban communities occurs on Saturdays, when shoppers clog the roads. Thus "adequacy" appears to be applicable on a sliding scale related to the urban experience of local residents.

Standards can be used as a no- or slow-growth measure. It is not unheard of for "acceptable" levels to be set above current levels, thus putting a brake on future development until the condition is improved.

The second step in the adequacy test is measuring the potential impacts of proposed projects on facility capacities. For residential projects, this procedure begins with projecting the household characteristics—for example, the number of school-age children or automobiles per household, taking into account the type of housing to be built. (Projections for commercial or business developments usually focus on traffic and parking needs for employees and visitors.) Using measures of typical use of services—for example, average gallons of water per person per day, or proportions of elementary, middle, and high school students per household—capacity needs for various types of facilities are projected and then compared to available capacity in each type of facility. Clearly, although the estimates of project characteristics and projected use of facilities may be based on the best information available, they remain only estimates until the projects are built and occupied. Even then, capacity impacts forecast for a series of projects, along with ongoing changes in existing neighborhoods, often make estimates of facility adequacy less dependable than desired.

Unintended Consequences

The uncertainties produced by using these measures, standards, projections, and judgments to determine adequate capacity may lead to counterproductive results. One early consequence of the Florida concurrency requirement for transportation, for example, was that the regulations appeared to encourage development in rural areas where road capacities were available or could be inexpensively expanded. At the same time, the requirements were hampering development in congested urban areas considered prime targets for future development. Also, APF regulations commonly do not differentiate among sources of impacts. For example, traffic flowing into a growing area from surrounding communities can curtail development. Montgomery County experienced that problem in transit-station areas designated for denser development. The county eventually decided that its standards for highway levels of service should take lower priority than its planning goals for focusing concentrated development around Metrorail. In 1995, after twenty-two years of imposing adequate facilities requirements, the county modified them to allow development to continue in station areas. These problems in applying adequacy standards indicate that the premises underlying the standards must be continually examined for their reasonableness and appropriateness to the specific circumstances.

Issues of Public Responsibilities

Adequate facilities provisions, on the surface, are eminently reasonable: who can argue that development ought to be allowed to overload public facilities? Formulating regulatory requirements for adequate facilities, however, raises administrative issues that frequently create problems in applying APF requirements.

One issue regards the basic responsibility for providing public facilities in developing areas. Local governments traditionally have planned, financed, and administered public services for the common good. But, unlike Carlsbad's program, many APF provisions are silent about local governmental responsibilities for maintaining facility capacities in reasonable equilibrium with needs. Some local governments, having adopted an adequate facilities policy, appear to abdicate responsibility for maintaining facility capacity. By implication or in practice, part or all of that responsi-

BOX 5.2

Who Pays for Transportation? Inconvenient Truths

Robert Dunphy, Senior Fellow, The Urban Land Institute

The general public likes infrastructure—the more, the better, in most cases. And roads seem to catch most of their attention. But even while road capacity has been lagging well behind driver's needs, with consequent increases in highway congestion, most people are reluctant to ante up more taxes to pay for road improvements. And they're equally unwilling to spend on transit as an alternative to driving.

The truth is that the public's notion of transportation costs seems to take only partial costs into account. Most drivers consider only operating costs while most transit riders consider only the fares. In both cases, out-of-pocket costs amount to about one-third of actual costs.

Capital and operating costs for transportation vary widely. Transit costs per passenger mile in 2004 ranged from $ .60 for heavy rail (like subways) to $2.04 for light rail. Buses cost about $.90 per passenger mile because operating costs are much higher than capital costs. Costs for driving alone in a car are only $.53. Transit is heavily subsidized

These cost estimates do not include such hidden external costs as social and environmental impacts. Probably the largest costs not paid directly by car users arise from free parking. The 1990 national Personal Transportation Study estimated that 99 percent of all auto trips parked free. Adding parking charges to car capital and operating costs could result in a 60 percent or more jump in driving costs. Transit becomes the lower-priced alternative when downtown parking costs are considered.

Hard costs are important but time is even more important. Despite the publicity about growing congestion in most large metropolitan areas, the average commute time for drivers (who average longer trips) was about half of that for transit riders. Actually, even with slower speeds compared to driving, transit carries significant shares of travelers in six dominant transit cities, as well as moderate but important share of travel in other cities.

Transit costs can be brought down with a mix of technology and investment. Traffic congestion, gas price spikes, and an aging population provide more incentives for riding transit. But ambitious plans for transit expansions in places such as Phoenix, Orange County, and Seattle have run into the realities of ballooning costs in areas not built to make transit work well.

Is better transportation worth the cost?

bility is shifted to the private sector. A 2006 study by the National Center for Smart Growth Research and Education at the University of Maryland points out that "APF consistency with a local comprehensive plan is possible only if adequate funding is allocated to provide necessary infrastructure in the plan's designated [urban growth] areas."[6]

There are good reasons for local governments to remain active in planning, funding, and managing basic systems of public facilities. Leaving such functions totally to individual project developers creates physical and funding gaps in the systems. Fresno, California, for example, required developers to fund and construct several basic types of public facility systems. Developers' plans were guided by city-prepared functional plans, but funding is derived from impact fees tailored to each area and type of facility. Local builders credited the program with keeping costs down, but the city has had to step in from time to time to construct connections between developer-installed systems. Because these actions were not anticipated, planning and funding them has been troublesome.

Another problem in passing responsibility to the private sector is that local governments relinquish much control over the planning and timing of development, which is a vital part of most community development strategies. Even with the most elaborate standards and diligent public reviews, letting developers decide when, where, and how infrastructure will be constructed means that local officials risk losing touch with infrastructure needs and emerging problems in delivering basic services.

Another issue of public responsibility is that adequate facilities requirements frequently pertain to facilities not under control of the local government—a problem experienced in Ramapo. For example, transportation capacity deficiencies often occur on state and federal highways rather than on roads under local jurisdiction. Congestion on such roads can be cured only through regional or state action, yet local ordinances require the maintenance of a certain level of service before development will be approved. Local governments and developers caught in such a squeeze have only a few options:

- persuading the responsible agencies to act more quickly to correct deficiencies or stepping in with innovative financing methods to move construction schedules ahead;
- modifying standards or capacity measurements (after Florida adopted its concurrency requirement, local planners indulged in inventive ways to measure highway capacity to avoid development moratoriums); and
- waiving requirements for certain desirable types of development.

Yet another issue concerns public responsibilities for keeping up (or catching up, in most cases) with infrastructure needs. On the day that an APF ordinance takes effect, many communities' facilities are already inadequate and others face drastic declines in capacity because of long-term public failures to invest in improvements. Often, CIPs suffer the first cuts in local budget deliberations, and facility improvement programs fall short of meeting demands. Imposing adequate facilities requirements in these circumstances means that future development is hampered by the inadequacies of past governmental efforts.

Henry Fagin's original proposal for adequate facilities requirements is instructive in this regard. He recommended that such requirements be placed within a framework of public programs for scheduling and financing infrastructure. He wrote: "A municipality exercising this system for regulating the timing of urban development should be obliged by statute to carry forward programs of municipal facility and service expansion reasonably related to development trends."[7] He called, in other words, for a quid pro quo: a government that requires adequacy should take reasonable steps to ensure adequacy. However, many local governments, especially in western states, have coupled the Ramapo system with limits on annual growth to keep development in line with scheduled investments in infrastructure.

APF regulations, while apparently simple in concept, require long-term legislative commitments to responsible programming of public facilities and a great deal of administrative effort in application. They are not automatic devices that, once installed in local regulations, operate without further concern. APF effects on community development goals and on the development process need to be carefully tracked and the requirements occasionally modified to ensure an appropriate balance between infrastructure investments and community growth.

Requiring Developer Contributions for Financing Infrastructure

Traditionally, local governments have funded public improvements from general revenues (often based on property taxes), from issuance of municipal bonds repaid from local revenue sources, and from state and federal funding programs. Commonly, several sources are combined to fund improvements. Because many types of public facilities are expensive to construct but will have a lengthy useful life, they are usually funded by bond issues that spread costs over fifteen, twenty, or more years. General obligation bonds, backed by the full faith and credit of the municipality, are repaid through general revenues, including property taxes, and carry a fairly low interest rate. Revenue bonds are repaid from earmarked sources of revenue, usually fees and charges for services, and are sold at a somewhat higher interest rate. In addition, the bond market has invented many variations on general obligation and revenue bonds to suit the fiscal needs of local governments or conditions of the bond market.

For many years, local governments issued bonds for facility investments to be repaid by property taxes, but by the mid-1980s property taxes had dropped to less than half (47 percent) of all revenues from local sources. After dropping further to 42 percent in the mid-1990s, tax revenues from escalating real estate values propelled a return to the 47 percent level. By contrast, sales and income taxes and various types of excise taxes, fees, and charges are increasingly employed. Small increments of sales taxes are earmarked to improve roads and parks and to preserve open space. Excise taxes on specific goods and services, such as airport landings and hotel rooms, help fund airport improvements and convention centers. Communities have increased the variety of fees and charges they levy, such as landfill charges, fees for use of recreation areas, automobile license fees, and public parking charges, to raise funds from users of those services.

Public sentiment in recent years has favored wider use of such special taxes, fees, and charges to relieve the tax burden on the general public. Especially for facilities required to support new development, local governments increasingly impose funding requirements to be paid by developers, builders, and their client consumers. "Development should pay for itself" is a phrase heard across the nation. Thus an important element of many growth management programs is raising funds for infrastructure investments in developing areas, by stricter regulations for privately providing basic facilities, imposing impact fees, and forming special taxing districts.

Subdivision Requirements

Local governments continue to widen the variety of requirements for developers' provision of public facilities related to their developments. Often specifically prescribed in subdivision regulations, but at other times negotiated on a case-by-case basis (and termed *exactions, extractions,* and *proffers*), these contributions may include dedication of land for facilities, actual construction of facilities, or payment of fees to be used for facility construction. Typically, developers are required to fund, build, and dedicate for public use the basic facilities required for residents and tenants of their developments: local streets, sewer and water lines, drainage facilities, and parks and recreational facilities. In addition, many jurisdictions also require developers to fund other improvements to off-site facilities affected by their projects, such as improvements to major streets within or on the borders of their projects, nearby intersections, and drainage facilities in the general area. Developers may also be required to reserve school sites.

These kinds of requirements have become common across the nation and are broadly supported by law, as discussed later in this chapter. Although some states strictly limit requirements by local governments, while others allow a wide range of exactions, developers in many growing areas now expect to underwrite infrastructure costs as part of the development process. In fact, developers often prefer to control the quality and timing of such improvements to coincide with their project objectives and construction schedule.

Communities also have become quite adept at demanding other types of facility funding, such as for amenities that may benefit the larger public as much as or more than they do project residents. Such demands can occur when developers request rezoning or use special procedures that require subdivision approval by a legislative body. Public officials (and neighborhood groups) often find this an opportune time to wrest additional contributions from developers. Developers of office buildings in city and suburban downtowns, for example, have been asked to contribute public art and child care facilities as conditions of development approval. Other developers have had to offer scholarships for neighborhood youths and to restore existing neighborhood parks. Developers in suburban areas sometimes are advised to fund transportation management programs to diminish traffic congestion. Developers in rural counties sometimes find it necessary to build fire stations badly needed for the whole area. Although developers may be legally obligated to provide facilities and improvements that primarily benefit their developments, developers pressed to move forward with a project often agree to other contributions as well.

Impact Fees

Impact fees are a newer form of development requirement increasingly imposed by communities across the nation to defray the costs of public facilities required for newly developing areas. (Other terms for impact fees are *systems development charges* and *development fees*.) Fee schedules are adopted to identify impact fees for various types of facilities for each new dwelling or increment of new nonresidential space. Impact fees are usually paid when building permits are issued and thus generally fall on builders who acquire parcels from developers rather than the land developers. For local governments, impact fees have several advantages over traditional property taxes in paying for facility expansions:

- Fees, by requiring new development to absorb at least some of the costs of new services and facilities, relieve the tax burden on existing residents and businesses; in essence, they give public notice that developers must compensate communities for development impacts on community facilities.
- Fees are collected as development occurs (usually when building permits are issued), rather than a year or more later after residents receive tax bills.
- Fees provide a useful way to pool funds from individual projects to pay for facilities in locations outside specific development sites, such as highway and interchange improvements, water trunk lines, sewage treatment plant improvements, and community parks.

Impact fees are most often charged for sewer and water improvements, roads, and parks. Some local governments also charge fees for drainage, police and fire, and other municipal facilities affected by development. Fees for schools are complicated by boundary and administrative differences between local governments and school districts. Some communities, especially those in California, charge consolidated fees for a complete array of public facilities, including administrative buildings and libraries.

Fees on new development have been widely used for many years to help pay for off-site facility improvements. For example, many water and sewer authorities require builders to pay "hook-up" or "tap-in" fees to connect into water and sewer systems; revenues from such fees are used to improve trunk lines, pumping stations, treatment plants, and the like outside the project site. Subdivision regulations in many communities also provide for developer payments in lieu of on-site parks and recreational lands; the funds collected are aggregated to purchase parklands in the most desirable locations.

Ordinances imposing fees spell out methods for calculating them so that developers can determine in advance the level of expected payments. Most communities allow developers to construct facilities rather than pay fees.[8]

Impact fees can range from a few hundred dollars to many thousands of dollars. Clancy Mullen, of Duncan Associates, conducts an annual survey of impact fees across the nation. The 2005 survey of 245 local jurisdictions indicated an average fee of $7,669 for single-family homes, including all types of facilities for which fees were demanded. Average fees for multifamily units were $4,729; for each one thousand square feet of retail space, $4,544; for each one thousand square feet of office space, $3,195; and for each one thousand square feet of industrial space, $2,247. Most localities charged fees for roads and schools; half charged fees for water and sewer

BOX 5.3

Developing Defensible Impact Fees

Arthur C. Nelson, PhD, Professor, Virginia Polytechnic Institute

Development impact fees are onetime charges assessed on new development to pay for the proportionate share of facilities needed to serve it. To the surprise of many public officials who may view impact fees as a magical source of new revenue, impact fees should be conceived as part of a comprehensive growth management planning process. If viewed principally as a revenue-raising device, their legal defensibility is often lost.

Five distinct steps are required to formulate defensible impact fees. First, community goals that support the need for impact fees must be established, such as minimizing taxpayer burdens, fairly apportioning facility costs based on demand, providing adequate facilities when and where needed, and facilitating economic development by generating new revenues earmarked for expansion of community facilities.

The second step is to prepare projections of growth, land area, and required facilities to portray an overall picture of current and future community characteristics and demands for infrastructure. Included should be determinations of desired facility standards for all community facilities (e.g., acres of park land per one thousand residents, peak-hour traffic per land mile).

Third, based on growth projections and facility standards, needs for future facilities should be determined. This involves a combination of spatial analyses, such as the location and densities of future development, and financial analyses focusing on the costs of providing facilities in various locations and with various characteristics. In addition, analyses of the extent to which existing facilities have the capacity to meet future demands and the cost of building or expanding facilities must be determined. The result of this step is a fairly clear picture of where development will go, how it will be served, and how much facilities will cost.

The fourth step is to determine the phasing and funding of needed capital facilities over time—a capital improvements program. Specific facility costs and revenue sources should be identified. The gap between costs and revenues can be filled, at least in part, by impact fees. This step, in other words, defines the magnitude of fee revenues required to meet future infrastructure needs.

Finally, along with zoning, design review, and other implementation measures for growth management, impact fee programs should be determined. Calculating and administering impact fees involves many technical details, which are explained in a number of publications. Impact fees basically serve a regulatory function by ensuring the provision of adequate public facilities when and where needed. As such, they are one component of a growth management program—the tail on the dog, so to speak (although, in some controversial cases, they seem to be the tail that wags the dog).

facilities; and less than 40 percent charged fees for drainage, parks, libraries, fire and police, general government, and other facilities.[9]

Fees charged by California jurisdictions are considerably higher than the national averages, in part because of higher housing costs and in part because of state restrictions on local infrastructure funding, such as those imposed by Proposition 13. Mullen's survey shows that total fees $20,000 and more for single-family homes are not uncommon in California communities and that some jurisdictions' fees reach more than $60,000 per home. When Mullen calculated average fees for non-California communities, the average single-family home fee for all types of facilities was $5,361 in 2005, 30 percent lower than the average for all communities surveyed. Averages in rapidly growing areas, such as Florida, Arizona, and Maryland, tended to be somewhat higher. Especially in an era of surging home prices, and considering their contribution to fundamental product value, these fee levels are a rather small increment of total development costs.

A few communities have adopted special types of fees, often called "linkage fees," which are intended to help finance housing programs and special public amenities. The best known and most stringent is San Francisco's Office Housing Production Program, which requires developers of downtown office buildings of more than fifty thousand square feet of floor space to pay fees for improvements to transit, housing, public art, child care, and public open space. Boston levies fees on nonresidential development, including institutions, to provide funds for housing improvements. Several such programs enacted by other cities in the 1980s, when downtown office building was booming, are no longer operational.

Issues in Imposing Facility Requirements and Fees

Facility regulations and fees raise four major concerns that must be considered in establishing local policies for financing facilities: legal constraints, equity issues, technical issues, and administrative concerns.

Legal Constraints

The extent to which local governments can demand contributions from developers, and for what purposes, has generated a considerable amount of litigation in state and federal courts. (See the summary of major court cases in chapter 1 for some details.) Three constitutional guarantees—awarding property owners compensation for public taking of property, equal protection, and due process—limit local governments' powers to require exactions. Requirements must be clearly related to a public purpose, must be applied equally to all types of development to avoid an exclusionary effect, and must not be arbitrary and capricious.

The general test, applicable in virtually all states, is that requirements should bear a "rational nexus" to a development's impacts on local public facilities. A local government may, for example, require a developer to improve a certain road intersection if the developer's project will generate enough traffic to warrant the improvement. However, the local government cannot legitimately require developers to pay for improvements to intersections many miles away that traffic from their projects will seldom use.[10]

The legal foundation for impact fees is more complicated. First, it must be established that fees are allowable under the police powers granted by the state to the local government, rather than defined as a form of tax for which specific state authorization is usually required. In some states, local governments have adopted impact fees under liberal home rule provisions. In other states, local governments have secured special state legislation allowing them to adopt fees. A number of states have adopted state enabling legislation allowing communities to adopt impact fees under certain conditions and restrictions.

Assuming that impact fees are allowable local acts, their calculation and administration must meet stiffer criteria than those used for other types of tax revenues. To avoid double taxation, the amounts of fees should take into account regular taxes that property owners will pay for public improvements and must not include funds needed to correct existing deficiencies (for which existing residents are responsible). In administering impact fee programs, fees collected from specific developments must be expended within a reasonable time for facilities in areas that will benefit those developments.

To establish impact fee programs, communities usually conduct studies to determine their legal status and appropriate levels of fees. These studies consider level-of-service standards, the costs of developing various types of facilities, the proportion of costs directly attributable to new developments, and credits for other payments that may contribute to facility costs, such as property taxes. In general, however, to avoid legal challenges and because fees are often charged for only a few types of facilities, local impact fees typically cover only part of the actual costs incurred by communities as development occurs.

Equity Considerations

Exactions and fees also raise some issues about who should pay for infrastructure improvements. At one time, it was assumed that the general community should be responsible for funding major infrastructure systems, the theory being that long-lasting facilities are enjoyed by generations of beneficiaries who gradually contribute to facility expansion through taxes. Then, in response to rapid postwar growth, local governments began shifting responsibilities to developers for funding facilities on their development sites. But taxpayers increasingly insist that developers contribute to overcoming any and all impacts of growth, with the result, developers complain, that improvements may benefit many residents throughout the community.

A more fundamental issue concerns governmental services that are financed on the basis of ability to pay—that is, people who earn more pay more. Elementary and secondary education, for example, is normally considered important enough to society as a whole that it has been financed largely by property tax revenues, which reflect levels of personal income within communities. However, that practice has resulted in have and have-not school districts dependent on starkly different levels of school funding support. Some states provide redistribution measures to better balance school funding among jurisdictions, but school funding issues are currently fomenting intense political and legal battles. A similar problem arises when requirements and fees in developing neighborhoods provide high-quality facilities without corresponding improvements taking place in existing developed areas. San Diego experienced severe community conflicts when its fee-based system for financing capital facilities failed to provide funds for upgrading facilities in older neighborhoods. The city first had waived impact fees to stimulate reinvestment in those areas but then found that development was too anemic to produce adequate funds for improvements.

In general, funding measures for many infrastructure improvements appear to favor greater use of user fees, excise taxes, and sales taxes to fund community needs, thus cutting access to some facilities and services by lower-income people and communities.

Finally, a major equity issue concerns the effects of requirements and fees on market factors, such as the price of housing. (This issue is discussed in chapter 9.)

Administrative Concerns

Facility requirements and fees pose two major administrative concerns: the frequent lack of administrative guidelines or rules for determining facility requirements and the planning and management complexities inherent in the use of impact fees. As noted earlier, many public requirements for set-asides of land or funding of improvements, especially those located outside development sites, are negotiated during project approval procedures. Guidelines are sketchy or nonexistent for determining the appropriate types or amounts of such requirements or to frame the sharing of financial responsibilities among public and private interests. As a result, developers often complain of extortionary requirements unrelated to the impacts of their projects, while public officials maintain that developers are not being required to do enough.

These problems supposedly are resolved by the use of impact fees that provide predictable measures of impact and resulting payments. It takes expert knowledge, time, and effort, however, to create legally sound and politically stable fee programs. Once enacted, correct fees must be collected for each project, accounting for any direct provision of facilities by developers, and timely expenditures must be made for constructing facilities that benefit the payers. Cities, such as San Diego, that use impact fees as a major mechanism of financing facilities employ full-time staffs to administer their programs. Thus, fees tend to complicate the development process by introducing intricate accounting and administrative requirements.

Also, requiring developers to construct facilities and pay fees does not replace serious public planning for expanding infrastructure systems in growing city and suburban areas. Developers' contributions seldom cover all infrastructure needs associated with growth and development and depend on market behavior: when development downturns occur, developers stop delivering facilities and paying fees, leaving system gaps difficult to connect. Furthermore, it may take time for fee revenues to build up enough to fund specific improvements. For these reasons, developer requirements and fees should be employed as one of several sources of revenue within an overall public program for financing capital facilities.

In their favor, exactions and impact fees help to improve the predictability of the process, since they promise permission to develop once the exactions are made and the fees paid. Particularly when conceived as one element of a comprehensive program for funding and scheduling construction of facilities necessary to support development, they can play a significant role in community growth management.

Forming Special Taxing Districts to Fund Facilities

Searching for new ways to finance infrastructure, many communities have borrowed and updated an old technique: special taxing districts. Special districts—which have many titles, including *authorities* and *commissions*—provide facilities to serve residents within designated areas. New facilities are funded by assessments on property owners who benefit directly from the services. Local governments often form assessment districts or public improvement districts to permit levying a special tax on property owners. For example, such districts can extend sewer systems to areas once dependent on septic tanks or fund new libraries in areas not previously served. Many local governments organize tax increment financing (TIF) districts to fund improvements in redevelopment areas. Alternatively, property owners, including developers, may initiate the formation of districts to provide financing for public facilities within their properties.

State laws, which differ markedly from state to state, have generated a great variety of districts. Special taxing districts are allowed in all states; in some—including Illinois, Texas, California, Florida, and Pennsylvania—they are particularly numerous. In every state, statutes spell out requirements and responsibilities for initiating, financing, and operating specific types of districts. Some districts are given powers to function as almost completely independent entities, much like local governments; others are formed and guided by local governments or regional public agencies and may be governed by local legislative bodies. Most districts have a single purpose, such as constructing roads, building junior colleges, or promoting soil conservation.

Some districts are organized to help fund roads and transit systems in certain corridors or areas. New Jersey's Transportation Development Act of 1989, for example, allows counties to apply for state approval of special transportation improvement districts to fund the construction of roads and transit systems in designated corridors or areas. Once approved, the districts draw up transportation improvement plans, issue bonds, and construct improvements. The county manages the process and approves all expenditures.

Special Taxing Districts to Support New Development

Some states enable the formation of multipurpose districts that can supply almost all of the facilities and services required to serve new development. Landowners may petition a local government to approve the establishment of a special district for that purpose. Prior to circulating the petition, landowners work out a general plan for developing desired facilities and determine the costs and construction phasing. They hire consultants to draw up detailed development plans, impact and costs analyses, and phasing and financing programs. Once the local government (and sometimes a regional or state agency) approves formation of the district, the district elects a governing board, which organizes a bond issue based on estimated infrastructure construction costs. Bond proceeds then are used to construct the planned facilities. Bonds are repaid through assessments on properties within the district, with the expectation that as land is sold for development and values increase, revenues will rise to meet costs.[11]

The developers of Pelican Bay, a resort development on 2,100 acres near Naples, Florida, formed an improvement district in 1974 with the approval of the city and surrounding county. (The special state act to allow the district was later the basis for a general state act enabling the formation of community development districts.) At the time, Naples's water and sewer facilities were inadequate to support the proposed development. The new district allowed the sale of bond issues to fund new wells and a water treatment and distribution system, wastewater collection and treatment, a drainage control system, and street lighting. (Roads and recreation facilities were funded by the developer and turned over to the community association for maintenance.) As development proceeded, additional bond issues were sold to pay for system expansions. The bonded debt, as well as all maintenance and management costs, was funded through annual assessments and specific service charges. In 1989, in accordance with the original agreement, the district was reorganized as a dependent district under the responsibility of the county.

A type of special district popular in a number of states is a TIF district. TIF districts depend on earmarked tax revenues raised from only new development to finance capital improvements. Assessments are based on net increases over the existing property tax base. For this reason, TIF districts are often used for redevelopment areas that need fresh infusions of capital for improvements. For example, Arlington Heights, Illinois, formed a series of TIF districts to provide funding for the planned redevelopment of its downtown area. The plan proposed several mixed-use projects centered around a new train station on the Metra transit system that leads to downtown Chicago. Working with developers selected for the developments, village officials provided substantial funding for infrastructure improvements based on expected tax revenues from the TIFs. The resulting highly successful redevelopment efforts are now projected to pay off the TIF bonds ahead of schedule.[12]

District Advantages and Disadvantages

Special taxing districts are especially useful as a way to fund facilities for new development. Forming a district avoids taxing the general public or existing residents for facilities required by new residents. Instead, districts spread the costs of improvements over a targeted group of consumers, who directly benefit from the facilities they pay for. In addition, because most districts can issue bonds to finance improvements, they extend the payment period over fifteen to twenty years. They are also invaluable in developing and redevelopment areas where local governments have administrative capacity or financial resources to fund facility improvements. District bond issues are usually not subject to local governmental bonding limits and thus add to, rather than detract from, local governmental bonding resources.

Some public finance analysts also claim that special districts, because they focus on delivering specific services outside the local political process, can deliver services more efficiently than general-purpose local governments.

However, political scientists tend to look askance at special districts because districts substitute for, and may compete with, local governmental functions. The proliferation of districts, they believe, weakens the powers of local governments and increases administrative inefficiencies and fiscal inequalities. The existence of many special districts providing a variety of services can also lead to confusion and complexity in the governance process. Citizens rarely know district board members, and boards frequently act with little direct accountability to the public or in coordination with other governments. Most districts function with little oversight from the state or any other governmental entity. One of the most difficult tasks in many local and regional growth management programs is to win cooperation from special districts that provide key services to developing areas.

Most of these issues can be resolved by ensuring that local governments retain significant control over district activities and budgets, rather than allowing districts to act independently. King County, Washington, in the Seattle area, for example, obtained legislation to require the numerous water and sewer districts in growth areas to conform the expansion of service areas with local comprehensive plans. Similar measures to ensure the coordination of facility improvements with planning policies, as well as careful attention to the financial basis for establishing districts, can allow districts to function as useful partners in local governmental financing of infrastructure.

Privatization

In recent years, a number of local governments have experimented with the idea of having private companies build and operate public facilities. It is not a new idea: private water companies, private solid waste disposal facilities, and private transit companies are not uncommon. Special taxing districts that provide basic services are often managed by private companies under contract to the districts, and public-private authorities manage many toll roads and bridges. The states of California and Indiana have entered into agreements with private companies to build and operate special toll lanes or roads in congested commuter corridors.

Proponents of such ventures assert that private companies provide superior service at lower cost, partly as a result of more efficient management and lower employment costs. In 2006, the governor of Indiana backed legislation to allow private operation of a toll facility in the Chicago area because it had proven impossible to obtain legislative agreement to raise tolls to a level that would support maintaining and improving the road-way. The private operators are expected to hike tolls but also to improve highway maintenance. Public officials, however, often worry that private companies may make unreasonable profits or fail to provide equal and ade-quate service to all residents. Perhaps for these reasons, despite a great deal of interest in privatization and some highly publicized examples, local and state governments have been slow to convert public facilities to private ones. Privatization appears to be the exception rather than the rule in financing infrastructure improvements.

Combining Funding Resources

Most communities realize that adequate funding of infrastructure to sup-port development requires reaching out to a variety of financing sources to structure a program that balances public and private contributions. Sarasota County's experience in funding its ambitious capital improve-ments program (as described at the beginning of this chapter) is instruc-tive. The county has employed a number of financing mechanisms that draw from both public and private resources. In 1982, voters approved the issuance of revenue bonds to acquire the large tract of land in the rural area needed as a water supply resource. In 1983, the county instituted impact fees on new development for roads and parks. In 1973 and 1986, general obligation bonds were approved for beach acquisition. Voters approved a one-cent gas tax increase in 1988 to pay for road improvements. In 1989, a one-cent local-option sales tax was approved to pay for a variety of road, park, school, and library improvements to correct existing deficiencies.

These measures provided adequate funding for the county's infrastructure needs for many years. But managing facility funding is an ongoing process, and the county constantly faces new decisions. Until recently, impact fees and developer exactions were fairly effective in providing for new infrastruc-ture needs, but recent cuts in residential fees and waivers for economic development have reduced fee collections. In 1995 the planning commis-sion voted against expanding the growth boundary due to infrastructure funding backlogs, and county officials over the last ten years have yet to plug the widening gap between infrastructure needs and available funding.

"Green" Alternatives to Traditional Facilities

Advocates of sustainable development and green building propose alterna-tives to the types of infrastructure facilities frequently employed in urban and suburban development. Their aim is to retain, as much as possible, the natural aspects of the landscape and hydrology while providing essential services within developing areas. They favor adaptation, preservation, and restoration of natural systems (as discussed in chapter 4) rather than constructing traditional pipelines, pavements, and massive structures, and they suggest development layouts and building designs that accomplish that purpose. Without delving into the technologies involved, some of the alternatives to standard structural systems for basic public services include:

- stormwater drainage through vegetative swales, detention ponds and on-site storage, and permeable pavements to promote infiltration into the underground water table and aquifers;
- planted building roofs and tree cover that promote rainwater transpiration into the atmosphere;
- water quality protection through preservation and restoration of natural landscapes, stream buffers, and wetlands that filter and remove pollutants, and water conservation through the use of native vegetation and gray water reuse;
- household wastewater disposal through constructed or restored wetlands that filter and remove pollutants and through alternative septic systems that serve clusters of housing;
- multimodal transportation networks that foster connectivity between roads and highways, transit lines, and pedestrian and biking pathways as well as proximity to residents and workers;
- schools, libraries, and other civic facilities clustered to reduce site sizes, improve multiuse opportunities, and optimize nonmotorized access; and
- parks and recreation facilities planted with native vegetation and landscaped to preserve natural features.

The challenge in applying such alternatives is to balance the retention of natural areas with the need for achieving compact development, while at the same time determining approaches that are both financially feasible and satisfactory from a regulatory standpoint. Yet examples exist: the design of the Coffee Creek development near Chicago incorporates many of these alternative modes of public infrastructure. Another Chicago-area development, Prairie Crossing, preserved and restored native prairie lands and historic hedgerows and employs restored wetlands to clarify stormwater runoff. It also has not just one but two rail stations to improve the transportation mix.

In general, the costs of these alternative technologies seldom pose significant barriers to their use. However, many communities still have requirements on the books that make it difficult to avoid the use of standard types of systems.

Managing growth by managing infrastructure programs is a powerful tool for accommodating and directing community development. Local governments concerned with managing growth are combining basic planning approaches—projecting future needs and detailing priorities and schedules of facility improvements—with requirements for integrating development with the availability of infrastructure capacity and innovative financing mechanisms. The job is difficult, but the rewards are significant.

CHAPTER 6

Design to Preserve and Improve Community Character and Quality

The growth management approaches discussed in the previous chapters largely focus on guiding the amount, rate, and location of growth and change, all important factors in the development process. This chapter deals with growth management concerns that, while less quantifiable, are arguably most important to most people: improving the design quality of community development. Over decades of planning for growth, it has become more and more apparent that conventional planning and zoning techniques cannot be depended on to produce superior urban and suburban development, although they may succeed in screening out the worst examples. Something more is required: attention to urban design, which is gaining renewed respect as a central concern in managing growth and change.

It has not always been so. The lists of growth management techniques propounded in the 1960s and 1970s include no examples specifically addressing the quality of urban design, although one or two techniques (e.g., zoning bonuses and incentives) have been employed for that purpose. The most vivid legal battles over growth management techniques were fought over restrictive growth limits and infrastructure requirements rather than over the form and appearance of resulting development. For many people, however, design quality is what public management of the development process is all about. Jan Krasnowiecki, in his incisive 1986 critique of the effectiveness of zoning for guiding development, spotlighted most residents' and voters' principal concerns about development: what it looks like and how it changes community life.[1]

Without doubt, most anti-growth movements around the nation have evolved from widespread fears that new development will harm the character of existing communities. Indeed, community vision and goal statements commonly highlight the need to develop in accordance with an individual community's unique character. And increasingly, residents express concerns about establishing a desirable community image—place-making—as well as a livable community. Many community residents and public officials insist that quality, not quantity, should be the first objective of growth management.

The Resurgence of Urban Design

Inspired urban design of the sort practiced by Frederick Law Olmsted and Daniel Burnham at the turn of the twentieth century was once considered the hallmark of city planning. They and other notable designers of growing cities, such as John Nolan, focused on designing cities and neighborhoods to be beautiful as well as functional places. In 1907, Nolan was commissioned by the city council of Roanoke, Virginia, then home to forty thousand residents, to recommend civic improvements that would upgrade the city's image and pride of place. Nolan observed that Roanoke was made up of commonplace and even unsightly individual developments, "developing rapidly from its humble beginning, from Big Lick [the original town] to Bigger Lick." Nolan proposed the addition of eye-catching civic works: a grouping of public buildings as a central focus for community activities; a network of urban streets, parkways, and boulevards to improve access to major city features; and a variety of open spaces (in a city then lacking parks or recreation facilities) for public pleasure.[2]

In the years before World War II, urban designers continued to focus on creating appealing communities, especially practical yet attractive settings for residential development. They were concerned with adapting street systems to serve growing numbers of automobiles, nesting buildings in natural landscapes, and planning convenient centers of civic and commercial activities—as demonstrated in plans for Radburn, New Jersey; Baldwin Hills, California; and the three Greenbelt towns developed with federal backing in the Washington, Cincinnati, and Milwaukee areas. And postwar designs for such large-scale new communities as Columbia, Maryland; Reston, Virginia; and Irvine, California, attempted to replicate complete communities, providing central commercial and civic complexes, expansive employment areas, a mix of residential types and designs, systems of local and arterial streets, and a wide range of public facilities.

However, in the postwar decades, in response to demands long stifled during the depression and the war years, multitudes of smaller developments dominated most market areas—and still do. Designed to appeal to families with children seeking an alternative to crowded conditions in big-city neighborhoods, subdivisions were planned as enclaves of single-family housing set back on expansive lots—the larger, the better. Floor plans typically emphasized the use of backyards away from the street frontage, while driveways and garages dominated the view from the street. Curvilinear street systems were considered a refreshing alternative to "dull" city grid systems and adapted well to rolling topography. Cars were a necessity; residents depended on highways to link them to commercial services and employment areas, often in distant locations. Sidewalks were dispensed with. Subdivision entrances tended to focus on a single entry point from an arterial street or highway, and the scattershot siting and timing of such developments often discouraged connections of internal streets across subdivision boundaries. Among other ramifications, the postwar subdivision layouts tended to isolate households from schools, shopping, and other day-to-day services, requiring car trips or special transportation for these purposes.

These approaches to residential design, and the zoning and subdivision regulations that encouraged them, remained in high gear through the postwar years and continue to be popular today, especially on the fringes of developing metropolitan areas. In 1961, however, Jane Jacobs published *The Death and Life of Great American Cities*, which stridently advocated the interactive lifestyle of city folks against the remoteness of suburban life. She saw cities as being "organic, spontaneous, and untidy" in their mixture of different types and uses of buildings.[3] She reaffirmed the value of diversity and density as a way of life and the city as central to civilization, both precepts that continue to influence the design of cities and suburbs. It might be said that Jane Jacobs's book had much the same impact on changing attitudes about the desirable form of community development as Rachel Carson's *Silent Spring* (published just the year before) had on the environmental movement. Jacobs's book continues to be considered a touchstone for contemporary views on the design of urban places.

Urban design is getting more respect these days. Dissatisfied with the disorderly jumble of sprawling development, proponents of sustainable development, smart growth, new urbanism, and other like-minded concepts have rallied around alternative approaches for designing the built environment. These sizeable constituencies, which have gained considerable momentum over the past decade, are reviving the traditional role of physical design to create more livable cities and suburbs. The extension of the LEED (Leadership in Energy and Environmental Design) green building rating system to promote sustainable neighborhood design (LEED-ND) will undoubtedly bolster the revival.

BOX 6.1

Urban Design: The Elusive Elixir of Growth Management

Richard E. Tustian, FAICP

Quality of life is an often-cited but seldom-defined concept. Usually, it includes two ways of experiencing the public dimension of a place: how it "looks" and how it "works," or its form and its function. Until recently, most growth management programs focused only on functional, and quantitatively measurable, elements, such as jobs, housing, transportation, education, and natural systems. Such programs miss the important contribution of the "form" dimension to the composite experience of quality of life. This dimension is important in its own right, for the beauty, meaning, and sense of identity it gives to individual inhabitants of the community.

It is in this dimension that urban design finds its central mission. Urban design is commonly called the art of relating structures to one another and to their natural setting to serve contemporary society. Like the architecture of buildings, urban design is a social art. Its products must be judged against criteria in both aesthetics and efficiency. But how to do this within the political setting of growth management decision making presents some real challenges.

The first challenge is the dichotomy created by the U.S. Constitution between private-sector rights and public-sector rights in determining the use of land. Public regulations affecting land must (1) declare the regulation's public purpose; (2) articulate a clear, close relationship (a nexus) between this public purpose and the regulation; and (3) show that the regulation does not constitute a disproportionate burden on the individual property owners involved. For example, the public purpose of environmental regulation is to preserve specific things (e.g., endangered species) or states (e.g., water quality) in the natural environment. To satisfy judicial review, these things and states must be measurable to some degree.

The aesthetic purposes of urban design, however, are more difficult to define

(Continued on next page)

Designers who follow the principles of the new urbanism/smart growth/traditional neighborhood movement (hereafter referenced as "new urbanism") turn conventional approaches to subdivision design on their head by promoting compact development instead of sweeping lawns; a mix of uses rather than more of the-same; roadways and sidewalks that invite walking instead of streets that lead only to highways; and civic buildings and spaces that bring people together rather than the one-dimensional conventional subdivisions. New urbanist designs for residential neighborhoods and mixed-use town centers may not reproduce Jane Jacobs's vision of big-city ambiance, but the results are certainly much nearer to urban forms of development than the conventional suburban subdivisions and strip malls they replace.

The irony is that the resurgence of traditional forms of development demands more attention to the quality of urban design. For example, to be livable and marketable, higher-density development must carefully relate build-

BOX 6.1

(Continued)

objectively. Spatial shapes and relationships are difficult to translate into functional terms or to quantify. Although great advances have been made in recent years in environmental and behavioral science, the subtleties of the form-to-function relationship are still not well understood in commonly accepted measurable terms.

The second major challenge facing urban design is to understand what people really want in terms of community form and to determine whether achieving that form is legally and fiscally possible. Public attitudes seem to be veering away from the perceived sterility of mass-produced, large-scale, sleek, and rationally derived forms of community development. People seem to be looking instead for comfort and pleasure in forms that are custom tailored, smaller scale, idiosyncratic, and culturally derived. As the world becomes more "high tech," people seem to want more "high touch," although still with high-tech convenience.

The most popular coalescence of these trends applied to urban form is the new urbanism movement, which is attracting an expanding constituency interested in its challenges to the orthodoxies of contemporary society. New urbanism seems to reflect two desires: (1) to shift society's attention from the products of our industrial economy to the places in the natural environment they affect, and (2) to shift the scale of concern from one appropriate for automobiles to one appropriate for pedestrians.

To fully satisfy these two desires, many issues need resolution, including the role of public transportation, the conversion of building industry prototypes, the marketability of such prototypes, the revision of building and public works codes to permit construction at the pedestrian scale, the articulation of public purpose rationales that can withstand judicial scrutiny, and the invention of market and regulatory tools that work at the finer grain of detail demanded by "small is beautiful" notions. Only time will tell whether a major paradigm shift will emerge broad enough to embrace this range of issues.

ing designs and the character of urban spaces. Retrofitting older shopping and business centers into mixed-use centers demands sensitive melding of new design treatments with existing structures. Turning suburban transit-station sites into walkable town centers requires close attention to refurbishing streetscapes. Design for development inserted into existing neighborhoods must respect the historic and architectural character already present.

Getting the design right is necessary for overcoming the reluctance of many residents to see their neighborhoods change. Bitter experience tells us that the grand strategies of growth management that advocate the establishment of growth boundaries, conservation of rural land, coordinated provision of infrastructure, and greater emphasis on infill and redevelopment can succeed only if detailed attention is paid to maintaining and enhancing the quality of existing and emerging neighborhoods and community centers. In both San Diego, California, and Portland, Oregon, to name but two of many examples, policies to curb urban sprawl by encouraging infill development in existing neighborhoods have had to buck residents' complaints about incompatible building designs and other impacts of infill projects.

Yet good design stimulates value in the form of both direct and indirect benefits for investors in development and the public at large. Developers and builders understand the importance of design in improving financial values, such as an accelerated sales pace and more rapid appreciation of real estate assets. Likewise, the public may reap countable benefits from increased public revenues derived from well-designed development. More intangible, but still significant, benefits of high-quality design include the enhanced reputation or greater visibility of project developers and investors in the community and, for local residents, the strengthening of a sense of community identity and civic pride.

Thus growth management programs must incorporate ways and means of ensuring that the design of new development and community amenities and the preservation of historic areas and buildings are taken into account in the development process.

Some Knotty Issues

Despite the rising respect for urban design, ensuring support for high-quality design of development is still only an occasional victory. Some localities are committed to serious guidance of design quality; others are less interested in quality than quantity; and still other communities are fearful of treading on landowner rights by insisting on good design of proposed projects. Techniques for improving the quality of design in growing communities must consider three issues: (1) the reluctance of the courts to accept aesthetic controls on development; (2) the difficulties of defining distinct qualities of "good" design for the wide range of development types and locations in every community; and (3) the problem of how to stimulate innovative design while maintaining a certain level of standards.

The Question of Legality

Legal support for zoning and subdivision requirements relating to the aesthetic qualities of land use was equivocal, at best, for many years. But design quality is finding increasing support in the law. The U.S. Supreme Court first spoke out on the issue in *Berman v. Parker* (348 U.S. 33 [1954]), writing that "the concept of the public welfare is broad and inclusive. . . . The values it represents are spiritual as well as physical, aesthetic as well as monetary. It is within the power of the legislature to determine that the community should be beautiful as well as healthy."

Berman, however, was really an eminent domain case; the application of these statements to zoning was unclear. Then the U.S. Supreme Court's decision in the Grand Central Terminal case (*Penn Central Transportation Company v. New York City*, 438 U.S. 104 [1978]) signaled that local controls over landmarks—and by implication, other aesthetic concerns—were constitutional. Several court cases involving billboard controls in the early 1980s, especially *Metromedia, Inc. v. City of San Diego* (453 U.S. 490 [1981]) added strength to the aesthetic rationale by allowing local governments to phase out nonconforming billboards to improve community appearance.

For many years after *Berman v. Parker*, state courts generally continued to regard aesthetics as an unsound rationale for development regulations. However, a number of state courts now reflect the views of the Florida Supreme Court: "Zoning for aesthetic purposes is an idea whose time has come; it is not outside the scope of the police power" (*City of Lake Wales v. Lamar Advertising Association of Lakeland*, 414 So. 2d 11030 [Fla. 1982]). These and other cases have established local governments' powers in most states to regulate for enhancing community character and livability. Yet the subjectivity of many regulatory measures and an ongoing concern in most communities over allowing wide latitude for landowners' use of property continue to cause debate over these types of regulations.

Defining "Design Quality"

Definitions of desired development qualities are tricky to pin down. Achieving good design is not as simple as requiring a thirty-five-foot zoning setback or a maximum building height of three stories. How does one specify, for example, "attractive" appearance or "well-related" buildings or in what ways new buildings can be "compatible" with historic buildings? General descriptions of desired qualities usually raise more questions than they answer. More precise definitions can ramble on for paragraphs. Sketches and photographs help but do not necessarily bridge the gap between intent and outcome. These issues have caused many local governments to depend on advisory committees to interpret design guidelines and regulations (as discussed below).

Promoting Innovative Designs

Designers frequently come up with new ideas for site layouts and architectural forms. Such innovations, by their very nature, tend to align poorly with standard measures or criteria that define "good" design and may be uniquely suited to the site or other conditions affecting of the proposed project. This issue underscores the need for broad statements of purposes and goals to guide design decisions, as a framework for more specific guidelines, and the usefulness of advisory committees or boards capable of evaluating innovative proposals against such statements.

Three techniques that help promote high-quality design include (1) establishing support for good design, (2) creating design guidelines, and (3) preparing plans that specify design goals and standards.

Creating a Nurturing Context for Design Excellence

Communities can adopt a number of measures to promote a development environment that values high-quality design, short of enacting specific guidelines and regulations. The goal is to foster an understanding in the design and development community, and among public officials who make decisions about proposed projects, that design excellence is an important objective—that well-designed development can add to civic pride, identity, and image. In some communities, this perspective seems to take hold as the community grows, but even so, and in other communities, the quality of design needs to be carefully tended and promoted through a variety of programs and activities instituted by public agencies and private organizations.

Employing Design Staff in Public Agencies

Nothing beats in-house knowledge and experience, and that goes too for public agencies that regularly review proposed developments. Having staff capabilities for evaluating design qualities and innovative ideas can make all the difference in decision making, since it allows for conferring and reaching agreement with applicants on technical issues that might otherwise be overlooked or short-changed. Staff design expertise also enables the institution of educational programs about design goals and issues within the administration and among the public at large. As urban designer Mark Hinshaw demonstrated in his work in Seattle, the presence of even one knowledgeable local expert on design matters can accomplish much.

Design Competitions for Public Buildings

The architecture of city halls, libraries, and concert halls can heighten community image and thus deserve avid attention to their quality of design. Often, they can establish expectations for design excellence in development throughout the community. Although competitions are not easy to organize and administer, they can generate favorable publicity, and even controversies over the submitted and chosen designs can elevate the level of discussion about civic design. Of course, the availability of staff designers can aid the process.

Sponsoring Design Awards

Most professional organizations involved in development, whether public or private, sponsor award programs to highlight well-designed development projects. Although each may have a unique perspective on the design qualities that merit attention, they have a common objective: to demonstrate that the community admires and supports high-quality development. Local sponsorship of an annual award program, perhaps through an organizational alliance, can encourage more attention to design.

Stating the Public Interest in Good Design

Short of enacting specific requirements regarding design excellence and innovation, or perhaps as a policy framework for them, local governments can publicly state their interest in promoting higher-quality design of projects and buildings. This may occur in the form of a mayor's policy statement or a declaration by the local legislative body, with references to existing programs and regulatory processes for which the policy can serve as a guide. It can also allude to the community benefits to be derived from such a policy, including elevating the community's image and competitive economic position as well as improving citizens' quality of life.

Extending the Reach of Existing Regulations

Gone are the days when zoning regulations and subdivision regulations provided a few straightforward requirements for allowable uses in various districts, yard setbacks and building height limits, and the basic standards for subdivision layouts. Public officials have heard and responded to citizens' irritations about the appearance of new development and its compatibility with adjacent neighborhoods. Over time, sections have been added to zoning and subdivision regulations on sign controls, fence heights and placement, landscaping for parking lots, off-street loading and storage areas for businesses, landscaped buffers between residential and commercial areas, and other concerns. (Box 6.2 lists some of the development aspects that generate appearance and nuisance issues.)

One recent subject included in zoning ordinances regards the location, height, and appearance of cellular network towers, a complicated topic that in one city's ordinance sprawled for more than twelve pages of text. A number of communities have adopted tree conservation ordinances to protect existing trees and wooded areas and to require replacement of trees removed during construction. Subdivision regulations increasingly spell out the types of native vegetation that are considered appropriate for required landscaping or new subdivisions and streetscapes. Entire books have been written about these types of aesthetic controls, and the regulations themselves are often extensive and complex.[4]

In the hands of competent designers and responsible developers, these rather cosmetic approaches to quality control can increase voter satisfaction. In other hands, all bets are off. Elaborate sign controls adopted by many communities commonly fail to mitigate the clutter and distraction of signage, especially along commercial highway corridors. Landscaping and tree conservation requirements are only as good as their follow-up inspections, especially after the first growing season has passed. Much of the enforcement of aesthetic requirements depends on angry neighbors calling attention to lapses.

Nevertheless, the continuing expansion of ordinances to cover new subjects testifies to the interest of communities in influencing the quality of design, not just the quantity and location of development.

The "Guidelines" Route to Quality Control

Because of the difficulty of writing definitive requirements for controlling site and building design, and the uncertainty about the legality of strict regulatory provisions, planners and public officials have tended to employ more subtle means to induce quality in development. They adopt guidelines rather than mandatory, prescriptive requirements. Using guidelines has several benefits:

- Guidelines announce public objectives and visions for future community character and appearance, thereby alerting developers, designers, and citizens about the quality of design they hope to achieve.
- Guidelines are usually advisory in nature, providing descriptions of development traits by which proposed projects can be evaluated.
- Because they frequently are employed within a regulatory framework that establishes ground rules and requirements for project approval, guidelines tend to prompt conciliatory approaches to resolving issues.
- Generally, guidelines offer opportunities for a range of design choices that allow developers and builders to tailor responses to specific site and market constraints.

BOX 6.2

A Partial List of "Supplemental" Regulations Related to Design

Zoning Ordinance, Scottsdale, Arizona
Mobile homes and construction trailers
Vehicle repair in residential districts
Model dwelling units and preconstruction sales offices
Accessory structures
Enclosure of existing porches
Garage and yard sales
Buffers and screening
Home occupations
Solid waste storage area
Fence and wall regulations
Antennas
Commercial communication towers regulations
Swimming pools
Open storage
Screening of open display areas
Screen enclosures
Tents
Vendors

Common Approaches

San Francisco's Urban Design Plan of 1971 provided an early and influential formulation of design guidelines; urban designer Mark Hinshaw calls it "the single most important document . . . in rethinking the value of design rules."[5] An example of the plan's detailed advice on the desired character of design is shown in figure 6.1.

Planners and designers have borrowed many of the plan's ideas in preparing guidelines for today's development. For example, the small town of Arlington, Washington (population fifteen thousand), north of Seattle, prepared an extensive and well-illustrated set of design guidelines for desired qualities of development, particularly in its "oldtown" neighborhood and central business district. Like San Francisco's guidelines, the Arlington guidelines focus particularly on making new development fit in with the character of existing buildings and neighborhoods, addressing such concerns as making streets lively and interesting, placing parking, retaining privacy, and designing to a human scale. Two examples of the guidelines follow:

3.1 [for "Neighborhood Character"] Within the context of higher density, mixed residential and commercial zones, buildings should be sited to orient to the street and respect adjacent residential projects.

FIGURE 6.1
The pathbreaking urban design guidelines adopted by San Francisco in 1971 provided sketches of examples for conserving the character of existing neighborhoods while allowing new development.

4.1 [For "Building Character and Massing"] [In designing large buildings] use modulation and articulation in a clear rhythm to reduce the perceived size of all large buildings.

To further explain the term *modulation*, one of several subsequent guidelines describes it as follows:

4.3.1 Façade modulation: Stepping back or extending forward a portion of the façade at least six feet, measured perpendicular to the front façade for each interval.[6]

Fourteen sets of general guidelines describing aspects of site and building design are included, and another section describes additional guidelines for the central business district, all with helpful drawings illustrating the design goals. Cliff Strong, Arlington's planning director, says that Arlington had adopted downtown design guidelines in the mid-1990s. After he was employed in Arlington, Strong assembled the citywide guidelines, primarily based on Snohomish County's residential design guidelines published several years earlier. The citywide guidelines were formally adopted in 2003.[7]

The Tampa, Florida, illustrated design standards for the West Tampa Overlay District differ markedly. Intended to encourage context-friendly development in a rundown but historic black and Hispanic district, twelve brief statements, each accompanied by an illustrative drawing, describe development design qualities, including this one: "Unobstructed pedestrian access and shelter, shade, and/or weather protection shall be provided along streets, public rights-of-way and next to areas used by the public through the use of shade trees, awnings, arcades, balconies, overhangs, etc."[8]

Scottsdale, Arizona, has put together perhaps the most ambitious array of design guidelines in a comprehensive effort to address quality and appearance issues in growth management. Its residents, although generally conservative in their regulatory outlook, have taken great pains to maintain the quality of development during a period of rapid growth. The city's particular concern is maintaining the character and aesthetic qualities of its Sonoran Desert location. Building on earlier design statements in the general plan and other policies and ordinances, Scottsdale formulated a "Sensitive Design Program" that includes guiding principles, architectural design guidelines, and guidelines for scenic corridors and streetscapes and for exterior lighting (a major concern for a desert city). In brief, the design principles adopted in 2000 and amended in 2001 call for new development to enhance the character of the city's physical context; preserve scenic views, ecological processes, and historical resources; respond to the desert environment and unique terrain; provide for continuity in the public realm; promote walkability and human scale; incorporate sustainable products and practices; and conserve water and energy.[9]

The architectural design guidelines pertain to restaurants, gas stations, commercial retail shops and services, and offices. The guidelines for the first three uses, adopted in 1999 and 2000, generally conform in the wording and subjects addressed, including elements of site, architectural, and landscape design; lighting; and signage. The guidelines for office uses, however, were adopted in 2003 and are considerably more detailed (running to twenty-seven pages, compared to eight or nine pages for the other sets), indicating the intense concern of local officials about the design quality of the various types of office buildings in the Scottsdale area.

Scenic corridor guidelines set standards for six major thoroughfares to preserve or restore the desert setting and scenery and to buffer landowners from the effects of traffic. Guidelines establish the character of "landscape setback" areas along the thoroughfares to retain the desert scenery for a minimum of one hundred feet from the right-of-way. Exterior and site lighting design guidelines reflect Scottdale residents' concerns about ambient lighting disturbing the nighttime scene.

Unlike design guidelines adopted by many communities, Scottsdale's do not incorporate illustrations of desired designs. Nevertheless, Scottsdale public officials and residents believe that design guidelines are a key to retaining and upgrading the quality of life in the city. The city continues to update and expand the coverage of the design guidelines.

Appearance Codes

A number of Chicago-area communities take a somewhat different approach to design guidelines. Their ordinances tend to spell out broad design goals, such as selection of building materials to promote "good architectural character" and "harmony with the building and adjoining buildings," and landscape treatment to "enhance architectural features, strengthen vistas and important axes, and provide shade."[10] The primary concern of some appearance codes, locally called "anti-monotony" codes, is to vary the styles of single-family homes in subdivisions by requiring variations in rooflines, window treatments, construction materials, and colors.

This approach is echoed in the residential development design guidelines adopted in 2005 by San Jacinto, California, a fast-growing city eighty miles east of Los Angeles. The site-planning guidelines intend to "discourage subdivisions where identical homes march down long, uninterrupted straight streets with no variation in building placement or the street scene." Accordingly, site-planning guidelines encourage the use of "knuckles, cul-de-sacs and curvilinear streets" and call for varied lot widths and not less than a five-foot setback for at least one in every three homes. Architectural guidelines advocate, for example, the "integration of varied texture, relief, and design accents on building walls," second-story setbacks on all street-side facades, and "roof lines representative of the design and scale of the homes under them."[11]

Comprehensive Guidelines

The *Grand Traverse Bay Region Development Guidebook* provides yet another approach to use of guidelines.[12] Produced through the leadership of the Traverse City (Michigan) Area Chamber of Commerce, the guidebook describes comparative "common" and "better" approaches for a broad array of design concerns, with the overall goal of retaining the region's natural beauty on which its economy is based (figure 6.2). It includes guidelines for maintaining natural landscapes and wetlands as well as providing lighting and curb cuts. On the subject of community appearance, for example, it contrasts the typical clashes of individual architectural styles along a com-

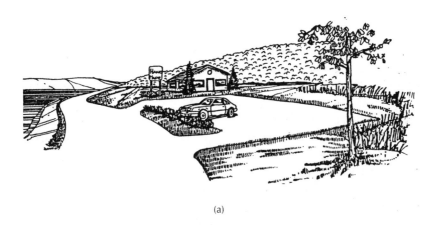

(a)

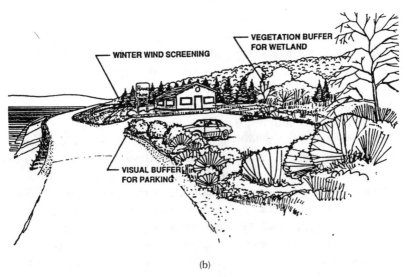

(b)

FIGURE 6.2

The "Grand Traverse Bay Region Development Guide Book" incorporated many sketches showing "common" and "better" practices for development, such as buffering parking and wetlands with plantings for roadside commercial uses.

mercial corridor with the better approach of limiting the range of building styles, shapes, roof angles, and other design features to be compatible with the character of neighborhood buildings. The guidelines were recommended for adoption by local counties, towns, and townships; in just a few years, nineteen jurisdictions had adopted some form of the guidelines for use in reviewing development proposals. Now the guidebook has been updated as the *New Designs for Growth Development Guidebook,* with a similar objective.

Crafting Guidelines

The examples of guidelines described above frequently resort to general language, using broad statements that leave plenty of room for subjective decisions. Guidelines commonly suggest an "I know what I like when I see it" approach. Such terms as *compatible* and *desirable* are sprinkled throughout the design criteria with little attempt to further define them. The more general the guidelines, the greater the burden of review boards to translate them into sensible determinations, and the more likely that the individual whims of reviewers will prevail.

On the other hand, guidelines should not be detailed so closely that they amount to regulatory absolutes. Mark Hinshaw, whose support for design guidelines was mentioned earlier, observes that design review processes based on guidelines are a more creative approach to development design than are narrowly specified requirements. He comments: "Design review should be broadly oriented and encourage the creative application of design principles to a specific site. [Detailed] aesthetic controls seek to severely limit choices, while design review attempts to expand choices. Aesthetic control is concerned with product, while design review is concerned with performance. Aesthetic control is exclusionary; design review embraces different solutions to general criteria."[13]

However, it is impossible to lay down a hard-and-fast rule about the appropriate specificity of guidelines. It depends too much on the complexity of the guideline subjects, their statutory status, the competence and attitudes of the review boards and their staffs, and the general development climate of the community (e.g., rancorous or supportive). It is clear from experience, however, that highly detailed guidelines cannot guarantee design excellence and that highly flexible guidelines leave much to discretionary decision making. Somewhere between those extremes is the place to be.

Design Review Procedures

The examples of design guidelines presented above, like those of many other communities, provide guidance for design reviews by appointed boards and commissions. Such entities are usually made up of five to seven members and generally include persons with professional expertise, such as architects and landscape architects, although most boards also include some lay citizens. Decisions of review boards may be advisory, with final decisions left to planning commission or council action, or may be final subject to appeals. In some cities capable of employing specialized staff, design reviews are carried out as an administrative function by public staff.

In Scottsdale, for example, design guidelines are generally applied during site plan reviews, when the city's design review board examines proposals for all development except individual single-family homes. Based on the board's interpretation of the guidelines, the board can request changes in site layout, exterior finishes and colors, roof lines, and other site and building design factors. Applicants can appeal board decisions to the city council; however, the board is chaired on a revolving basis by council members, which means that relatively few council decisions reverse board decisions.

Design reviews should be conducted with public notice of hearings and decisions. Preapplication conferences can help explain required information and potential issues. Review boards also benefit from staff analyses of proposals. Approvals often are conditioned on design changes worked out in discussions among board members, staff, and developers, a process that Mark Hinshaw, in his primer on design review, calls "communication, cooperation, collaboration, and negotiation."[14] An appeals procedure must be established and approvals enforced through monitoring of construction. In Arlington, Washington, the design review process was set up to be "rather painless," according to its planning director, Cliff Strong.[15] Projects are reviewed by a design review board, but as public meetings rather than hearings, avoiding the need for special notification and establishing a somewhat informal setting for agreeing on application of the guidelines.

Clearly, design review takes time and effort, not just by review board members but by applicants and public staff as well. Because design reviews are highly discretionary processes, procedural rules and guideline language must be carefully formulated to provide a sound basis for board decisions. Even then, conflicts are likely to arise over design details. Sometimes problems arise from underlying concerns over the scale or density of proposed projects, which may mean that design reviews can become protracted and time intensive. It pays for review boards to consider thoughtfully the intent of design guidelines and to seriously evaluate proposed development to provide both a legal basis for decisions and broad community understanding of the desired goals of the process.

Adopting Detailed Plans and Zoning to Improve Design Quality

The quality of community character and appearance can be improved by adopting detailed plans and special zoning districts that establish design contexts and policies for important areas, such as downtowns, neighborhood retail centers, historic districts, and commercial corridors. Many communities prepare "specific" or "special" plans to identify important area attributes, to indicate desired design qualities, and to ensure that the plans identify future actions, such as redevelopment actions and zoning overlay districts. These detailed planning processes allow close attention to the qualities that make up the special character of the community and its components. Especially important are plans and zoning that foster context-reflective design of development in infill and redevelopment areas. Actions by local governments to promote good design in newly developing areas are also challenging.

Enhancing Design Quality in Developed Areas

Baltimore's rejuvenated waterfront and San Diego's Horton Plaza and Gaslight District are well-known for their inspired planning and design within the existing urban fabric. But particularly in recent years, many cities and suburban communities throughout the United States have succeeded in attracting well-designed development that caters to the surging interest of young professionals and older "empty nester" households for living in in-town locations, close to shopping, entertainment, and cultural opportunities. Several examples depict creative local planning and design efforts that establish a positive context for high-quality development within existing developed areas.

Rebuilding Downtown with a Plan

The Village of Arlington Heights, Illinois, a pleasant suburban commuter hub of about seventy-seven thousand residents eighteen miles northwest of downtown Chicago, had suffered through the withering of downtown activity as outlying shopping malls proliferated. By the mid-1980s, when vacant storefronts, rundown buildings, and parking lots were all too common, the village council began to fight back, establishing a tax increment financing [TIF] district and adopting a central business district master plan that proposed strategic public improvements and redevelopment efforts to promote mixed-use, high-density development. With the intensive involvement of council members, planning commissioners, and other boards, the village invested in parking garages, new parks, improved streetscapes, and the rebuilding of the train station on the commuter-rail system.

BOX 6.3

Design Review in Seattle: The Tribecca Example

Seattle adopted twenty-six citywide design guidelines for multifamily and commercial buildings, plus design guidelines tailored to individual neighborhoods. For the proposed Tribecca project at 17 West Mercer Street in the Queen Anne/Magnolia neighborhood, which was to consist of a grocery store and additional retail space, 50 condominium units, and 140 parking spaces, the neighborhood review board identified six important citywide guidelines to be addressed by the design and satisfied all of them. The guidelines and the design responses can be summarized as follows.

Entrances visible from the street. All entrances—residential, retail, and parking—were clearly designated and conveyed each entry's function.

Pedestrian open spaces and entrances. The building's facades were successfully treated at the pedestrian level to increase comfort and interest through warm building materials, planters, wall openings into the buildings, public benches, and overhead canopies.

Architectural concept and consistency. The building modulation and exterior cladding materials were derived from the urban fabric of neighboring buildings and detailed to help articulate the appropriate massing and fenestration.

Corner lots. In response to the busy corner, the design accentuated rooflines; incorporated a major sign, balconies, and an entry; and provided human-scale facades and other design treatment to support pedestrian activity.

Architectural context. The building complements its surroundings through the use of similar building materials, modulation, and articulation.

Height, bulk, scale. Tribecca provides a model for the use of a small lot without adversely affecting its surroundings, while keeping within the allowed building height and lot coverage.

Source: Seattle Department of Planning and Development, "Design Review Program: What We Do: Gallery of Great Examples: Tribecca," at http://www.seattle.gov/dpd/Planning/Design_Review _Program/What_We_Do/Gallery_of_Great_Examples/DPD_001553.asp.

The strategy worked. New development occurred, marked most dramatically by the 1999 opening of Arlington Town Square, a public-private project combining retail and office space, a movie theater, and a thirteen-story condominium building, all grouped around an urban plaza and above an underground parking garage. In tandem came a cluster of three residential condominium buildings and a performing arts center, increasing downtown housing units to 1,160 in 2001, with more still planned. In early 2004, the village completed a new park that planning director Bill Enright calls its "urban centerpiece." The village-directed redevelopment process, much of it carefully phased on former commuter parking lots, has re-created downtown Arlington Heights as a walkable, attractive, busy town center.

Crafting a Design Strategy

At a very different scale from Arlington Heights, Portland, Oregon, has employed detailed plans and design guidelines, prepared through a highly inclusive process of citizen involvement, as part of the city's development efforts over many years. Of particular note are its Special Design Guidelines prepared in 1992 for the Lloyd District, a booming commercial and employment center adjacent to downtown. The guidelines defined specific design concepts for the district to express the special identity and image of Portland, an emphasis on improving pedestrian movements, and specific aspects of project design. The guidelines were followed in 2001 by the adoption of an Area Development Strategy that proposed a number of major new projects and infill developments, to be guided by an urban design concept with the overall goals of increasing connectivity among major district landmarks and creating a network of parks and open spaces.[16] A 2004 study produced its ambitious *Sustainable Urban Design Plan for Lloyd Crossing*, the central part of the Lloyd District. The study proposes to extend the typical architectural focus of urban design to include the integration of proposals for ecosystem preservation, green infrastructure, and innovative public-private financial models. The ultimate aim is "to create an identifiable and sustainable place within the central city."[17]

Neighbors Designing Neighborhoods

Like Portland, the city of Pittsburgh, Pennsylvania, has fought urban decline in its central area with a series of creatively designed redevelopment projects. Even so, the development of Crawford Square, a 17.5-acre residential project adjacent to downtown, called for special treatment. Much of the neighborhood had been demolished through clearance and subsequent decay over a forty-year period. Local residents, deeply distrustful of official agencies, were determined to see it rebuilt as an attractive area affordable for lower-income households. The redevelopment agency brought in a St. Louis development company, McCormack Baron Salazar, a firm nationally recognized for its collaborative and comprehensive approach to rebuilding old neighborhoods.

The developer and his design team engaged members of the community in a series of workshops and small-group meetings that ultimately turned out a plan developed with and for the neighborhood. The plan is based on the historic gridiron street pattern, with grass and trees along the sidewalks, traditionally designed apartments and townhomes, three small parks, and a community center with a swimming pool—in some ways, the suburban ideal sized for an urban location. Some eight hundred residents live there now in 409 housing units; more than half the households pay rents pegged at 60 percent or less of the area median.

Using Zoning Incentives to Shape Design

Big cities, such as New York and San Francisco, have employed zoning density incentives to encourage desirable building design features for many years. Seattle based its downtown plan on allowing density increases in return for up to twenty-five "public benefit" features, from day care facilities and rooftop gardens to plazas and transit station access. At a less exalted scale, the zoning of Montgomery County, Maryland, encourages high-density development in transit station areas by permitting discretionary density increases in designated areas; the negotiated agreements also allow the planning board to condition approvals on special design features and public benefits, such as public art and streetscape improvements. For example, in the Bethesda business center, a highly attractive regional location in a "first suburb" of Washington, D.C., the zoning density incentive combined with a area-wide ceiling on potential development to generate intense developer interest in projects around the Bethesda Metrorail station. County planners announced that projects offering a high quality of construction and significant public amenities would be first in line for approval. Eight major office complexes and a hotel were constructed through the optional zoning procedure (which has since become known as the "beauty contest"). In the competition, developers offered open spaces, public art, community cultural spaces, and other public-use facilities to satisfy the plan's design criteria. In addition, the Bethesda Urban District raised funds to redesign and redevelop the downtown streetscape. In a matter of a few years, Bethesda's downtown was transformed into a modern regional center, leading to substantial residential development as well as such mixed-use projects as Bethesda Row.

However, incentive zoning programs depend on real estate market activity and pricing levels to produce positive results. During the downtown office building heyday of the 1980s, developers eagerly seized on incentives to build as much space as quickly as possible. With potential rents soaring, project income could digest the costs of providing special features. In many cities, however, sharp reductions in market activity and profit levels in the late 1980s meant that some developers' promises for public benefits went unfulfilled.

Incentives also raise issues of "zoning for sale" and highly discretionary decision making by public officials about proposed "extras" to gain project approvals. Negotiations for rezoning or to gain density bonuses open up possibilities for playing politics rather than playing by the rules. Terry Lassar, in her book on public-private deal making on development projects, observes that "the public bodies that must wheel and deal to secure [public benefits] often resemble hard-driving entrepreneurs more than disengaged protectors of the public interest."[18] Public officials understand, however, that public objectives for high-quality development are well served by incentive techniques. The essential ingredients for achieving a fair result in such negotiations are well-conceived design objectives and detailed guidelines to aid decisions.

Special Plans in Outlying Places

Developers across the nation have stepped up to the challenge of building well-designed projects and large-scale communities in growing suburban locations.

They commonly employ optional planning and design processes provided by local zoning and subdivision ordinances, such as planned unit developments (PUDs) and cluster subdivisions, that allow developers greater freedom in site layout and building design. In the 1960s, new towns such as Reston, Virginia, and Columbia, Maryland, were developed through these types of provisions. Other large-scale suburban developments launched in the 1990s—such as Anthem in the Phoenix area, Weston near Fort Lauderdale, Florida, and Hidden Springs, Idaho—have been based on developers' preparation of overall, phased plans and special zoning procedures to win local governmental approval. Their designs featured clustered groups of residential development and small commercial centers, all bordered by bands of conserved natural areas. A somewhat smaller development of 342 acres—Bailey's Grove near Grand Rapids, Michigan—was planned for a mix of 1,075 varied types of housing units within a green setting of conserved wetlands and trails. As a PUD development, the site design required special hearings and rezoning by the town of Kentwood. In 2003, the design won a National Arbor Day Foundation award for tree conservation.[19]

Typically, the provisions call for preparing detailed plans, often marked by distinctive designs (such as compact clusters and mixed uses) that would be difficult to implement under normal zoning provisions. Plans are subject to intensive reviews, frequently involving lengthy public discussion procedures. Final plans are usually cemented with formal public-private agreements and translated into zoning proposals and even first-phase subdivision plans for final approval by the local legislative body. The "specific" or "special" plan widely used in California and increasingly in other communities for unusual or important developments offers such an approach. In addition, traditional neighborhood and new urbanist designs for developments in many suburban market areas—designs that generally represent a poor "fit" within local zoning and subdivision regulations—generally require special regulatory treatment. The special plan, in effect, allows developers and their designers, working with public agencies, to fashion plans and zoning proposals to suit their understanding of market trends and other local conditions affecting development.

New Urbanist Developments

Designs of suburban developments based on traditional neighborhood and new urbanist concepts have become more common since the mid-1990s. As described in chapter 1, these design approaches envision a return to earlier, small-town forms of development where homes are close together and near the street, walking is made easy, street systems are interconnected to reduce traffic congestion, and many kinds of open spaces are readily accessible.

Addison Circle, in Addison, Texas, fourteen miles north of Dallas, was a relatively early example. In 1991, city officials adopted a comprehensive plan that called for development of a new town center providing a pedestrian-oriented mix of uses. Subsequently, a Vision 2020 process identified a seventy-acre site for such a center, and the city worked with the landowner to develop a specific plan and new zoning classification that allowed for construction of an urban district in a distinctly suburban area. The plan established two subareas, one composed of midrise housing and associated retail, community services, and parks. The other, bordering the North Dallas Tollway, featured high-density office, hotel, retail, and residential development. Design and development standards dealt with density, streetscape, building materials, and lot coverage. Although almost one third of the site is dedicated to open space and public parks, the overall density of development reaches 37.5 dwelling units per acre. Sidewalks are generous, while roadways are narrow and lined by trees. Construction began in 1995 and was virtually complete ten years later.[20]

About the same time as construction began in Addison Circle, planning started for another new urbanist development, this one in nearby Southlake. For a 130-acre site surrounded by developing areas, a developer worked with a designer to formulate a detailed plan based on new urbanist forms for a mixed-use town center bordered by townhome areas. Since opening in 1999, the town center has been quite successful; in 2003, residential development was initiated, with satisfying results.[21]

Elements of new urbanist designs are also popular in developments on the edge of metropolitan development, as demonstrated by the Coffee Creek project outside Chicago (described in chapter 4). A more typical example is a development named Carothers Crossing, fourteen miles from downtown Nashville. The development will incorporate a mix of home types and a retail center. Because the three thousand units in the seven-hundred-acre community are to be developed in compact clusters, the project conserves almost 60 percent of the total acreage in green space, much of it along several creeks that meander through the site. Development began in 2006 and will be conducted in several phases.[22]

Obstacles to New Urbanist Designs

Although new urbanist design concepts have won a devoted following among designers and many developers for encouraging higher-density and mixed-use development, conventional subdivisions of single-family homes on large lots continue to be popular, especially in newly developing areas where families are looking for inexpensive homes with plenty of space around them. Land use regulations in these areas, aided by local voters' antipathy toward denser developments, tend to encourage conventional layouts and create obstacles for new urbanist designs. However, a recent study indicates that at least 30 percent of home buyers and renters surveyed prefer dense, walkable neighborhoods, similar to new urbanist designs. Moreover, the study projects potential increases in that preference level to 55 percent or more in coming years. The study concludes that "New Urbanism is poised to boom. The only question is by how much."[23]

The fact that many new urbanist developments produce homes higher priced (though with plenty of amenities) than those in conventional subdivisions is another obstacle, especially for entry-level home buyers. Sometimes this hindrance results from local restrictions rather than from the developer of new urbanist designs. For example, the development of I'On, in an upscale suburb of Charleston, South Carolina, was to feature a broad range of home types and prices, including significant amounts of housing for moderate-income households. The Mount Pleasant city council, after lengthy and bitter wrangling, approved a plan that cut out almost all of the lower-priced units and left a distinctly upper-income, superbly designed enclave.

FIGURE 6.3
Distinctive architecture and a pedestrian-oriented design make the Southlake town center outside Dallas more than just another suburban commercial area.

Implementing New Urbanism through Form-based Zoning

To achieve the goals of new urbanism, advocates have been disposed to focus on rather detailed design concerns appropriate for development in towns, villages, and city neighborhoods, such as architectural compatibility among buildings, relations of residences to streets, facade treatments in commercial areas, pedestrian walkway networks, landscaping and streetscapes, and locations and designs of parking areas and garages. In 2005, the Duany Plater-Zyberk firm published the "SmartCode" to provide an alternative to conventional zoning ordinances. The SmartCode derives from regulations written in 1982 to guide the development of Seaside, Florida, plus some two hundred sets of regulations written for projects since then.[24]

Form-based regulations avoid pinning down the specific uses of buildings and focus instead on the design character of the buildings' siting and architecture. In its simplest outline, form-based zoning begins with an illustrative plan for an area and perspective drawings that identify specific building shapes and features, public spaces, and important natural features on a planned street system. The plan is then translated into requirements for building heights, shapes, maximum and minimum setbacks from the street frontage, facade features (such as windows, door placement, and signs), uses of various floors, and other site and building provisions, including roof types and balconies or arcades. The regulations may define multiple building types (e.g., retail, cottage) and key the requirements to the individual types. In the newest version, that of the 2005 SmartCode, the requirements vary by the type of area involved—six categories from rural to urban core—which are labeled the "transect" sequence of building environments. Sections of the regulations also incorporate provisions and standards for regional and community-wide plans, street cross sections, parking, civic spaces, and other details of site and building plans.

The SmartCode is characterized as a model code, a guide that can be adapted for individual communities and projects. Although the regulations ease the specific requirements of typical zoning for land and building use, they increase requirements for aspects of block and building design that have tended to be addressed by design guidelines. The code appears to be framed in the first instance for designing new building complexes, such as town centers, residential neighborhoods, and sections of large-scale communities, where most construction will occur within a few years. It seems less useful for managing intermittent, individual developments in existing communities, where development opportunities may bloom and decay over time. In some ways, the SmartCode reminds one of the statements of covenants, conditions, and restrictions (CC & Rs) placed on numerous developments, which are notoriously resistant to modification to suit changing conditions or needs.

Green Building and LEED Ratings

Another major influence on urban design stems from the increasing interest by environmental activists, architects, and planners for incorporating "green" attributes in development. The term *green building* generally refers to sustainable site and building designs that conserve rather than consume resources, support and restore rather than destroy natural systems, and mitigate rather than worsen development impacts on the environment. Designs for green buildings aim to reduce energy consumption and greenhouse gas emissions, decrease the use of raw and irreplaceable resources in favor of recycled building materials, and lessen consumption of potable water. For example, designers of green buildings reduce energy requirements for heating and cooling buildings by specifying new types of high-performance window glass, installing passive and active solar heating, planting roof gardens to absorb rainwater and sunlight, placing buildings for best use of sun and shade, and increasing use of natural light. These attributes not only decrease operational costs but create a more pleasant living and working environment.

The green building concept also propounds development layouts that lessen environmental impacts and take advantage of the natural character of project sites. Many site designers and developers are aware of techniques for retaining natural systems and weaving them into the built environment—approaches such as the green infrastructure concept (described in chapter 4), which promotes ecologically healthy natural settings for human settlements.

Many designers work to meet the standards of the green building rating system (LEED) established by the U.S. Green Building Council. Designers of commercial buildings can submit documentation to obtain certification by the council that buildings have met a sufficient number of standards to be rated as green buildings. A new LEED certification process for neighborhood-related development is being tested for implementation in 2009. The LEED-ND system rates projects according to a score derived from listed prerequisites and credits for location and linkage, development pattern and design, construction and technology, and innovation and design process.

Often, the standards and criteria provide options. For example, one of the five prerequisites for "smart location" lists five options, from an infill site or proximity to transit service to a location with lower average vehicle miles traveled than the regional average. A prerequisite for compact development is a density of seven or more dwelling units per acre of buildable residential land or the minimum density required to support transit service. The criterion for diversity of housing types is more complex, using the Simpson Diversity Index based on the types of housing to be developed to calculate credits.[25]

Designers and their developer or builder clients seek LEED certification in part to indicate their concern for conservation of natural resources but also to increase the potential market value of the end product. Given the relative newness of the program, the question of how often the latter goal is achieved is still unclear. Nevertheless, the LEED process, by establishing clear standards and criteria for evaluating green buildings and neighborhood developments, provides significant guidance for improving the environmental qualities of development.

Transit-oriented Design

Transit-oriented development (TOD) has become popular across the nation not just as a partial solution for rampant highway traffic congestion but also as a way of life. The emphasis of TODs on creating a close-knit, pedestrian-friendly, distinctively designed form of urban and suburban development is solidly ensconced as a significant component of smart growth, sustainable development, and new urbanism. Many public officials view the concept as a valuable building block for developing accessible and attractive communities, while transit agencies value the increased ridership it generates. However, the results of construction and expansion of rail transit systems in many cities over the past three decades demonstrate that most suburban patterns of development lend poor support for transit use. Transit planners have understood for decades that both bus and rail transit depend to a great extent on drawing riders from concentrations of residents and workers within walking distance of transit. In addition, ridership is increased if pedestrian access is convenient, pleasant, and safe and if pedestrians can satisfy a variety of trip demands near transit.

These conditions are being met in dozens of transit-oriented developments across the nation, where mixed-use projects and transit locations are finding many interested developers. A 2002 national survey found more than one hundred transit-oriented projects developed in markets in all parts of the United States, including such older transit cities as New York, Boston, and Chicago as well as many newer transit cities in the south and west, such as Dallas, Denver, and Salt Lake City. Many more projects exist in the planning stages.

The developments in Arlington Heights, Contra Costa County, and Bethesda (highlighted earlier) provide examples of successful TOD that served a variety of public purposes. Plano, Texas, is as another example. When the Dallas Area Rapid Transit (DART) advanced its extension of light-rail service to Plano by eight years, the city saw the change as a call to action. At the planned downtown station, using a combination of city-owned, DART-owned, and private properties, the city facilitated public-private development (before the station opened) of a three- and four-story, high-density apartment and retail development and initiated a second mixed-use project a block away. New and existing businesses began investing in renovation along downtown streets, and a city-supported arts and theater complex began taking shape. In just two years, Plano's downtown had become a transit-oriented place, building on a vision and years of preparation (figure 6.6).

Plano (and other Dallas-area cities) got the message: transit can spark placemaking with the right timing and the right ingredients—attractive development clustered closely around stations, energetic public support, and an aggressive rail system ready to roll. Now Denver, Colorado, is planning transit-oriented development around two dozen or so stations on the projected extensions of its rail system.

Preserving the Historic Scene

Preserving historic buildings and areas is a major objective for maintaining the unique character and appearance of communities. Planning for protection of historic resources has spread rapidly; surveys by the National Trust for Historic Preservation of communities with historic preservation ordinances found 421 in 1975, 1,863 in 1993, and 2,300 in 2002. Historic preservation ordinances are local laws through which owners of historic properties are usually prohibited from demolishing their property or making major alterations to it without local government approval. The ordinances typically provide a process for officially designating historic buildings and areas, after which proposed building demolitions and renovations must be reviewed by a commission or board. Most such reviews are advisory in nature; they may recommend against demolition or for certain design changes.

But property owners can oppose designation as a historic district, believing that such an action would drive down property values. This was the case in Denver, when in 1988 the city council proposed the designation of the Lower Downtown (LoDo) neighborhood—consisting of twenty-three square blocks and 127 historic structures—as a historic district. The idea raised a storm of protest from many of the area's property owners, who feared further erosion of already dropping property values. Instead, after designation of the historic district, LoDo experienced a renaissance. As of 2006, it had more than fifty-five restaurants, thirty art galleries, and more than one thousand new residential units. Property values have soared as the charm and historic character of the area, and its protected status as a historic district, created real estate value. Businesses and investors knew that their investment in rehabilitating old buildings would not be undermined by scattershot demolition.[26]

Many states urge or require local governments to prepare comprehensive plans that include a historic preservation plan. Preservation plans usually define the goals of preservation and the historic characteristics of the buildings and areas to be preserved, identify the historic resources present in the community, and propose public responsibilities, actions, and incentives to achieve preservation. Preservation plans may be implemented by a wide assortment of state or local financial and tax incentives.

Among other benefits, such plans provide a process for considering historic resources for official designation as landmarks by federal, state, and local governments. Section 106 of the National Historic Preservation Act requires that any federal undertakings—funding facilities and programs, for example—that might affect historic resources must be reviewed to consider the potential adverse effects of such undertakings and possible alternative actions. State and local laws may require similar reviews. The "consideration of potential adverse effects" does not prohibit demolition or changes in historic resources, especially those in private ownership. Listing of areas and buildings as landmarks simply gives the governments and owner advance notice of those possibilities. The review process, however, does cost time and money (meaning a delay in the proposed governmental action) and opens up possibilities for litigation and associated additional delays and costs.

Zoning offers possibilities for greater control over historic resources, frequently in the form of overlay districts that establish and may require adherence to design guidelines. Some states require that local historic districts be classified as official zoning districts.

However, zoning that allows major density increases for new development in historic areas provides incentives for tearing down old buildings rather than preserving them, and the indiscriminate granting of zoning variances and special exceptions can erode the special character of a historic district.

Planning policies that promote maintenance of older neighborhoods will support preservation of historic buildings. This is a way of saying that historic preservation efforts must be part of a community's overall growth management strategy, not a separate and unequal element.

This recitation of activities on the "soft" side of growth management—preserving community character and livability through close attention to design aspects of development—indicates the range and intensity of concerns being pursued by communities across the nation. Two implications should be drawn from the description of regulatory and other efforts being practiced today. First, design and appearance initiatives should be closely interrelated with other growth management activities. They can strongly support and reinforce elements of growth management programs and, in turn, can benefit from operating in a broad policy context established by the growth management program.

Second is the extent to which techniques and actions for preserving community character and promoting high-quality design must work in conjunction with the development marketplace. Fine points of project and building design are significant only if and when development takes place. Even historic preservation depends on attracting profitable uses for old buildings and neighborhoods.

CHAPTER 7

Managing Growth to Advance Social and Economic Equity

The principles of sustainable development and smart growth highlight a dimension of growth management that is often overlooked: the quest for advancing economic and social equity during the process of urban development. Moving toward sustainable development requires the balancing of environmental, economic, and social goals across the globe and among nations—and within developing urban regions and communities. Taken as a whole, smart growth principles aim to increase the variety of living and traveling choices available for America's increasingly diverse population and to encourage forms of development that support community interaction and inclusiveness. In recognition of these needs, growth management policies and programs are focusing more and more on reducing the disparate treatment of neighborhoods and communities across urbanizing regions.

Timothy Beatley and Kristy Manning's book *The Ecology of Place* describes how these ideas form an "alternative vision" for growing cities and towns:

> This future is one in which land is consumed sparingly, landscapes are cherished, and cities and towns are compact and vibrant and green. These are places that have much to offer in the way of social, cultural, and recreational activity, where the young and the old are not marginalized, and where there is a feeling of community, an active civic life, . . . a concern for social justice . . . [and an economic base that] is viable as well as environmentally and socially restorative.[1]

This dazzling view of the possibilities offered by sustainable and smart growth approaches to development underscores the critical role of social and economic concerns in growth management. For many communities, in fact, issues of economic and social well-being pose fundamental difficulties in managing development. For example:

- Rapid development of housing in "bedroom" communities on the outskirts of metropolitan areas, without accompanying economic development, generates fiscal shortages that hobble the provision of basic services to new residents.
- Workers find affordable housing only in places remote from their jobs, creating long and costly commutes that affect family life and household budgets.
- Rising housing prices in desirable residential areas displace or screen out young and low- to medium-income households.
- Older suburban communities undergo declines in business and neighborhood conditions as firms and residents move to more attractive locations in newer suburbs.
- Minority residents of central cities and many inner suburbs continue to face low-wage job opportunities, unchecked crime, poor schools, and deteriorating housing conditions.

These problems arise from crosscutting economic and social forces affecting all parts of the nation. National and regional economic trends promote the expansion of some types of industries while others wane in importance, affecting labor and locational needs that lead to employment shifts from region to region and within regions. In turn, these movements generate population changes that commonly intensify social tensions and affect settlement patterns. One such trend is the surge of immigration from foreign nations over the past two decades. According to William Frey, the largest and fastest-growing metropolitan areas are now prominent centers of minority population growth, and although minority groups tend to favor central locations, they are increasingly fueling growth in outer suburban and even exurban areas.[2]

In fact, the United States has become a largely suburban nation. Since 1950, more than 90 percent of all growth in U.S. metropolitan areas has occurred in the suburbs. Today, half of the nation's population resides in suburban jurisdictions. Many fast-growing metropolitan areas, such as Atlanta, Phoenix, and Dallas, are really collections of suburban jurisdictions. Although downtown populations grew by 10 percent during the 1990s, leading some analysts to assume the rebirth of central cities, downtown gains have tapered off as more residents leave than arrive.[3] Most suburban jurisdictions, like central cities, find growth a troublesome issue, particularly as they must deal with shifting social and economic conditions in the community and region.

Growing Economic and Social Disparities

Social and economic change through the past half century has extended major disparities in economic and social conditions across metropolitan regions. Central cities still lag in economic strength, and a large proportion of their residents represent poor and minority populations. At the same time, suburban communities formed to ensure desirable living environments are bombarded by external forces that hamper efforts to maintain their way of life. Besides altering the balance of jobs and housing that is so desirable for livable communities, economic trends have gravely affected the fiscal status of many local jurisdictions. Declines in business and neighborhood conditions are paralleled by decreasing investments in maintaining infrastructure systems. Tax bases erode even as social costs rise. Competition among local governments for tax ratables generates friction and unforeseen impacts on fiscal conditions and community character. Small towns and rural settlements experiencing rapid growth can easily fall prey to footloose industries, giant retail operations, and fly-by-night developers who build cheaply and not well.

Throughout metropolitan areas, household income and tax-base differences between rich and poor jurisdictions continue to widen, isolating the poor from jobs, housing, and educational opportunities and heightening racial and other social tensions. The U.S. Census Bureau reports that the number of households living in poverty conditions has continued to increase since 2000.[4] A new study of housing prices and income growth from 1950 to 2000 reports that although the number of families in U.S. metropolitan areas doubled, the number earning more than $140,000 (in year 2000 terms) increased more than eightfold.[5] One consequence is an ever-widening gap in housing values and incomes between the highest-priced places (such as San Francisco and Boston) and typical communities.

Increasingly, cities and suburbs are being separated into "have" and "have-not" places, or what Christopher Leinberger classifies as the "favored quarter" and, by implication, what amounts to the "leftovers" of urban regions.[6] The 2000 Census demonstrated that over the past thirty years, higher-income families have been increasingly likely to live in higher-income neighborhoods and lower-income families in low-income neighborhoods.[7] Enclaves of the wealthy and well housed—many of them living in new suburbs built since the 1970s—expect high-level public services or are able to pay for private services (as denoted by the clusters of private schools and country clubs in wealthy suburban locales). High-priced homes guarantee the exclusion of families with more modest incomes from their neighborhoods and schools.

Those who cannot afford the best often must make do with the least. Trapped on an uneven playing field, poor neighborhoods and communities cannot compete successfully for the businesses and amenities that can boost employment and the tax base. Such places lack the means to overcome concentrated poverty, unemployment, and poor schools, and their living environments are commonly degraded by abandoned industries, solid waste dump sites, and other uninviting neighbors. According to a recent Brookings Institution study, families in lower-income neighborhoods tend to pay higher-than-average prices for basic household necessities than do those in higher-income neighborhoods, and businesses in lower-income neighborhoods face greater market risks and higher costs of providing sales and services.[8]

Meanwhile, middle-income families and neighborhoods, once considered the bedrock of America's economy and society, are waning. An analysis of thirty years of data for the one hundred largest metropolitan areas found that the proportion of middle-income neighborhoods in metropolitan areas had declined from 58 percent in 1970 to 41 percent in 2000, decreasing faster than the proportion of middle-income families. Middle-income neighborhoods appear to be increasingly vulnerable to "tipping" to high-income or low-income neighborhoods. Middle-class neighborhoods in older cities are declining into poverty as middle-class residents leave for the suburbs, while in other cities and suburbs affordable homes are difficult to find. The resulting disparities among residents of these changing neighborhoods create new challenges for struggling locales to deliver public services and promote private investment.[9]

Toward Balanced Growth

Growth management programs can be oriented to address these problems. They can work to redirect economic and social forces (1) by balancing the spread of new development with efforts to stabilize or revive existing neighborhoods and business centers and (2) by modifying tax and infrastructure investment policies that influence the location of growth. They can mitigate the adverse outcomes of economic and social forces by improving opportunities for economic and social advancement, including better access by disadvantaged residents to jobs, decent housing, and good public facilities and services. They can avoid furthering inequities by conscientiously siting public facilities and making investment decisions that improve the quality of life of nearby residents. Proponents of social and economic equity call for ensuring the full participation of all members of society in community life and an equal share in the benefits and costs of economic activities.

These efforts almost always involve a wide spectrum of activities that are normally the provenance of disciplines outside the usual realm of growth managers. Maintaining stable neighborhoods, for example, often depends as much or more on the quality of local schools as on keeping up with street repairs or achieving an open space ratio of three acres per one thousand residents. Addressing the influences of poverty and joblessness requires the efforts of skilled health and social welfare staffs in addition to programs for housing or infrastructure improvements. Growth management programs should more strongly emphasize reaching out to these professional disciplines to find solutions to social and economic problems affecting community development.

Fundamentally, the management of community growth and change must establish a link between physical and human development. Following are some common techniques for making this connection:

- making broadly inclusive plans and decisions about community and neighborhood development;
- strengthening community economic and employment bases;
- expanding the stock of affordable housing for low-income, moderate-income, and workforce residents; and
- revitalizing existing neighborhoods and local business centers
- reducing regional disparities.

Inclusive Planning and Decision Making

Not too many years ago, decisions about community growth and change generally were made by a relatively small leadership group of political, business, and property interests. It was assumed that the opinions of such leaders would represent the best interests of the community, so consultation with the people most affected by the decisions was scanty at best. This approach has changed as community and neighborhood groups have fought planning and development proposals that they believed might unreasonably damage their living environments. Public officials have become wary of generating contentious arguments about future plans and projects, and developers have learned that controversies often extend project approvals. Now, meaningful community outreach and participation processes are the norm in many jurisdictions—involving not just a formal public hearing or two but informative, interactive discussions that can lead to support for what to do and how to do it.

Communities and neighborhoods gain strength by participating in development decision making that will affect the character of their living and working environments. Building the civic infrastructure needed to recognize and agree on how to act on opportunities for positive change is the key to advancing socially and economically. Whether the issues concern the blighting influences of abandoned properties or public trash dumps or the potential displacement of current residents by increases in housing costs, coping with change in a positive manner builds social capital— defined by John Parr as "the networks and norms of trust and reciprocity that facilitate coordination and cooperation for mutual benefit."[10]

Citizens can participate in various formats (which will be described in detail in chapter 9). Examples of community collaborative procedures include the Lee-Harvard shopping center renovation in Cleveland and the Freetown neighborhood redevelopment process in Greenville County, North Carolina, each profiled later in this chapter. Both demonstrate that collaborative decision making for planning and development can build social capital and spur economic development.

Stimulating Beneficial Economic Development

Since colonial days, communities have used various tactics to stimulate local economic development. In modern times, growth management programs contribute to community economic vitality by expanding infrastructure systems to support economic growth and by making communities desirable places to live and work. In addition, local public officials hope to expand the tax base and retain or expand employment opportunities for residents by adopting programs to attract new industries, stimulate growth of existing industries, and revitalize declining business districts. Public officials understand that economic vitality is one key to maintaining the fiscal stability crucial to providing needed services and facilities and enhancing residents' quality of life.

During the Great Depression of the 1930s, federal public works and housing programs poured money into efforts to stimulate economic activity. The years after World War II saw federal programs expand in such areas as small business assistance, manpower training, and promotion of investments in declining areas. Although small business assistance and manpower training continue to receive federal support, federal efforts in recent decades have focused on establishing local enterprise zones and empowerment zones as channels for federal and state assistance. Within enterprise zones, most states allow local governments to offer tax and other incentives for locating or expanding business within the zones, hiring disadvantaged workers, establishing employer-funded child care programs, and other actions calculated to improve employment opportunities. The empowerment zone program initiated in 1994 provides federal grants to assist economically distressed communities in strategic planning to address local development problems. The enterprise and empowerment zones encourage cities, counties, and towns to target their efforts to particularly needy neighborhoods and to use various tax benefits and regulatory waivers.

Local Promotion of Economic Expansion

Public officials and administrators of economic development programs are often tempted to focus on offering large tax breaks and other subsidies to attract business interest. Most local governments have relatively limited capacities for financial offerings, but states have been making news for years with major deals to attract major companies. Many economists decry such public payments to industries, many of which expect to locate within a particular region. Instead, they argue, states and local governments should invest in schools and improvements of community amenities that would provide long-lasting lures to new business. These are precisely the areas in which communities, through their growth management programs, can most broadly influence economic development.

However, many towns, cities, and counties are quite skilled at structuring economic development programs that can help expand existing businesses and attract new businesses without major tax concessions. Typical approaches include the following:

- Formulating an economic development strategy that targets types of businesses and employment most compatible with other community objectives and most feasible given existing and potential community resources.
- Developing a marketing program that emphasizes community assets, such as labor availability, transportation facilities, tax structure, accessibility to natural resources or existing related businesses, and well-located sites.
- Arranging financing tools to aid development, including short-term tax abatements and waivers, establishment of community develop-

ment corporations as conduits for public grants and low-cost loans to promising firms, and targeted financing mechanisms such as special taxing districts.

- Assembling and improving potential sites for business development, including appropriate zoning, addressing hazardous waste and other environmental site problems, and installing basic infrastructure.
- Making available publicly owned land or facilities as potential sites; offering public lease commitments in proposed developments; providing supportive facilities such as parking, port facilities, and child care centers; and supporting services such as job training programs.

The rebuilding of downtown Arlington Heights, Illinois (described in chapter 6), pursued these approaches. Interestingly, Arlington Heights benefited from the newly strong market for in-town housing, which is generating substantial momentum for downtown renewal in many cities, large and small. Downtown Springfield, Missouri, for example, languished for decades until 1998, when a developer converted a vacant building to loft units. In a few short years, a community development corporation was formed, a downtown plan was prepared, and thirteen banks pooled funds for gap financing, followed by a surge in residential construction and the opening of a number of pubs and restaurants, almost all featuring the adaptive reuse of existing buildings. The city's economy and employment were boosted by this burst of activity.

Improving Job Opportunities for Inner-city Workers

Analysts of urban social ills ranging from low educational attainment to crime and dysfunctional families point to employment as the essential foundation for improving social conditions. For decades, federal- and state-sponsored job training programs have struggled to provide unemployed and underemployed workers with marketable skills. And local governments try to incorporate job training programs in every development and redevelopment project that is partially supported by public funding.

But job training is only one part of the picture. Access to jobs is equally important. Since World War II, industries and businesses have streamed out of central cities to locate in the suburbs. Inner-city workers—many of whom depend on public transportation—find it difficult to take advantage of the unskilled and semiskilled jobs available in communities miles from their homes. Programs to improve transportation access to suburban jobs have succeeded moderately in some areas. Central-city employment programs can also choose to emphasize retaining and expanding employment in existing industries and businesses in core locations. Downtown development and redevelopment has improved service employment opportunities for inner-city workers. But demands for renovated office and residential space in close-in areas have displaced existing industries that typically paid higher wages than service jobs, which emphasizes the need to improve access to outlying job centers.

Rebuilding Declining Neighborhood Business Centers

The historical hopscotching of retailing and business services from downtown locations to outer highway commercial strips and then to ever-larger shopping centers has created leftover business areas in many communities. We know them by their forlorn facades, marginal uses, vacancies, and bedraggled appearance. Some continue to provide valuable merchandise and services to residents of surrounding neighborhoods. Some have evolved into specialty shopping or entertainment areas, perhaps inelegant but still active. Some are simply catchalls for firms seeking cheap space.

Efforts to bolster the economic health of left-behind business districts and older shopping centers generally face major obstacles. Typically, neither owners nor tenants can afford costly renovations, which often are complicated by building code requirements and lengthy project review procedures. Property and building values may be too high to allow private redevelopment without increases in development intensities, a solution often unsupported by market demands and opposed by NIMBY-minded neighbors. Assembly of sites to allow redevelopment can be difficult, given the diverse ownerships and small parcels usually involved. For these reasons, investing in improving ailing business districts, especially those in declining neighborhoods, can be risky for both tenants and developers.

The key is to tailor an improvement program to the realities of the area—to its market opportunities and the kinds of public improvements needed to spur business development and private investment and to attract the cooperation of business and property owners. Some declining business areas can benefit from public efforts to encourage improvement of the business environment, such as providing new sidewalks and curbside plantings and adding public parking, which can spruce up an area enough to spur private fix-up efforts. Public programs also can arrange low-interest loans to stimulate business development and allow tenant improvements. Business owners can formulate a unified marketing program to attract more business.

A public-private effort to re-create the aging High Street business district serving the Ohio State University campus in Columbus, Ohio, focused on a strategic plan for stimulating private construction and rehabilitation in the area. The corridor had suffered from more than thirty years of disinvestments. Many buildings had been torn down for parking lots, bars had displaced many other uses, and students and nearby residents had turned to shopping centers elsewhere. The plan called for re-creating a integrated mix of uses along the corridor through public-private actions to upgrade existing buildings and uses combined with site assembly and promoting new development, improving streetscapes, establishing a parking authority, and implementing design and development guidelines. The cooperation of the university and the business community with public agencies has begun transforming the district, with the initial development of Gateway Center, a 500,000-square-foot, mixed-use anchor at the heart of the High Street corridor.[11]

For business centers in serious decline, however, stronger measures may be required, including rebuilding or redevelopment. The public and private investments necessary to undertake such projects may be difficult to arrange but may pay off economically in expanded sales and services for the area. The "demographics" of surrounding neighborhoods commonly offer unrecognized opportunities for improving business activity. Residents of inner-city neighborhoods represent a substantial market for retail sales and services. The architectural or historic character of some neighborhoods may suggest possibilities for specialty markets.

The rebuilding of the Lee-Harvard shopping center in Cleveland exemplifies the business opportunities that may be found in such neighborhoods. Once the dominant commercial center for the area, the Lee-Harvard center was suffering from declining maintenance and decreasing sales, threatening the livability of the surrounding inner-city, working-class neighborhood. When residents demanded attention to the problem, the nonprofit New Village Corporation, one of dozens of community organizations fighting to revive the declining fortunes of Cleveland neighborhoods, acquired and proposed to revamp the shopping center. New Village teamed up with the neighborhood's Amistad Community Development Corporation and brought Forest City Enterprises, an experienced Cleveland-based development firm, on board. Forest City contributed advice on a development strategy, financing sources, and reconfiguration of the tenant mix and then managed the design and reconstruction of the center. The team drew up a plan for a $26 million reconstruction project to renovate the structural condition, sales functions, and appearance of the shopping center.

The team sought out a variety of short- and long-term funding sources, including a $1 million city grant, a $500,000 federal grant, low-interest loans from several Cleveland nonprofit organizations, a first mortgage loan by a three-bank consortium, and equity and construction financing from Fannie Mae's American Community Fund. The collaborative effort allowed the Lee-Harvard shopping center to retain more than thirty local businesses and 650 jobs, which generated annual incomes of about $12 million. Best of all, residents of the Lee-Harvard neighborhood can once again shop at an attractive and convenient center, one that adds to the neighborhood's long-term vitality.

Projects such as the Lee-Harvard shopping center might benefit from the New Markets Tax Credit program, a federal program created by the U.S. Congress in 2000. It provides tax credits to taxpayers who make investments in or loans to qualified businesses or organizations located in low-income communities. The credits are allocated to local community development groups to channel to local businesses and organizations. Since an investor's rate of return is subsidized by the tax credits, the investor can make loans and equity investments to qualified organizations at very favorable terms—as much as 2 or 3 percent below market rates. Historic tax credits can be combined with New Market credits to enhance equity contributions.[12]

Even in small towns and cities, intensive public-private efforts over many years have channeled public and private investments into face-lifts and significant new projects. The Main Street project of the National Trust for Historic Preservation, which has helped many small communities gear up for downtown revitalization, advocates four key steps: (1) forming an organization to hatch ideas and lead revitalization efforts, (2) developing a dynamic promotion campaign, (3) building on downtown assets through attention to design, and (4) expanding business through economic restructuring.[13]

Economic Revitalization through Environmental Cleanup

Many inner-city sites are affected by the lingering effects of past practices in toxic waste storage and disposal—known as the "brownfields" syndrome. Acres of abandoned buildings, old railroad yards, and uses that pollute the air and contaminate the land cast a pall on surrounding residential areas. Often, the neighborhoods most affected are occupied by poor and needy residents. In addition to the equity issues raised by these circumstances, local public officials recognize that cleaning up such contaminated industrial and commercial sites raises significant obstacles for productive reuse of the properties. Problems may range from large quantities of buried waste of unknown toxicity to the fairly frequent problem of leaking gasoline tanks at automobile service stations. The former are typically identified in the 1,200 sites listed by EPA as national priorities; the latter types, called "brownfields," usually are easier to clean up but pose questions of who is financially responsible and able to conduct the needed work. Total cleanup may be prohibitively expensive, and much confusion surrounds how to identify and appropriately treat toxic substances. Federal, state, and local agencies often disagree about remediation standards and procedures. When faced with these issues, lenders are reluctant to finance development on such sites. They fear loss of collateral value and potential liability if contamination is found.

For these reasons, local or regional agencies often must take the lead in assessing and financing cleanup to make sites and buildings available for reuse. These efforts commonly are assisted by state agencies that provide tax incentives for cleanup or limit the liability of purchasers of brownfield sites. Meanwhile, developers now know to anticipate the possibility of contamination in buildings (such as asbestos and lead-based paint) and sites (such as toxic wastes in the soil), and specialists are now widely available for treating such conditions.

Washington's Landing, a mixed-use development in Pittsburgh, is one of several brownfield sites in that city redeveloped through public-private efforts. Herr's Island, a severely contaminated former manufacturing area located just two miles from downtown, was a prime candidate for redevelopment. The Pittsburgh Urban Redevelopment Authority purchased the land, came up with a plan for a mix of residential and commercial uses, and managed a two-year cleanup effort using city and state funding sources. The Authority also constructed basic infrastructure systems, a public park, and a riverside pathway. In 1995, builders Montgomery and Rust were selected to initiate a mixed-use development that involved construction of upscale townhomes and an office park, flanked by a rowing club, tennis courts, and a marina, all now completed.

Such proven techniques for expanding local economies through strategic redevelopments are available to every community and need only committed leadership to initiate and carry them out.

Affordable Housing Programs

Programs to increase the supply of affordable housing have a long history, beginning with the U.S. Housing Act of 1937, which provided federal backing for public housing, and continuing through the Housing Act of 1949 and its many amendments. In the decades following the 1949 legislation, federal housing subsidies enabled many communities to form housing authorities and conduct housing programs that produced millions of units priced or rented at levels affordable to low- and moderate-income residents.

Since the mid-1970s, however, federal funds for construction of affordable housing have been drastically cut. Housing starts for construction or substantial rehabilitation assisted by the U.S. Department of Housing and Urban Development (HUD) fell from an annual average of 135,298 units during the 1970s to 61,245 per year during the 1980s and then to 20,000 units by the 1990s.[14]

Many communities receive Community Development Block Grants (CDBGs), which have become more and more important in supporting local housing programs, although communities often spread the annual funding over many areas with little attention to long-term housing or revitalization strategies. Although HUD requires communities receiving federal housing assistance to prepare Housing Assistance Plans (HAPs) and Comprehensive Housing Affordability Strategies (CHASs), the plans often fall short of providing real direction for housing programs.

With federal programs on the wane and with local efforts overwhelmed by growing needs, state housing programs have taken up some of the slack, as have public-private housing organizations and local governments. Local public-private partnerships for housing development use various funding sources, including low-income housing tax credits. Such nongovernmental organizations as BRIDGE (the Bay Area Residential Investment and Development Group), Jubilee Housing, and the Local Initiatives Support Corporation and Enterprise Foundation have become major players in stimulating the production of affordable housing.

Recognizing the growing need for affordable housing, many local governments have forged programs that blend public, semipublic, and private resources, tapping a wide range of leadership. Typically, they set specific targets for the rehabilitation and production of various types of affordable housing and budget local funds to augment state and federal assistance programs and to help support private and semipublic housing activities. Communities across the nation also combine these types of actions with other programs, such as inclusionary zoning, housing trust funds, and community land trusts.

Inclusionary Zoning

Zoning regulations became popular primarily as a means of protecting neighborhood and residential values. Ironically, many communities also have been using zoning to escalate housing values, first by restricting most housing construction to single-family homes, and second by raising standards for lot sizes, setbacks, and required amenities to levels that push housing costs beyond those affordable for average-income and lower-income home owners and renters.

The exclusionary effects of these regulations, which became especially evident during the 1960s in the nation's newly developing suburbs, were answered by a movement to "open up the suburbs." Publications in the early 1970s by Paul and Linda Davidoff and Anthony Downs proposed that communities adopt "inclusionary" regulations that would require developers of residential subdivisions to earmark a proportion of new housing units for lower-income households.[15] Although the concept was considered a radical idea and was accepted only slowly by local governments, the mounting needs for affordable housing have since stimulated greater interest. Today, about 250 local governments have adopted inclusionary zoning, and inclusionary programs have generated production of an estimated eighty to ninety thousand affordable housing units since the 1970s.[16] Many other communities negotiate the inclusion of affordable housing as a condition of approval for special zoning or other regulatory requirements, particularly for public-private and mixed-use projects.

Inclusionary zoning leverages thriving residential development markets where developers and builders can expect sizeable price premiums, especially growing suburban jurisdictions and historic neighborhoods in central cities and established suburbs.

Most programs mandate participation by all projects of a certain size, but some offer incentives for voluntary participation and others simply negotiate case-by-case understandings with developers needing rezoning or variances. Most inclusionary programs are designed to:

- focus on projects large enough to absorb the costs involved (typically, thresholds for participation are set at twenty to fifty units);
- require or, rarely, encourage voluntary participation to incorporate a specific minimum percentage of affordable units, usually in the range of 15 to 20 percent;
- provide incentives to at least partially compensate for the inclusion of lower-priced housing, such as density bonuses and variances;
- target certain income levels of households, from moderate to very low income;
- give priority to on-site construction but in some circumstances allow off-site construction or in-lieu payments;
- require the distribution of affordable units throughout the project with exterior designs that blend in with market-rate units; and

- establish a control period before resales are allowed to maintain the stock of affordable housing.

Inclusionary programs tend to be clustered in certain states and metropolitan areas. California, Massachusetts, New Jersey, and a few other states require communities to provide housing for all income classes and offer a variety of program options, including inclusionary zoning, to help them reach that goal. Many communities in metropolitan areas with a history of housing price escalation, such as San Francisco, Washington, Boston, and Denver, have adopted inclusionary programs. By most accounts, Montgomery County, Maryland, administers one of the most successful, longest-running, and most copied programs. Termed the *Moderately-Priced Dwelling Unit* (MPDU) law, since 1974 the program has produced more than eleven thousand units affordable to moderate-income households, scattered in nearly three hundred subdivisions developed by dozens of developers and builders. The ordinance requires residential developments of thirty-five units or more to set aside from 12.5 to 15 percent of the units as affordable to households with incomes at or below 60 percent of the area's median income. A sliding scale of density bonuses based on the percentage of units provides for an increase in density up to 22 percent over as-of-right zoning.

Inclusionary zoning programs almost always operate within a framework of interrelated housing programs that draw from a variety of funding sources, produce various forms of affordable units, and involve public, non-profit, and private developers of housing. For example, Montgomery County's eleven thousand moderate-income units generated by its inclusionary requirements are matched by another eleven thousand units for lower-income households produced through other programs. Cambridge, Massachusetts, has a similarly coordinated group of programs to help reinforce and augment its inclusionary zoning program. Cambridge's zoning program adopted in 1998 requires low- and moderate-income units in every new residential development of ten or more units and offers a density bonus of 30 percent in the permitted floor-area ratio. Cambridge also gives developers a compensatory incentive by allowing them to build one market-rate unit (above the as-of-right zoning density) for each affordable unit produced.

The latest trend is for big cities to adopt requirements for inclusionary units, sometimes in designated areas in which redevelopment is expected. New York, Chicago, Boston, San Diego, San Francisco, and Denver administer programs that require lower-cost units in market-rate developments. The inclusionary concept also is used by some communities to provide lower-cost housing for certain types of employees. Communities whose economies

FIGURE 7.1
Inclusionary Housing in Palo Alto, CA. This attractive development of 12 townhomes built in 2000 in Palo Alto, California, includes one below-market-rate, three-bedroom unit, which was sold for $240,000, well under market-rate prices.

depend on housing workers within or near their jobs, such as ski resorts in remote mountain locations, sometimes require developers of commercial projects to provide housing at affordable prices and rents for future employees (not unlike the towns erected by mining and mill corporations in earlier days). Breckenridge, Colorado, gives preference to projects that produce housing units for employees—units defined as deed restricted for either long-term leasing or sale to a person residing in and employed in the county. The city has followed up on its May 2000 *Affordable Housing Strategy* report to encourage production of affordable housing units in a variety of ways, including site acquisition, density increases, and accelerated project approvals, especially for employees of local businesses. The Wellington Neighborhood project described in chapter 2 is one such outcome. Some cities also require or provide incentives for developers to provide affordable housing for employees of public agencies, hospitals, and universities.

Is it fair to expect developers and builders to cure what appears to be a community-wide problem? Bernard Tetreault, who directed Montgomery County's housing program for many years, says that developers and builders should not have to bear that responsibility. "But," he says, "given that they produce the housing stock, and that the density bonuses alleviate any economic harm, the affordable housing requirement (like similar infrastructure and amenity requirements) is not an undue burden."[17] Builders of inclusionary projects tend to regard inclusionary requirements as a cost of doing business in highly desirable housing markets (although, for public consumption, builders and real estate salespeople rail against proposals for such programs). To ease any real or imagined burden, public officials work hard to reward builders of such projects with fee deferrals or waivers, variances on site and lot standards, and other means of reducing development costs.

Housing Trust Funds and Community Land Trusts

These two nonprofit vehicles for collecting funds and obtaining land to enable the production of affordable housing are widely used throughout the United States. They were invented largely to help fill the void left by sharp reductions in federal assistance for housing. Both housing and land trusts function as collectives—or "banks"—for gathering funds and sites from a broad range of sources, then directing these assets for the production of affordable housing.

More than four hundred housing trust funds have been established in cities and counties to provide financial resources for satisfying the unmet housing needs of low- and moderate-income community residents. They are organized locally to take advantage of unique opportunities to attract resources from within the community and to target specific housing needs of the community. For example, the Cambridge, Massachusetts, Affordable Housing Trust focuses on creating new affordable units, assisting with multifamily rehabilitation, acquiring and rehabilitating limited equity housing cooperatives, and preserving existing affordable housing. Housing trust funds have demonstrated a capacity to provide a range of flexible funding arrangements.

Generally, housing trust funds are administered by a city housing agency and are overseen by a board that represents nonprofit developers, service providers, housing advocates, private industries, unions, low-income citizens, and others. The trusts tap as many sources of funds as possible—the Housing Trust Fund Project estimates that housing trusts have attracted about forty different sources of revenue—but often benefits from obtaining one or more dedicated funding sources, such as fees paid by developers and real estate transfer taxes. For example, in addition to private corporate donations, the Indianapolis City/County Council recently approved the dedication of fee revenues—about $300,000 a year—from the electronic filing of property sales disclosure forms for the Indianapolis/Marion County Housing Trust Fund. The fund also is receiving $2 million from the city's sale of the former arena site to a private owner and is hoping to attain a funding level of $5 million per year through a coalition-backed fund-raising effort begun in May 2006.[18] Many states have also organized housing trust funds to provide funding pools for various housing projects and programs.

Community land trusts are private, nonprofit corporations created to acquire and hold land in order to help provide affordable housing that promotes resident ownership and control of the supply of low-cost housing. Land trusts retain ownership of the acquired land to ensure that it will continue to benefit the community. Land trusts may sell homes but lease the land under them, usually for a ninety-nine-year renewable period. If home owners subsequently decide to move, the land lease requires the sale of the homes at an affordable price to another lower-income household or to the land trust.

Multifamily housing on land trust land can be owned by the land trust, other nonprofit organizations, or cooperatives and condominiums owned by residents. Land trusts can also make land available for community gardens, playgrounds, and other activities. Like housing trust funds, community land trusts obtain funds for acquiring property from many sources, including governments, foundations, private corporations, and nonprofit groups. They are governed by boards elected by all residents who live on or use land trust land and other housing interests from the community.

Burlington, Vermont, has one of the country's most successful community land trusts. Established in 1984, the Burlington Community Land Trust has grown to control nearly five hundred units of housing, including single-family homes, housing cooperatives, condominiums, and rental housing. It has improved affordable housing opportunities in a low-income neighborhood as well as in suburban locations.

Reducing Housing Costs by Streamlining Regulations

In the past, subdivision development and building construction required only simple onetime permits issued with a minimum of fuss. In most communities today, however, developers and builders face a bewildering array of zoning and rezoning procedures, subdivision plan and plat approvals, conditional and special-use zoning permits, construction and environmental clearances at several levels of government, design and other special reviews by various boards and commissions, and specific permits for site grading, foundations, and sewer and water hookups. In some places, the permitting process seems like less a system than an obstacle course.

Most regulations benefit the community at large, but they also have costs, among them the amount of preparation needed for permit approvals, delays in the approval process, and the risks posed by these investments of effort and time. Complex regulatory processes can also be manipulated by opponents of proposed projects to further delay approvals and increase costs of development. The upshot is that regulations can substantially affect housing costs, especially in the more affordable ranges. As discussed in the section on growth management effects on housing prices in chapter 9, a $5,000 impact fee, for example, may be a relatively insignificant addition to the cost of a house priced at $300,000 but a major problem for one priced at $90,000.

Federal and state agencies, as well as local governments in many areas, have promoted regulatory reform for many years as a way to achieve more affordable housing. Most studies identify the effects on housing costs stemming from NIMBY-driven exclusionary zoning, a reluctance to zone for multifamily housing, "gold-plated" subdivision and building standards, large impact fees, and overburdensome permitting procedures. Dozens of

BOX 7.1

Highland Park: Putting It All Together

As one of Chicago's older suburbs, Highland Park has always taken pride in its housing diversity. Since its founding in 1869, Highland Park developers and residents marketed the community as an inclusive place of "great harmony." According to Betsy Lassar, the city's housing planner, that tradition remains a strong force in the community's outlook. The city's 1976 master plan identified as a planning goal the maintenance of the stock of low- and moderate-income housing. But Highland Park has become an attractive market for higher-priced housing. Worried that Highland Park would lose part of its civic heritage, citizens established a Housing Commission in 1973 and set about developing three projects providing 153 apartments and townhouses for low- and moderate-income families and seniors, using federal Section 8 grants.

Then, in 2001, after people began buying and tearing down low-priced houses to build expensive homes, Highland Park developed a four-part affordable housing strategy. Revenues from a *tear-down tax*, plus other funding sources as available, provide revenues for a city-administered *affordable housing trust fund*, which provide a major source of funding for a *community land trust*. An *inclusionary zoning ordinance* expands production of affordable units by requiring developers to incorporate them within market-rate residential projects. The city council adopted ordinances establishing the trust fund and the tear-down tax in May 2002. A year later, the council approved a resolution launching the community land trust and an ordinance establishing the inclusionary zoning program. For a city of thirty-one thousand residents, this remarkable achievement is already paying dividends in preserving housing affordability in an increasingly upscale community.

228 MANAGING GROWTH IN AMERICA'S COMMUNITIES

publications produced by federal, state, and local agencies over several decades suggest specific ways of streamlining regulations to reduce costs of developing affordable housing.[19] These methods include:

- clarifying the organization and language of ordinances;
- periodically evaluating and updating standards and procedures;
- simplifying and clarifying procedures and spelling out standards and criteria for discretionary approvals;
- publishing guidebooks and checklists for applicants; and
- improving review procedures, including combined or simultaneous reviews by several departments and expedited processes for noncontroversial or high-priority projects.

One regulatory issue that has only recently begun to receive attention by public officials is the negative effects on rehabilitation projects of building codes written primarily to guide new construction. The volume of rehabilitation work to upgrade buildings is growing throughout the nation. But many local building code provisions make it difficult and prohibitively expensive to renovate structures for new or adaptive reuse. For example, the code might force improvements in plumbing and electrical systems that necessitate costly reconstruction of walls or floors. A home owner intending to modernize a kitchen might be required to upgrade wiring, plumbing, and framing just to obtain building permits for the work. Simple upgrades and repairs may become too costly to undertake, making building codes into barriers for rejuvenating neighborhoods.

The state of New Jersey tackled this problem by preparing a new Rehabilitation Subcode, which based the application of code provisions on the type of project (rehabilitation, additions, or change of use) and the scope of work to be undertaken (repair, renovation, alteration, or reconstruction). Simple alterations do not necessarily require major reconstruction to bring a building up to a general standard. Maryland took a somewhat different route to the same end by identifying specific provisions of existing codes that would apply to rehabilitation work. Although other states have been slow to change building codes to encourage rehabilitation, "The Nationally Applicable Recommended Rehabilitation Provisions," prepared by HUD, adapted the New Jersey proposals into a form easily used by other states and code organizations.[20]

Although recommendations for regulatory changes to promote housing affordability have been circulated for years, many communities continue to manage growth in ways that defy housing needs. On the positive side, where communities have seriously assessed housing demands, created incentives to produce affordable housing, and tapped a variety of organizational and funding sources to assist the process, they have managed to make substantial contributions to the stock of affordable housing.

Revitalizing Declining Neighborhoods

Chapter 3 discussed the role of infill and redevelopment in promoting compact development within urban and urbanizing areas. But redevelopment also serves to revitalize declining neighborhoods. Neighborhoods are more than residential areas; they are also social networks, suppliers of workers and services, sources of livelihoods and recreation, and much more. Declining and decaying neighborhoods are losing their ability to deliver these important functions of everyday life. This is why neighborhood revitalization requires more than physical improvements, more than fixing up houses; rebuilding sustainable neighborhoods also means reconstructing their social and economic capacities. Communities must plan carefully to identify areas susceptible to improvement and then formulate reinvestment strategies tailored to the specific needs and resources of the areas. Neighborhood revitalization takes a broad menu of approaches, including public facility improvements, crime, beautification, traffic, tenant-landlord relationships, and other issues.

Communities have learned to focus programs and investments in the following ways:

- Target specific neighborhoods with a battery of coordinated, mutually reinforcing programs that will leverage the existing assets of such areas to the greatest effect.
- Build on economic and social forces at work in the community to take full advantage of untapped or unfulfilled markets and consumer needs.
- Cast a wide net to assemble federal, state, and local governmental funding, as well as corporate and community assistance, to promote investments in revitalizing designated areas.
- Establish a collaborative process for decision making and community investment that provides an interlocking, multilayered structure of government, civic, business, and other interests in community revitalization.

The city of Champaign, Illinois, emphasized neighborhood revitalization needs in its comprehensive plan and adopted a Neighborhood

Wellness Action Plan in 1992 to coordinate service delivery to fifteen neighborhoods. Elements of the plan included stepping up code enforcement to improve property maintenance, targeting street and other improvements, and creating neighborhood centers to coordinate residents' voluntary cleanup, housing maintenance, and neighborhood watch programs. The plan designated "healthy," "conservation," "preservation," and "restoration" neighborhoods to establish priorities for city attention. To implement the plan, the city created a neighborhood services department with an annual budget of $2.8 million, funded mostly through utility taxes and federal CDBG grants.

In 2006, Champaign updated its Neighborhood Wellness Action Plan, now for seventeen neighborhoods. The new plan reflects current information on the city's growth and a vision statement based on the city's 2002 comprehensive plan. As with the 1992 document, the plan covers four categories of city concerns: housing and property maintenance, public infrastructure and facilities, public safety, and civic involvement. Within each category, the plan spells out general goals, defines several strategies to reach each goal, and identifies "wellness indicators" or measures of success by which to measure how well the strategies are being implemented. Then a "Prognosis" is spelled out for each neighborhood, and a "Prescription" report details the city actions anticipated in the individual neighborhoods.[21] Overall, the plan lays out a comprehensive program to support neighborhood revitalization in Champaign.

Communities such as Champaign help to prepare the way for neighborhood renewal by identifying developable properties and making them available at a reasonable price. Using computer searches of vacant or tax-delinquent properties, public agencies can provide local brokers and developers with lists of potentially developable parcels, including information on size, current assessments, and any tax or legal problems attached to the property records. Many communities have taken the next step of formally acquiring tax-delinquent properties by foreclosure and packaging them for development. In addition, other city-owned, unused parcels can be combined with tax-foreclosed properties to assemble developable sites. Public agencies frequently hold unused properties that can be declared surplus for city needs and sold for infill and redevelopment.

Three neighborhood revitalization projects demonstrate these approaches. The site of the redevelopment initiative by the city of Dayton, Ohio, in the Wright-Dunbar neighborhood was once slated for total clearance and rebuilding. Located adjacent to the national historic park marking the Wright brothers' home and workshop site and the Dunbar State

Memorial for the home of African American poet Paul Dunbar, the neighborhood had evolved into a cultural and commercial center for Dayton's African American community. However, much of the neighborhood had been lost in the 1950s and 1960s to highway construction, urban renewal, and civil unrest. By the 1990s, it contained more than seventy-five abandoned houses and about as many vacant lots; fewer than twenty families remained as residents when the city scrapped its demolition plan.

The city began the rescue of the neighborhood by investing $22 million for infrastructure improvements (including the creation of a seven-acre park) and then jump-started housing redevelopment and rehabilitation by aggressively acquiring and reselling abandoned properties for rebuilding. The local home builders' association sponsored new-home shows that drew up to ten thousand visitors. People are now buying lots and building their own homes. The neighborhood currently contains 107 occupied homes, including at least two dozen restored houses. The neighborhood business district, with the help of the National Trust for Historic Preservation's Main Street program, is being restored to active use. Through the years, the city has invested about $75 million in city, state, federal, and foundation funds.

The Freetown neighborhood in Greenville, South Carolina, which was developed in the 1880s as a haven for freed slaves, has undergone a complete makeover that has replaced decaying housing and junk-strewn lots with eighty affordable new homes, ten rehabilitated residences, a new community center, and upgraded neighborhood infrastructure. Greenville County's Redevelopment Authority accomplished all of this by acquiring blighted properties to assemble buildable sites for new homes and working with local residents to upgrade some existing homes and provide needed public improvements.. The Authority completed its carefully phased redevelopment activities in 2006 with the successful relocation of more than a third of the displaced households back into the Freetown community.[22]

The Dudley Street neighborhood in Boston's Roxbury district had suffered property abandonment and arson, trash dumping, and widespread poverty among the multicultural population of twenty-four thousand residents. A grassroots community organization, the Dudley Street Neighborhood Initiative, countered the city's plans for large-scale redevelopment with a different vision. The Neighborhood Initiative's strategy focused on reinvigorating the sixty-four-acre heart of the neighborhood, including consolidating vacant and intermingled public and private properties that would provide sufficient development sufficient to change the neighborhood's economic environment. The Neighborhood Initiative requested and received city authorization to use eminent domain to over-come the complex process of acquiring tax-delinquent and abandoned properties. The organization assembled enough land to allow for construction of more than 400 single-family homes, in addition to the refurbishment of 740 existing houses and the construction of a new town common, a community center and gym, a child care center, and a community greenhouse. Boston's willingness to entrust the eminent domain power to the Neighborhood Initiative proved a key to successful redevelopment.[23]

Schools: A Critical Ingredient for Neighborhood Rejuvenation

Good schools can play a major role in restoring livable neighborhoods. Schools function not only as learning centers but as gathering places for social interaction and neighborhood meetings, as voting sites, as venues for local music and theater groups, and as facilities for sports programs. In many cities and towns, schools also function as centers of social interaction for families with children. Neighborhoods are known by the quality of their schools, and over time desirable schools go hand in hand with desirable neighborhoods. Education also enables effective participation in an evolving society and economy, which plays a vital role in building desirable communities.

But schools also contribute to the problem of sprawl in many communities. School standards, especially for elementary schools, commonly require single-story buildings set well back from streets on large sites that preclude many schoolchildren from walking to school. Middle and high schools, already surrounded by acres of sports fields, frequently are designed to be almost unapproachable by foot from nearby neighborhoods. These educational oases in the midst of low-density suburban subdivisions ignore the need for more compact development and walkable neighborhoods. Every school should be designed to enhance pedestrian and transit access from the surrounding area, to use no more land than necessary for an efficient building and associated outdoor spaces, and to be contiguous to or within an urbanizing area.

St. Louis-based developer Richard Baron takes a lead role in promoting better schools in every neighborhood where his firm conducts residential redevelopment projects. In his acceptance speech for the St. Louis Award for civic service in 1999, Baron said: "Good schools drive housing markets. Redevelopment plans for a neighborhood must be 'school centered,' where schools are in fact magnets . . . as the crucial ingredient in the process of neighborhood revitalization."

In 1996, when Baron's firm began planning for redevelopment of a St.

Louis public housing project into a mixed-income development, the school system's antidiscrimination and special education policies dispersed the neighborhood's children to more than twenty-five schools throughout the city. Baron became convinced that neighborhood restoration required a school that would bring neighborhood children and their families together in a facility that could serve as a multifaceted community center. He worked with the Board of Education to revamp the nearby Jefferson elementary school as a neighborhood school, raising $3.5 million in contributions from twenty corporations for that purpose. Today, 70 percent of the schoolchildren in the redeveloped neighborhood live within walking distance of their schools.[24]

The common threads in these examples are a close-knit collaboration among city officials, neighborhood residents, and property owners or developers (true public-private partnerships); a holistic approach to improving neighborhood physical, social, and economic conditions; and a targeted approach to using a broad range of resources. In addition, and significant for the purposes of growth management, all the efforts took place within a framework of community-wide policies and regulations that stimulated and reinforced actions by specific neighborhoods.

Seeking Interjurisdictional Parity

Differences in the economic and social status of communities seem inevitable in a competitive world. Yet developing metropolitan areas are built through the collective interplay of economic and social forces across jurisdictional boundaries. Municipalities that have garnered major shares of regional business growth depend on other communities to supply affordable housing for many employees of those businesses. Residents of suburban communities may shop in other jurisdictions and work in still others. Their quality of life is supported by teachers, police, maintenance and repair workers, and gardeners who live elsewhere, often long commuting distances away. Traffic generated by employment and shopping centers in some communities generates congestion in neighboring jurisdictions that reap no fiscal benefits from income and sales from those activities. Who wins and who loses in these transactions? And is there a better path to equitable sharing of a region's common wealth, whether measured by fiscal, income, quality-of-life, or other standards?

Many states and some regional agencies have adopted practices to reduce disparities. From a fiscal standpoint, federal and state programs frequently are structured to help overcome inequitable differences in the wealth and status of local jurisdictions. For example, most federal housing and education programs give funding priority to cities and towns that are most in need of assistance. State funds collected from income, sales, and excise taxes, for example, may be redistributed to local jurisdictions according to "equalization" formulas that give more assistance to jurisdictions with greater needs than others.

In many states, however, this approach to matching fiscal resources to demands fails to close the fiscal gap between well-off and less advantaged jurisdictions. Sometimes, shortfalls are due to state legislators' reluctance to redirect state revenue streams from jurisdictions that contribute a major share of the revenues—so-called donor governments—to needy jurisdictions that contribute relatively limited revenues. Legislators may also give priority for state funding to supporting development in growing rather than established communities. However, court decisions in recent years have tended to emphasize the importance of equitable fiscal treatment of needy jurisdictions. Courts in some states have ruled that school funding, for example, should be based on pupil and poverty indicators rather than a jurisdiction's population size or the strength of the local property tax base.

Residents of the Minneapolis–St. Paul region have been concerned about these issues for decades. Although the Twin Cities Metropolitan Council had gained a reputation as an unusually effective regional organization, the results of the 1990 census showed significant and widening economic and social disparities among jurisdictions in the metropolitan area. Businesses, public investments, and affluent taxpayers were flowing to outer suburbs, leaving the central cities and inner suburbs with sharp increases in concentrations of poverty and unemployment. Myron Orfield, then a state legislator, prepared a series of definitive maps to highlight shifts in growth patterns and demonstrate their origin in suburban communities' adoption of exclusionary housing policies and state spending practices that invested heavily in suburban infrastructure—common circumstances in many, if not most, metropolitan areas.

Orfield proposed legislation to address these issues by barring state aid to jurisdictions that restricted construction of multifamily and low-income housing and by requiring that road improvements be planned to relieve widespread congestion and promote access for low-income people to job opportunities. Although the legislature approved the bills, the governor vetoed them as punitive and "premature." In 1995, however, the state enacted the Metropolitan Livable Communities Act, which enables the Metropolitan Council to provide grants to local governments for cleaning up polluted land for redevelopment, jobs growth, and affordable housing;

undertaking strategically located development and redevelopment that links housing, jobs, and services; and creating affordable housing opportunities. From 1996 through 2005, the Metropolitan Council awarded 427 grants totaling more than $144 million, which are expected to leverage billions of dollars in private and other public investments. Some outcomes have included more than nineteen thousand new and retained jobs through brownfield cleanup, dozens of development and redevelopment projects that produced more than 22,000 new and 600 rehabilitated housing units, and production of more than 2,500 new and rehabilitated affordable rental units in fifty cities throughout the region.[25]

A number of state and regional agencies are pursuing similar grant programs to provide incentives for communities to focus more attention on revitalizing urbanized areas. In addition, a movement has begun among "first suburbs"—America's older, inner-ring suburban jurisdictions—to recapture federal and state attention to their needs. Home to one fifth of the nation's population, these jurisdictions just outside central cities have aged in place, becoming less suburban and more urban in their makeup and interests. Some are enclaves of expensive housing and highly educated residents with high incomes; others are faced with major needs for improved infrastructure and public services. A recent study of first suburbs observes that as a group they are highly racially diverse, home to more and more foreign-born residents, and struggling with changing needs for affordable housing but lacking access to the kinds of tax subsidies that help outer suburbs grow.[26] William Hudnut's book *Halfway to Everywhere: A Portrait of America's First-tier Suburbs* tells the stories of more than seventy such communities that, he says, are coping with aging populations, housing stock, and infrastructure; diminishing fiscal capacity and rising social service needs; rapidly changing ethnic makeups; and declining retail centers.[27] Several groups of local governments around cities in Ohio and elsewhere have formed consortiums to press for assistance in revitalizing mature, development communities as an antidote to sprawl.[28]

Two notable types of initiatives for addressing regional disparities are the "fair-share" housing programs administered by several states and regions and the concept of sharing revenues among jurisdictions within a region.

Fair-share Housing Requirements

Decent, affordable housing is a critical social need. A number of court decisions, as well as several state legislatures, have urged or even mandated the production of affordable housing as an essential component of community growth and development. Perhaps the best known is New Jersey's "Mount Laurel" series of court decisions, which were followed by the state's enactment of a "fair housing" law in 1985 and the establishment of the Council on Affordable Housing. The judicial decisions and the state act require New Jersey municipalities to meet their "fair share" of regional needs for low- and moderate-income housing. Aimed at overcoming communities' reluctance to zone for higher-density and multifamily housing, the act provides builders legal standing to force communities to allow development of affordable housing.

Court decisions in other states, including New York, Pennsylvania, and New Hampshire, have invalidated exclusionary zoning practices by local governments. Several states, through special legislation or state growth management programs, require or encourage local governments to provide a range of housing for all income groups. Massachusetts enacted an "anti-snob" law in 1979 to ensure that at least 10 percent of a community's housing stock is available to low-income households. The act provides for local governments to issue a "comprehensive permit" for publicly subsidized housing projects that replaces all other required local permits. Permit applications are reviewed by local zoning boards of appeal, which may approve projects not otherwise complying with existing zoning. More than twenty thousand housing units in more than four hundred projects have been approved through this process. Versions of the Massachusetts approach were later adapted by Connecticut and Rhode Island.[29]

Other examples of state efforts include California's requirement that local governments include housing elements in their general plans that respond to overall housing needs and requirements, as well as both Oregon's and Florida's state growth management laws that require local governments to formulate comprehensive housing programs. California's law requires that all jurisdictions provide their fair share of regional housing needs. Based on a statewide estimate of housing needs for various levels of household incomes, regional organizations and local governments are charged with determining their share of housing needs. Cities and counties must incorporate a housing element in their general plans to establish programs and policies to respond to housing needs. They must be able to demonstrate a "good faith" effort to plan and zone to allow the variety of housing types needed to meet the fair-share targets.

Regional agencies are positioned to encourage local government attention to affordable housing needs. For example, the San Diego Association of Governments and the Metro regional organization in Portland, Oregon, have actively promoted the production of affordable housing by establishing regional and local targets for housing needs and by encouraging local governments to meet their housing targets by allowing the densities and housing types most appropriate for achieving affordability.

However, many communities continue to resist the need to produce affordable housing. Although they may establish favorable policies and even appropriate zoning, public officials frequently bow to NIMBY-ist pressures when proposed projects come up for approval. Even the strong court decisions more than a quarter century ago against local governments' tendencies to zone out affordable housing have not prevailed in many New Jersey jurisdictions, and many California communities, faced with escalating land and development costs, disregard the state's requirements to establish regulatory conditions suitable for affordable housing production. In many locales, "fair housing" is kept at bay—considered a disregarded aspect of growth that some other jurisdiction will address.

Tax-base Sharing Programs

For many years, the concept of regionwide sharing of tax revenues generated by development has tantalized planners and others concerned with reducing fiscal disparities among jurisdictions. Communities with low tax bases must impose higher tax rates to deliver the same services as communities with high tax bases. At the same time, regional development may benefit some communities while hurting others. Tax-base sharing spreads a proportion of the fiscal benefits of development, such as revenues from property and sales taxes, among a region's local jurisdictions according to their individual needs more than their fiscal resources. Revenue-sharing programs tend to reduce competition between communities for tax-generating development that might lead them to make inappropriate land use decisions. For example, a community might forgo development of affordable housing in favor of expensive homes that will yield higher property tax revenues. Competition between neighboring jurisdictions may devolve into bidding wars to offer developers tax breaks or lower design and environmental standards.

Best known is the tax-sharing program of Minneapolis–St. Paul. It was adopted in 1971 to reduce competition among local governments for tax-producing commercial and industrial development and to prevent severe tax-base disparities among jurisdictions. The Metropolitan Revenue Distribution Act provides that 40 percent of local tax revenue increases derived from industrial and commercial development since 1971 must be deposited in a general fund, which is then shared regionally through a formula that takes into account population and fiscal capacity. The intention was that this program would allow local governments to make more rational decisions about development policies and that it would also spread revenues from new development among communities that might be affected by new development outside their borders.

The system has succeeded in reducing tax-base disparities among Twin Cities communities from 50:1 to roughly 12:1. It has not entirely eliminated disparities, because 60 percent of any new revenue from commercial development remains in the host community. But about 20 percent of the region's total tax base, or about $393 million a year, is shared annually.

Clearly, the tax-sharing concept has merit for reducing fiscal disparities among jurisdictions. After many years of consideration, however, tax-base sharing has been adopted only in the Twin Cities and Hackensack Meadowlands regions and in Charlottesville, Virginia (where the county returns revenues from tax-base increases to the city in return for a nonannexation agreement). One planner in the Twin Cities commented that the tax-sharing program probably would be voted down if proposed today, given continuing local competition for tax base. Regional tax-base sharing remains an intriguing but largely unused concept.

Growth management programs originated as creatures of the boom in suburban development spreading across the nation in the post–World War II period. Early manifestations of growth controls by suburban communities focused primarily on ensuring the quality of emerging development while safeguarding a jurisdiction's fiscal status. Policies and actions were aimed at protecting established neighborhoods and business centers from the negative effects of rampant development. As a suburban phenomenon, rarely did these programs address social and economic issues, least of all the problems of disadvantaged households and neighborhoods.

But effective management of growth requires a wider outlook. Many aging suburbs are being forced to cope with issues arising from economic and social trends that are diversifying the resident population and altering the economic makeup. At the same time, newer suburban cities and counties are struggling to establish a fiscally sound base of development capable of supporting residents' desires for public services. And central cities, while enjoying economic gains from influxes of new residents, still must contend with aging infrastructure, unemployment, and a growing lack of decent, affordable housing. These disparate effects of growth and change demand attention throughout metropolitan regions. They require a better means of sharing the prosperity gained through regional growth—a firm commitment to improving social and economic equity for all residents.

Several strategies can help to achieve this ambitious goal.[30]

1. Strengthen regional economies in ways that widen opportunities for low-income residents and working families.
   - Work to promote economic development that will improve access by low-income workers to jobs in regional growth industries.
   - Focus public investments to maintain neighborhoods, housing, and social services that will support such employment.
   - Use the community resources of educational and medical institutions, corporations, and nonprofit organizations to form supportive partnerships for accomplishing these aims.
2. Invest in transportation systems that improve mobility for all.
   - Balance spending on highways with support for other modes of transportation to improve access by all residents to jobs and services throughout the region.
   - Focus neighborhoods and business centers around transit stations and corridors that provide low-cost alternatives to driving cars.
   - Improve transportation access between low-income communities and neighborhoods to suburban employment centers.
3. Stimulate equitable reinvestment in vacant, abandoned, and underused properties.
   - Reclaim used or poorly used properties for development that generates economic and social benefits for neighborhoods and communities.
   - Prepare well-laid plans for reinvestment that engage local residents, community groups, and businesses in decision making and that correspond with community comprehensive plans.
4. Make all neighborhoods desirable and healthful living environments.
   - Work to equalize disparities in public facilities and services that support livable neighborhoods and provide opportunities for social and economic advancement.
   - Capitalize on the dynamics of community and regional market forces and build on existing neighborhood character and resources to maintain or revitalize neighborhood assets.
   - Increase affordable housing opportunities by dismantling exclusionary land use policies across the region and creating innovative financing strategies and housing coalitions.

This list of potential actions only hints at the magnitude of the task. But the programs and projects described in this chapter demonstrate the extraordinary efforts mounted by cities and towns to revive older areas, improve employment and housing opportunities, and stimulate neighborhood conservation. Imagine the power and effect of such efforts linked to a regionwide growth policy that encourages the full use of existing urban areas and discourages sprawl into the countryside! The next chapter describes some ways states and regions are working to achieve such ends.

CHAPTER 8

Regional and
State Growth Management

Ever since local governments began to plan and regulate development, the constraints of their jurisdictional boundaries have limited their capabilities for managing growth. Most individual towns, cities, and counties have only marginal control over development beyond their boundaries, leaving them vulnerable to the actions of adjacent jurisdictions. A fairly common example is the traffic jams a town may experience emanating from the construction of a new shopping center in a bordering jurisdiction town, which also reaps the tax benefits of the new development. Another example is a county that carefully guides growth while officials in an adjacent county gladly allow poorly controlled development with little concern for spillover effects on other jurisdictions.

Many consequences of development reach beyond the responsibilities of individual local governments. Construction and expansion of basic infrastructure for water supply, wastewater treatment, and highway improvements, for example, involve watersheds, drainage basins, and interstate connections that extend across many local communities. Natural landscapes that can provide green space for future generations stretch past jurisdictional lines. Social and economic disparities among jurisdictions threaten to disrupt regional economies unless addressed on an intergovernmental basis. The fact is that our communities' economic, social, and environmental interests function within regional, state, national, and even global contexts. And intergovernmental concerns have become more important as metropolitan areas have increased in size and complexity and as uneasiness about global economic competition and sustainable development has intensified. Communities attempting to manage growth and change, therefore, must recognize the many external forces that demand coordination and cooperation with other jurisdictions.

Regional planning agencies and state growth management programs have been established in many areas to help meet that goal. Many varieties of regional agencies have been formed to prescribe regional strategies and coordinate local actions to resolve issues of development and natural conservation. States have encouraged regional activities and enacted laws to encourage the consideration of state and regional concerns in local planning and regulation of development.

The Intergovernmental Dilemma

All such efforts have been and continue to be stoutly resisted by local governments and their constituents. Americans traditionally value public decision making at the lowest possible rung on the ladder of governmental entities. They decry the "meddling" of state and regional agencies in local development matters and oppose requirements for recognizing state and regional interests in local development policies. They defend their wariness of any diminishing of their authority over development by claiming the need to maintain the unique character of the community and particularly the community's competitive position in the region's economy and tax structure.

However, despite resistance by community officials and many voters eager to control development locally, concerns about coordinating growth management efforts and establishing intergovernmental management of growth arise time and again. Officials are challenged to translate state and regional interests into specific policies and actions while retaining a large measure of local government control over growth and development.

Regional Growth Management

During the "good government" movement in the early decades of the twentieth century, political reformers paid much attention to regional governance. Their enthusiasm led to the establishment of a number of regional planning organizations, state planning commissions, and multistate river basin commissions during the 1920s and especially during the New Deal years of the 1930s. The concept of region-based planning gained currency among geographers, planners, and political scientists as urban growth spread past city boundaries, new suburban jurisdictions proliferated, and threats to natural and rural environments became more perceptible. Lewis Mumford, in *The Culture of Cities*, characterized the emerging regional outlook in 1938: "The re-animation and re-building of regions as deliberate works of collective art, is the grand task of politics for the coming generation."[1]

With the rapid growth following World War II, the federal government encouraged the formation of regional planning councils and substate districts to coordinate the many federal grant programs flowing to local governments. Federal funds were available for regional planning and various regionally managed programs. Federal encouragement proved so successful that by the end of the 1970s, local governments in most parts of the nation were participating in regional organizations. Every state included regional agencies of some kind, and many states had formed regional organizations for all sections of the state.

Federal funding was drastically curtailed in the early 1980s, however, forcing severe cuts or the termination of regional programs. Only the metropolitan transportation planning organizations required by law continued to receive support, although their funding dwindled as well. The regional councils that had been engaged in regionwide planning regrouped, attracting local support by performing services useful to their constituent local governments, such as data collection and projections, special studies, and certain services that local governments perceived as regional in nature.

Regional planning declined in many areas. Local governments frequently took dim views of the regional planning efforts of the 1960s and 1970s, seeing them as theoretical exercises of little practical value or as potential threats to their local decision making. Once regional agencies became dependent on local governments for survival, many regional agencies gave up serious attempts at strategic regionwide planning, opting instead to stitch together local plans or formulate airy statements of planning goals and toothless policies that had little influence on local actions.

Yet regional organizations persist in most metropolitan areas and provide significant services to aid growth management. The regional transportation planning function, especially, continues to draw sustenance from federal programs, and regional organizations have been given serious coordinating duties in state growth management programs. Other regional groups gain support from business, environmental, and other constituencies. Across the nation, a number of regional organizations have managed to gain enough credibility to substantially influence the development process in their regions.

A Range of Regional Approaches

Regional organizations that participate in growth management take multiple forms and are involved in a variety of growth management efforts, including:

- regional planning councils or districts;
- metropolitan transportation planning organizations;
- federal or state-chartered commissions or authorities charged with;
- protection of environmentally sensitive areas;
- regional public service authorities, such as airport or transit authorities or water districts;
- regional business and civic leadership groups promoting regionwide planning;
- ad hoc groups established to support defined regional goals; and
- consolidated city-county governments and, in some states, county planning organizations.

Large metropolitan areas generally harbor dozens of these organizations, often with overlapping interests and powers. The most effective regional organizations have accumulated several functions that permit strategic regional planning and some control over implementing regional plans.

Regional Planning Councils

The most common type of regional agency is the regional planning council (or association of governments or council of governments). Such councils exist in some form in every state, and some states have designated councils across the entire state. Typically, their membership and governing body consist of representatives of the local governments within the defined region, and they constitute an official forum for identifying, exploring, and making recommendations on intergovernmental issues. Regional councils commonly organize standing subgroups of local administrative staffs, such as planners or finance officers, to recommend solutions to technical issues. Councils' responsibilities vary widely but may include assembling statistical information and projecting regional growth trends, conducting other research and educational programs, coordinating selected federal and state programs that affect the region, preparing strategic regional plans, planning and managing selected regional services, and coordinating or assisting local planning programs.

The Achilles' heel of regional planning councils is the typical requirement for consensus on policy positions by a council's local government members. In theory, this arrangement might stimulate local governments to define and carry out regionwide development strategies that could guide local actions. In practice, the requirement for consensus allows member local governments to exercise virtual veto power over policy positions, resulting in regional statements that are so broad as to be almost meaningless. Regional councils are also unable to implement strategies and policies without the acquiescence of the affected local governments. As a result, most regional planning is limited by three factors:

- Most planning by regional councils is only advisory in nature, leaving local governments to ignore or implement regional policies at will.
- Even where regional councils can require conformance of local plans to regional goals, the agencies are reluctant to do so in the face of local government control of regional administrative and financial matters.
- Jurisdictions of regional agencies seldom coincide with metropolitan growth patterns, which may encompass vast rural areas with issues quite different from urban growth areas or may exclude urbanizing fringe areas outside the defined region.

Regional plans, therefore, commonly lack incisive direction for metropolitan development and, worse, are often unenforceable and ignored almost at will by member local governments.

Notwithstanding these limitations on the powers of regional councils, some agencies have managed to influence metropolitan growth, aided in some cases by state support for regional actions and also by the technical prowess and political acumen of regional administrators, as illustrated by Portland's Metro organization, widely viewed as the most successful metropolitan planning organization in the nation. Why is the most effective agency in Portland? Some posit Oregonians' passionate environmental concerns; others cite the Willamette Valley's world-class agricultural fertility, which begs for protection, or the Portland area's decades of slow economic growth, which allowed thoughtful consideration of policies for shaping a desirable living environment.

Oregon's growth management law, adopted in 1973, provides for strong state guidance of local development policies, including a requirement for all communities to adopt a growth boundary. Portland was challenged to invent an organization that could work with dozens of local governments to draw a growth boundary around the metropolitan area. The solution was to combine into one agency the planning functions of the regional association of governments with the service functions of the three-county service district, and to have voters directly elect the agency's governing body and executive. The proposal was adopted by the state legislature in 1977 and by the state's voters in 1978.[2] A state constitutional amendment in 1990 gave Metro a home rule charter.

Within that state policy context, Portland's Metro has interwoven state and local development policies to form a cohesive growth strategy for the entire metropolitan area. Metro's definition of the original growth boundary and subsequent reviews encouraged coordination of local plans and widened citizen participation in planning. Metro manages solid waste management operations for the region. It took the lead in planning the state convention center and then formed a commission to build and operate the center and to manage the Civic Stadium, the Portland Center for the Performing Arts, and the Expo Center. To carry out the federal transportation planning mandate, Metro established and staffed a joint advisory committee (as an ad hoc council of governments) to make key decisions on regional transportation policies. An affordable housing policy worked out with the state requires half of all residential zoning to allow multifamily use and establishes minimum housing density targets for each jurisdiction in the region. Metro also launched a Metropolitan Greenspaces program to inventory and protect open spaces and natural areas.

Metro set out in 1992 to formulate a fifty-year strategic concept plan for the year 2040, recognizing that regional development patterns evolve over decades. After evaluating four alternative regional patterns of development, Metro adopted a plan that called for minimum expansion of the current urban growth boundary and substantial development and redevelopment in compact centers connected by rail and bus transit lines. Metro then prepared a regional framework plan for 2020, composed of eight "fundamental" policy statements and sections describing substantive planning policies for land use, transportation, and other aspects of the concept plan. Adopted in 1997, the framework plan was updated in 2005. In addition, the Metro board enacted an Urban Growth Management Functional Plan, which prescribes performance measures used to determine the progress of individual cities and counties toward implementing the policies.[3]

Metro's relationships with local governments are sometimes contentious but are ultimately productive. For example, Metro established regional targets for developing higher-density, affordable housing and then worked with local governments to define affordable housing programs and amend planning and zoning to allow development of such housing. Metro also works with cities and counties to encourage development in regional and town centers and transit-station areas.

Two other regional councils—the San Diego Association of Governments (SANDAG) and the Minneapolis–St. Paul Metropolitan Council—provide somewhat different examples of regional approaches to growth management.

The San Diego Association of Governments brings together representatives of eighteen city governments and the San Diego County government plus nonvoting representatives of more than a dozen agencies and nonprofit organizations. Through skillful administration over many years, SANDAG established solid credentials throughout the region for providing useful data and projections, functioning as the metropolitan transportation planning organization, and conducting innovative planning and management of multiple regional programs, including wildlife habitat preservation, solid waste recycling, airport siting, and open space planning. The agency provides leadership in considering regional issues through collaborative relationships with local governments. Its procedures envision a cross-acceptance process: the regional growth strategy will incorporate principles and policies *generated from* and *directed to* local jurisdictions.

This fast-growing region demands all the planning attention it can get. In 1988, after several years of controversy over regional growth management issues, the county's voters resoundingly approved a proposal to establish a regional organization with special powers to manage a regional growth management program. After due deliberation, a Blue Ribbon Committee proposed to designate SANDAG as the lead regional agency by amending existing joint powers (intergovernmental) agreements among the local governments. The amendments were confirmed by 1990, assigning SANDAG the responsibilities for developing a regional growth management strategy, including growth rate policies, phasing and distribution of growth, open space preservation, site and financing of regional facilities, and quality-of-life concerns. The amendments called for local governments and agencies to "self-certify" the consistency of their general plans with the Regional Board's regional plans, subject to the review of consistency findings by the board. The strategy assumed that local jurisdictions would respond to pressures for making decisions that corresponded to regional goals. By 1993, SANDAG had defined measurable quality-of-life standards as well as the actions required to respond to federal and state mandates for such issues as water supply and quality and housing needs.

Ten years later, SANDAG took two major steps toward coordinating regional decision making on growth issues. One step was the implementation of a new state law that took effect on January 1, 2003, which consolidated all of the roles and responsibilities of SANDAG with many of the transit functions of the Metropolitan Transit System and the North County Transit District. The new law made SANDAG responsible for transit planning, funding allocation, project development, and construction management in the San Diego region. It was followed in November 2004 by voter approval of a forty-year extension of a local sales tax to generate $14 billion in funding for transportation improvements.[4]

The second step was SANDAG's approval in July 2004 of a new regional comprehensive plan (RCP). The plan is viewed as a consensus statement of the region's vision, core values, key issues, goals, objectives, and needed actions. The RCP included a list of "strategic initiatives" to implement the plan's recommended actions and concepts. To demonstrate the range of issues involved, several early actions identified in the list were already under way, including:

- preparation of a Smart Growth Concept Map (adopted in October 2006);
- development of a regional funding program for transportation;
- evaluation of the use of transportation impact funding;
- adoption of an updated regional housing needs assessment; and
- development of a regional habitat funding program.[5]

SANDAG also prepared a "baseline" of performance measures to monitor progress in meeting the regional plan's goals, such as the proportion of housing units and jobs in smart growth opportunity areas and the share of energy produced from renewable resources. For example, the 2006 report found that nearly one third of the new housing units built in 2005 were located in designated smart growth opportunity areas but that the region continues to experience a serious housing affordability problem.[6]

SANDAG's unique blend of regional and local policy making and implementation through persuasion has established tangible regionwide policies for guiding local governmental actions. An evaluation of SANDAG's effectiveness by the independent California Legislative Analyst Office in 2006 found that SANDAG plays a more prominent role in managing growth than most other California councils of governments. However, the agency's authority to address most regional issues is limited, and its members are mostly unaccountable for meeting regional objectives—a common problem for regional agencies.[7] But SANDAG's administrative responsibilities for transit service give it additional powers of persuasion and makes funding available as incentives for promoting transit-oriented development.

The Metropolitan Council of Minneapolis–St. Paul was established in 1967 to coordinate development in a seven-county, 140-jurisdiction region of three thousand square miles and 2.5 million people. It has some similarities with and differences from SANDAG. The Minnesota legislature created the Metropolitan Council in response to a severe water pollution problem that required immediate planning for an expanded regional sewer system. Once established, the council accrued responsibilities for other regionwide problems, such as solid waste disposal, park and open space acquisition, airport siting, and transportation systems. The council is responsible for preparing a regional plan and also functions as the metropolitan transportation planning organization. The council maintains a regional perspective through its appointment by the governor of council members from sixteen multimunicipal districts. It is given some freedom of action by the financial support provided by a mill levy on all property in the region, which generates a substantial part of its budget requirements.

Although the council possesses more powers than most regional organizations, it influences metropolitan development mostly through its planning and consensus-building functions—especially for basic infrastructure systems and services—rather than by regulatory means. For example, the council defines a metropolitan urban service area for sewer service that is quite similar to an urban growth boundary. The urban service area constitutes less than a third of the total metropolitan area. Development outside the urban service area is limited to low densities that can be served by septic systems. The urban service area functioned relatively successfully to achieve contiguous urban development, but most development within the area has remained at fairly low densities. The Metropolitan Waste Control Commission provides the actual sewer service, but eight of the nine commission members are appointed by the Metropolitan Council and the council must approve the commission's implementation program, including its financial program, as consistent with the council's sewer policies.

Transportation planning and management is directed by the council in much the same manner as the sewer system. The Regional Transit Board carries out metropolitan transit planning, operates the metropolitan bus company, and contracts with other bus companies and specialized vendors. The board's chairperson is appointed by the governor, and its members are appointed by the Metropolitan Council. As with sewer service, the council develops a transit policy plan as part of its metropolitan transportation plan and the board carries out the plan with an implementation program approved by the council. Despite the close relationships between the council and the board, the two have disagreed sharply, including the council's refusal of the board's proposal to develop a heavy-rail system in the 1970s that delayed the advent of rail transit service in the Twin Cities by thirty years.

Highway construction remains the responsibility of the Minnesota Department of Transportation. Although not required to follow the council's transportation plan, the department usually does because the council has veto power over department plans for controlled-access highways and also manages relationships between the department and local govern-ments and groups. A transportation advisory board, made up largely of local officials, advises the council in choosing highway priorities and allo-cating federal funds. In practice, the council almost always follows the board's recommendations.[8]

Despite this broad range of interlocking planning, the Twin Cities' trans-portation problems look much like those in other metropolitan areas. Rail transit service was held up by disagreements over plans and costs; for exam-ple, a task force once proposed fourteen corridors (more miles than the Paris rail system) and a $2 billion investment to provide service to all jurisdictions represented on the task force. One result was that regional bus services flour-ished, as did traffic congestion. As of 2007, rail transit service was finally becoming available along one corridor and other corridors are planned.

The council's famous tax-base sharing program was adopted in 1971 to provide a compensation mechanism for regional land use and facility-siting actions that might favor one jurisdiction over another. Particularly, the program was meant to reduce competition over high-value commercial and industrial development and to reduce tax-base disparities. Since its inception, 40 percent of property tax revenues from new commercial and industrial development have been pooled in a regional fund and redis-tributed based on population and other factors. In effect, the tax-base sharing program compensates jurisdictions that attract less high-value development than do other jurisdictions. Although tax sharing remains a significant part of the council's program, its importance has declined as property tax proportions of total revenues have dropped.

The Metropolitan Council prepared its first regional plan in the early 1970s with an elaborate process that led to adoption of the Metropolitan Development Framework in 1975. The framework combined both a policy plan and an implementation program. In 1976, the state legislature expanded the council's powers by requiring all cities in the metropolitan area to formulate comprehensive plans every ten years that are consistent with the council's functional plans for infrastructure systems and services. If the council determines that a local plan will adversely affect regional sys-tems (e.g., highways), the council can demand plan changes.

The interjurisdictional consensus that supported the council for so many decades was shaken in the 1990s as minorities' migration into the central cities and fiscal and other disparities between suburban jurisdic-tions and the Twin Cities began to surface. The council was criticized for responding too slowly to new regional imperatives for social and eco-nomic development. Development trends at that time also demonstrated that much development was occurring outside of the metropolitan region. Then-governor Arne Carlson called for the council to become either "relevant or extinct." The council issued a series of "Blueprint" regional policy plans, and in 1994, new legislation merged the regional waste control and transit agencies with the council, broadening the council's mission to incorporate operating as well as planning functions. Around the turn of the century, the council appeared to recover its influence in regional development.

The council's most recent regional plan is the 2030 Regional Development Framework, adopted in January 2004. It is based on four fundamental strategies:

- accommodating growth in a flexible, connected, and efficient manner;
- slowing the growth in traffic congestion and improving mobility;
- encouraging expanded choices in housing locations and types; and
- working to conserve, protect, and enhance the region's vital natural resources.

Emphasizing that the framework plan is not a one-size-fits-all process, the plan incorporates a Regional Growth Strategy Map, which identifies urban and rural geographic planning areas. The map and accompanying tables specify applications of the fundamental strategies for all communities, including developed and developing urban communities and four categories of rural areas. For example, to accommodate projected growth, all communities are to plan for development that accommodates growth forecasts at appropriate densities, while developed communities are to accommodate growth forecasts through reinvestment in infill, adaptive reuse, and redevelopment at densities of five or units in developed areas and even higher densities near transportation corridors and with adequate sewer capacity. The council works with local officials and provides incentive grants to achieve these goals, aided by Regional Framework Benchmarks issued in 2006 to help track and measure progress.

The stories of Portland, San Diego, and Minneapolis–St. Paul offer useful lessons for other regional organizations. Both Portland's and the Twin Cities' agencies were established with state support. All three manage important regional services, are governed by boards with regional membership or state membership (or both), and were assigned selected but significant powers to influence key elements of the development process, such as transportation and sewers. As the major urban areas in their respective states, they receive much attention from state legislators.

Metropolitan Planning Organizations

Metropolitan planning organizations (MPOs), which the Federal Aid Highway Act of 1962 requires for all metropolitan areas with more than fifty thousand in population, are responsible for "continuing, comprehensive, and cooperative" planning for regional transportation systems. To accomplish this goal, MPOs collect detailed data about travel patterns, forecasts of growth throughout the region, and other trends and use sophisticated computer models to project future travel patterns and volumes. The results help them determine needs for highway and other improvements in the metropolitan transportation systems. MPOs are charged with adopting annual multiyear transportation programs that indicate priorities for improvements and funding sources, including federal and state contributions.

An example is the Ohio-Kentucky-Indiana Regional Council of Governments based in Cincinnati, Ohio, which conducts transportation planning for a 2,636-square-mile region with a population of 1.9 million. The council is governed by a board made up of representatives of each county, each municipality of more than five thousand in population, county and city planning agencies, state departments of transportation, and up to ten nonelected residents of the region. The council's primary mission is to prepare and adopt regional transportation plans and two-year proposals for transportation improvements. It is also responsible for tracking air quality and determining compliance plans for nonattainment areas. It has no authority—and announces that it seeks none—over local land uses but promotes a regional policy plan to guide land use decisions of local governments.[9] A December 2006 news report described the upcoming launch of "yet another exercise" to prepare a plan for the region, this one promoted by the Cincinnati USA Regional Chamber and the United Way of Greater Cincinnati. The reporter, Cliff Peale, asked whether this effort would be more successful than many similar programs in the past. He recalled a "Quest Vision" process in Northern Kentucky in 1996, and another try in 2005 labeled "Quest 2015," but little follow-up action and only a cool response from Cincinnati officials.[10]

Commonly, MPOs are combined administratively with regional planning agencies. However, MPOs retain their individual responsibilities for transportation planning and are administered by boards that include some members appointed by state governors. MPOs also maintain close affiliation with state transportation agencies, which are major sources of funding, as well as with local elected officials. Some MPOs are established as separate agencies, and others are administered by state transportation departments. The latter are powerful agencies well connected to state legislators and construction contractors, with relatively little concern for regional planning.

MPOs have an uneasy relationship with regional planning agencies charged with laying out plans for metropolitan development. MPO programs that reflect the priorities of state transportation departments and local governments for transportation improvements may or may not correspond to regional strategies for metropolitan development. Whereas regional planning agencies may wish to promote patterns of growth that will support the expansion of public transit systems, state highway departments focus on highway construction and local governments plan and zone in ways that support highway rather than transit use. MPOs and regional planning agencies find it difficult to bridge the jurisdictional gap between state control of transportation funding and local determination of land use patterns. The Intermodal Surface Transportation Efficiency Act of 1991 and subsequent acts have prodded MPOs to plan for multimodal transportation systems and to recognize funding limits in satisfying metropolitan transportation needs. But the gulf between local governments and regional agencies, on the one hand, and state agencies and regional agencies, on the other, continues to hobble collaboration to promote regional development strategies.

Regional Environmental Conservation Agencies

Regional agencies formed to conserve valued environmental qualities have proven most effective at managing the development process, chiefly because many are given regulatory as well as planning powers. Such well-known agencies as the Adirondack Park Commission, the Tahoe Regional Planning Agency, the Cape Cod Regional Commission, and the Chesapeake Bay Commission (the latter described in chapter 4) have demonstrated their capabilities for protecting environmental qualities. Perhaps the best example of such agencies is the New Jersey Pinelands Commission because its major features echo many of those in other agencies: established after public clamor to protect a cherished resource, mandated by federal or state action, given narrow powers to override local development policies, administered with intensive efforts at intergovernmental cooperation, and funded by sources not dependent on local governments.

The New Jersey pine barrens occupy about a third of the state's land, generally located south and east of the New Jersey Turnpike. An ecosystem with a high water table, many marshes and bogs, stunted trees, and multiple species of plants and animals, the pine barrens is truly a backwater area.

Scattered small settlements persisted from colonial days, their economies dependent on small farms, bog-iron foundries, and cranberry bogs. In the 1960s, however, development threatened to spread east from Princeton and inland from the coast; proposals for new towns and major second-home projects were broached. Although many local officials and property owners were elated by prospects for development, environmentally minded residents and people outside the pine barrens were concerned about potential damage to the pine barrens ecosystem and particularly to the 17-trillion gallon aquifer of exceptionally pure water underlying the area.

The federal government acted first, with passage of the National Parks and Recreation Act of 1978, which created the pinelands as a national reserve. A year later, the state followed suit with the Pinelands Protection Act. The act created the New Jersey Pinelands Commission, a fifteen-member board of national, state, and local representatives, to oversee conservation and development in a 1-million-acre area with fifty-two municipalities and seven counties.

The act required the commission to adopt a comprehensive management plan. Commission members defined plan goals: protecting the forested core, water quality, and associated ecological features; accommodating population growth but directing development to the edges; providing homes for residents employed in the region rather than second homes for residents of other areas; and adopting a process for mitigating economic impacts and recognizing vested rights. The plan designated four types of areas. The preservation area, delineated in the state act, prohibits residential uses unless a landowner can demonstrate two-generation ownership. The protection area allows development of one dwelling unit for each thirty-nine acres. Agricultural production areas are scattered throughout the other areas and provide for continued cranberry and blueberry production of great economic value. Regional growth centers were designated to accommodate future development. The plan was supplemented with a variety of environmental management programs and a transferable development rights (TDR) program to compensate landowners for refraining from development.

Once the plan was adopted, local plans and regulations were required to conform to it through a certification by the commission. The state helped by establishing the Pinelands Development Credit Bank in 1985 to buy development credits in restricted areas and sell them to enable higher densities in regional growth centers (similar in many ways to the TDR program at Lake Tahoe). Also in 1985, New Jersey voters approved a $30 million Pinelands Infrastructure Trust Bond Act to fund sewer and other capital improvements in regional growth centers.

The Pinelands plan benefited from federal and state mandates that established environmental values as prime objectives and carefully crafted provisions to respond to economic as well as environmental needs. It also benefited from an empathetic administrative staff that worked consistently to attain consensus with local officials and residents without wielding the state/federal hammer too visibly or often. The Pinelands experience demonstrates several important factors in the relative success of environmentally oriented regional organizations:

- the focus on a *clear objective*—preserving a significant environmental feature that called for extraordinary action, whether the unique ecosystem and valuable aquifer of the Pinelands, the alpine clarity of Lake Tahoe, or the fishing and recreational qualities of the Chesapeake Bay;
- federal and state actions that permitted *overrides of local decision making* on development matters by requiring conformity of local plans to agency goals and rules;
- significant *financial support* to compensate affected landowners through TDRs or outright acquisition of severely affected properties, and the funding of planning and economic development programs to help local governments respond to regional objectives;
- regional agency efforts to establish *cooperative relationships* with local governments and residents to build consensus instead of promoting conflict; and
- the existence of an *organized constituency* of environmental interests that continues to monitor and support agency actions.

The experience of the Tahoe Regional Planning Agency is instructive on at least two of these points. The agency, established in 1969 as a bistate organization, adopted a strong "command-and-control" stance toward regulating conformance with the agency's goals. Its plans and regulations promised to virtually wipe out the values of nine thousand platted lots around the lake, and development approvals were made on a case-by-case basis, often with formidable conditions. Local governments retained little control over the development process. Political conflicts and litigation raised storms of controversy in both states throughout several administrations. Not until the agency reformulated requirements to provide more predictability and potential compensation for affected property owners did a conservation plan obtain approval. Even then, the bitter attitudes stirred by years of strife continued to affect implementation of the plan.

Other Regional Organizations

Regional coordination is also carried out in less official ways by a variety of other regional organizations formed as ad hoc groups to support regional actions for specific purposes. The report of a forum on ad hoc efforts across the nation noted that they "often begin with an opportunistic handle: a crisis that mobilizes the interests of community leaders, a commonly held perception that growth is rapidly destroying valued open space, or the realization that an area is losing its competitive edge."[11] The movement that generated the Task Force on Growth and Change in southeastern Massachusetts, for example, brought public officials and representatives of interest groups together to focus on impending urban and rural growth issues stirred by Boston-area growth in that region. Other organizations are formed simply to raise the level of attention toward regional concerns, such as the Treasure Valley Partnership in Boise, Idaho, which provides a forum for local officials to focus on growth issues in the Boise region. Some are business groups, such as the Greater Baltimore Committee, which provided much of the leadership for revitalizing the Baltimore waterfront; the Allegheny Conference, which for decades has promoted economic development in the Pittsburgh region; and the Bay Area Council, which supports high-quality development in the San Francisco area.

In moderately sized to midsized cities especially, such groups often provide the primary stimulus for regionwide planning and action. The New Designs for Growth project of the Traverse City Area Chamber of Commerce in Michigan, described in chapter 6, for example, improved growth control practices in the five-county region of Grand Traverse Bay on Lake Michigan. Its initial efforts began in 1992 with publication of the *Grand Traverse Bay Region Development Guidebook*. The guidebook provided a compendium of model development practices, using simple drawings to contrast inadequate and superior techniques for developing, building, designing, and protecting land. The book became a valuable tool for educating public officials and citizens and for instilling better standards of development in township and county plans and regulations.

At a somewhat larger scale, the New York Regional Plan Association (RPA) was founded by business and civic leaders in the 1920s to create a long-term plan for the New York region and to promote its implementation across political boundaries. For more than eight decades, the RPA has sponsored highly regarded research studies, formulated three regional plans, and acted as a regional advocate to influence public and private decisions throughout the region. Its 1929 *Regional Plan of New York and Its Environs* provided an authoritative analysis of regional development issues and a breathtaking vision of future growth. The 1968 and 1996 plans both emphasize the need to maintain and revitalize older urban areas and to preserve open space.

The RPA implements these ideas through the hard work of informing, persuading, nudging, and brandishing the banner of regionalism through countless meetings, hearings, discussions, and conversations. Its board and staff put prestige, lengthy experience, and a regional outlook into service for regional development. In a region with few other regional advocates, the RPA provides a constant reminder of the value of thinking regionally.

In addition to business-led organizations, civic federations, coalitions, and alliances also promote discussion of regional issues in many areas. Citizens' planning and zoning groups, for example, commonly sponsor regionwide discussions of current development issues. These educational efforts often pay off by enlarging the constituency for regional action.

Lessons for Regional Growth Management

The various organizational models and experiences in regional management of growth described above provide some general themes to guide regional efforts.

- Identify and build a broad *constituency of interests* for regional action. This is admittedly a tough job but one absolutely necessary for overcoming current obstacles to regional cooperation.
- Focus on a *clear objective* for which a persuasive case for regional action can be made. Successful regional agencies have been created to preserve highly valued environmental features or to solve specific, grave regionwide problems, such as water pollution. Regional agencies are accepted more readily if they control key components of the development process; multipurpose "regional governments" are beyond the pale and do not exist.[12]
- Recognize that effective regional strategic planning and implementation depend on the capability of saying "no" to individual local proposals, if necessary. The power to override local governments realistically comes only from *state and federal authority* for regional action, rather than from voluntary local assent to regional decisions.
- Establish procedures to make *local governments accountable to regional interests,* such as requiring the conformity of local plans to regional objectives. Accountability requires *auditing or monitoring* local plans and regulations and providing an *enforcement process.*

- Share decision-making responsibilities in such a way that *local governments retain major responsibilities* for development policies and regulations and for day-to-day development decisions. The alternative is the almost certain rejection of regional governance.

State Growth Management

As the first edition of this book was being written, eight states had enacted statutes that established comprehensive statewide procedures for managing growth. In general, the laws went beyond the states' planning, enabling statutes to require or provide incentives for local governments to plan and zone according to listed planning goals or principles. The new acts also provided for some degree of state oversight of local growth management programs. By 2006, three states—Oregon, Florida, and Rhode Island—had administered such comprehensive programs for almost three decades. Five other states—Vermont, Maine, New Jersey, Georgia, and Washington—have administered comprehensive laws similar to the earlier statutes for a decade or two.

But the enactment in 1998 of Maryland's Smart Growth program and Tennessee's Growth Policy Act broke the mold—Maryland by tying state infrastructure spending to locally designated growth areas and Tennessee by requiring city-county definition of growth areas as the basis for annexation programs. These variations on the previous state comprehensive programs set the stage for a surge in state actions to better control community development. It has been calculated that from 1999 through 2001, according to one reckoning, seventeen governors issued nine executive orders on planning and smart growth and eight states issued legislative task force reports on these topics.[13] As of 2007, more than a dozen states require local governments to plan according to explicit goals for managing growth and another dozen are providing various types of incentives and encouragement for improving local governments' guidance of development. All in all, state growth management programs illustrate a wide spectrum of approaches to state leadership and intergovernmental coordination in managing urban development.[14]

State Planning: A Long, Arduous Road

States have been practicing some form of growth management since the early twentieth century when, in 1915, Massachusetts prepared a general outline of a state conservation plan. In the 1920s and 1930s, states began establishing state-level planning offices in response to conservation and economic development concerns. At the urging of the National Planning

Board appointed by President Roosevelt, forty-seven states had formed permanent state planning boards by 1938. Although federal funding disappeared with the outbreak of World War II, causing the dismantling of two thirds of the state planning agencies, state planning was revived by the Housing Act of 1954, which provided funding for state planning, especially to help channel federal program funds to local governments. In the 1970s, the Nixon administration's emphasis on "New Federalism" reduced federal funding for state programs, which instigated widespread reorganization of state governments and frequently relegated state planning functions to "back-office" status in other agencies.[15]

Also in the early 1970s, however, at roughly the same time that Petaluma, Ramapo, and Boulder were pioneering local growth management concepts (see chapter 2), several states moved to strengthen public controls over development. Their actions were prompted in part by proposals for state planning in the Model Land Development Code then being prepared for the American Law Institute by the nation's top land use attorneys. The code provided for state involvement in planning for areas of critical state concern (such as sensitive natural areas) and for state oversight of planning by local governments. These concepts were highlighted in an influential book by Fred Bosselman and David Callies, *The Quiet Revolution in Land Use Control*, which claimed urgent needs "to provide some degree of state or regional participation in the major decisions that affect the use of our increasingly limited supply of land."[16]

Indeed, in 1970, just a year before the book's publication, Vermont's Act 250 was enacted in response to rampant resort development and land speculation that sent land prices soaring and threatened the state's bucolic environment. The act required state permits for most sizeable developments and established district environmental commissions to determine whether proposed projects satisfied ten criteria stated in the law. For more than thirty-five years, the commissions' deliberations have formed a political flash point for controversial projects. Although generally the commissions have approved rather than refused projects, increasingly they have attached rigorous conditions to mitigate development impacts. Since the mid-1990s, the commissions have been intensely involved in conflicts over proposals for development of Wal-Mart and similar stores in small Vermont towns. In some cases, the commissions have required substantial revisions in site designs, and in one or two cases they have denied an application because of its probable impact on the town's economy. (A later statute, Act 200, described below, expanded Vermont's state requirements to include local and regional planning according to state goals.)

California also got an early start in state growth management. As early as 1955, it required local governments to plan according to state policies, although state enforcement of the requirements was largely ineffectual. California's big step came when legislation in 1972 imposed strict restrictions on the use of coastal lands. Regional commissions were constituted to work with local governments to conform local plans to state criteria. Although the criteria were not formally adopted for many years, the commissions reviewed and required changes in major projects, generating extensive controversy among local governments and developers. It was the California Coastal Commission, for example, that issued the requirement for public beachfront access across Patrick Nollan's property, a decision reversed by the U.S. Supreme Court in *Nollan v. California Coastal Commission* (cited in box 1.4 in chapter 1). To this day, California's requirements for local planning, while quite strict on the printed page, are hobbled by inconsistent state oversight amid a development climate constantly in legal and economic turmoil.

As California established its coastal program, Florida initiated a series of land and water management acts that required regional and state approval of "developments of regional impact" and encouraged the formulation of plans in areas of critical state concern. These acts were followed by the 1975 Comprehensive Planning Act, which required all local governments to engage in comprehensive planning. Later, in 1974, Colorado adopted a limited statewide planning act that soon met political resistance that led to its demise, and North Carolina approved legislation restricting development in twenty coastal-area counties that is still on the books but may be faltering in execution.

These early state programs suggested some new approaches to managing growth and helped set the stage for the initiation of comprehensive state growth management acts. Beginning with Oregon's legislation in 1973, eight states adopted comprehensive acts through the early 1990s, when an economic recession swept the nation and reduced enthusiasm for restricting development at any level of government. Then the 1998 growth management acts in Maryland and Tennessee began another series of state initiatives quite different in scope and effect than the comprehensive acts. The earlier comprehensive acts, however, established an influential model that remains a significant guide to state involvement in managing growth.

Comprehensive State Acts

Oregon's law established a Land Conservation and Development Commission, whose first task was to adopt state goals and guidelines for development to which local governments' plans must conform. Later, the commission would preside over reviews and approvals of those plans, unlike the situation in Florida, where the state had no mechanism for enforcing the 1975 requirements for local planning. In 1978, Rhode Island consolidated a number of previous actions into a statewide planning program that required local planning and adoption of a state land use plan. A flurry of state enactments followed:

- Florida led the way in 1985 by strengthening its local planning requirements and engaging in state-level planning.
- In 1986, New Jersey created a state planning commission to formulate a state development and redevelopment plan to which local plans would be made to conform through a "cross-acceptance" negotiation process.
- The states of Maine, Vermont, and Rhode Island enacted new legislation in 1988 requiring local governments to adopt plans consistent with state planning goals. Maine and Vermont also gave regional councils responsibility for reviewing and commenting on local plans.
- Georgia adopted a complicated law in 1989 calling for multitiered planning similar in some respects to Florida's program.
- Washington followed suit in 1990 (expanding the law in 1991) with a statute similar in many ways to other states'.

Although the momentum of new state growth management acts waned in the wake of the real estate downturn of the late 1980s through the early 1990s, the eight state acts promote planning at state, regional, and local levels of government and encourage consistency and coordination between the resulting plans. Frequently, the statutes also require preparation of plans by regional and state agencies. Most mandate consistency between local plans and development regulations. In essence, the states fundamentally reconfigured state-local relationships for dealing with urban development issues by emphasizing the state's interest in responsible planning for growth.

State officials and growth management supporters in all eight states understood the importance of retaining a significant role for local governments in growth management. The various statutes reflect that concern: provisions typically express the principle of maintaining local control over day-to-day decisions. Maine's law, for example, finds that "the most effective land use planning can only occur at the local level of government and comprehensive plans and land use ordinances developed and implemented at the local level are the key in planning for Maine's future."[17] But the state statutes also assert that states have legitimate statewide interests that justify some oversight of local actions.

Six types of intergovernmental planning responsibilities may be discerned in the statutes: state plans, state agency planning and coordination, requirements for local planning, provisions for regional coordination, processes for achieving consistency between local and agency plans and state goals, and appeals or conflict resolution procedures.

State Plans: Goal Statements and Mapped Plans

The eight comprehensive acts incorporate or provide for preparation of statewide plans to express state interests in growth and development. In every state except New Jersey and Rhode Island, the plans are expressed as statements of goals and policies to guide planning activities throughout the state. State goal and policy statements define state interests that must be addressed by plans and regulations of local governments, regional agencies, and state agencies. For example, Oregon's 1973 act contained fourteen goal statements, later expanded to nineteen by the addition of five coastal management goals. Two goals refer to citizen involvement and the planning process to be followed by local governments; regional, state, and federal agencies; and special districts. Six deal with environmental concerns and six with development issues. The goals are spelled out in some detail and include both mandatory and suggested implementation policies—for example, the agricultural lands goal that calls for preserving and maintaining agricultural lands cites criteria for determining the appropriateness of converting such lands and guidelines for separating urban from agricultural uses.[18]

Although Florida's Comprehensive Planning Act of 1972 required the formulation of a state comprehensive plan, little progress was made until new legislation in 1984 mandated preparation of a draft plan by December 1, 1984.[19] The plan that the legislature rewrote and adopted in 1985 is an extensive statement of goals, each with multiple policies, covering twenty-five topic areas.[20] In contrast, Maryland's 1992 statute incorporates seven quite general "visions" as the state's overall growth policies to be implemented by local plans. A backlash to Vermont's 1988 Act 200 resulted in Vermont's 1990 legislature reducing the original thirty-two goals to twelve and rewriting them to weaken their authority.[21]

Several states have attempted to go beyond policy statements to geographic applications of urban growth policies, similar in concept to local comprehensive plans. Hawaii's 1961 plan designated urban, agricultural, and conservation areas (a rural area was later added) that placed the state in the role of directly controlling the location of urban development.

Vermont's Act 250, adopted in 1970, required the adoption of a state plan in three phases over one year. The first phase of the plan contained general policies and a map of land capabilities for certain uses, such as agriculture. The second phase depicted land capabilities in more detail, and the third-phase plan, which began in some people's eyes to look like state zoning, was emphatically rejected and the Act 250 provision pertaining to plan preparation was repealed.[22] New York attempted to craft a geographically defined state plan in the mid-1970s but encountered a highly resistant legislature, which killed the plan and dismantled the state planning office.

State plans in New Jersey and Rhode Island list goals and policies but have incorporated maps depicting geographic locations in which the planning policies are applied. Rhode Island's Comprehensive Planning and Land Use Regulation Act of 1988 establishes eleven general goals "to provide overall direction and consistency for state and municipal agencies in the comprehensive planning process." The State Land Use Policies and Plan, "Land Use 2010," published in 1989, however, expands on those goals with explanatory discussions and adds a statement of policies in seven categories (e.g., "Housing"). The plan includes a computer-generated land capability map identifying four categories of land use intensity, from high-intensity development potential to positive conservation potential. The map is to be used by cities and towns in determining allocations of land for development and conservation.[23]

New Jersey's State Development and Redevelopment Plan, adopted in 1992, is unique among state growth management programs. The State Planning Act, adopted by the legislature in 1985 and signed by the governor in 1986, provided a short list of general goals but also required preparation of a state plan that would "identify areas for growth, agriculture, open space conservation, and other appropriate designations."[24] Adopted after lengthy and contentious negotiations, the plan expands the general goals into dozens of more definitive policies and blends state and local plans into a statewide map depicting growth centers and preservation areas. Applications of policies to geographic areas were further detailed through continuing discussions between local governments and state agencies that led to formal delineations of growth centers.[25]

In subsequent years, the plan maps have been revised as state-local agreements about changes in land use patterns are negotiated. The extent of urbanization and existing planning in New Jersey possibly explains the appropriateness of this approach. Oregon, for example, although it requires local governments to define urban, agricultural, and forest areas around urban centers, has not moved in more than thirty years of administering the statute to consolidate these mapped areas into anything resembling a statewide plan.

State Agency Planning and Coordination

Many local government officials would like to see state agencies spend more time planning and coordinating their own programs than prodding local governments to plan. State agencies are notoriously independent and reluctant to act cooperatively with one another other or with local governments. John DeGrove, the dean of state growth managers, has observed that "the notion that state agencies will actually move in the direction of coordinated behavior to further a clear and well-understood set of state goals and policies is no less than revolutionary."[26] Yet most state growth management statutes promise just that. Vermont's Act 200 is typical: "State agencies that have programs or take actions affecting land use . . . shall engage in a continuing planning process to assure those programs are consistent with [state] goals . . . and compatible with regional and approved municipal plans."[27]

Vermont is one of the few states that have actually responded to this mandate. After two years of discussions, Vermont's agencies pulled together a draft agreement for interagency cooperation and coordination. Plans were adopted for seventeen agencies and departments, but changes in administration and agency personnel over the years made continued coordination difficult to sustain. In 2001, Governor Howard Dean strengthened interagency coordination by his executive order establishing a Governor's Development Cabinet to support a new initiative regarding conservation around interstate highway interchanges.[28]

Oregon's law empowers the Land Conservation and Development Commission to coordinate state agency planning with local plans and state goals. DeGrove reported in 1984 that the commission was making some progress but observed that it had to move cautiously to avoid the appearance of becoming a superagency.[29] In the mid-1980s, the commission stepped up efforts to secure interagency coordinating agreements, revising rules to incorporate periodic reviews and conflict resolution procedures. By 1990, the plans of twenty agencies had been certified as consistent with local plans and state goals.[30]

Shortly thereafter, the Oregon Department of Transportation developed a transportation rule in concert with the Land Conservation and Development Commission that laid out a ten-point program for coordinating transportation improvements with land use planning at state and local levels of planning. By the late 1990s, however, state agencies were increasingly focused on the growing opposition to Oregon's constraints on land development, which eventually led to the Measure 37 statewide vote in 2004, which severely undercut the planning and zoning process throughout the state.

In general, state agencies have been slow to respond to directives to prepare functional plans and coordinate them with other agencies and with state goals. Florida established a process for accomplishing this through a 1991 interagency agreement, but DeGrove comments that the variety of agency missions and constituencies, a hostile legislature, and weak oversight by the Office of Management and Budget diluted the collaborative effort.[31] In New Jersey, because the state plan relies on state agencies to implement many of its provisions, the Office of State Planning has worked hard to establish interagency ties, with some success. Then-governor Parris Glendening of Maryland emphasized the importance of his Smart Growth program by establishing the Governor's Office of Smart Growth, headed by a special secretary for smart growth and guided by a "subcabinet" group of agency representatives. Governor Glendening also issued an executive order requiring the cooperation of state agencies in implementing smart growth policies. Although, given changing administrations, coordinating state agency planning is an uphill endeavor, the concept continues to promise a more effective state role in managing growth.

Requirements for Local Planning

The most visible and significant accomplishment of state growth management acts is their encouragement for local governmental planning and plan implementation in a responsible manner. The state growth management statutes have moved the states involved from simply authorizing local government planning and regulation of future development to mandating or providing incentives for local government planning according to defined standards of purpose and content, and for plan implementation through consistent regulatory programs.

The Oregon model—also employed in general terms by Florida, Rhode Island, Maine, Washington, Maryland, Tennessee, and Wisconsin—requires local governments to prepare or revise comprehensive plans to conform to state goals and to state requirements for plan elements. (Washington requires counties over a certain population threshold, and cities within them, to plan; others may volunteer to plan. Tennessee requires counties to plan in cooperation with municipalities.) In Vermont, Georgia, and New Jersey, planning by local governments is voluntary, although in each case the act provides incentives to encourage planning. Vermont's and Georgia's statutes also provide that local governments who decide to plan must satisfy the act's planning requirements.

Typically, the state statutes spell out the required or recommended elements of local comprehensive plans. For example, Rhode Island's statute provides that the local comprehensive plans "shall be a statement (in text, maps, illustrations or other media of communication) that is designed to provide a basis for rational decision-making regarding the long-term physical development of the municipality."[32] It should include a statement of goals and policies consistent with the state guide plan and should incorporate elements for land use, housing, economic development, natural and cultural resources, services and facilities, open space and recreation, and circulation. Rhode Island also mandates that an implementation program be prepared, including a capital improvement program and other public actions needed to carry out the plan.

Securing the cooperation of local governments in meeting these requirements has been difficult and time-consuming. Oregon's program was administered for twelve years before all cities and counties had completed state-approved plans. Florida's approval process dragged on for more than eight years after the statute was enacted. In Maine, enforcement of the requirement is essentially on hold because of the lack of state funds to assist in planning. In the meantime, in Maine and the other states, some local governments have refused to plan at all or have refused to plan according to state officials' interpretation of state goals and objectives and have gone to court and to the electorate to assert their independence of these requirements.

The local comprehensive plans produced through state programs have come under criticism. Charles Siemon observed that the shortage of funding and brief time frames allotted to local planning in Florida "led to the use of 'cookbook' approaches and other short cuts that are antithetical to rational, comprehensive planning."[33] He noted that in the rush to comply with statutory deadlines, many policy decisions were simply postponed to the regulatory phase. Undoubtedly, this problem also appeared in other states. Certainly in Washington, which established a timetable for plan submissions and required counties and cities to agree on designation of urban growth areas within that period, the initial plans of many local governments were truncated and imprecise. The second and third rounds of required plans produced more complete versions. In Tennessee, many counties solved political battles over designating growth areas by drawing huge areas unrelated to fiscal reality or logical planning, a problem that the state has little power to influence.

Have the state requirements resulted in more planning by local governments? Certainly. More public officials have been introduced to planning concepts, and more have been pressed to use them in their regulatory programs and for other decision making on urban development issues. The state requirements can be and have been used as leverage by citizens and interest groups to curb planning abuses, either through appeals procedures or in the courts. Have the requirements produced better plans? Possibly, although the jury is still out in most states. State requirements clearly have set new standards for planning content and procedures. But state planning offices often review local plans full of "correct" language but empty policies unsupported by specific implementation actions. Whether the requirements stimulate a better quality of development—the bottom line—is discussed in the final section of this chapter.

The Regional Role in Planning

States also defined a regional role in growth management systems. Regional agencies were required to plan and to coordinate local plans in Florida, Vermont, and Georgia. In those states, regional agencies also review developments of regional impact, linking them more directly with the development process.[34] In addition, Maine's regional councils are required to comment on plans of local governments within their areas. New Jersey's statute requires counties to coordinate local plans and to participate in negotiating the compatibility of local plans with state plans. Although Washington's statute does not specify county coordination of local plans, it does require counties to delineate urban growth areas in consultation with cities, as well as natural resource lands, critical areas, and open space corridors, driving many counties to prepare their own comprehensive plans.

The effectiveness of regional agencies in reviewing plans is mixed. Vermont's Act 250 called for regional agencies to provide testimony before the environmental boards on projects determined to be regionally significant. The regional agencies also prepare regional plans that require collaboration with local governments. But Act 250's authority to review local plans for conformance to state goals was postponed indefinitely at the insistence of local governments. Florida gave regional agencies important responsibilities to prepare regional plans that would guide local planning and to review Developments of Regional Impact prior to state approval of such projects. But many councils were ineffective, and others were viewed as overly aggressive in pursuing their mandates, stimulating calls for their abolition. Nevertheless, the state recognized the valuable role of regional agencies in reaching collaborative understandings with other regional agencies, such as the powerful water management districts, allowing the regional planning agencies to survive Florida's periodic attempts to reduce or eliminate their powers, even through Governor Bush administration's attempts to whittle down state leadership in growth management.

New Jersey has taken a different approach to addressing regional concerns; it has created separate agencies in the Hackensack Meadowlands, the Pinelands, and most recently the Highlands area of northeastern New Jersey, granting each substantial powers to plan and carry out development and conservation.

Enforcing Consistency: The Intergovernmental Challenge

One measure of the success of state growth management programs is their effectiveness at achieving consistency of local, regional, and state agency plans with state goals. The eight states with comprehensive programs set up review processes to encourage consistency among levels of government, compatibility among plans of adjoining jurisdictions, and consistency between plans and implementing programs and regulations within jurisdictions—procedures that provide the ultimate test of intergovernmental relationships in growth management.

State agencies in all of the states except Vermont review local plans for consistency with state goals. (Vermont reviews only the housing element for consistency with affordable housing policies.) Oregon, Florida, Georgia, Rhode Island, and Maine retain ultimate authority to approve local plans. Washington reviews and comments on plans.[35] New Jersey negotiated agreements with individual local governments to reach some level of consistency between local plans and the state plan. In Florida and Georgia, regional agencies also review and approve local plans for consistency with regional plans and state goals.

State differences in review approaches and consistency requirements have led to characterizing some states as "bottom up" and others as "top down." In "bottom up" states (including, by most accounts, Vermont, Georgia, Rhode Island, Maine, and Washington), state or regional reviewing agencies have relatively little leverage to determine the substance of local plans. In "top down" states, including Florida, New Jersey, and Oregon, state planning agencies have exerted a considerable amount of leadership in determining the appropriate strategies and policies in local plans.

Florida's Department of Community Affairs and Oregon's Land Conservation and Development Commission, the administering agencies for the respective state growth management programs, retain ultimate approval authority over local plans. Both agencies have aggressively interpreted applications of state goals to local plans. For example, they have turned back plans that permitted densities deemed too low to satisfy the goal of compact development. New Jersey's Office of State Planning, although it negotiates agreements with local governments for compliance with state goals and policies, still retains strong influence over the ways that future state actions may be used to encourage greater compliance—such as future state actions to officially designate growth centers depicted on local plans.

Maryland's status in the review process appears ambivalent. The state planning office can only comment on local plan compliance with state goals, including smart growth requirements. But state agencies cannot provide state funding (except under "extraordinary circumstances") for any projects that are not consistent with state goals or local plans, a significant pressure point. The sanction written into Maryland's law is echoed in other state statutes, all of which may deny eligibility for various state grants to local governments whose plans are not brought into conformance with state goals. Florida, for example, may suspend recreation and state revenue-sharing grants as well as federally funded community development grants. Some states allow communities to impose impact fees only if they have achieved compliance. Both Florida and Rhode Island provide for state preparation of comprehensive plans if local governments fail to prepare them. In Maine, recalcitrant municipalities may find their zoning ordinance invalid. Thus far, state agencies have imposed penalties very sparingly for failure to comply with state mandates. Generally, states have been more interested in negotiating agreements with local governments for increased levels of compliance than in issuing politically embarrassing sanctions.

Appeals and Conflict Resolution

State planning review processes frequently have created animosities between state and local officials. Most state statutes foresaw this and provided procedures to negotiate agreements or appeal to higher authorities, which have proved a boon for the participants as well as attorneys. The earlier acts tended to set up administrative procedures that include litigation; the later statutes emphasize conflict resolution techniques.

The 1973 statute in Oregon established a Land Use Board of Appeals with three judges who decide nothing but land use cases. Their decisions may be appealed to state courts. Rhode Island has a similar process. Florida set up an elaborate system that allows regional bodies to mediate local conflicts, provides hearing officers at the state agency level, and establishes final authority in the governor and cabinet sitting as an appeals board. The 1988 act in Georgia, by contrast, directs the state Department of Community Affairs to establish a mediation or other conflict resolution process for resolving state, regional, and local differences over plans. The

1990 Washington statute set up three hearings boards to address disputes over delineating urban growth areas and other matters.

The appeals procedures have been heavily used. Oregon communities frequently challenge state decisions that reject local plans for noncompliance with state goals. The procedures are also used by landowners and developers aggrieved by local planning decisions and by 1000 Friends of Oregon, a watchdog organization that monitors local, state, and private actions and often chooses to enter the fray. Florida's appeals process also has heard many objections to state decisions on plan reviews, not least of which are citizen complaints about specific aspects of local plans. Vermont's Act 250 process of reviewing proposals for developments of substantial size begin with three-member District Environmental Commissions, whose decisions may be appealed to a state Environmental Court (established in 2005). The appeals processes are given credit for providing a pressure release valve for disagreements with state, regional, and local decisions. They are equally valuable for helping to establish more specific interpretations of state goals.

State Requirements for Specific Growth Management Techniques

All of the state growth management acts include strictures to prevent urban sprawl, protect rural and natural areas from undesirable development, and develop efficient systems of public facilities and services to support anticipated growth and economic development. In many cases, the statutes have promoted these goals by directing local governments and regional agencies to adopt specific growth management techniques. The most common requirements are for designation of urban growth boundaries or areas to promote compact development and protect rural areas, adoption of infrastructure programs and financing approaches to support development, and special provisions for dealing with large-scale development and critical areas.

Urban and Rural Demarcation

Since 1973, when Oregon required all cities to define urban growth boundaries to contain urban development and to conserve natural resource areas, several other states have required or promoted similar provisions. New Jersey calls for urban development to occur within compact centers designated on local and state plans. Maine requires municipalities to identify and designate growth areas and rural areas. Washington and Tennessee require counties to designate urban growth areas, and Washington requires counties and cities to designate natural resource lands and critical areas.

Other state statutes include goals that, while less specific, encourage the demarcation of urban lands from rural lands. Maryland provides that local plans and regulations must implement goals to concentrate development in suitable areas and protect sensitive lands. Florida's state goals contain multiple statements that discourage the proliferation of urban sprawl, on which the Department of Community Affairs has based its policy— enforced through a rule—to insist that local plans promote compact patterns of development. The department has encouraged local governments to consider adopting such mechanisms as urban growth boundaries and urban service limits.[36]

Securing local compliance with these requirements has been difficult. As described in chapter 4, market forces and citizen attitudes still favor low-density development; single-family, detached homes and reliance on automobiles remain prime objectives of many Americans. Translated through the political process to local plans and regulations, these attitudes appear almost intractable.

Oregon's and Washington's experience is telling. Although all municipalities adopted urban growth boundaries as required by the state statute, much development still takes place outside them. Widespread development on Oregon's "exception" lands (deemed unsuitable for agriculture or forestry) and waivers by local governments have undermined the state's policy. In addition, in both Oregon and Florida, development within urban growth boundaries has tended to result in lower densities than would be appropriate to achieve compact growth. Plans and regulations may permit higher densities, but developers often choose to finesse local residents' opposition by proposing lower-density development. Only in Portland, which has adopted special rules to promote higher-density housing, including minimum-density provisions, have densities increased.

The upshot is that state goals and inducements to encourage compact development and preserve rural areas have been only partially successful in the face of countervailing market and political forces.

Infrastructure Planning and Financing

Another purpose of most state growth management acts is to get a grip on infrastructure needs and costs, which in many areas appear to be totally out of control. State statutes refer to the inefficiencies of extending public facilities to serve sprawl development, the advantages of promoting better use of existing facilities, and the need to provide adequate capacities of facilities in step with development. The New Jersey state plan expresses the policy in this way: "The essential element of statewide policies for infrastructure investment is to provide infrastructure and related services more efficiently by restoring systems in distressed areas, maintaining existing infrastructure investments, creating more compact settlement patterns . . . and timing and sequencing the maintenance of capital facilities service levels with development throughout the state."[37]

At least four approaches to achieving these goals have been incorporated into state acts: (1) encouraging more attention to capital facilities programs; (2) requiring "concurrency" of facility capacities with development; and (3) linking infrastructure funding sources, including impact fees, to plans that conform to state goals.

Most state statutes have prompted local governments to strengthen the connections between comprehensive plans and capital improvement programs, emphasizing the need to formulate realistic implementation efforts. Rhode Island's statute, for example, requires an implementation program as part of the requirements for local comprehensive plans, including the definition and scheduling of "expansion or replacement of public facilities and the anticipated costs and revenue sources proposed to meet those costs."[38] Similar requirements are found in all other state acts except Georgia's and Maryland's, although Maryland's statute requires that funding to achieve state goals must be addressed. (Maryland's financing incentives are enhanced by the 1998 smart growth law described in the next section.)

Perhaps the best-known state requirements that connect public facilities to development plans are the "concurrency" provisions of the Florida and Washington statutes. Although many local governments have enacted provisions making development approvals contingent on the availability of adequate facilities, Florida raised the requirement to the state level by providing that no local government can issue a development permit unless adequate public facilities are available to serve it. Unfortunately, Florida did so at a time when state highways were demonstrably lacking in capacity and when the state was unprepared to fund improvements to make up deficiencies. The results (as described in chapter 5) have been major controversies over the concurrency requirement, numerous law journal articles on the subject, and highly imaginative calculations of levels of service to avoid development moratoriums. Also, in 1992 and 1993, Florida authorized local governments to designate exceptions to the concurrency law for urban infill and redevelopment in already developed areas, projects promoting public transportation, "part-time" developments such as stadiums, and areas for which long-term plans provide for correction of existing deficiencies.

Facility funding is another point of leverage used by some states to secure compliance with state goals. Maryland's requirement that projects receiving state funds be consistent with approved plans and state goals has already been referenced. But other states threaten to withhold various types of state funding if local plans remain out of compliance with state goals. New Jersey's plan, for example, suggests that state funding of capital projects depend in part on adherence by local governments to state goals.[39] Thus far, however, it does not appear that any states have actually withdrawn funding for this reason.

On a more positive note, several states permit local governments that secure approval for local plans to levy impact fees, and Washington allows local governments to levy an excise tax on real estate transfers to help fund capital improvements.

Large-scale Development and Critical Area Concerns

As noted in the earlier section on regional roles in state growth management, several state statutes pay special attention to large-scale developments. Vermont's Act 250 is focused directly on such projects. Florida set up special review procedures for developments of regional impact many years ago. Georgia's statute builds on the Atlanta Regional Commission's past experience with reviewing developments of regional impact by giving all regions that responsibility. Washington's act provides for recognition of large-scale resort developments when delineating growth areas. These states value addressing the regional and statewide impacts that major projects may engender.

Similar attention is given to critical natural areas, such as wetlands, aquifer recharge areas, wildlife habitats, and flood plains. Washington required an immediate delineation of critical areas to be followed by recognition of such areas within local comprehensive plans. Maryland's act singles out "sensitive" and critical areas for attention in state and local plans.

The State Role in the "Smart Growth" Era

The concept of smart growth (described in chapter 1), which emerged during the 1990s as a popular theme for guiding development, immediately became a touchstone for additional state laws and programs. The benefits of smart growth principles were espoused by many nongovernmental organizations, including the American Planning Association, which began publishing editions of the *Growing Smart Legislative Guidebook* in 1996. The *Guidebook* compiled and recommended model state planning statutes, with two chapters focused on programs such as those adopted in Oregon and Florida.

However, the Maryland statute adopted in 1998 sparked the particular interest of many states in promoting the ideals of smart growth. It provided for fiscal and other incentives to focus development in designated areas, including infill and brownfield sites, and to conserve open lands. Although many of Maryland's cities and counties had a solid, long-term record of managing growth, concerns about pollution levels in the Chesapeake Bay and the spread of low-density development around the Washington metropolitan area engendered support for tougher state intervention in the development process. A 1992 Maryland law encouraging local adherence to seven "visions" for the state was viewed as ineffective, and support grew for greater state control of development.

The legislation signed into law by then-governor Parris Glendening in 1998 employed the simple notion that the state should direct its investments in roads, schools, and other infrastructure to areas designated for growth. Such areas, termed *priority funding areas*, would be defined by local jurisdictions according to criteria in the legislation. Although cities and counties could choose to allow development in rural and lightly populated areas, state monies would not be available to pay for infrastructure to support that development.

Putting state powers of the purse to work in favoring development within urban and urbanizing areas became a mantra for other states. Many such programs have been initiated by executive orders of the governors. For example, Massachusetts governor Paul Cellucci issued Executive Order 385 in 1996 (predating the Maryland law) to manage state-sponsored development and resource protection. The order primarily addresses infrastructure spending, urging agencies to give preference to assisting infrastructure improvements in previously developed sites and areas. In 2001, Governor Ruth Ann Minner of Delaware issued Executive Order 14, directing state agencies to implement policies created in the former administration to determine how and where the state will focus its financial resources for new and expanded infrastructure. Governor Jeanne Shaheen of New Hampshire issued an executive order in 2002 endorsing a list of smart growth principles to be used by state agencies in making decisions about expending state or federal funds or providing advice for public works, transportation, or major capital improvements projects.

Maryland's program has been fairly successful in redirecting state capital facility funding to promote improvements within designated growth areas, including urbanized areas. For example, the state approved funding for construction of a community college only after the college's proposed location was moved from outside the city of Hagerstown to downtown; several proposals for state highway bypasses have been modified to favor improvements of existing roads. However, problems have arisen when local governments have disregarded criteria for establishing priority funding areas, and more than one county has chosen to approve "nonsmart" growth locations in rural areas that required little or no state infrastructure funding. Furthermore, with a change in governors in 2002, the program's administration has been considerably more lenient than the previous administration in determining state-funded facility locations.

Another focus of smart growth programs is conserving green space, which has attracted major attention by states in recent years. Along with the Smart Growth statute, Maryland also enacted a Rural Legacy program to add fiscal muscle to its already strong conservation programs. The program was especially notable for its requirement for interjurisdictional planning and land acquisition to conserve connected natural systems. Pennsylvania, a state that has stoutly resisted strengthening its local planning laws to manage growth, has authorized $1.8 billion in funding since 1999 for programs packaged by three consecutive governors as "Growing Greener," "Growing Smarter," and "Growing Greener II." The funds go to communities for acquiring parklands and conservation areas of many kinds. In 2003, New Jersey announced new priorities in its "Green Acres" open space acquisition program that more strongly emphasize funding recreational lands and parks in cities and older, densely developed suburban communities, as well as increased funding for conserving water resources and wildlife habitats.

Another tack taken by many states is to authorize incentives for local governments to improve management of growth. Florida has sponsored several grant programs for communities willing to try out innovative approaches for meeting concurrency requirements, new forms of urban design and design regulations, and affordable housing programs. Vermont initiated a "growth centers" program that provides tax credits and other incentives for communities to steer growth to designated centers, such as downtowns and village centers with existing infrastructure. Wisconsin authorized a "Smart Growth Dividend" that was available beginning in 2005 for local governments that adopt plans meeting state standards (discussed later in this chapter) or that increase compact development and moderately priced housing within their borders; at least two agencies have announced policies to award points to project evaluations for such localities. Many states provide tax credits and other incentives for redevelopment of brownfields and development in infill neighborhoods. Many states also offer special grants to stimulate intergovernmental planning among local jurisdictions.

Meanwhile, two states, Tennessee and Wisconsin, have adopted growth management laws that replicate some of the ideas laid out in the eight "comprehensive" state statutes discussed earlier in this chapter. To the surprise of many planners, Tennessee's General Assembly enacted a Growth Policy Act in 1998. It was initially aimed at correcting uncontrolled annexations that were creating conflicts between cities and counties. Part of the solution to that problem, however, lay in improving local planning and management of growth. The act required cities and counties to collaborate in designating areas for future growth and to plan for providing urban services to those areas prior to annexations. Lacking firm state oversight, however, most Tennessee local governments and cities complied on paper but tended to stake out growth areas unrelated to probable rates of growth and heedless of potential infrastructure costs. Some local governments, chiefly in high-growth areas, have continued to improve their growth management programs, but many lack serious intentions to guide the course of private development.[40]

Wisconsin's Comprehensive Planning Law, which took effect in 2000, was deliberately written to spur local planning while leaving decisions about the use of specific techniques, such as growth boundaries, to local officials. State involvement was limited to requiring all local governments to prepare comprehensive plans with nine defined elements by 2010, ensuring consistency of community actions with local plans, and requiring public participation and notice to adjoining jurisdictions and regional agencies at every step of the planning process. As might be expected, the goals and qualities of the 369 plans submitted to the state by mid-2005 vary tremendously; Tom Larsen, the head of the state Realtors' association commented: "This is a messy process, involving people with many kinds of interests." The state's jurisdictions are learning more about planning, but opponents continue to fight for the law's repeal. Governor Jim Doyle had to veto legislation to abolish the act in 2005.

Nevertheless, many states have taken little or no action to become more responsible for managing growth, and several fast-growing states that appeared to be in the forefront of adopting new programs have stumbled badly. Arizona governor Jane Dee Hull led action in 1998 to pass the Growing Smarter Act, which urged local jurisdictions to consider how and where growth should occur and how to finance it. This rather mild bill led to the Growing Smarter Plus Act in 2000, which required large or fast-growing communities to prepare voter-approved general plans incorporating designated growth areas and ordered municipalities to adopt citizen review processes for rezonings, plus several other provisions. However, in November 2000, voters defeated two high-profile ballot initiatives that would have created a conservation reserve and a constitutional amendment requiring most local governments to adopt urban growth boundaries. Further progress on state encouragement of local growth management has stalled.

Meanwhile, Colorado, thought to be at the forefront of planning reform and smart growth measures at the turn of the century, has held several special legislative sessions, experienced an acrimonious ballot initiative, and entertained numerous legislative proposals that have produced only minor improvements in existing legislation. Development and local interests in North Carolina have successfully opposed anything but minor changes in its planning laws. Across the nation, the wave of interest in smart growth has stimulated countless state-sponsored conferences, commissions, studies, and legislative proposals, but substantive action by states to promote effective growth management has occurred in less than half the states.

The Balance Sheet for State Growth Management

Some two dozen states have embarked on programs for managing future development that establish new relationships among state and local governments and, in some cases, regional agencies. About ten states have gained a substantial amount of experience, while others are still working through initial requirements or focusing on specific aspects of planning. The record thus far shows that the tensions and strains that mark most intergovernmental relationships are not allayed by state growth management activities. Indeed, by forcing recurring confrontations between conflicting state and local interests in managing growth, the state statutes could be said to have increased at least the perception of divisiveness and disagreement. The continuing tensions are evident in state legislative sessions, where proposals for repealing parts or all of the state programs make annual appearances. The state programs also have attracted charges that they engender stultifyingly complex regulations and intractable bureaucracies in addition to misguided development policies.

To the extent that these program "costs" are real and substantial, they should be matched to the real benefits being achieved through the state programs. Whether one agrees that these benefits are without blemish, the programs have accomplished some important objectives.

- The states have succeeded in promoting increased attention to state and regional interests in development issues while retaining significant decision-making roles for local governments in the development process. In all states involved in administering growth management statutes, local governments maintain much autonomy in determining the character of future community development.

- The state programs have stimulated a greater understanding of the planning process among local officials, prodding municipalities, regional agencies, and state agencies to define development trends, identify future needs, and plan and program public actions to meet those needs.
- The state programs have structured a framework for coordinating the growth management efforts of all jurisdictions and levels of government and have encouraged negotiated agreements among them regarding development issues.
- State agencies have been prompted to recognize the programs and plans of other agencies and local governments in their own planning for future projects.
- The private sector has gained certainty and predictability from the state requirements that set standards for local governmental planning, implementation programs, and regulations and that provide procedures for ensuring some degree of consistency among individual jurisdictions.
- The state programs have stimulated a growing recognition that plans must be linked to workable implementation programs and that public guidance of urban development is a long-term process that should be incorporated into every jurisdiction's administrative structure.
- Experience in Oregon, Vermont, and Florida demonstrates that state programs take time to mature and require continual fine-tuning and reevaluation to maintain effective, creative intergovernmental relationships for managing growth and development.
- State programs that promote specific aspects of growth management, such as conservation of green space or infill development, typically promote local planning by requiring that local proposals be consistent with an adopted comprehensive plan.

At the same time, experience with state growth management programs has raised some questions and issues that should be considered in formulating future state programs.

- In general, state programs have not recognized differences in local governments' planning needs or capabilities to respond to state mandates. Although some states, such as Washington and Vermont, have provided for optional participation by some local governments, planning requirements in all programs have failed to distinguish among community size, growth rate, and other characteristics that might affect the nature of local planning. State programs should not assume that "one size fits all."

- State agencies administering growth management statutes have found that statements of state goals and policies require further definition for guiding how consistency between state and local plans is determined. Interpreting broad goals often entails formulating detailed guidelines and administrative rules to guide preparation of plans and plan reviews, requirements that generally were not foreseen in the original statutes.

- The long-term nature of state growth management programs demands continuity of administration in a political arena—state government— that traditionally has been highly changeable. For years, Oregon's and Florida's programs benefited from strong constituent support that helped to maintain staff and budget priorities for growth management programs through several state administrations. In 2007, however, Florida's programs are beset with growing restrictions and an apparent waning of Governor Bush's administration in upholding the goals of the state plan, while Oregon is still trying to recover some semblance of planning continuity after the voter approval and court ratification of Measure 37, which emasculates local zoning powers. In both cases, the foundations of state planning initiatives once firmly emplaced are eroding. Also, many state programs, notably in Maine and Vermont, have been severely affected by national and state economic recessions that affected grant-making and staffing.

- Several states, having mandated more planning or specific mechanisms for managing growth, have provided inadequate financial assistance for local governments to meet requirements. Florida's example of requiring concurrency but not providing adequate funding to correct state highway deficiencies remains a sore point in its intergovernmental relations.

- Some evaluations of Oregon and Florida programs suggest that their focus on establishing procedures for planning according to state goals has succeeded overall but that results "on the ground" have fallen short of desired objectives for urban development and protection of open spaces, natural resources, and environmentally sensitive lands. In the future, state programs may consider becoming more involved in setting minimum development standards (such as the minimum-density provisions adopted in Portland, Oregon) to be incorporated in local plans.

Regional and state growth management is in a revolutionary but also evolutionary stage—revolutionary in establishing new administrative frameworks for managing development; evolutionary in adapting to circumstances and issues that arise during program administration. Experience over time confirms that such programs are suspended not in equilibrium but in a political sea of forces that can unite or divide public interests in urban development.[41]

CHAPTER 9

Deciding How
to Manage Growth

State governments and regional agencies may influence local governments' choices for managing growth and development (as described in the previous chapter), but local governments still figure prominently in determining how communities manage future growth and development. Their state-given authority for planning and regulating development is a powerful tool. Some local public officials may dodge the responsibility for guiding growth in favor of giving private market forces free rein. Others may clamp down on growth in ways that stifle opportunities for creative forms of development. Local governments also may blame state restrictions for hobbling the range of regulatory techniques available, or they may cite political opposition to expanding public controls over growth. But in every state and region, local public officials possess significant powers to determine the course of community development—if they choose to employ them.

Every state gives local governments powers to prepare comprehensive plans for future growth and to impose zoning and subdivision regulations to implement such plans. Plans, zoning, and subdivision requirements can embody many, if not most, of the growth management techniques that this book describes. For example, comprehensive plans can designate urban growth areas, zoning can spell out the desired types of development within growth areas, and subdivision regulations can specify the required and optional standards for layout and construction of development.

In particular, the state-given powers enable communities to implement the urban design principles espoused by advocates of sustainable development, smart growth, new urbanism, and green building. Typically, for example, local governments have powers to require or promote the development of compact densities and appealing streetscapes in designated areas. Zoning and subdivision regulations can be oriented to encourage specific qualities of site and building designs. Even growth management tools that may appear to require special state authorization, such as impact fees or transferable development rights, can be offered as incentives rather than requirements for specified areas and types of development. To cite an old aphorism: where there's a will, there's a way.

How can public officials acquire the will to prepare and carry out an effective program for managing community growth? This chapter advises that local governments can succeed by maximizing the benefits and minimizing the potential downsides of growth management policies, programs, and regulations. Such a balance is best accomplished by seeking early and frequent participation by citizens and community leaders in decision-making procedures.

Reaching an Equitable Balance in Managing Growth

The pathway to creating a fair and politically acceptable growth management program requires careful footwork. Communities adopt growth management policies and techniques to improve the community development process—to ensure the creation of well-designed neighborhoods and business centers, for example; to provide necessary facilities and services for growing areas; and, overall, to enhance the quality of life for area residents and workers. But growth management techniques can be problematic. Sometimes their use can have unintended and unwanted consequences as well as positive effects. For example, unless carefully crafted, growth management efforts may impose unwise restrictions on development choices that lead to increased development costs.

A prominent theme in considering growth management approaches is finding the right balance between the benefits of publicly guiding the development process and the costs entailed by additional public policies and regulations. Establishing that balance nearly always requires tempering growth management goals to acceptable levels and mitigating or offsetting the resulting costs in time, effort, and materials.

Potential Costs of Growth Management

The advent of growth management programs stirred immediate and lasting criticism that public restrictions on the location of growth and stepped-up requirements and standards raised development costs (an issue explored extensively in chapter 3). In addition, growth management programs have been blamed for skewing patterns of development considered desirable in the marketplace and for increasing the costs of doing business under greater public oversight and more complex regulations. The criticisms, taken individually and without considering the offsetting benefits, have some basis in fact. Growth management programs do affect the development process in ways that can raise the costs of development.

Suppressing Development

Growth limits and moratoriums that limit the amount of development to levels below market demands tend to create artificial shortages and quasi-monopolistic conditions that can boost land prices and thus prices for the finished product. This effect has generated many studies, several by John Landis at the University of California at Berkeley, whose work was cited in chapter 3. His latest findings, published in the Autumn 2006 edition of the *Journal of the American Planning Association*, indicated that "all local regulatory policies, programs, and actions that significantly limit new housing production adversely affect housing prices."[1] Landis counted more than 120 California cities and counties that limit the annual amount of new residential construction. Generally, however, the restrictions lower population growth and housing prices only if the limits are below a jurisdiction's normal share of regional housing development. Restrictions on annexations and requirements for supermajority voter approval of major projects produce similar consequences. Landis found that other kinds of growth management limits, such as growth boundaries, appear to redistribute development from fringe areas into central locations or into nearby communities.

Restricting Land Supply

Several growth management techniques—growth boundaries, designated growth areas, and urban service areas, for example—define certain areas as appropriate for development and restrict it elsewhere. A common rule of thumb (as in Oregon and Washington) is to draw boundaries that allow a twenty-year supply of developable land. However, bureaucratic inertia and political indecision sometimes get in the way of keeping that supply up-to-date, or developers contend that a significant amount of the designated land is unsuitable for development because of topography, wetlands, and so forth. As discussed in chapter 3, a shortage of developable sites in prime market locations inflates land prices and can alter the character of the community—known as the "Boulder effect," in which steep increases in land and housing prices in that highly desirable Colorado city brought smaller and wealthier households to town and drove many families to find affordable housing elsewhere.

Adding to Development Costs

Communities may adopt growth management techniques that shift the costs of some types of infrastructure from public agencies to developers. For example, amendments of subdivision regulations may require developers to build wider streets or install sidewalks or may impose impact fees for off-site parks and highway improvements. Although these measures may be defended as reasonable public requirements, they result in additional costs for development and, when first adopted, can reduce the profitability of projects for which sites have been acquired and designs initiated. Subsequent developments, however, can take such costs into account before major investments in land and design have been undertaken.

Raising Approval Costs

By their very nature, growth management programs tend to enlarge the number of regulatory requirements and steps in the project approval process faced by developers and builders. Some regulatory options and flexible approaches may be intended to provide incentives for desired types of development (such as clustered residential layouts), but they also often entail more elaborate studies, detailed documentation, and multiagency involvement that raise costs. Also, allowing more discretion for official decisions increases opportunities for delays and interventions by various interest groups. The consequences often mean extra expenditures by developers and greater time investments for agency staffs.

Increasing Exclusionary Effects

Communities that adopt growth limits and restrictive development standards, or that limit zoning to only certain types of residential and commercial development, may unintentionally—or intentionally—shut out certain classes of residents and businesses. The most often cited example is a community that raises minimum lot sizes to levels that ensure that new residential development will be affordable only to upper-income households. In 2005, a county outside Atlanta decided to dampen rapid growth by doubling minimum residential lot sizes to 3.6 acres; the tactic substantially slowed down growth but also increased housing prices for new residents—effects perhaps desirable for existing residents but that exclude much of the area's housing market. Local governments pursue similar goals by excluding mobile homes, establishing minimum housing space standards, and adopting onerous zoning procedures for certain types of development.

A Note about Mismanaging Growth

Growth management programs can also fail to achieve their objectives because of glitches or mistakes in program design and administration. Many communities have mismanaged growth by reacting slowly and inadequately to growth pressures or by refusing to tackle the difficult choices they must make to exercise reasonable control over the development process. When decisions are made, public officials may quickly adopt techniques without thoroughly considering administrative requirements, needs for interagency coordination, and potential impacts on the development process.

Some public officials in once-rural settlements and small suburbs find it difficult to picture the character of the community beyond the status quo. They are reluctant to formulate a realistic vision of the future community and are inclined to put aside difficult decisions concerning growth. Furthermore, making long-term policy decisions and adhering to them cramps the style of many elected officials. But by neglecting to engage in strategic planning and management, they miss opportunities to positively guide and support development.

For example, the discussion of Sarasota County's growth management efforts (in chapter 3) described how county commissioners delayed responding to spreading urbanization, hoping that a lack of infrastructure would discourage development. The failure of that strategy—or the lack of one—forced the county into frantic reorganization to deal with crises in infrastructure capacity. Fortunately, the county commissioners did not fall into the trap of crisis management, trying out quick-fix solutions as problems arise. Too often, public officials in growing communities seize on one or two techniques as "the answer" without considering offsetting negative consequences. Over time, they learn that in managing growth there are no easy answers.

It has become popular in some areas, particularly in California, for voters to rebel against growth problems by passing ballot measures that freeze annexations or restrict the amount of allowable growth or prohibit large-scale developments without a special vote by citizens. In a number of places, "supermajority" approval by two thirds or three quarters of the voters is needed to approve such developments. That style of "management" disregards the needs of communities to adapt to changing circumstances and opportunities.

Many communities manage growth through programs that resemble a grab bag of programs and regulations rather than a strategic, comprehensive, and coordinated approach to community development. They add new requirements, bit by bit, without thinking through the relationships with existing regulations. Often, programs offer simple methods to address complex problems and are administered by insufficient staff. No attempts are made to evaluate how the regulations are working. For growth management to work well requires constant attention to changing needs, budgetary support, knowledgeable staff, and the willingness to try out new ideas now and then.

The Benefits of Managing Growth

Despite the difficulties of formulating and administering growth management programs, they can improve the overall character of the built environment and help to achieve important public objectives for economic growth, social advancement, and preservation of natural qualities.

Support for Community Livability

Perhaps the most direct benefit of growth management programs stems from the way wise management encourages better growth. The practice of growth management is intended to anticipate and resolve development issues connected with community growth and change before they degrade a community's quality of life. By providing ways and means to accommodate urban and suburban expansion in a positive manner, growth management programs ensure that community changes are compatible with local values and standards. Done well, growth management heads off and alleviates problems in developing communities by resolving issues as varied as those that arise in building affordable housing, protecting green space, and creating transit-oriented activity centers.

Covering All the Bases—A Holistic Approach

Growth management programs work best when they provide a comprehensive, integrated framework of policies and regulations that acknowledge the complexities of urban and suburban development. Designating growth areas and expanding community green infrastructure systems go hand in hand with revitalizing existing neighborhoods and business centers. Policies to encourage more compact growth are supported by design guidelines and zoning for mixed uses. Programs to expand the supply of affordable housing are coordinated with improved access to transit facilities. Community development goals are compatible with those of bordering communities. Policies and programs are not hatched as individual actions but are crafted as part of an overall strategy for managing growth.

Improving Public Investments in Growth

Growth management programs promote a thoughtful approach to selecting and coordinating public investments that assist development. Public investments in infrastructure systems; in other public facilities, such as museums and convention centers; and in redeveloping and revitalizing declining areas are best guided by firm planning decisions concerning the location and character of community growth, as laid out in comprehensive plans. Plans provide a menu of actions that will require public capital investments in development, and they often indicate priorities for such actions. Annual determinations by public officials about investment needs are incorporated in capital improvement programs, which indicate the timing of investment projects and the sources of required funding to meet development needs defined by plans. Funding sources may include such growth management techniques as impact fees and special financing districts and may be driven by requirements for adequate public facilities in proposed developments. This linking of long-range plans to action programs, including coordinated funding approaches, provides a more predictable, coordinated process for public investments in growth.

Establishing a Predictable Development Process

Growth management reduces both public and private risks in the development process by providing public backing of policies, plans, and programs. Adopting a public policy framework to guide development puts everyone on notice about community needs and public objectives to be achieved as growth and change occur. Developers who orient their projects to accomplishing recognized public objectives limit the risks and costs of doing business. Definitive public policies and regulations also provide measures for evaluating proposed developments. Residents gain the security of knowing what to expect in their neighborhoods. Growth management programs that spell out expectations for the quality, quantity, and location of development thus benefit all stakeholders.

Expanding Economic and Social Opportunities

In an ever-changing economy and society, communities can use growth management programs to widen housing and employment opportunities, maintain the vitality of older neighborhoods and business districts, and improve fiscal and social equities throughout the community. Reaching these important goals can be woven into the strategic aims of growth policies and accomplished through various programmatic initiatives that benefit the entire community.

Balancing Benefits and Costs

Growth management programs must somehow steer a course for community development that achieves a reasonable and equitable balance among competing concerns and objectives. A collaborative planning and decision-making process can help to moderate differences, especially by improving the flow of reliable information and building a sense of trust among citizens throughout the community. In addition, civic participation processes can be particularly useful in defining and evaluating the benefits and costs of specific growth management proposals, such as new comprehensive and neighborhood plans, new subdivision standards, designations of growth areas or urban service areas, additions to conservation areas, and revisions of adequate public facility requirements.

The most common procedure is for agency staffs and consultants to pre-

BOX 9.1

Collaborative Planning and Shared Governance

A New Paradigm for Reconciling Urban Growth and Conservation

Lindell L. Marsh, Attorney/Facilitator, Newport Beach, CA

Decision-making about land use in this nation has been fragmented among landowners and local, state, and federal governments. In the aftermath of World War II, this arrangement worked quite well to promote economic development in the growing nation. It became apparent in the 1960s, however, that exuberant economic growth was fostering environmental impacts on the quality of the nation's air, water, and natural resources. The environmental laws enacted in response in the early 1970s mirrored traditional regulatory approaches, utilizing hierarchical, narrowly focused agencies and quasi-judicial processes.

While the electorate has continued to support environmental protection, the strong reliance on command-and-control measures has been relatively inefficient and, in many cases, inequitable (e.g., habitat preservation costs imposed primarily on new development), resulting in reactive political efforts to roll back regulations. Commencing in the early 1980s, and reflective of the emphasis on cooperation between agencies and interests in the National Environmental Policy Act of 1969, a new and different approach has been emerging to resolve conflicts between development and environmental objectives. It focuses on transcending the boundaries of our project-by-project quasi-judicial permitting, and is epitomized by the habitat conservation planning (HCP) process authorized by the 1982 amendments to the federal Endangered Species Act, as well as the critical areas planning process allowed by Section 380 of the Florida Comprehensive Land and Water Management Act. These approaches encourage the constituency of affected agencies and interests to collaboratively design a plan that reconciles their individual concerns for conserving wildlife and wetlands while allowing development to proceed.

After a slow start, we have seen a blooming of hundreds of conservation planning efforts addressing urban, water, timber, and other development issues

(Continued next page)

pare proposals in preliminary or sketch form, perhaps with suggested options or employing the "what if?" mode of throwing out untested ideas for consideration. Or with sufficient time and effort, several scenarios or alternative plans might be prepared to provide a range of possibilities to open up discussions. These processes offer a way to work out questions and concerns about community growth and change that can satisfy most of the participants involved. They also provide opportunities to test ideas, assess their potential benefits and costs, and determine a reasonable balance among them.

To guide follow-up implementation of growth management policies and techniques, communities—assisted by participatory processes—can take the next step of determining benchmarks or measurable indicators of progress that can periodically assess the effectiveness of growth management programs. Examples are measures of the proportion of development

BOX 9.1

(Continued)

in all parts of the nation. Among major initiatives is the California Natural Community Conservation Planning (NCCP) program that is applying the HCP concept to ecosystems of virtually all of urbanizing Southern California. The promise of such an approach extends in many directions. It overcomes the national's historic institutional fragmentation. It is based on the collaboration of interests and shared leadership. Historically, the stakeholders formulate a plan, a kind of social contract, which reconciles the underlying interests and concerns. The process has much in common with ideas such as "partnering," "public/private partnerships," "horizontal management," and "management by principle" that now pervade our culture.

The breadth of this approach can be expected to contribute to resolving broad growth management issues such as central city/suburban conflicts and regional approaches to economic development. It is currently being explored as a means of addressing the impacts of massive freight movements from the Los Angeles metropolitan area ports through existing urbanized regions to the rest of the nation. A more recent variation on this theme, "shared governance," works through a multi-agency group of "principal conveners" who establish a virtual roundtable of initiatives and assist affected agencies and interests to scope the concerns, issues, and opportunities involved. This approach is being initiated in the examination of goods movement impacts in the Los Angeles region.

For me, the metaphor that best characterizes the evolving notions of collaborative planning and shared governance is traditional American quilt making. Typically a group process, quilt making engages individual creativity to create sections that are then stitched together to reflect broader themes determined through a collective, often facilitated process. This reflects our nation's qualities observed by De Toqueville: fierce individual independence coupled with a willingness to share ideas and responsibilities when necessary. Collaborative planning and shared governance are examples of collaborative processes—stitching together a shared vision—that respects individual creativity.

taking place within designated growth areas, or completion of planned infrastructure extensions, or increases in production of affordable housing units. Some communities report annually on progress in meeting goals; others conduct such assessments as part of updating comprehensive plans. These types of measures allow public officials and the general public to understand how well the community's growth management program is functioning to improve their quality of life.

Civic Participation: The Gateway to Managing Growth

People tend to be suspicious of changes in their community. Fearing the worst, they commonly react to growth as a threat rather than an opportunity. Often, they lack essential information by which they can sort out the potentially good effects of future development from the bad. And until recent years, citizens and civic leaders alike were often kept in the dark about community goals for growth and the benefits they might bring. The result in many communities is controversy over every proposal for development and little attention to the consequences of inadequate preparation for growth. Even projects shaped to reflect a civic consciousness, sensitivity to environmental preservation, and innovative design can be thwarted by opposition to growth in any form.

The omnipresent popularity of the principles of sustainable development, smart growth, new urbanism, and green building promises a breakthrough in understanding how to manage growth. The principles appear to lay out clear policy directions for guiding development and appear to be easily translated into community plans and regulations. However, applying the principles in specific communities and neighborhoods requires much further definition. What is a desirable level of "compact" development? Should every project or neighborhood have a mix of uses, and of what kind? How much and what type of green space should be preserved as the community grows? Although advocates of new urbanism and green building profess to have the answers to these questions, there are no "correct" answers to these issues that can be applied in every locality, only guidelines that must be translated into reasonable goals according to the specific conditions and desires of each community.

However, broad principles set up the need for intense community discussions that can specify the right answer for the right place—yet another reason to involve community residents in decision making about important aspects of future development. After all, public interests in community development demand difficult choices about the benefits and costs of growth and a delicate weighing of offsetting factors. Moreover, growth management approaches have become more complicated as they deal with redevelopment and adaptive reuse in existing neighborhoods and commercial centers in addition to greenfield development.

The experience in Fort Collins, Colorado (described in chapter 1) emphasized how city officials, with intensive involvement by local citizens and community leaders, have worked long and hard to understand growth trends and to adopt a variety of strategies and policies to guide the community toward desired objectives. Whether the process is meant to update a comprehensive plan, define a regional vision, or determine urban design policies, the days of a small group of civic leaders—elected or otherwise—acting alone to fashion a community's future are gone. Instead, elected and planning officials increasingly expect—and state laws frequently require them—to engage the citizenry in thinking through community development issues and reaching conclusions about growth management strategies and programs.

Forms of Collaborative Civic Engagement

Long-range planning by public agencies typically involves complex concepts, large quantities of information, and long-term commitments by participants who are called to understand and ultimately consent to policies and regulations. The process may reach out to dozens or even thousands of residents. It may require a series of midpoint products along the way, such as formulating a community vision and determining basic policies to guide community development. Frequently, it will end with a formal adoption by elected officials of a vision statement, a plan, or an ordinance.

An example is the civic engagement process sponsored by St. Lucie County, a rapidly growing area on Florida's east coast. In 2005, the county involved citizens in determining a plan for the northern area then under pressures for development. The process, led by a consultant team organized by the Treasure Coast Regional Planning Commission, involved more than 350 participants in a seven-day series of meetings and concentrated discussions called a charrette (figure 9.1). It required weeks of research and meeting preparation by consultants and, following the charrette, numerous technical discussions with county staff to reach a conclusion. Even then, the process was just an important stepping stone to further detailed work to create a comprehensive plan and implementing regulations for future development.

No small affair, these community consultation processes can absorb large amounts of time and energy by local officials, but they also generate a new clarity about the direction of future community development. They

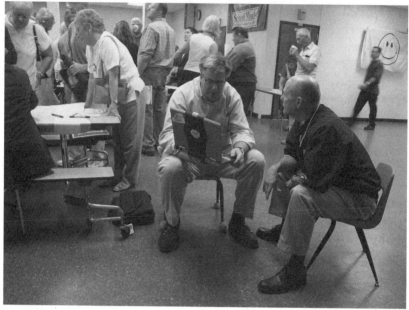

FIGURE 9.1

The County's planning for future development and conservation in the western half of the county involved a seven-day charrette process, which gave residents many opportunities to participate in the planning decisions.

provide a constellation of techniques for engaging the attention, input, and ultimate support of community residents in improving the quality of community development. The defining characteristic of such efforts is collaboration: recognizing, respecting, and working with individual residents and businesses, interest groups of all kinds, and public officials to agree on community policies and programs for managing growth and development. The involvement of citizens, public officials, and interest groups in learning about community growth issues and making decisions about future directions of community development invests their energies in determining positive approaches to managing growth.

Getting Started

All the activities and commotion generated by a process of community engagement demand a thoughtful period of organization; "planning ahead" is necessary because these processes can take many forms. As indicated by the example of St. Lucie County, organizers of engagement processes work with community groups and local officials to shape the scope and character of outreach efforts, which can involve an elaborate sequence of research, events, and media communications over months or years, or just a few meetings with interested parties to work out the details of a program or policy. Preparations for meetings can benefit from the involvement of specialists in facilitating discussions, visualizing design options, and many other techniques for presenting and interactively discussing information and ideas. The efforts can be assisted by public agency staff and one or more consulting firms.[2]

To organize the most effective process, the organizers must carefully define the purpose(s) and magnitude of the effort, including:

- the major issues that are driving consideration of growth management strategies and techniques, which will help define the content of the process (e.g., growth in general, schools and traffic, fiscal concerns, the changing character of the community);
- the nature of the desired outcome or end product (e.g., a list of overall policies for guiding community development, a ratified strategic program, a detailed set of growth management techniques to be adopted, a "next steps" action agenda);
- the allowable timeline for reaching agreement on the conclusions, which will be influenced by upcoming project approvals, budget decisions, annexation requests, elections, and other events that may trigger needs for decisions;
- the number and roles of people who need to be involved (e.g., decision makers, influential civic leaders, interest group representatives, regular citizens); and
- the official "convener" of the process and the "receiver" of the outcomes (e.g., the planning commission, the mayor and council, a task force, a civic group, a blue-ribbon committee formed for the purpose).

The planning study for Eastern Cambridge followed this course. The City of Cambridge expected a building boom in a large area along the Charles River that consisted of several old neighborhoods mixed with a fast-growing complex of research and technology firms and substantial open areas. Citizens in Eastern Cambridge had watched development of more than 2.5 million square feet of building space and knew that proposed zoning would allow construction of 9 million square feet more. Alarmed about the encroachment of commercial development, increasing traffic congestion, real estate price escalation, and the inadequacy of public open space, they petitioned for City Council imposition of a moratorium on major development projects until a study could recommend appropriate policies and zoning to guide development in the area. The Council established an eighteen-month moratorium and formed an Eastern Cambridge Planning Study Committee (ECaPS) to resolve development issues and agree on an overall plan and zoning recommendations.

Working with a consultant team, the committee met weekly, then two or three times a week, learning about conditions in the neighborhood and talking over possible directions for future growth. They sponsored public meetings to obtain more neighborhood input. The committee evolved a stance that instead of protecting the area against growth, they could harness growth to accomplish useful ends. The plan proposed modest zoning reductions of about 1 million square feet, with a somewhat higher proportion of residential development. But it also recognized opportunities—for strengthening existing neighborhoods by additional housing construction, including affordable housing, as well as some retail services, pedestrian-friendly streets, and new parks. Design guidelines were also drawn up to address the built form of development and the public realm. Since the adoption of the plan and the moratorium's end, 2.2 million square feet of office and research-and-development space and about 2,700 dwelling units have been approved for development.[3]

The Cambridge experience contrasts with that in Pleasant Hill in the Bay Area of California, where the process for reaching agreement on a workable plan was riddled with conflicts. In 1981, ten years after the Pleasant Hill station opened on the Bay Area Rapid Transit (BART) rail system in San Francisco, officials in Contra Costa County, the cities of Walnut Creek and Pleasant Hill, and BART commissioned preparation of a plan for the 140-acre station area. But for almost twenty years thereafter, gradual development of office, retail, and residential development occurred but never quite gelled to create an attractive, walkable center. By 1995, more than half the land remained undeveloped.

At that point, hoping to stimulate development, BART selected a development team to develop eleven acres of parking lots on the nineteen-acre BART property. Strong opposition by the cities, park-and-ride commuters, and neighbors led the county redevelopment agency to cut planned densities, but the plan still failed to achieve unanimity among the various interests. Finally, in 2001, a design team was commissioned to work intensively with citizens and various interest groups to agree on a development plan for the station area. The final agreement on a plan, made after a number of negotiated trade-offs among the organizations' objectives, emphasized residential development and cut back on potential office and retail

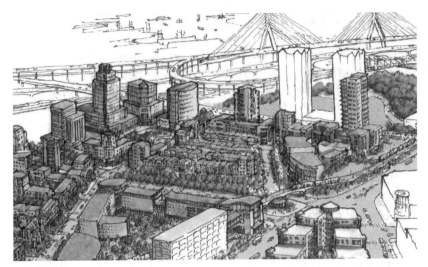

FIGURE 9.2
Neighborhood meetings in Eastern Cambridge brought residents together to work out issues about future development.

space; it also established a strong design plan, incorporating a formal civic space at Station Square surrounded by a mix of commercial and civic uses, an elegant residential street, a twelve-story office building visually linking the station to existing office buildings, and accommodation of all parking needs. A year later, the Contra Costa County Board of Supervisors accepted the plan and the regulatory documents to implement it.

A Variety of Potential Activities

Once these basic aspects of a collaborative process have been pinned down, the organizers can shape the types and order of events that will generate the desired result. These can consist of one meeting or many, discussions among large and small groups or one-on-one conversations, technical reports and mapped or drawn presentations, open houses or focus groups, and sessions focused on exchanging information or building consensus. The series of events should build a base of information about needs and approaches for managing growth and establish a discussion environment in which proposals, options, and issues can be freely explored, leading ever closer to forming some consensus among the participants about recommended policies and actions. (Total consensus is seldom possible and might even mean that proposals are so broadly stated as to be meaningless as guides to future action.)

Many kinds of agreements reached through engagement processes can provide useful outcomes. The strongest are group concurrence on specific strategies or resolutions to one or more issues, or binding statements not contingent on further actions; the weakest are agreements to conduct further discussions or proposals for more studies. The measure of the strength of an agreement is how far it takes the community toward concrete action. Agreements that acknowledge trade-offs among the interests involved are preferable to weak-kneed statements that do not promise advancement toward the objective.

In Eastern Cambridge, the consultant team began by identifying and evaluating the key issues raised by the prospect of changes in the neighborhood and then facilitated ongoing discussions to sound out the views of an appointed committee on these issues. Subsequently, the consultants drew up sketches to illustrate possible approaches to guiding future growth in ways that would improve the neighborhood while allowing additional development. Through further discussions and public meetings over a six-month period, as well as additional studies of technical questions, the committee voted to support a plan that would significantly improve the neighborhood while providing sites for 12 million square feet of office and technology space. Submitted to the city council, the plan was approved and substantial construction followed.

Ground Rules

Collaborative outreach processes tackle complex but negotiable issues involving a number of parties who are willing to work with rather than against one another. The aim is to build a common understanding of the existing and forecast circumstances of the area under consideration, to develop and test ideas, and to design workable and reasonable solutions that will gain general support. That goal is accomplished through following some rules that may appear simple but that are sometimes difficult to apply consistently.

- Participation includes representation from all parties with a stake in the results.
- Participants understand that they are responsible for ensuring the success of the process and that they will share in implementing the conclusions.
- A common sense of the purpose and problem is agreed upon prior to engaging in discussion.
- Participants help to educate one another about issues, concerns, and opportunities.

- Options to proposals and ideas are identified and evaluated.
- Decisions are made by general agreement, not by voting that creates winners and losers, although disagreements should be noted.
- Participants and the public are kept informed about the process and its results.[4]

Current Approaches and Technologies

Reaching agreements through collaborative processes can profit from leadership by skilled facilitators who know how to establish and maintain a positive environment for evocative discussion. Specialists in organizing and managing public meetings, charrettes, visioning processes, and other forms of community involvement are increasingly in demand as community participation in development planning has become more widely used. Also, consultants can bring valuable perspectives to the table and can point out courses of action that have worked in other communities. Consultants are useful not only in providing a broad range of skills and experience but also for providing the manpower to staff the intensive public events that often are scheduled within a brief time frame and attract wide participation.

Leaders, moderators, and facilitators of meetings use many tools to engage participants in fruitful discussions of development strategies and policies.

FIGURE 9.3
Planners have learned to involve citizens in thinking through and making decisions about community plans and regulations that will affect them; often such meetings function best as small gatherings that spark stimulating discussions.

Asking provocative questions, making certain to define terms just introduced in the discussion, restating the immediate issue before the group, summarizing the ideas or concerns offered at some point, calling for greater definition of proposed approaches or solutions—all are ways that facilitators keep discussions going productively. Charrettes, especially, demand knowledgeable leadership because these processes usually involve concentrated, multidiscussion efforts over a two- to seven-day period. Like the St. Lucie planning process, charrettes usually include on-site preparation of visual aids illustrating proposed plans and potential applications of growth management techniques (figure 9.2) as well as a series of follow-up meetings focused on specific issues.

Discussion leaders may employ a variety of visual techniques, especially for processes that involve distinctive designs or redesigns of existing areas. Besides the traditional drawings, sketches, and slides of desired types of development, leaders are making greater use of digital photo simulations of potential design approaches in significant areas, such as commercial centers and major streetscapes. With the proper equipment and know-how, three-dimensional views can be animated to indicate changing perspectives along a route or through a project area.

Facilitators also use various methods of "voting" to indicate aspects of a plan or program that are considered most desirable. This can be as simple as pinning a series of sketch plans or plans showing alternative locations of proposed growth areas on the wall and asking participants to provide a show of hands or apply stickers to indicate their preferences. Increasingly, more structured methods, many using computer assistance, are being used in group discussions to elicit the responses and comments that promote a shared understanding of issues, ideas, and possibilities. Many of these methods focus on helping participants visualize plans and the effects of policies being considered.

In addition to reaching agreements on specific policies and projects, citizen participation processes help to educate community officials and residents about ongoing issues that must be faced as growth continues. The long learning process undertaken by citizens of Fort Collins (described in chapter 1) built a core of knowledge and understanding about community development that has guided its growth ever since.

Guides for Managing Growth and Change

The growth management policies and practices described in this book demonstrate that many communities have built on fundamental planning and regulatory techniques to structure policy frameworks and action programs to better manage community development. Managing growth and change is a difficult, time-consuming, and perplexing chore. Yet communities have crafted imaginative and rational ways to deal with the fact of growth. Their experiences show us that certain understandings are important to success.

Aim for Comprehensiveness and Connectivity

This analysis of growth management techniques and practices has stressed the importance of viewing growth management both as a comprehensive strategy and as an interactive system of public policies and regulations. The four cornerstones of planning—comprehensive plans, zoning, subdivision regulations, and capital improvement programs—form one level of community approaches to governing growth. On this broad foundation, other growth management techniques can be added and interrelated to build a strong policy and action framework for guiding community development.

Understanding the linkages and interactions among the components of growth management programs is a key to effective management. Growth boundaries, for example, are most successful when accompanied by efforts to promote compact development within the boundaries, including revitalizing and redeveloping existing urbanized areas. Programs to efficiently expand infrastructure systems must consider needs for protecting environmentally sensitive lands and other green spaces of value to the community and region.

Communities are using a broad and inventive array of growth management techniques today, but they do not always match up well. Stopgap measures can do more harm than good. For example, efforts to curb sprawl can generate stresses in existing neighborhoods and business areas, which may be afflicted with incompatible new development. These problems should be anticipated and steps taken to avoid them. Growth management programs should always recognize the interactions between growth management practices and the secondary effects they may engender. They may generate opportunities for even more effective management of community growth.

Expect Complexity and Change

"Keep it simple, stupid," may be a political catchphrase, but administrators managing growth should understand that community development is a complicated adventure. In practice, growth management programs mirror the ever-changing climate of community attitudes and market forces within which they operate. All communities experience shifts in citizen and consumer preferences, real estate booms and busts, changing federal and state policy contexts, and turnover among community decision makers. The context of community programs for managing growth is always changing, and unforeseen consequences occur. To remain effective, growth management programs must be continually evaluated and adapted to respond to new circumstances.

Recognize Regional Forces and Relationships

Communities do not exist in a vacuum, and community efforts to manage growth should not be regarded as independent of activities in their surrounding regions. Communities are part of and will be conditioned by larger systems of land use, transportation, economic activities, social forces, natural ecosystems, and other intrinsic elements of urban and metropolitan areas. Metropolitan regions are widely recognized as competitive centers within the global economy and places with distinctive heritages that form desirable living environments. Local governments can choose to act as good citizens of the regional "community of communities" by participating in and supporting regional evaluations and decisions that will affect current and future growth patterns. They can build collaborative relationships with adjacent communities to work out growth management strategies that benefit all rather than one or a few communities. As William Hudnut observes: "Regional stewardship represents an expression of our collective self-interest."[5]

In closing, this book confirms that growth management is here to stay. It has proven invaluable for communities coping with growth and change. Growth management strategies and techniques enable the grand ideas for community betterment described in comprehensive plans to be implemented. They also supply a proactive public policy environment essential to support development of the splendid designs for urban life being promoted by campaigns for smart growth, new urbanism, and green building. The spirited efforts of many towns, cities, and counties in managing development demonstrate the rewards of anticipating and finding ways to accommodate growth and change.

Notes

Chapter 1. Introduction to Managing Community Development

1. Joel Kotkin, *The New Suburbanism: A Realist's Guide to the American Future* (report, The Planning Center, Costa Mesa, CA, November 2005).
2. For more information on these trends, consult William H. Frey, *Metropolitan America in the New Century: Metropolitan and Central City Demographic Shifts Since 2000* (report, The Brookings Institution Metropolitan Policy Program, 2005).
3. Eugenie L. Birch, *Who Lives Downtown* (report, The Brookings Institution Metropolitan Policy Program, 2005).
4. Bruce Katz and Robert E. Lang, eds. *Redefining Urban and Suburban America: Evidence from Census 2000* (Washington, DC: Brookings Institution Press, 2005).
5. William Goodman and Eric Freund, *The Principles and Practices of Urban Planning* (Washington, DC: International City Managers' Association, 1968), 13.
6. Randall W. Scott, David J. Brower, and Dallas D. Miner, eds., *Management and Control of Growth*, vol. 1 (Washington, DC: Urban Land Institute, 1975), 6.
7. William K. Reilly, ed., *The Use of Land: A Citizen's Policy Guide to Urban Growth*, A Task Force Report sponsored by the Rockefeller Brothers Fund (New York: Thomas Y. Crowell, 1973), 6.
8. Reilly, *The Use of Land*, 40.
9. David R. Godschalk et al., *Constitutional Issues of Growth Management* (Chicago: ASPO Press, 1977), 8.
10. Scott, Brower, and Miner, *Management and Control of Growth*, 1:4.
11. Benjamin Chinitz, "Growth Management: Good for the Town, Bad for the Nation?" *Journal of the American Planning Association* 56, no. 1 (1990): 3–8.
12. Vincent Scully, "The Architecture of Community," reprinted in Neil Levine, *Modern Architecture and Other Essays by Vincent Scully* (Princeton, NJ: Princeton University Press, 2003), 346.
13. Vincent Scully, "Urban Architecture Awakens from a Bad Dream," *City Journal*, Autumn 1994, http://www.city-journal.org/article02.php?aid=1373 http://www.city-journal.org (accessed April 7, 2004).
14. New Urbanism.org, home page, http://www.newurbanism.org.
15. See http://www.cnu.org for more information.
16. For more information on smart codes and form-based zoning, see Congress for the New Urbanism, *Codifying New Urbanism: How to Reform Municipal Land Development Regulations*, Planning Advisory Service Report no. 526 (Chicago: American Planning Association, 2004); and David Rouse and Nancy Zobl, "Form-based Zoning," Zoning Practice 5 (May 2004).

17. Peter Katz, "Form First: The New Urbanist Alternative to Conventional Zoning." *Planning*, November 2004, 6.

18. For helpful discussions of the density issue, see Richard M. Haughey, *Higher-density Development: Myth and Fact* (Washington, DC: Urban Land Institute, 2005); Steven Fader, *Density by Design* (Washington, DC: Urban Land Institute, 2000); and Douglas R. Porter, *Making Smart Growth Work* (Washington, DC: Urban Land Institute, 2002), esp. 14–21.

19. Peter Calthorpe and William Fulton, *The Regional City* (Washington, DC: Island Press, 2001), 279.

Chapter 2. The Practice of Growth Management

1. For guides to comprehensive planning, see Charles J. Hoch, Linda C. Dalton, and Frank S. So, eds., *Practice of Local Government Planning*, 3rd ed. (Washington, DC: International City Management Association, 2000); and Eric Damian Kelly and Barbara Becker, *Community Planning* (Washington, DC: Island Press, 2000).

2. For a guide to the content of zoning ordinances, see Charles A. Lerable, *Preparing a Conventional Zoning Ordinance*, Planning Advisory Service Report no. 460 (Chicago: American Planning Association, 1995). A refreshingly infor-mal but knowledgeable treatise on preparing for zoning hearings is Dwight H. Merriam, *The Complete Guide to Zoning* (New York: McGraw-Hill, 2005).

3. For a guide to drafting subdivision regulations, see Robert H. Freilich and Michael Shultz, *Model Subdivision Regulations*, 2nd ed. (Chicago: APA Planners Press, 1995).

4. Robert C. Einsweiler et al., "Comparative Descriptions of Selected Municipal Growth Guidance Systems," in *Management and Control of Growth*, vol. 2, eds. Randall Scott, David J. Brower, and Dallas Miner, (Washington, DC: Urban Land Institute, 1975), 283–329.

5. For more on the controversies over limits to growth, see series of articles in "Limits to Growth and Zero Growth," ch. 5 in *Management and Control of Growth*, eds. Randall Scott, David J. Brower, and Dallas Miner, vol. 1 (Washington, DC: Urban Land Institute, 1975), 303–426.

6. Montgomery County Department of Park and Planning, "Revitalizing Centers . . . Reshaping Boulevards . . . Creating Great Public Spaces: A Planning Framework Report" (working draft, November 2005), 6.

Chapter 3. Managing Community Expansion: Where to Grow

1. Urban Land Institute, *Sarasota County, Florida: Strategies for Managing Future Growth* (Washington, DC: Urban Land Institute, 1999).

2. Arthur C. Nelson and Casey J. Dawkins, *Urban Containment in the United States*, Planning Advisory Service Report no. 520 (Chicago: American Planning Association, 2004), 16.

3. A commentary by Peter Applebome in the *New York Times*, January 8, 2006, 19, called attention to the overly organized and circumscribed lives of children in many suburban areas: "Who could have imagined that today's suburbs, with children their prime reason for being, would end up excising the one thing kids always had before: a sense of freedom, room to explore, time to wander around to see what you could find? Who could have imagined today's fortresslike homes and grand green lawns as quiet as an empty church?"

4. Joel Garreau, *Edge City: Life on the New Frontier* (New York: Doubleday, 1991).

5. Robert Lang and Jennifer LeFurgy, "Edgeless Cities: Examining the Noncentered Metropolis," *Housing Policy Debate*, 14, no. 3 (2003): 427–60.

6. Nelson and Dawkins, *Urban Containment in the United States*, 16.

7. Nelson and Dawkins, *Urban Containment in the United States*, 47–68.

8. Nelson and Dawkins, *Urban Containment in the United States*, 74.

9. John D. Landis, "Do Growth Controls Work?" *Journal of the American Planning Association* 58, no. 4 (Autumn 1992): 489–508.

10. Landis, "Do Growth Controls Work?" 506.

11. John D. Landis, "Growth Management Revisited," *Journal of the American Planning Association* 72, no. 4 (Autumn 2006): 411–30.

12. Arthur C. Nelson, Rolf Pendall, Casey J. Dawkins, and Gerrit J. Knaap, "The Link between Growth Management and Housing Affordability: The Academic Evidence," in *Growth Management and Affordable Housing: Do They Conflict?*, ed. Anthony Downs (Washington, DC: Brookings Institution Press, 2004), 154.

13. Nelson et al., "The Link between Growth Management and Housing Affordability," 153.

14. William A. Fischel, "Comment," in *Growth Management and Affordable Housing: Do They Conflict?*, ed. Anthony Downs (Washington, DC: Brookings Institution Press, 2004), 161–62.

15. Nelson and Dawkins, *Urban Containment in the United States*, 19.

16. See Douglas R. Porter, "Evaluation of Local Implementation of the Washington State Growth Management Act," report prepared for the National Association of Realtors, March 2005, available at http://www.realtor.org/smart_growth.nsf/Pages/washingtongma.

17. Samuel R. Staley and Leonard C. Gilroy, *Smart Growth and Housing Affordability: Evidence from Statewide Planning Laws*, Policy Study No. 287 (Los Angeles: Reason Public Policy Institute, 2001).

18. Jerry Anthony, "The Effects of Florida's Growth Management Act on Housing Affordability," *Journal of the American Planning Association* 69, no. 3 (Summer 2003): 282–93.

19. Michael H. Schill, "Regulations and Housing Development: What We Know and What We Need to Know" (paper presented at the Conference on Regulatory Barriers to Affordable Housing sponsored by the U.S. Department of Housing and Urban Development, Washington, DC, April, 2004), 2.

20. Schill, "Regulations and Housing Development," 2.

21. For a detailed history of Kane County's planning process over a fifty-year span, see http://www.co.kane.il.us/Development.

22. ECO Northwest, *Urban Growth Management Study: Case Studies Report* (report prepared for the Oregon Department of Land Conservation and Development, January 1991).

23. Information from the Oregon Department of Land Conservation and Development, 1995.

24. Donovan D. Rypkema, "Preserving for Profit," *Urban Land*, December 1998, 68–69.

25. Quoted in G. Allan Kingston, "Worker's Growth Need for Housing," *Multifamily Trends*, Summer 2004, 66.

26. David Takesuye, "A Common Landmark: Millennium Place," *Urban Land*, August 2004, 130–31.

27. Mark Johnson, "Brownfields Are Looking Greener," *Planning*, June 2002, 14.

28. "Smart Growth in Action: Wellington Neighborhood," http://www.smart-growth.org/library/articles.asp?art=1829 (accessed April 16, 2007).

29. Forest City Development, *Stapleton: Where Denver Is Moving Next* (Denver: Forest City Development, 2002).

30. Douglas R. Porter, "Building Homes in America's Cities: A Progress Report" (report prepared for the U.S. Conference of Mayors, 2000).

31. Eric Damien Kelly, "*Robinson vs. Boulder*, a Balance to *Ramapo* and *Petaluma*," *Real Estate Law Journal* 5 (1976): 170–4.

32. Larimer County and City of Fort Collins, *Intergovernmental Agreements*, November 2000, http://www.ci.fort-collins.co.us/advanceplanning/pdf/iga-doc.pdf.

33. References for the Lincoln-Lancaster County case study include interviews in
1989 with Garner Stoll, Lincoln director of planning; Kent Morgan, assistant
director of planning; William Smith, First Tier Bank of Lincoln; Robert Hans,
former chairman, Lincoln/Lancaster County Planning Commission; and Patrick
Malloy, Lincoln Chamber of Commerce; in 1993, with John Bradley, assistant
planning director; in 1995, with Timothy M. Stewart, planning director; and in
2006, Marvin Krout, planning director. Documents include the *Lincoln-
Lancaster County Comprehensive Plan*, prepared by the Lincoln City–Lancaster
County Planning Department, 1985 and 1994; proposals for updating of the
plan in 2005; a residential land inventory in 2005; the capital improvements
program of 2005 and various memoranda and newsletters. The 2005 materials
are available at http://www.lincoln.ne.gov/city/plan.
34. See "Evaluation of Growth Slowing Policies for the San Diego Region," Oct. 21,
2001 (prepared by the San Diego Association of Governments); and
EcoNorthwest, *Evaluation of Slow-growth and No-Growth Policies for the Portland
Region* (prepared for Metro, 1994). Both studies determined that regional
growth could be slowed only by actions that would adversely affect the economy, such as imposing taxes and fees that would increase the price of doing
business or that would reduce the quality of living in the area, such as allowing
degradation of public services or raising the cost of living. The studies concluded that not only were these actions unlikely to be supported by area residents
and businesses but that, if adopted, they were likely to lead to unforeseen consequences—that is, they concluded that tampering with regional economic
functions was risky.
35. Daniel R. Mandelker, *Land Use Law*, 2nd ed. (Charlottesville, VA: Michie,
1988), 209.
36. Roger Lewis, "Planning—A More Sensible Choice," *Urban Land*, September
1989, 37.
37. Eric Damien Kelly, *Managing Community Growth* (Westport, CT: Praeger, 1993), 46.
38. Kelly, *Managing Community Growth*, 47.

Chapter 4. Protecting Environmental and Natural Resources: Where Not to Grow

1. Dan L. Perlman and Jeffrey C. Milder, *Practical Ecology for Planners, Developers,
and Citizens* (Washington, DC: Island Press, 2005), 3.
2. Ian L. McHarg, *Design with Nature*, 2nd ed. (New York: Wiley, 1992), 56.
3. Perlman and Milder, *Practical Ecology*, 1.
4. Christine Meisner Rosen and Joel A. Tarr, "The Importance of an Urban
Perspective in Environmental History," *Journal of Urban History* 20, no. 3
(May 1994): 307.
5. Maryland Office of Planning, "Achieving Environmentally Sensitive Design,"
no. 11 of a series on Flexible and Innovative Zoning for Managing Maryland's
Growth (Baltimore: Maryland Office of Planning, 1995), 5.
6. Florida Local Government Comprehensive Planning and Land Development
Regulation Act, 1985, sec. 163.3177(d), Florida Statutes.
7. An early but still valid analysis of the carrying capacity concept is Rice Odell,
"Carrying Capacity Analysis: Useful but Limited," *Management and Control of
Growth*, Randall Scott, David J. Brower, and Dallas Miner. vol. 3 (Washington,
DC: Urban Land Institute, 1975), 22–28.
8. A helpful description of the green infrastructure concept is in Mark A. Benedict
and Edward T. McMahon, *Green Infrastructure: Smart Conservation for the 21st
Century* (Washington, DC: Sprawl Watch Clearinghouse, 2001).
9. Washington State Growth Management Act. RCW Chapter 36.70A, sec. 030
and 170.
10. The Natural Community Conservation Planning (NCCP) program,
www.dfg.ca.gov/nccp.

11. Information about the Highlands Coalition is taken from Douglas R. Porter and Allan D. Wallis, *Exploring Ad Hoc Regionalism* (Cambridge, MA: Lincoln Institute of Land Policy, 2002), 26, 27, and the following Web sites: http://www.highlandscoalition.org; http://www.rce.rutgers.edu/Highlands; and http://www.nynjtc.org/issues/advocacy.html#issues.
12. For more information on the Chesapeake Bay program, see Erik Meyers, Robert Fischman, and Anne Marsh, "Maryland Chesapeake Bay Critical Areas Program: Wetlands Protection and Future Growth," in *Collaborative Planning for Wetlands and Wildlife* ed. Douglas R. Porter and David A. Salvesen (Washington, DC: Island Press, 1995), 181–202.
13. Laura Thompson, "The Long Good Buy," *Planning*, May 2001, 4–9.
14. Author's telephone interview with Christopher Coover, March 2, 2006.
15. City of San Diego, *Multi-species Conservation Plan* (public review draft, 1995). A description of the plan is also published in "Natural Habitats in the San Diego Region: Balancing Development and Habitat Preservation," *Info* (published by San Diego Association of Governments, January-February 1995).
16. "Support for Land Conservation Continues in 2005," http://www.tpl.org /special topic: landvote
17. Mary Manross, mayor of Scottsdale, State of the City speech, February 23, 2006.
18. Jim Carlton, "Cities Spend Millions on Land to Protect Water," *Wall Street Journal*, January 4, 2006.
19. Richard Shaw, "Conservation Easements," *Urban Land*, May 2005, 26. Shaw discusses issues that developers should consider in using conservation easements.
20. Jeff Pidot, *Reinventing Conservation Easements: A Critical Examination and Ideas for Reform* (Cambridge, MA: Lincoln Institute of Land Policy, 2005), 1.
21. The town's experience is further detailed by Robert Lemire, "An Overview of an Innovative Land Protection Technique," *Exchange* (journal of the Land Trust Exchange) 7, no. 4 (Fall 1988): 1, 4–6. The issue also contains descriptions of a number of additional limited development projects.
22. See, for example, Randall Arendt, *Conservation Design for Subdivisions* (Washington, DC: Island Press, 1996).
23. Frederick County Zoning Ordinance, Resource Conservation District, Sec. 1-19-238.
24. Loudoun County Planning Commission, *Choices and Changes: Loudoun County General Plan, 1990–2010* (adopted September 17, 1991).
25. Robert H. Freilich and Wayne M. Senville, "Takings, TDRs, and Environmental Preservation: 'Fairness' and the Hollywood North Beach Case," *Land Use Law*, September 1983, 5.
26. Aldo Leopold, "Conservation Economics," in Susan L. Flader and J. Baird Callicott, eds., *The River of the Mother of God and Other Essays by Aldo Leopold* (Madison: University of Wisconsin Press, 1991), 202.

Chapter 5. Supporting Growth by Managing Infrastructure Development

1. Madelyn Glickfeld and Ned Levine, *Regional Growth—Local Reaction: The Enactment and Effects of Local Growth Control and Management Measures in California* (Cambridge, MA: Lincoln Institute of Land Policy, 1992).
2. National Center for Smart Growth Research and Education, University of Maryland, *Adequate Public Facilities in Maryland* (report for the Home Builders Association of Maryland and the Maryland National Capital Building Industry Association, April 20, 2006).
3. Henry Fagin, "Regulating the Timing of Urban Development," *Law and Contemporary Problems* (published by the Duke University Law School) 20, no. 2 (1955): 298–304.
4. Chula Vista's program is fully described by its planning director, Robert Leiter, in "The Use of Threshold Standards in Chula Vista's Growth Management

Program," in *Performance Standards in Growth Management,* ed. Douglas R. Porter, Planning Advisory Service Report no. 461 (Chicago: American Planning Association, 1995), 13–18.

5. By now, the reader will observe the number of California examples in this chapter. It is no accident that so many California cities have gone to great lengths to manage infrastructure development and funding. State restrictions on levying property taxes, including Proposition 13, have severely hampered California cities' ability to raise revenues for public facility construction. This drives those cities not only to employ impact fees and other user-based funding mechanisms almost exclusively to fund facilities but also to ensure that development occurs only as facilities are made available.

6. National Center for Smart Growth Research and Education, "Adequate Public Facilities in Maryland, Executive Summary," 4.

7. Fagin, "Regulating the Timing of Urban Development," 298.

8. For detailed information on methods of calculating and administering impact fees, plus model ordinances, see James C. Nicholas, Arthur C. Nelson, and Julian C. Juergensmeyer, *A Practitioner's Guide to Development Impact Fees* (Chicago: APA Planners Press, 1991).

9. See http://www.impactfees.com.

10. Detailed discussions of court decisions affecting exactions and fees can be found in Nicholas, Nelson, and Juergensmeyer, *A Practitioner's Guide to Development Impact Fees,* and in Nancy E. Stroud and Susan L. Trevarthen, "Defensible Exactions after *Nollan v. California Coastal Commission* and *Dolan v. City of Tigard,*" *Stetson Law Review* 25, no.3 (Spring 1996): 719–822.

11. For more information on trends in special district formation, types of districts, funding approaches, and specific examples, see Douglas R. Porter, Ben C. Lin, Susan Jakubiak, and Richard B. Peiser, *Special Districts: A Useful Technique for Financing Infrastructure,* 2nd ed. (Washington, DC: Urban Land Institute, 1992).

12. For an analysis of the pros and cons of TIF districts, see Jim Krohe, Jr., "At the Tipping Point," *Planning* 73, no. 3 (March 2007): 20–25.

Chapter 6: Design to Preserve and Improve Community Character and Quality

1. Jan Krasnowiecki, "The Fallacy of the End-state System of Land Use Control," *Land Use Law,* April 1986, 1–30, decries the ineffectiveness of zoning to deliver desired qualities of development.

2. John Nolen, *Remodeling Roanoke: Report to the Committee on Civic Improvement* (Cambridge, MA, 1907), 11.

3. Jane Jacobs, *The Death and Life of Great American Cities* (New York: Vintage, 1961), 47.

4. Publications that offer specific guidance on some of the more common approaches include Eric Damian Kelly and Gary J. Ruso, *Sign Regulation for Small and Midsize Communities,* Planning Advisory Service Report no. 419 (1989); Thomas P. Smith, *The Aesthetics of Parking,* Planning Advisory Service Report no. 411 (1989); and Wendelyn A. Martz with Marya Morris, *Preparing a Landscaping Ordinance,* Planning Advisory Service Report no. 431 (1990), all published by the American Planning Association, Chicago. Lane Kendig, *Performance Zoning* (Chicago: American Planning Association, 1980), provides much information about various types of landscaped buffers.

5. Mark L. Hinshaw, *Design Review,* Planning Advisory Service Report no. 454 (Chicago: American Planning Association, 1995), 3. Hinshaw's monograph provides an excellent overview of design guidelines and review processes in many types of circumstances.

6. City of Arlington, Washington, *Development Design Guidelines and Central Business District Design Guidelines,* September 2003, sec. 5.3, 16, and sec. 10.1, 34.

7. E-mail communication to author from Cliff Strong, July 27, 2006.
8. City of Tampa Land Development Coordination Division, *West Tampa Overlay District Illustrated Design Standards*, [n.d.], sec. (F)(1)(c)(1).
9. Descriptions and details of the guidelines can be found online at the city's Web site, http://www.scottsdaleaz.gov.
10. A complete discussion of appearance codes, including sample provisions, can be found in Peggy Glassford, *Appearance Codes for Small Communities*, Planning Advisory Service Report no. 379 (Chicago: American Planning Association, 1983). 11. City of San Jacinto, California, *Residential Development Design Guidelines*, 2005, http://www.ci.san-jacinto.ca.s/maps&guidelines.
12. Traverse City Area Chamber of Commerce, *Grand Traverse Bay Region Development Guidebook*, 1992.
13. Hinshaw, *Design Review*, 15.
14. Hinshaw, *Design Review*, 28.
15. Cliff Strong, e-mail to author, July 27, 2006.
16. Portland Development Commission, *Lloyd District Area Development Strategy*, June 2004, 22, http://www.pdc.us/ura.
17. Portland Development Commission, "Executive Summary," Lloyd Crossing Sustainable Urban Design Plan, August 2005, http://www.pdc.us/ura.
18. Terry Jill Lassar, *City Deal Making* (Washington, DC: Urban Land Institute, 1990), 2.
19. Information from David Jensen of David Jensen Associates Inc. in Denver, and from Julie Makarewicz, "Bailey's Grove Recognized for Conservation Efforts," *Grand Rapids Press*, May 8, 2003.
20. Local Government Commission, "Addison Circle Brings Urban Environment to Dallas Suburbs," http://www.lgc.org/freepub/land_use/models/addison _circle.html.
21. Shannon Canard, "Stebbins' Southlake Center Is Urban Development Jewel," *Fort Worth Star-Telegram*, January 31–February 6, 2003; Jennifer Packer, "Square Roots: Southlake's Old-fashioned Downtown Quickly Becoming Centerpiece of Community," *Dallas Morning News*, March 23, 2001.
22. Steve Wright, "New Urbanism Is Being Used to Build Traditional Neighborhoods," *On Common Ground* (published by the National Association of Realtors), Summer 2006, 31–35.
23. Congress for the New Urbanism, *The Coming Demand* (report, October 9, 2001), 8, http://www.cnu.org/node/359.
24. A version of the SmartCode (V-6.5, Spring 2005) can be found at http://www.placemakers.com or http://www.dpz.com. A helpful explanation of the regulations by Peter Katz, "Form First: The New Urbanist Alternative to Conventional Zoning," November 2004, can be found at http://www.nh.gov /oep/resource library/referencelibrary/f/formbasedzoning.
25. The rating systems and explanations of the process can be found at http://www.usgbc.org.
26. Edward T. McMahon, "Sustainability and Property Rights," *Urban Land*, June 2006, 30–33, and information from http://www.LoDo.org.

Chapter 7. Managing Growth to Advance Social and Economic Equity

1. Timothy Beatley and Kristy Manning, *The Ecology of Place: Planning for Environment, Economy, and Community* (Washington, DC: Island Press, 1997), 1, 2.
2. William H. Frey, "Diversity Spreads Out: Metropolitan Shifts in Hispanic, Asian, and Black Populations since 2000" (report of the Brookings Institution Metropolitan Policy Program, March 2006), http://www.brookings.edu/Metro /pubs/20060307_Frey.pdf.
3. Joel Kotkin, *The New Suburbanism: A Realist's Guide to the American Future* (report, The Planning Center, Costa Mesa, CA, November 2005).

4. Alan Berube, "The Geography of U.S. Poverty and Its Implications" (testimony before the Committee on Ways and Means, Subcommittee on Income Security and Family Support, February 13, 2007), http://www.brook.edu/views /berube20070213_povertytestimony.htm.

5. Joseph Gyourko, Christopher Mayer, and Todd Sinai, Superstar Cities. June 16, 2006, http://realestate.wharton.upenn.edu/newsletter.

6. Christopher Leinberger, "The Connection Between Sustainability and Economic Development," in *The Practice of Sustainable Development*, ed. Douglas R. Porter (Washington, DC: Urban Land Institute, 2000), 56.

7. Jason C. Booza, Jackie Cutsinger, and George Galster, "Where Did They Go? The Decline of Middle-income Neighborhoods in Metropolitan America" (report of the Brookings Institution Metropolitan Policy Program, June 2006), http://www.brookings.edu/metro/pubs.

8. Matt Fellowes, "From Poverty, Opportunity: Putting the Market to Work for Lower Income Families" (report of the Brookings Institution Metropolitan Policy Program, July 2006), 1–2, http://www.brook.edu/scholars/mfellowes.htm.

9. Fellowes, "From Poverty, Opportunity," 1–2.

10. John Parr, "Visions of a Renegotiated Social Contract," *National Civic Review*, 82, no. 2 (Spring 1993): 96.

11. For more information on the High Street project, see http://www.goodyclancy .com/html/proj_descr.asp?pageID=1201.

12. See Gordon Goldie and Tim Frens, "Financing Activities in Low-income Communities," *Urban Land*, November/December 2005, 30.

13. For more information on the National Trust for Historic Preservation's Main Street program, see http://www.mainstreet.org.

14. Mary K. Nenno, *Ending the Stalemate* (Lanham, MD: University Press of America, 1996), 90.

15. Paul Davidoff and Linda Davidoff, "Opening the Suburbs: Toward Inclusionary Land-use Controls," *Syracuse Law Review* 22 (1972): 510; and Anthony Downs, *Opening Up the Suburbs* (New Haven, CT: Yale University Press, 1973).

16. These estimates and much of the information in this section are based on Douglas R. Porter, *Inclusionary Zoning for Affordable Housing* (Washington, DC: Urban Land Institute, 2004).

17. Bernard Tetreault, "Arguments against Inclusionary Zoning You Can Anticipate Hearing," *New Century Housing* 1, no. 2 (October 2000): 19.

18. "Indianapolis City/County Council Finds Revenue for Marion County Housing Trust Fund," *Housing Trust Fund Project News* (Summer 2006), http://www.communitychange.org/issues/housing/trustfundproject.

19. See, for example, Edward Stromberg, ed., "Regulatory Barriers to Affordable Housing," *Cityscape: A Journal of Policy Development and Research* 8, no. 1 (2005); "Not in My Back Yard": Removing Barriers to Affordable Housing, report to President Bush and Secretary Kemp by the Advisory Commission on Regulatory Barriers to Affordable Housing (Washington, DC: U.S. Department of Housing and Urban Development, 1991); and Welford Sanders and David Mosena, *Changing Development Standards for Affordable Housing*, Planning Advisory Service Report no. 371 (Chicago: American Planning Association, 1982).

20. For more information on rehabilitation codes, see Matt Syal, Chris Shay, and Faron Supanich-Goldner, "Streamlining Building Rehabilitation Codes to Encourage Revitalization," *Housing Facts And Findings*, Fannie Mae Foundation, 3, no. 2 (2001). Also at http://www.fanniemaefoundation.org/programs/hff /v3i2-streamline.html.

21. City of Champaign, Illinois, "2006 Neighborhood Wellness Action Plan," at www.ci.champaign.il.us/quicklinks/neighborhoods/neighborhoodactionplan.

22. Author's telephone interviews on August 9, 2006, with Martin Livingston, director of the Greenville County Redevelopment Authority, and Gwen

Kennedy, former director; the *Authority's Community Report, 2004*; and John
Boyanoski, "Three's the Charm," *Planning*, April, 2005, 22–25.

23. Beth Williams Prior, Jennifer Blake, Henrique Caine, Diana Meyer, "Dudley
Street Neighborhood Initiative (Case Study)," The Enterprise Foundation, 2000
at www.knowledge.plex.org/showdoc.
24. Information based the author's research for Douglas R. Porter and Terry Lassar,
The Power of Ideas: Five People Who Changed the Urban Landscape (Washington,
DC: Urban Land Institute, 2004).
25. "Livable Communities Grant Program," http://www.metrocouncil.org/servic-
es/planningassistance.
26. Robert Puentes and David Warren, *One Fifth of America: A Comprehensive Guide
to America's First Suburbs* (Washington, DC: Brookings Institution, February
2006), http://www.brookings.edu/metro/pubs/20060215_firstsuburbs.htm.
27. William H. Hudnut III, *Halfway to Everywhere: A Portrait of America's First-tier
Suburbs* (Washington, DC: Urban Land Institute, 2003).
28. See, for example, the Web page of the First Suburbs Consortium at
http://www.firstsuburbs.org.
29. The section on inclusionary zoning is based on Porter, *Inclusionary Zoning for
Affordable Housing.*
30. The strategies are loosely based on recommendations in Radhika K. Fox and
Sarah Treuhaft, *Shared Prosperity, Stronger Regions: An Agenda for Rebuilding
America's Older Core Cities* (Washington, DC: Policy Link, 2005).

Chapter 8. Regional and State Growth Management

1. Lewis Mumford, *The Culture of Cities* (New York: Harcourt, Brace, 1938), 48.
2. Historical information in this section is drawn from Carl and Margery Post
Abbott, *Historical Development of the Metropolitan Service District* (prepared for
the Metro Home Rule Charter Committee, May 1991).
3. The 2040 Concept Plan, 2020 Regional Framework Plan, and Urban Growth
Management Functional Plan are all available on Metro's Web site,
http://www.metro-region.org.
4. San Diego Association of Governments, "2006 Progress Report on Consolidation
in the San Diego Region" (report, December 2006).
5. San Diego Association of Governments, "Regional Comprehensive Plan for the
San Diego Region" (report, July 2004), http://www.sandag.org.
6. San Diego Association of Governments, "The Regional Comprehensive Plan:
Establishing a Baseline for Monitoring Performance" (report, November 2006).
7. San Diego Association of Governments, 2006 Progress Report on Consolidation
in the San Diego Region, December 2006, at www.sandag.org/publicationid
_1269_6128.pdf.
8. For an extended discussion of the council's political and planning evolution into
the 1990s, see Steve Keefe, "Twin Cities Federalism: The Politics of Metropolitan
Governance," in *State and Regional Initiatives for Managing Development*, ed.
Douglas R. Porter (Washington, DC: Urban Land Institute, 1992).
9. Ohio-Kentucky-Indiana Regional Council of Governments, *Unified Planning
Work Program, Executive Summary, FY 2007*, April 11, 2006, http://www.oki.org.
10. Cliff Peale, "Regional Becoming a Leader in Visions," *Cincinnati Enquirer*,
December 10, 2006, http://news.enquirer.com.
11. Douglas R. Porter and Allan D. Wallis, *Exploring Ad Hoc Regionalism*
(Cambridge, MA: Lincoln Institute of Land Policy, 2002), 24.
12. Some will argue that Portland's Metro organization, with an elected regional
council, comes close to being a regional government. An analysis of Metro's
actual responsibilities, however, demonstrates that it has only a few selected
powers to guide development in the Portland region and virtually no general-
purpose governmental responsibilities. Moreover, it has attained its present

position by carefully building consensus with local governments rather than challenging them on every front.

13. American Planning Association, "Planning for Smart Growth: 2002 State of the States," February 2002, http://www.planning.org.

14. The growth management statutes of the states specifically mentioned, by date of enactment, are as follows:

Oregon: Oregon Land Use Act, Senate Bill 100, 1973. Oregon Revised Statutes 197.005-197.650, 215.055, 215.510, 215.515, 215.535, and 453.345.

Florida: Omnibus Growth Management Act, 1985, House Bill 287. Laws of Florida Chapter 85-55. State Comprehensive Planning Act, House Bill 1338, 1985. Laws of Florida Chapter 85-57.

New Jersey: State Planning Act, 1986, Senate No. 1464-L, 1985. New Jersey State Acts 52:18.

Maine: Comprehensive Planning and Land Use Act, 1988, H.P. 1588—L.D. 2317. Sec. 4 30 Maine Revised Statutes Annotated 4960-4960-F.

Rhode Island: Comprehensive Planning and Land Use Regulation Act, 1988. PL 88-601, Chapter 45-22.1, Rhode Island General Laws.

Vermont: Growth Management Act, 1988, Act 200, General Assembly.

Georgia: Georgia Planning Act, 1989, House Bill 215. Georgia Laws 1317–1391.

Washington: Growth Management Act, 1990, House Bill 2929. Chapter 17, 51st Legislature. Growth Management Act Amendments, 1991, House Bill 1025, 52nd Legislature.

Maryland: Economic Growth, Resource Protection, and Planning Act, 1992, House Bill No. 1195. Article 66B; State Finance and Procurement Article, secs. 5-402, 5-701 through 5-710; and State Government Article sec. 8-403(h), Annotated Code of Maryland.

Tennessee: Growth Policy Act, 1998, Public Chapter 1101 of the Laws of Tennessee.

15. For a detailed history of state planning, see Robert G. Benko and Irving Hand, "State Planning Today," in State and Regional Planning, ed. Frank So (Chicago: American Planning Association, 1986).

16. Fred P. Bosselman and David Callies, The Quiet Revolution in Land Use Control (Washington, DC: Council on Environmental Quality, 1971), 1.

17. Comprehensive Planning and Land Use Act, 1988, H.P. 1588-L.D. 2317. Sec. 4960-A.1.E.

18. Pursuant to secs. 197.225ff, the Oregon Land Conservation and Development Commission prepared and adopted an administrative rule defining the goals. Published in "Oregon's State Planning Goals," Land Conservation and Development Commission, 1985.

19. Charles L. Siemon, "Growth Management in Florida: An Overview and Brief Critique," in State and Regional Initiatives for Managing Development, ed. Douglas R. Porter (Washington, DC: Urban Land Institute, 1992), 40.

20. State Comprehensive Planning Act, H.B. 1338, 1985. Laws of Florida Chapter 85-57, sec. 2.

21. John M. DeGrove, Land, Growth and Politics (Chicago: Planners Press/American Planning Association, 1984), 195.

22. Jeffrey F. Squires, "Growth Management Redux: Vermont's Act 250 and Act 200," in State and Regional Initiatives for Managing Development, ed. Douglas R. Porter (Washington, DC: Urban Land Institute, 1992), 14.

23. The original goals are cited in the Comprehensive Planning and Land Use Regulation Act, 45-22.2-3(C). Expanded goals, policies, and the land capability map are included in "Land Use 2010, State Land Use Policies and Plan," Element 121 of the State Guide Plan, published in report no. 64 by the Division of Planning, Rhode Island Department of Administration, in

Providence (1989). As a note of interest, Rhode Island prepared and adopted a state land use plan, incorporating twelve categories of land uses, in 1975.

24. New Jersey State Planning Act of 1985, N.J.S.A. 52:18A-199.
25. For a detailed discussion of the procedures for delineating growth centers, see "The Centers Designation Process," document no. 99 (prepared by the New Jersey Office of State Planning, February 1993).
26. DeGrove, *Land, Growth and Politics*, 288. For an extensive discussion of state agency responses to state growth management requirements, see Douglas R. Porter, "State Agency Coordination in State Growth Management Programs," in *Modernizing State Planning Statutes: The Growing Smart Working Papers*, vol. 1, Planning Advisory Service Report no. 462/463 (Chicago: American Planning Association, 1996).
27. 3 V.S.A. ch. 67, sec. 4020A.
28. Executive Order 01-07, 2001, in John M. DeGrove, *Planning Policy and Politics: Smart Growth and the States* (Cambridge, MA: Lincoln Institute of Land Policy, 2005), 200.
29. DeGrove, *Land, Growth and Politics*, 284.
30. Deborah A. Howe, "Review of Growth Management Strategies Used in Other States" (prepared for the Oregon Department of Land Conservation and Development, 1991).
31. DeGrove, *Planning Policy and Politics*, 52.
32. Comprehensive Planning and Land Use Regulation Act 1988. PL 88-601 Chapter 45-22.1, Rhode Island General Laws Sec. 45-22.2-6.
33. Siemon, "Growth Management in Florida," 48.
34. Vermont's regional councils were given approval powers over local plans under Act 200, but subsequent legislation postponed these actions to 1996. Vermont's district environmental commissions retain their authority to review and approve large-scale developments.
35. Maryland's 1992 law does not expressly call for local governments to submit plans for review and comment by the state agency. Instead, local governments are required to submit a schedule showing when they expect to achieve conformance with state requirements, which mandate the inclusion of state "vision" goals in local plans. The state agency is required to submit an annual report assessing the progress of state and local governments in achieving the goals and recommending appropriate actions to overcome any problems identified (H.B. 1195, sec. 5-708). Clearly, in order to prepare the report, it is necessary for the agency to review local plans.
36. The Florida Department of Community Affairs published a "Technical Memo" (vol. 4, no. 4) in 1989 that cited aspects of the Florida statute that supported compact development, described the legal basis for its position, defined a number of indicators of sprawl found in local plans, and suggested a variety of techniques for avoiding sprawl.
37. *Communities of Place: The New Jersey State Development and Redevelopment Plan* (prepared and published by the New Jersey State Planning Commission, 1992), 35.
38. Comprehension Planning and Land Use Regulaton Act, 1988. Sec. 45-22.2-6(I).
39. See, for example, the introduction to *Communities of Place*, which observes that "the State Plan also will be important when the State of New Jersey makes infrastructure investment decisions. The State Plan will serve as a guide to when and where available State funds should be expended to achieve the Goals of the State Planning Act" (p. 6).
40. Information based on a paper by Douglas R. Porter, "Tennessee's Growth Policy Act: Purposes, Implementation, and Effects on Development." Prepared for the National Association of Realtors, 2002.
41. For an extended critique of existing state programs and proposals for improving state growth management systems, see *Modernizing State Planning Statutes*

(vol. 1 of a research project to improve the statutory basis for American planning), Planning Advisory Service Report no. 462/463 (Chicago: American Planning Association, 1996).

Chapter 9. Deciding How to Manage Growth

1. John D. Landis, "Growth Management Revisited: Efficacy, Price Effects, and Displacement," *Journal of the American Planning Association* 72, no. 4 (Autumn 2006): 426.
2. Many of these approaches are further described in Douglas R. Porter, *Breaking the Logjam: Strategies for Building Community Support* (Washington, DC: Urban Land Institute, 2006).
3. For more information on Eastern Cambridge planning, see Douglas R. Porter, *Breaking the Development Logjam: New Strategies for Building Community Support* (Washington, DC: Urban Land Institute, 2006).
4. Adapted from Susan L. Carpenter, *Solving Community Problems by Consensus* (Washington, DC: Program for Community Problem Solving, 1990), 33.
5. William H. Hudnut III, *Cities on the Rebound: A Vision for Urban America* (Washington, DC: Urban Land Institute, 1998), 42.

Index

A

Abercorn Common (GA), 33
Accountability, 54–55, 257
Act 200 (VT), 259
Act 250 (VT), 259, 263, 267, 270, 273
Adaptive reuse, 22–23, 88–91
Addison Circle (TX), 201–202
Adequate public facilities provisions (APF):
   overview of, 58–59, 152–53;
   public responsibilities and, 161–64;
   regulation of development using, 154–59;
   standards issue and, 159–61;
   unintended consequences of, 161
Administrative issues, 171–72
Adverse effects, 208
Aesthetics:
   guidelines for, 188–95;
   issues surrounding design for, 184–86;
   promotion of design for, 185–86;
   urban design and, 182–83
Affordability, 202, 283
Affordable housing:
   community land trusts and, 225, 226;
   housing trust funds and, 225–26;
   inclusionary zoning and, 221–25;

interjurisdictional parity and, 233–38;
land supply and, 71–75;
overview of, 39;
programs for, 220–21;
revitalization of declining neighborhoods and, 229–33;
streamlining of regulations and, 226–29
Agins v. City of Tiburon, 16
Agricultural districts, 51
Agricultural land, 51, 58
Agricultural production areas, 254
Agricultural zoning, 51
Ambler Realty Co., Village of Euclid, Ohio v., 15, 16
American Can Factory buildings (MD), 43
American Community Fund, 99, 219
Amistad Community Development Corporation, 218
Annexation, 41, 101–2, 258, 285
Anthony, Jerry, 74
Anticipation, importance of, 12
Anti-snob laws, 236
APF. See Adequate public facilities provisions (APF)
Appalachian Trail, 126
Appeals, 269–70
Appearance codes, 192
Approval costs, 284

Area Development Strategy, 198
Arendt, Randall, 138
Arizona Trail, 126
Arlington, WA, 189–91, 195
Arlington Heights, IL, 94, 174, 196–97, 216
Atlanta Regional Commission, 273
Automobiles, 68–69. *See also* Transportation
Avco Community Builders, Inc. v. South Coastal Regional Commission, 16
Avenue Community Development Corporation, 91–92
Awards, design, 187

B

Baby boomers, 5
Balanced growth, 12–13, 212–13
Baltimore Enterprise Zone, 43
Baron, Richard, 232–33
BART, 294–95
Bass Lofts, 89
Beatley, Timothy, 209
Beechwood Manor, 90
Benefits of growth management, 286–90
Berman v. Parker, 184–85
Bethesda Row (MD), 92, 199
Bielinski Homes, 138
Blacksburg, VA, 102
Blue Devil Ventures, 88–89
Blue lines, 76

Boca Raton, FL, 47
Boca Raton (City of) v. Boca Villas Corporation, 47
Bonds, 164–65, 254
Bosselman, Fred, 259
Boston, MA, 231–32
Bottom up states, 268
Boulder, CO:
    blue line of, 76;
    Danish Plan of, 47;
    effects of land supply restrictions in, 283;
    greenspace protection in, 132;
    growth management in, 109;
    water and sewer services in, 103–4
Boulder effect, 283
Boundaries:
    community expansion and, 49;
    effects of, 283;
    establishment and administration of, 78–83;
    jurisdiction and, 99–104;
    local governments and, 75–78;
    requirements for delineation of, 270–71;
    unexpected results of, 83–85
Breckenridge, CO, 91–92, 93, 224
BRIDGE, 221
Brookings Institution, 72
Brownfields, 50, 54, 91–92, 219–20
Brownfields Redevelopment Program (TX), 91–92
Brundtland Commission, 21
Buildable lands analyses, 73–74
Buildable Lands Program (WA), 80
Building codes, 37
Burlington Community Land Trust, 226
Burnham, Daniel, 180

C

California Coastal Commission, 260
California Coastal Commission, Nollan v., 16, 17, 260

Callies, David, 259
Calthorpe, Peter, 25–26, 137
Calvert County, MD, 110, 111, 137
Cambridge, MA, 223, 225, 293–94, 295, 296
Capacity:
    provisions for, 58–59, 152–53;
    public responsibilities and, 161–64;
    regulation of development and, 154–59;
    standards issue and, 159–61;
    unintended consequences regulations and, 161
Capital costs, 151
Capital facilities, 39
Capital improvement plans (CIP), 42, 59, 154–55
Capital Improvement Program (MD), 59
Carlsbad, CA, 146, 155–59
Carlson, Arne, 251
Carothers Crossing (TN), 202
Carrying capacity, 119–20
Cars, 68–69. *See also* Transportation
Carson, Rachel, 10, 181
Celebration (FL), 33
Cell phone towers, 187–88
Cellucci, Paul, 274
Champaign, IL, 229–30
Charrettes, 291–92, 298
CHASs (Comprehensive Housing Affordability Strategies), 221
Chesapeake Bay Agreement, 124
Chesapeake Bay Commission, 253
Chesapeake Bay Critical Areas Law, 124–25
Chinitz, Benjamin, 12
Chula Vista, CA, 154
Cincinnati, OH, 252
Cities, 4–5, 70, 270–71
City Beautiful movement, 7–8
City of New London, Kelo v., 17, 98
Citywide Facilities and Improvement Plan (CA), 156–57
Civic participation, 18, 42–43, 187, 290–98

Clean Air Act, 116
Clean Water Act, 116–17
Clustered development, 135–37
Cluster zoning, 40
Coastal Barrier Resources Act, 117
Coastal Commission (South Carolina), Lucas v., 16, 17–18
Coastal Commission (California), Nollan v., 16, 17, 260
Coastal Zone Management Act, 117, 122
Coffee Creek Center (IL), 138, 177, 202
Collaboration:
    citizens and, 290–98;
    greenways and, 121;
    planning, decision making and, 214;
    regional planning and, 54;
    urban growth, conservation and, 288–89
Columbia, MD, 200
Columbian Exposition of 1893, 7
Columbus, OH, 217–19
Community Development Block Grants (CDBGs), 221
Community land trusts, 54, 225, 226, 227
Community vision, 23–24
Compaction, 30–31
Compensation:
    environmental regional conservation agencies and, 255;
    growth boundaries and, 81–82;
    Measure 37 (OR) and, 21;
    takings of private property and, 17;
    transferable development rights (TDR) and, 59–60
Competitions, design, 186–87
Complexity, allowing for, 299–300
Comprehensive guidelines, 192–94
Comprehensive Housing Affordability Strategies (CHASs), 221

Comprehensive Land and
Water Management Act
(FL), 288
Comprehensiveness, impor-
tance of, 299
Comprehensive Planning
Act (FL), 260, 262
Comprehensive Planning
and Land Use Regulation
Act (RI), 263
Comprehensive Planning
Law (WI), 276
Comprehensive plans, 38,
39, 57–58, 105–6
Concurrency rule, 154, 161,
272
Condemnation, 21, 98, 185
Conflict resolution, 269–70
Congress for the New
Urbanism, 26
Connectivity, importance of,
299
Consensus, 244–45, 295
Conservation.
See also Green space
collaborative planning
and, 288–89;
compensation and, 255;
planning for, 118–20;
transfer of conservation
rights and, 144
Conservation easements,
134–35
Conservation Fund, 132, 134
Conservation rights, transfer
of, 144
Conservation subdivisions,
51, 137–39
Consistency, enforcement of,
268–69
*Constitutional Issues of
Growth Management*, 11
Constructed wetlands, 177
Consultants, 297–98
Convention centers, 42
Cooperation. *See also*
Regional growth
management
environmental regional
conservation agencies
and, 255;
importance of, 300;
need for, 241–42;
state growth manage-
ment and, 264–65
Coover, Christopher, 128
Costs of Sprawl study, 68–69

Council of Environmental
Quality, 144–45
Covenants, conditions, and
restrictions, 204
Crawford Square (PA), 95,
198–99
Critical areas, 51, 122,
124–25, 260, 273
The Crossings (CA), 33

D

Dallas Area Rapid Transit
Station, 43, 206
Danish Plan, 47
Davidoff, Paul and Linda,
222
Dayton, OH, 230–31
Dean, Howard, 263
Decision making, 213–14,
258, 281–90
DeGrove, John, 263
Denver, CO, 108
Department of Community
Affairs (FL), 268, 271
Department of Community
Affairs(GA), 269–70
Desert Lands Conservation
Master Plan, 128
Desert Spaces Management
Plan, 126–28, 133
Designated growth areas, 49
Design awards, 187
Design competitions, 186–87
Design excellence, 186–87
Design reviews, 194–95
Design with Nature (McHarg),
114–15, 119
Developable land, calcula-
tion of, 80
Development:
greening of, 27–29;
increased costs of, 284;
infrastructure financing
and, 164–72;
predictability in, 287;
regulation of by local
governments, 8–9;
regulation of vs. proper-
ty rights, 20–21;
suppression of, 283
Development centers, 50
Development fees, 142,
166–69, 169–72
Development policy areas, 49
Development rights, 81
Development rights,

transferrable (TDR):
Montgomery County,
MD and, 58, 59–60;
New Jersey Pinelands
Commission and,
254;
overview of, 51;
preservation of green
space and, 143–44
Developments of regional
impact, 260
Discretionary procedures, 44
Distinct areas, 77–78
District Environmental
Commissions, 270
Dolan v. City of Tigard, 17, 18
Donor governments, 234
Downs, Anthony, 72, 222
Drainage, impact fees and,
167
Drinking water, 133–34, 167
Duany, Andrés, 25–26, 30,
137, 202
Dudley Street neighborhood
(MA), 231–32
Dunbar, Paul, 231
Dunphy, Robert, 162
Dynamic processes, 12

E

Easements, 134–35
Eastern Cambridge Planning
Study Committee (ECaPS),
293–94, 295, 296
East Pointe (WI), 94
The Ecology of Place (Beatley
and Manning), 209
Economic development. *See
also* Affordable housing;
Equity
balanced growth and,
212–13;
comprehensive plan-
ning and, 39;
equitable development
and, 214–20;
expanded opportunities
in, 287;
increasing disparity in,
211–12;
methods for, 53–54;
revitalization through
environmental
cleanup and, 219–20
Economic impact
analyses, 151
Edge cities, 70

Edgeless cities, 70
Education. *See* Schools
Edwards Aquifer, 133–34
Eminent domain, 21, 98, 185
Employment, 216–17
Endangered species, 9
Endangered Species Act (ESA), 117, 122, 288
Enright, Bill, 197
Enterprise Foundation, 221
Environment, 219–20, 253–55
Environmentally Sensitive Lands Ordinance, 139
Environmental threshold standards, 50, 51
Equity:
    balanced growth and, 212–13;
    decision making and, 282–90;
    decreasing, 211–12;
    economic development and, 214–20;
    facility regulations and fees and, 170–71;
    improvement of, 53–54;
    inclusive planning and decision making and, 213–14;
    interjurisdictional, 233–38;
    strategies for, 239–40
Euclid, Ohio (Village of) v. Ambler Realty Co., 15, 16
Exactions, extractions, and proffers, 165–66
Exceptions, boundaries and, 84
Exclusionary effects, 284. *See also* Inclusionary zoning
Existing infrastructure, standards and, 159–61
Expansion, management of, 49–50
Extra-jurisdictional controls, 50
Extraterritorial jurisdiction, 100–101

F

Facilities, adequate. *See* Adequate public facilities provisions (APF)
Factories, adaptive reuse of, 88–89

Fagin, Henry, 153, 164
Fair-share housing programs, 235–37
Fannie Mae, 99, 219
Favored quarter, 211
Fayette County, KY, 67
Federal Aid Highway Act, 252
Federal government, 9, 116–18, 220–21
Federal Transit Administration, 68
Fees, impact, 142, 166–69, 169–72
Fee simple ownership, 131
Fields of St. Croix, 137
Fifth Amendment, 20
Financing, 272–73
Fire stations, 69
First Evangelical Lutheran Church of Glendale v. County of Los Angeles, 16, 17
First suburbs, 235
Fiscal analyses, 151
Fischel, William A., 73
Flexibility, 52–53
Flexible zoning, 40
Floating zones, 40
Ford Model T factory, 89
Forest City Enterprises, 218
Form and function, 24–27
Form-based zoning (smart codes), 26, 40, 53, 203–4
Fort Collins (CO), 1–3, 5, 104, 291
Fourteenth Amendment, 20
Frank, James, 68
Free market system, 6–7
Freetown neighborhood redevelopment process, 214, 231
Freilich, Robert, 143
Fresno, CA, 100, 163
Frey, William, 210
Frick Park (PA), 130, 131
Functional plans, 51

G

Garreau, Joel, 70, 137
Gateway Center (OH), 218
General plans, 38–39, 57–58, 105–6, 260–63, 276
Gentrification, 5
Geographic information systems (GIS), 119
Germantown, WI, 138

Glendening, Parris, 265, 274
Go-it-alone syndrome, 29–30
Golden v. Planning Board of Town of Ramapo, 16, 46, 153–54
Governments, 7–8, 12, 241–42. *See also* Specific governments
Grand Traverse Bay Region Development Guidebook, 192–94
Great Rivers Greenway District, 126
Green Acres program, 275
Green Book framework, 96
Green building, 27–29, 53, 204–5
Green infrastructure, 28–29, 50, 120–22
Green lines, 76
Green space:
    clustered development and, 135–37;
    conservation easements and, 134–35;
    conservation subdivisions and, 137–39;
    federal and state agencies and, 122–25;
    integration of with built areas, 114–17;
    land acquisition and, 130–34;
    local planning for, 126–30;
    mitigation banking and, 144–46;
    planning for, 118–20;
    regional planning for, 125–26;
    regulatory approaches for conservation of, 137–39;
    rural development and, 142–43;
    subdivisions and, 141–42;
    transferable development rights and, 143–44;
    value of, 113–14;
    zoning codes and, 139–41
Greenville, SC, 231
Greenways, 29, 125–26, 127
Greyfields, 50
Grove Hall Mecca Mall (MA), 33

Growing Smarter Act, 276
Growing Smart Legislative Guidebook, 273
Growth centers program, 275
Growth management:
  benefits of, 286–90;
  boundaries and, 50, 76–77;
  defined, 11–14;
  emergence of, 9–11;
  evolution of, 19–29;
  fiscal issues of, 151;
  housing affordability and, 71–75;
  legal basis for, 14–19;
  methods of, 108–10;
  new concepts in, 29–34;
  overview of, 34–35
Growth Management Act (FL), 74
Growth Management Act (WA), 39, 122
Growth Management and Affordable Housing, 72
Growth Policy Act (TN), 276
Guidelines, aesthetics and, 188–95

H

Habitat conservation plans (HCP), 122, 288–89
Hadacheck v. Sebastian, 15, 16
HAPs (Housing Assistance Plans), 221
Herr's Island (PA), 220
Highland Park (IL), 227
Highlands Coalition, 123–24
Highlands Conservation Act, 124
Highlands Water Protection and Planning Act, 124
Hinshaw, Mark, 186, 189, 194, 195
Historic preservation, 207–8
Historic tax credits, 90
Holistic approaches, 286
Hookup fees, 167
Housing, affordable:
  community land trusts and, 225, 226;
  housing trust funds and, 225–26;
  inclusionary zoning and, 221–25;
  interjurisdictional parity and, 233–38;

land supply and, 71–75;
  overview of, 39;
  programs for, 220–21;
  revitalization of declining neighborhoods and, 229–33;
  streamlining of regulations and, 226–29
Housing and Urban Development (HUD), 221, 228
Housing Assistance Plans (HAPs), 221
Housing Trust Fund Project, 225
Housing trust funds, 54, 225–26, 227
Hubs, 120
Hudnut, William, 235
Hull, Jane Dee, 276

I

Immigration, 4
Impact fees, 142, 166–69, 169–72
Incentives, 53, 54, 55, 275
Incentive zoning, 40, 199–200
Inclusionary housing programs, 58, 60–61
Inclusionary zoning, 54, 221–25, 227
Inclusiveness, 213–14
Indiana-Ohio-Kentucky Regional Council of Governments, 252
Indianapolis, IN, 225–26
Individuals, role of, 290–98
Infill development, 50, 86, 91–93, 151, 183–84
Infrastructure. *See also* Adequate public facilities provisions (APF); Transportation
  boundary jurisdiction and, 102–3;
  complexity of responsibilities for, 149–50;
  cost increases of with sprawl, 69–70;
  Costs of Sprawl study and, 68–69;
  developer contributions to, 164–72;
  green, 28–29, 50, 120–22;
  green alternatives to, 176–78;

as heart of growth management problem, 147–49, 150–52;
  Maryland and, 258;
  methods for efficient provision of, 51–52;
  privatization and, 175–76;
  smart growth and, 23;
  sprawl and, 69;
  state growth management and, 271–73;
  urban service limits and, 75–76
Innovation, 185–86
Interlocal agreements, 103–4
Intermodal Surface Transportation Efficiency Act, 252
I'On (SC), 33, 202
Irvine Ranch (CA), 24
Issaquah Highlands (WA), 33

J

Jacobs, Jane, 181, 182
Jobs, 216–17
Johnson, Hunter, 90
Jubilee Housing, 221
Jurisdiction:
  annexation and, 101–2;
  boundaries and, 99–100;
  extraterritorial, 100–101;
  interlocal agreements and, 103–4;
  service extensions and, 102–3

K

Kaiser Aetna v. United States, 16
Kane County, IL, 78, 79
Katz, Peter, 29–30
Kelly, Eric, 111
Kelo v. City of New London, 17, 98
Kentlands (MD), 33
Kentucky-Indiana-Ohio Regional Council of Governments, 252
King County, WA, 76
Kotkin, Joel, 4
Krasnowiecki, Jan, 179

L

Lake Wales (City of) v. Lamar Advertising Association of Lakeland, 185

Land acquisition, 50, 130–34

Land and Water Conservation Fund, 130

Land Conservation and Development Commission (OR), 260–61, 264–65, 268

Landis, John, 72, 283

Land ownership, 6, 15, 16–18, 20–21

Land Resource Management Plan, 78, 79

Landscape design, 53

Landscrapers, 28

Land supply, 71–75

Land use, 10, 39, 202

Land Use 2010, 263

Land Use Board of Appeals (OR), 269

Lang, Robert, 4–5

LaQuatra Bonci, 130

Large-lot zoning, 51

Larsen, Tom, 276

Lassar, Betsy, 227

Lassar, Terry, 200

Leaking, 84

Leapfrogging, 84, 151

LEED (Leadership in Energy and Environmental Design), 181, 204–5

LEED for Neighborhood Development (LEED-ND), 28, 181, 205

Lee-Harvard shopping center (OH), 214, 218–19

Legal issues:
aesthetics and, 184–85;
affordable housing and, 236–37;
basis for growth management and, 14–19;
facility regulations and fees and, 169–70;
growth boundaries and, 83;
local government power and, 45–47;
moratoriums and, 110–11;
property rights and, 20–21

Legislative presumption of validity, 15

Leinberger, Christopher, 211

Leopold, Aldo, 146

Level-of-service standards (LOS), 159–60

LINC Housing, 90

Lincoln, MA, 136–37

Lincoln, NE, 75–76

Lincoln Institute of Land Policy, 135

Lincoln-Lancaster County (NE), 97, 104–7

Linkage, 109, 120, 169

Lloyd District (OR), 198

Local governments:
adaptive reuse, infill, redevelopment and, 96–99;
boundaries and, 75–78;
decision making and, 281–82;
economic expansion and, 215–16;
equity in decision making and, 282–90;
expansion of regulatory power of, 48–49;
growth management and, 13;
housing affordability and, 73;
legal basis for regulatory control by, 15, 45–47;
moratoriums and, 110–11;
overview of regulatory procedures of, 43–44;
state growth management and, 265–67;
support of by state governments, 54–55

Local Initiatives Support Foundation, 221

LoDo (CO), 207

Los Angeles (County of), First Evangelical Lutheran Church of Glendale v., 16, 17

LOS (level-of-service) standards, 159–60

Loudon County, VA, 142–43

Lower Colorado River Multispecies Conservation Program, 132

Lucas v. South Carolina Coastal Commission, 16, 17–18

M

Management and Control of Growth, 10, 11–12

Management guidelines, 298–300

Mandelker, David, 110–11

Manning, Kristy, 209

Maricopa Association of Governments, 126–28

Market factors, 73, 171

Maryville, TN, 100–101

Master plans, 38, 39, 57–58, 105–6

McCormack Baron Salazar, 198–99

McDowell Sonoran Preserve, 133, 138–39

McHarg, Ian, 114–16, 119

Measure 37 (OR), 21, 81, 279

Megapolitan regions, 5, 7

Metro (OR), 245–46

Metro Center, 60, 62

Metromedia, Inc. v. City of San Diego, 185

Metropolitan areas, growth of, 4

Metropolitan Development Framework, 250

Metropolitan Livable Communities Act, 234–35

Metropolitan planning organizations (MPOs), 252–53

Metropolitan Revenue Distribution Act, 237–38

Metropolitan Waste Control Commission, 249

Metrorail, 56, 58–59

Metro regional organization, 83–84

Middle-income families, decline in, 212

Military base closings, 96

Mill Creek Trail, 127

Millennium Place (MA), 91

Milwaukee Redevelopment Corporation, 94–95

Minneapolis-St. Paul, MN, 234, 237–38, 246, 248–51

Minner, Ruth Ann, 274

Minorities, 210, 211–12

Mismanagement, 285–86

Mitigation, 51, 54, 144–45

Mitigation banking, 144–46

Mixed-use zoning, 32, 52

Model Land Development Code, 259

Moderately-Priced Dwelling Unit (MPDU) law, 223

Modulation, 190

Montgomery and Rust, 220

Montgomery County, MD:
affordable housing and,
223–24;
green space preservation
in, 133, 139;
growth management in,
55–64;
infrastructure planning
and, 157–59;
zoning incentives and,
199
Moratoriums, 46–47,
110–12, 283, 293–94
Mortgages, 9
Mount Laurel court deci-
sions (NJ), 236
MPDU (moderately-priced
dwelling unit) law, 223
MSCP (Multi-Species
Comprehensive Plan),
128–29
*Mt. Laurel Township, Southern
Burlington County NAACP
v.*, 16
Mullen, Clancy, 167, 169
Multi-Species
Comprehensive Plan
(MSCP), 128–29
Mumford, Lewis, 242–43
Myers, Erik, 20–21

N
Nashville, TN, 95
Nassau County (NY), 10
National Environmental
Policy Act (NEPA), 10,
116, 117–18, 288
National Historical
Preservation Act, 207–8
National Parks and
Recreation Act, 254
National Trust for Historic
Preservation, 207, 219
Natural Community
Conservation Planning
(NCCP) program, 122–23,
289
Natural systems, 50–51,
113–14
The Nature Conservancy
(TNC), 132
NCCP (Natural Community
Conservation Planning)
program, 122–23, 289
Neighborhood Wellness
Action Plan, 229–30
Nelson, Arthur, 4–5, 72

NEPA (National
Environmental Policy
Act), 10, 116, 117–18, 288
*New Designs for Growth
Development Guidebook*, 193
New Federalism, 259
New Jersey Pinelands
Commission, 253–55
New London (City of), Kelo v.,
17, 98
New Markets Tax Credit
Program, 219
New urbanism, 25–26, 183,
201–4
New Village Corporation,
218
*New York City, Penn Central
Transportation Co. v.*, 16,
143, 185
Nine Mile Run, 130
Nolan, John, 180
*Nollan v. California Coastal
Commission*, 16, 17, 260
Northeast Corridor, 5

O
Office Housing Production
Program, 169
Oglethorpe, James, 6
Ohio-Kentucky-Indiana
Regional Council of
Governments, 252
Olmsted, Frederick Law, 180
Open space, defined, 32
Open space preservation,
30–32
Open Space Residential
District, 136–37
Ordinance of 1785, 6
Orenco Station (OR), 33
Orfield, Myron, 234–35
Overlay zoning, 40
Overrides, 255, 257

P
Palo Alto, CA, 224
Park and Planning
Commission (MD), 56
Parking, 52, 162
Parks, 39, 56, 254
Parr, John, 214
Peale, Cliff, 252
Pelican Bay (FL), 173–74
Penn, William, 6
*Penn Central Transportation
Co. v. New York City*, 16,
143, 185

Performance provisions, 53
Performance standards, 154,
156–58
Permitting, 118. *See also*
Zoning codes
Personal Transportation
Study, 162
Petaluma, CA, 46–47, 72,
109
Pine Barrens, 253–55
Pinelands Development
Credit Bank, 254
Pinelands Infrastructure
Trust Bond Act, 254
Planned infrastructure,
159–61
Planned Rural Residential
Conservation District, 141
Planned unit developments
(PUD), 40, 200–201
Planning, 262–64
Planning councils, regional,
244–51
Planning Framework Report
(MD), 63
Plano, TX, 43, 206
Plater-Zyberk, Elizabeth,
25–26, 202
Pleasant Hill (CA), 294
Police power, 14–17, 18, 185
Police protection, sprawl
and, 69
Politics, 80–81
Population growth, 3–6, 7,
20
Portland, OR:
affordable housing and,
236–37;
design guidelines of,
198;
green space preservation
and, 140;
growth limits and,
109–10;
regional boundary of,
67, 82, 83–84;
regional planning coun-
cils in, 245–46
Poverty, increasing, 211
Prairie Glen (WI), 138
Preservation, 30–32, 133,
139–44, 207–8
Preservation areas, 254
Preservation standards, 53
Priority funding areas, 274
Privatization, 175–76
Proffers, 165–66

Project rating systems, 53
Property rights, 6, 15, 16–18, 20–21
Property taxes, 164–65
Protection areas, 254
Public facilities, 52, 58–59, 102–3, 108–9
Public participation, 18, 42–43, 187, 290–98
Public use, eminent domain and, 98
PUD (planned unit developments), 40, 200–201

Q

Quality, 52–53, 185
Quality of life, urban design and, 182–83
Quest Vision process, 252

R

Railroads:
    greenways and, 29, 126;
    growth expansion and, 67–68;
    infrastructure planning and, 249–50;
    traditional neighborhood design (TND) and, 25–26
Rail-to-Trails Conservancy, 126
Ramapo (Planning Board of Town of), Golden v., 16, 46, 153–54
Ramapo, NY, 45–46
Rational nexus, 169–70
Reason Institute, 74
Receiving areas, 59, 144
Recreation, 39
Redevelopment:
    declining neighborhood business centers and, 217–18;
    declining neighborhoods and, 229–33;
    eminent domain and, 98;
    overview of, 93–96;
    programs for, 50, 86
Regional agencies, 253–56, 267–68
Regional Development Framework, 251
Regional environmental conservation agencies, 253–56

Regional Framework Benchmarks, 251
Regional growth centers, 254
Regional growth management:
    approaches for, 243–44;
    environmental conservation agencies and, 253–56;
    groups for, 256–57;
    important elements of, 257–58;
    metropolitan planning organizations (MPOs) and, 252–53;
    need for cooperation in, 241–42;
    overview of, 242–43;
    planning councils for, 244–51;
    state growth management and, 267–68
Regional Growth Strategy Map, 251
Regional Plan Association of New York, 153, 256–57
Regional planning, collaboration and, 54
Regional planning councils, 244–51
Regulations, 226–29, 284
Rehabilitation Subcode, 228
Research Triangle Park, 88–89
Resource Conservation, 117
Resource Conservation Zoning Districts, 138
Reston, VA, 24, 200
Reuse, 86
Revenue, 151
Revenue sharing, 235, 237–38, 250
Review procedures, 194–95
Right-to-farm laws, 51
River Ring, 126
Riverside County, CA, 142
RiverStation I (MN), 98–99
Roanoke, VA, 180
Rolling Hill, 95
Roofs, planted, 177
Rosen, Christine, 115
Rural clustering, 51
Rural development, 5, 142–43, 270–71
Rural Land Foundation, 136–37
Rural Legacy program, 275

Rypkema, Donovan D., 89–90

S

Saginaw Bay Greenways Collaborative, 121
San Diego, CA, 82, 108, 109–10, 236–37
San Diego (City of), Metromedia, Inc. v., 185
San Diego Association of Governments (SANDAG), 128–29, 246–48
San Francisco, CA, 126, 169, 189, 190
San Francisco Bay Trail, 126
San Jacinto, CA, 192
San Jose, CA, 77, 101
Santa Monica Mountains Conservancy, 125
Sarasota County, FL, 65–67, 82–83, 132–33, 285
Scenic corridors, 192
Schill, Michael, 74
Schools:
    facility regulations and fees and, 171;
    impact fees and, 167;
    infrastructure provision and, 52;
    Montgomery County, MD, and, 59;
    neighborhood rejuvenation and, 232–33;
    sprawl and, 69
Scott, Randall, 10
Scottsdale, AZ, 133, 138–39, 191
Scully, Vincent, 25
Seaside, FL, 25, 33
Seattle, WA, 109, 197
Sebastian, Hadacheck v., 15, 16
Sending areas, 144
Sensitive Design Program, 191
Septic systems, 75–76
Service extensions, 102–3
Service limits, 49
Setbacks, 141
Sewer, impact fees and, 167
Shaheen, Jeanne, 274
Shared governance, 289
Sharing of revenue, 235, 237–38, 250
Sidewalks, 181
Siemon, Charles, 266

Silent Spring (Carson), 10, 181
Sioux Falls, SD, 75–76
SmartCode, 202–3
Smart codes, 26, 40, 53, 203–4
Smart growth. *See also* New urbanism
 existing approaches and, 30;
 overview of, 19, 22–23;
 state growth management and, 273–77;
 state incentives for, 55
Smart Growth Concept Map, 248
Smart Growth Dividends, 275
Smart Growth program (MD), 258, 265
Smart Growth statutes, 77, 275
Social processes, 211–13, 287. *See also* Equity
South Carolina Coastal Commission, Lucas v., 16
South Coastal Regional Commission, Avco Community Builders, Inc. v., 16
Southeast Community Development Corporation, 43
Southern Burlington County NAACP v. Mt. Laurel Township, 16
South Florida Water Management District, 144
Special area management plans (SAMPs), 122
Special tax districts, 52, 172–75
Spheres of influence, 100
Sprawl, 151, 232
Springfield, MO, 216
Standards, 159–61
Stapleton Airport, 96
Stapleton Field (CO), 129–30
State Development and Redevelopment Plan (NJ), 263
State growth management:
 accomplishments in, 277–79;
 affordable housing and, 236–37;
 comprehensive acts for, 260–62;

conflict resolution and, 269–70;
 coordination and, 264–65;
 critical area concerns and, 273;
 development of, 258–60;
 enforcing consistency and, 268–69;
 infrastructure planning and financing and, 271–73;
 local planning and, 265–67;
 planning and, 262–64;
 reassertion of regulatory control by, 15;
 regional planning and, 267–68;
 regulatory control of, 9;
 smart growth and, 273–77;
 special tax districts and, 173;
 support of local growth management by, 54–55;
 urban and rural demarcation and, 270–71
State plans, 262–64
St. Lucie County (FL), 291, 292
Stormwater drainage, 177
Strathmore Music Center, 61
Strong, Cliff, 191, 195
Strong-accommodating urban containment programs, 71
Strong-restrictive urban containment programs, 71
Subdivision requirements, 41–42, 165–66, 188
Subdivisions, 51, 137–39, 141–42
Suburbs, 4, 235
Summerset at Frick Park (PA), 130, 131
Superfund Act, 117
Supplemental regulations, 189
Surveying, 6
Sustainable development, 19–22, 28–29, 55, 114–17
Swales, 177
Swasey, Welch v., 15, 16
Systems development

charges (impact fees), 142, 166–69, 169–72

T

Tacoma, WA, 87
Tahoe-Sierra Preservation Council, Inc. et al. v. Tahoe Regional Planning Agency et al., 17
Takings, 20, 81, 83, 141
Takings clause, 20
Tampa, FL, 191
Tarr, Joel, 115
Task Force on Growth and Change, 256
Taxes:
 historic tax credits and, 90;
 industry incentives and, 215;
 New Markets Tax Credit Program and, 219;
 property, 164–65;
 revenue sharing and, 235, 237–38, 250;
 special tax districts and, 52, 172–75;
 tear-down, 227
Tax increment financing (TIF) districts, 52, 172–73, 174, 196–97
TDR. *See* Transferable development rights
Tear-down taxes, 227
Tenth Amendment, 14–15
Terminology, 22
Tetreault, Bernard, 224–25
Threshold criteria, 50, 51
Thresholds, 154, 156–58
Tiburon (City of), Agins v., 16
Tiers, 77–78
TIF (tax increment financing) districts, 52, 172–73, 174, 196–97
Tigard (City of), Dolan v., 17, 18
Time, transportation costs and, 162
Tipping, 212
TNC (The Nature Conservancy), 132
TND (traditional neighborhood design), 25–26, 31–34, 53
TODs (transit-oriented developments), 26–27, 30, 61, 205–6

Top down states, 268
Traditional neighborhood design (TND), 25–26, 31–34, 53
Transferable development rights (TDR):
  Montgomery County, MD and, 58, 59–60;
  New Jersey Pinelands Commission and, 254;
  overview of, 51;
  preservation of green space and, 143–44
Transfer of conservation rights, 144
Transit-oriented developments (TODs), 26–27, 30, 61, 205–6
Transportation. *See also* Infrastructure
  comprehensive planning and, 39;
  employment access and, 216–17;
  equity and, 239;
  infrastructure provision and, 52;
  level-of-service standards and, 159–60;
  parties paying for, 162;
  regional coordination and, 249–50, 252–53;
  state growth management and, 264–65;
  transit-oriented developments (TODs) and, 26–27, 30, 61, 205–6
Transportation Development Act (NJ), 173
Traverse City, MI, 192–94, 256
Treasure Coast Regional Planning Commission, 291–92
Treasure Valley Partnership, 256
Tribecca project (WA), 197

Trusts, 54, 207, 219, 225–27, 254
Twin Cities Metropolitan Council, 234

U
United States, Kaiser Aetna v., 16
Urban areas, 4–5, 70, 270–71
Urban containment programs, 67, 70–71
Urban design, 180–84
Urban Design Plan (CA), 189, 190
Urban growth management areas, 100
Urban Growth Management Functional Plan, 246
Urban limit lines, 49
Urban renewal:
  declining neighborhood business centers and, 217–18;
  declining neighborhoods and, 229–33;
  eminent domain and, 98;
  overview of, 93–96;
  programs for, 50, 86
Urban reserve areas, 81
Urban/rural limits, 75
Use of Land: A Citizen's Policy Guide to Urban Growth, 10

V
Validity, legislative presumption of, 15
Visioning, 23–24
Voting methods, 298

W
Wal-Mart, 259
Warehouses, 88–89
Washington Courtyards (TX), 91–92
Washington's Landing (PA), 220

Water quality, 9, 52, 160
Weak-accommodating urban containment programs, 71
Weak-restrictive urban containment programs, 70
Wedges and Corridors, 57–58
Welch v. Swasey, 15, 16
Wellington Neighborhood (CO), 92, 224
Western Maryland Rail Trail, 126
Westminster, CO, 111
West Village (NC), 88–89
Wetlands, 9, 145, 177
Wright-Dunbar neighborhood (OH), 230–31

Z
Zero Population Growth, 47
Zoning codes. *See also* Smart codes
  design quality and, 196–208;
  extending reach of, 187–88;
  first adoption of, 8;
  green space preservation and, 139–41;
  historic preservation and, 208;
  incentives and, 40, 199–200;
  inclusionary, 54, 221–25, 227;
  legal basis for, 15;
  mixed-use, 32, 52;
  overview of, 38–41;
  property values and, 81;
  smart codes and, 26, 40, 53, 203–4;
  traditional neighborhood design (TND) and, 30–31

About the Author

DOUGLAS R. PORTER is nationally recognized as an authority on ways and means of managing community growth and change. For many years he has analyzed and written about programs, techniques, and issues on the topic of improving the quality of urban development. His work bridges traditional specialties in urban planning and development, from affordable housing programs to transportation/land-use relationships, regional growth strategies, transit-oriented development, community involvement, and local community development concerns, including the concepts of smart growth and sustainable development. In 1992 he founded The Growth Management Institute as a nonprofit organization to promote information exchange and research for public, organizational, and private clients.

These activities have built on twelve years as director of public policy research for the Urban Land Institute and twenty years of experience before that as a planning and development consultant. He works collaboratively with local and regional planning agencies and public officials, business groups, environmental organizations, state and federal agencies, and national organizations. In his current practice, he is especially concerned with integrating land-use patterns, transportation systems, and environmental features to create livable communities. Most recently he has advised Coweta County, Georgia; Maryville and Blount County, Tennessee; and Palm Beach County, Florida, on growth issues.

His recent publications include *Smart Growth Endorsement/Rating Systems* (APA); *Breaking the Logjam: Civic Engagement by Developers and Planners* (ULI); *Inclusionary Zoning for Affordable Housing* (ULI); *Developing Around Transit* (chapter on suburban TOD's) (ULI); *Exploring 'Ad Hoc' Regionalism* (Lincoln Institute); and *Making Smart Growth Work* (ULI). He is an AICP

Fellow and has been a ULI Fellow and Chair of the Maryland Transportation Commission. He received a B.S. and M.S. in Urban and Regional Planning from Michigan State University and the University of Illinois, respectively.

Island Press Board of Directors